GUIDE TO BETTER BRIDGE

Ron Klinger

For those who already know how to play bridge but need to grasp the fundamentals of sound bidding and sound play, *Bridge Basics* is the answer. The *Guide To Better Bridge* is addressed to the vast majority who are ready and keen to rise above the basics.

There is a higher plane to which players should aspire after they have managed to handle the early part of the auction. To reach the best contract time and time again, to understand and co-operate with partner, to get the most out of your cards . . . these are the objectives which the *Guide To Better Bridge* will help you to achieve. If you are able to master even 50% of the material in this book, your results will reflect your enhanced expertise.

We all like to win, and win regularly. There is a euphoria in winning at bridge that cannot be matched and with the knowldge contained in the *Guide To Better Bridge*, you will be on the road to winning more often. Even if your efforts are not crowned with success every time, you will certainly find that you are doing much better and consequently your extra confidence will be reflected by a significant improvement in the results you have been able to manage so far.

While the *Guide To Better Bridge* emphasises better bidding, each chapter also contains examples of play. These incorporate the bidding principles of the chapter and also highlight many areas of winning declarer technique and defense. The book can be used by teachers conducting intermediate courses or as a self-teacher. Each chapter contains plentiful exercises and partnership bidding practice. At the end of each section, a revision test enables the reader to measure the rate of progress.

Ron Klinger first played for Australia in 1970 when he was a member of the team that won the Far East Open Teams Championship. Since then he has competed in the world championships in 1976, 1978, 1980, 1984, 1986, 1988 and 1989. He won the Far East Open Pairs Championship in 1985 and again in 1987. He was a member of the Australian team which reached the semifinals of the 1989 Bermuda Bowl World Teams Championship. In addition to the many state and national titles to his credit, he is an Australian Grandmaster and a World Bridge Federation International Master. The Guide To Better Bridge has been compiled from his many successful intermediate to advanced classes conducted over the past twenty years.

Other books by Ron Klinger
published by Houghton Mifflin Company

Bridge Basics
Guide to Better Card Play

By Hugh Kelsey and Ron Klinger

Instant Guide to Bridge

Standard American Edition

GUIDE TO
BETTER
BRIDGE

♣ ♥ ♦ ♠

RON KLINGER

*A Master Bridge Series title
in conjunction with Peter Crawley*

Houghton Mifflin Company
Boston

For information about permission to reproduce selections from
this book, write to Permissions, Houghton Mifflin Company,
2 Park Street, Boston, Massachusetts 02108.

Library of Congress Cataloging-in-Publication Data

Klinger, Ron.
Guide to better bridge / Ron Klinger. — Standard American ed.
p.   cm.
"A Master bridge series title."
ISBN 0-395-59131-7
1. Contract bridge — Bidding.   I. Title.
GV1282.4.K57 1991   91-4494
795.41'52 — dc20   CIP

Printed in the United States of America

BP 10 9 8 7 6 5 4 3 2

To Mum

Acknowledgments

My thanks go to George Havas and to my wife Suzie who both spent considerable time proofreading the contents of this book. Through their efforts, there are far fewer flaws than there might have been and as a result, I sleep much better at night. My thanks go also to Ari and Keri who did not see as much of their father while the Guide was in production as he would have liked and who were very understanding about it all.

CONTENTS

INTRODUCING RON KLINGER

by Alan Truscott

Look around the world of bridge in search of someone who is at the top of the tree as a player, teacher and writer and you will find perhaps half a dozen candidates. One of them, and only one, is outside North America, which is why he is not as well known as he ought to be.

His name is Ron Klinger, and his residence is in Sydney, Australia, long the home of some of the world's best players. I first met him two decades ago when I took an expert team for a Down-Under tour and encountered a young Professor of Law who was describing the play for large audiences with intelligence and wit.

Soon afterwards he abandoned academic pursuits, which may have been a loss to the Law but was certainly a gain for the bridge community. He rapidly turned himself into Australia's Mr. Bridge, the equivalent perhaps of Charles Goren in his heyday in the forties and fifties. However the parallel is inexact, for Goren had many collaborators and Klinger is a one-man band.

Like Goren, Klinger made his name to the bridge public by a string of impressive playing performances. He has lost count of the number of major titles he has won, and enumerating his international appearances is not much easier. Down-Under, as Up-Over, every expert wants to carry the flag in foreign parts and fierce selection battles occur annually.

He is almost always in the thick of it, and is the most successful player of his generation. His total international appearances may soon rival that of the legendary Tim Seres, who helped earlier Australian teams to challenge effectively at world level.

Specifically Klinger has played five times in the Far East Championships, winning the Teams in 1970 and the Pairs twice, in 1985 and 1987. On a wider scene he has played in six of the biennial Olympiads — the bridge misnomer for an Olympic — and at three consecutive ones, in 1976, 1978 and 1980, he won the Bols Brilliancy Prize: for the best-played hand in 1976, and for his bridge journalism on the other occasions. Since there are hundreds of candidates for this prize his string is not only remarkable but unique. In the Bermuda Bowl, in which the representation is by zones, the South Pacific is represented by Australia and New Zealand. In this event Klinger made his second appearance in 1989, in Perth, and the team reached the semifinals before losing to the American defending champions after a hard fight.

For occasions such as this Klinger has created his own 'Power' system, which is a clever blend of the old and the new. Most of the opening bids follow the recipe that Dr. Paul Stern devised for the Austrian team which won the first world championship, played in 1937. An updated version, 'New South Wales', was popular in Sydney with Seres and his group. Klinger has taken some elements and added hypermodern two-bids and relays, a mixture that he does not offer to his students and readers. It is reserved for his partners, who are required to have good memories.

In a 13-year stint as Editor, starting in 1972, Klinger made *Australian Bridge* one of the world's best bridge magazines. At the same time he began writing a series of successful books on the game. One of them, 100 WINNING BRIDGE TIPS, has proved very popular in the United States and as these lines are written, he is at work on a sequel. He personally published many of the original Australian editions of his books using an early desk-top publishing set-up.

He is, as I know from hearing him, a superb teacher, and regularly projects his knowledge of the game to large groups in various parts of his continent. Like all the best bridge instructors, he provides his students with prepared deals to illustrate the lesson. This involves not only careful planning but also laborious work, as I know from personal experience.

When a vivacious lady named Suzie became his bride in 1974 she immediately found that bridge would have a big impact on her life. The money in the kitty was just sufficient either to take a honeymoon or to publish his first book. (It proved a great success.) Suzie attends to all the administrative details that her husband's work entails. Their children, Ari and Keri, join in much of the family travel, and if they miss some schooling, the parents promptly turn themselves into substitute teachers.

I began by saying that Klinger is a top player, writer and teacher. But he is also a commentator, game director, editor, publisher, game inventor, group travel co-ordinator and tour guide. What else is there? Time will tell.

Alan Truscott
January 1991

INTRODUCTION

Most players do not aspire to be world champions at bridge, but that does not mean there is a lack of ambition. We all would like to play better. We do not like to make a hash of our good hands and it pains us when we miss an easy opportunity or land in a woeful contract. We know that we are capable of doing better.

The *Guide To Better Bridge* is designed to remedy any shortcomings you may feel. Assuming you know the basics, the *Guide* aims to make you into an accomplished player, one who knows what to do and how to do it. It covers the areas which are beyond the basics but which are still part and parcel of sound, competent bridge.

It helps if you have regular partners with whom you can practise and play the topics you cover. This way you will gain confidence in each other and be able to trust partner when any new material crops up. Each chapter contains specific exercises for partnership bidding practice. If you do these with one of your partners, do not look at each other's cards as you do the bidding. Best of all is to have a book each and cover your partner's cards as you bid each hand. It is a sound idea to write the bidding down so that you can discuss the sequence and each bid later if need be. There are more than 350 sets of hands for partnership bidding and the recommended auction for each set is found in the answers at the back of the book. Before comparing hands and before consulting the recommended bidding, each partner should state what they know about the other's hand: shape, strength and any special features. If there is any significant discrepancy, determine how the misunderstanding arose and how to eliminate similar misunderstandings for the future. Needless to say, such practice sessions should be conducted in a spirit of keenness to learn, with a willingness to admit fallibility and a complete absence of acrimony or hostility. The aim is to fix any mistakes, not to fix the blame.

You do not need to wait for any partner, of course, in order to make the most of the exercises in this book. Glance through the subject headings within each chapter, then read through the chapter carefully. After your first reading, start on the exercises. In a few months time do the exercises again and check your improvement. If you are answering fewer than 80% correctly, it may pay you to read the relevant portions of the text again.

There is no reason why you cannot do the partnership bidding practice exercises on your own. Even if you do them on your own, you can still bid them again at a later date with a partner. There are so many hands that there is little risk that you will recall a significant number of them. To do the partnership bidding on your own, start on the West hands and cover the East cards. Each set contains 5 or 6 hands and West is the dealer unless stated otherwise. Write down the West action on all the hands in the set. Then uncover the East cards and cover the West cards. Now write down the East reply to the West action you have chosen on each of the hands in the set. Then uncover the West cards, cover the East cards and write down West's rebid on each hand. Continue this process until each auction is complete. Do not look at the East and West hands at the same time until you have completed the whole set. Then decide whether you feel you have reached the best contract and finally check the recommended auction in the answers. If the recommended auction does not agree with yours, sort out any discrepancy and re-read the text if necessary.

Do not cheat on any of the exercises by looking at the answers first or by looking at both the West and East hands when you are doing the bidding exercises. You are only cheating yourself and fooling nobody else. Your aim is to improve your standard, not to fake an achievement.

Practise also on the 4 play hands in each chapter. With a group of four players, you can play the hands at home by having each player sort out the appropriate hand from the lists of hands on pages 184-191. This way the hands can be arranged without anyone yet knowing the point of the hand. Bid the hand through — written bidding is useful — and when the auction is over, whoever is dummy should consult the relevant hand number in the text. The dummy should read out the recommended bidding and the contract to be played is the one in the text. (If this is not the same as the one reached, you may care to replay the hand later in the contract you reached, but initially, play the recommended contract.) The opening lead is made and dummy checks that it is the recommended lead. If not, replace it and make the lead suggested. The play is conducted without further reference to the text until the hand is over. Dummy can then indicate how the play should have gone if the play in the text differs from the actual play. It makes it easier if the cards are played duplicate style, keeping the cards in front of each player, so that the hand can be replayed conveniently. It also helps if everyone has their own book.

Even if you cannot organise a foursome, you can work on the 4 play hands by yourself. To practise the bidding, expose only one hand at a time, starting with the dealer, and write down how the bidding should go. To treat the hands as declarer play exercises, read the auction and cover the defenders' hands. Note the suggested opening lead and then decide on your plan of play before reading the 'correct play' section in the text.

After each part consisting of 8 chapters, there is a revision test of 50 questions. Answer all 50 questions before checking the answers at the back. If you score below 40, read the relevant chapter again. Errors here matter not a whit. The object is to eliminate them when you are actually playing when mistakes do cost.

If some of the areas in the *Guide* are new to you, read through the book again in about 3-6 months time and then again in a year's time. That way you may pick up something that slipped under your guard originally and refresh your memory as well. The more often you cover a topic, the easier it will become.

Above all, remember that bridge is a game and is meant to be enjoyed. It can and should be a lot of fun and that is how you should approach it. Who wants a grim, dour, humourless time? Play the game with a smile and a chuckle. I hope that you will derive as much pleasure and satisfaction from it as I have.

TO THE BRIDGE TEACHER

The *Guide To Better Bridge* is ideal for classroom use. It is set out as 4 courses of 8 lessons each. Parts 1 and 2 are suitable for Improver-Intermediate classes and Parts 3 and 4 are better for Intermediate-Advanced groups. Parts 1 and 3 cover constructive bidding with virtually no interference while Parts 2 and 4 deal with defensive and competitive bidding. The 4 play hands in each chapter are progressively more difficult. The hands in Parts 3 and 4 are significantly tougher than the ones in Parts 1 and 2.

The bidding throughout follows Standard American principles and the answers and the play hands are compatible with 4-card majors or 5-card majors and almost all local differences.

Each chapter contains more material than you will need in the normal 2-3 hour lesson. The subject matter can be covered in less than an hour but the exercises and the partnership bidding practice are often more than required. Choose the exercises which you wish to use in class and leave the rest for the students to do at home. The partnership bidding hands make ideal classroom practice. Allow the students to bid the hand completely before you deal with it. You should discuss the bidding hand by hand rather than wait for the students to bid all the hands. That way the problems are still fresh in their minds when you provide the solutions.

Most important of all are the 4 play hands which are prepared so that each player is declarer once. The hands incorporate the bidding area of the lesson and feature some significant declarer play technique. It is urged that these hands be included in each lesson for playing makes much greater impact than listening. Students learn more quickly and will enjoy your classes more with these practical examples. There are many who can grasp the essence of what you are trying to convey only by actually seeing it happen in play.

Let the students bid the hand through without help but do not let them start play until the recommended auction has been given. The students should play the given contract, not the one reached at the table if this differs. After you have explained the correct auction, the opening lead is chosen by the students without help. Explain the lead before the play continues. If a different lead has been chosen, have the card replaced and the stated lead made. Let the declarers play the hand without assistance. Cards are kept in front of each student in duplicate style. At the end of play, explain the correct play and have the students replay the hand if necessary.

Spend extra time on this play part. Students derive more benefit from it than from listening to a lecture, no matter how skilful and entertaining you might be. Some declarers will succeed, some will fail. Encourage those who fail and compliment those who make it. You achieve more by encouragement than by denigration. Be constructive at all times. Make sure that you never embarrass a student for failing to do the right thing.

It is hoped that the *Guide* will provide a useful tool for your students and make the teaching and learning of bridge an easier, pleasant and rewarding pastime.

Ron Klinger
January 1991

PART 1

CONSOLIDATE YOUR
CONSTRUCTIVE BIDDING

Constructive bidding refers to auctions where your side has opened the bidding. This part examines auctions between you and partner without significant interference by the opposition, about 25% of your bidding problems. Some of the areas should be familiar to you but do not skip over the chapters on that account. You will find more detail on the later bidding than is found in the average basic textbook. Even if you have been there before, it will not harm you to refresh your memory and note some new angles.

Chapter 1 deals with valuing your cards as opener or as responder; what adjustments are to be made; when you should use length points and when you should count shortages; using length points for superior valuation at no-trumps.

Chapter 2 covers responder's problems when holding a weak hand, up to 10 points; responder's strategy; resolving a choice of options depending on whether partner opened with a major suit or with a minor suit; opener's rebids and responder's rebids after an initial weak response; how often responder may bid; the skip-over principle; the barrier principle.

Chapter 3 pursues responder's strategy when holding a strong responding hand of 10 points or more; responder's options and priorities; how to develop a strong responding hand; opener's rebids and responder's rebids after a strong response initially.

Chapter 4 tackles the problems associated with raising partner's suit, whether you are opener or responder; how the bidding proceeds after a raise; raising partner's second suit; giving a preference; simple preference, jump preference and false preference; when and how to give delayed support; handling the 1♠ : 2♡ auction; bidding fake suits to elicit delayed support; bidding by a passed hand.

Chapter 5 deals with suit responses to 1NT and 2NT other than Stayman; when to give support and when to deny support; how to distinguish weak support and strong support; how to indicate weak support or strong support to partner to assist in slam exploration.

Chapter 6 covers the use of Stayman in response to a 1NT or 2NT opening; the requirements for Stayman; when to use Stayman and when not to; subsequent bidding after the reply to Stayman; how to make sure that the no-trump opener remains declarer.

Chapter 7 details the subsequent bidding after opener rebids 1NT or 2NT; responder's actions with a weak hand or with a strong hand; forcing bids and sign-off bids; opener's 2NT rebid after a 1-level response, after a 2-level response or after a jump-shift.

Chapter 8 is concerned with demand opening bids and slam bidding; when your hand is worth a demand; Goren Twos, Strong Twos and the 2♣ Demand; how the bidding proceeds in each of these methods; weak responses and strong responses; recognising slam potential; the use of Blackwood; when Blackwood is not necessary; when 4NT is not Blackwood; when to use the 5NT ask for kings; when to avoid using 5NT for kings; the use of 5NT when 4NT has not been used.

CHAPTER 1

HAND VALUATION FOR OPENER AND RESPONDER

THE HIGH CARD POINT COUNT

All standard systems start hand valuation by counting the high card content of the hand on this scale:

$$A = 4 \quad K = 3 \quad Q = 2 \quad J = 1$$

Other points are usually added to or subtracted from the high card point total but all hand valuation starts with the basic 4-3-2-1 count.

POINTS TO BE ADDED BY OPENER OR RESPONDER

Add 1 point when holding all four aces.

Add 1 point when holding 13 or more points consisting only of aces and kings.

POINTS TO BE SUBTRACTED BY OPENER OR RESPONDER

Deduct 1 point for a singleton king, singleton queen or singleton jack.
Deduct 1 point for a hand containing a queen-doubleton (Q-x), jack doubleton (J-x) or Q-J doubleton.
Deduct 1 point for a hand of 12 HCP or more which contains no aces.
Deduct 1 point for a 4-3-3-3 pattern unless bidding no-trumps.

POINTS USED WHEN OPENING THE BIDDING

To assess your hand for opening the bidding, count your High Card Points and add your Length Points (1 point for each card after the fourth card in any long suit, so that you count 1 extra point for a 5-card suit, 2 extra points for a 6-card suit, 3 extra points for a 7-card suit). The following hands are worth opening:

- **HANDS WITH 12 HCP OR MORE WITH NONE OF THE ABOVE POOR FEATURES**
- **HANDS WITH 13 POINTS COUNTING HCP PLUS LENGTH POINTS**

It follows that a hand with 11 HCP and a 6-card suit is worth opening, as is a hand with 11 HCP and two 5-card suits. A hand with 10 HCP and a 7-card suit would normally be opened with a pre-empt rather than a 1-opening. The best guide is that if most of the points are in the long suit, prefer the pre-empt, but if most of the points are outside the long suit, choose the 1-opening.

It is best not to count any shortage points when opening the bidding: to do so is counting your chickens before they hatch. The hand may end up in no-trumps where shortages are of no value or partner may hold length where you hold shortage and your shortage in partner's long suit is a defect, not an advantage. The opener should retain the HCP + Length Points count until a trump fit is located. Once a trump fit has come to light, opener then switches over to HCP + Shortage Points (Void = 5, Singleton = 3, Doubleton = 1). The point count assesses your trick-taking potential. In no-trumps or when there is no trump fit, tricks are usually taken by high cards or long suits. When there is a trump fit, tricks are normally won with high cards and by trumping.

Counting length points as part of your opening values is important. If you are using a 16-18 1NT opening, then a 5-3-3-2 pattern with 15 HCP is strong enough to open 1NT (because of the extra length point for the 5-card suit), while a 5-3-3-2 pattern with 18 HCP would be too strong for 1NT and should be treated as a 19-point hand. Likewise, if using a 22-24 2NT, a 5-3-3-2 hand of 21 HCP is worth 2NT.

Where the opener has a 5-4-2-2 pattern, it is not standard to open 1NT even if the point count is right, but if more than half of your HCP are in the short suits, 1NT is reasonable. Similarly, if you have opened a 5-4-2-2 with a 1-bid and received a suit response at the 1-level, then if more than half your points are in your short suits, a rebid of 1NT is attractive. However, if more than half your points are in your long suits, prefer to choose a suit rebid.

POINTS USED WHEN RESPONDING

In reply to a no-trump opening (or rebid), count HCP plus Length Points. Where a good trump fit is known to exist, such as when responder holds a 6-card or longer suit opposite a known balanced hand and responder intends to play in that suit, count HCP plus the 5-3-1 Shortage Point Count. If responder shows a 5-card suit and receives support, or if responder uses the Stayman enquiry (see Chapter 6) and locates a trump fit, again responder should use HCP plus the 5-3-1 Shortage Count.

In reply to a suit opening, if no trump fit has been located, responder should count only HCP, but may add 1 extra point only when holding a strong, long suit. If a trump fit has been found, responder should use HCP plus the 5-3-1 Shortage Point Count (Void = 5, Singleton = 3, Doubleton = 1).

Counting Length Points as responder is important after opener has shown a balanced hand. Since opener does not hold a void or a singleton, responder's long suit is more likely to be useful in producing additional tricks. Thus, opposite a 16-18 1NT, a 5-3-3-2 hand with 7 HCP is worth 2NT, showing 8-9 points, while a 5-3-3-2 with 9 HCP should be treated as 10 points and raise to 3NT. Likewise, a 6-3-2-2 with 8 HCP is worth a bid of game opposite a strong 1NT, because of the two extra points allowed for the long suit.

Where the responder to a no-trump opening has enough for a borderline game (combined total 25-27 points) and holds length in the minor suits, respond in no-trumps rather than in the long minor. It is much easier to score 3NT (9 tricks) than 5-in-a-minor (11 tricks).

Hands with honor cards in the long suits are more valuable than with honor cards in the short suits. Combined honors in one suit (A-K-Q) are superior to honors split among suits (A-x-x, K-x-x, Q-x-x).

PARTNERSHIP BIDDING PRACTICE : How should the following hands be bid? West is the dealer on all hands. Assume you are using a 16-18 1NT opening and and a 22-24 2NT opening.

SET 1 — WEST	SET 1 — EAST	SET 2 — WEST	SET 2 — EAST
1. ♠ A 9 2 ♡ A 5 4 ◇ A 8 4 ♣ A 9 7 5	1. ♠ Q 8 ♡ 7 6 3 ◇ K Q J 9 5 2 ♣ A 9 7 5	1. ♠ A K 7 3 ♡ K 9 8 ◇ A Q J 3 ♣ A J	1. ♠ 5 4 2 ♡ 7 6 ◇ 9 8 6 2 ♣ 8 5 4 3
2. ♠ A 4 3 ♡ 8 6 ◇ 9 2 ♣ A 10 9 6 4 2	2. ♠ K 7 5 ♡ A Q 3 ◇ A 10 8 6 ♣ K 7 3	2. ♠ 8 7 6 ♡ 8 4 ◇ K 9 7 6 2 ♣ 9 5 4	2. ♠ 9 5 2 ♡ A K 3 ◇ A Q J 4 ♣ A K J
3. ♠ K 2 ♡ 4 3 ◇ A 9 8 6 4 ♣ 9 5 4 3	3. ♠ A Q 3 ♡ A J 10 ◇ K 7 5 ♣ A 8 7 2	3. ♠ A K 4 ♡ A 8 7 ◇ A Q 5 ♣ A J 8 3	3. ♠ 8 6 3 ♡ 5 4 ◇ K 9 6 4 3 2 ♣ 5 4
4. ♠ A 5 ♡ A 6 5 4 ◇ A K J 8 ♣ 7 3 2	4. ♠ 8 4 ♡ 7 3 ◇ 6 2 ♣ A K 9 8 6 5 4	4. ♠ 5 4 ♡ 7 2 ◇ 7 5 3 ♣ K 7 6 5 3 2	4. ♠ A J ♡ A K Q 6 ◇ A 9 4 2 ♣ A 9 4
5. ♠ 7 2 ♡ K 8 6 ◇ 10 9 7 6 5 ♣ A Q 7	5. ♠ A Q ♡ A Q 3 ◇ 4 3 2 ♣ K 9 6 4 2	5. ♠ K 8 ♡ A Q 3 ◇ A K 8 ♣ A J 7 6 4	5. ♠ A 9 2 ♡ K 7 4 ◇ Q J 5 2 ♣ Q 10 5
6. ♠ A 4 3 ♡ J 10 3 ◇ A Q ♣ A K 9 6 5	6. ♠ 10 9 5 2 ♡ Q 6 5 ◇ K 8 4 ♣ Q 8 3	6. ♠ A K Q ♡ A Q 4 ◇ K Q 10 3 ♣ Q 7 6	6. ♠ J 5 4 ♡ K J 2 ◇ A 9 5 2 ♣ A K J

(handwritten margin notes: 3N, 3N, 2N, 3N next to items in SET 1 — WEST)

PLAY HANDS ON HAND VALUATION FOR OPENER AND RESPONDER

Hand 1 : Length points for no-trumps — Taking care not to block your long suit

Dealer North : Nil vulnerable

NORTH
- ♠ A 6
- ♡ 8 4 3
- ◇ Q 4 2
- ♣ A K Q 5 2

WEST
- ♠ Q 7 4 2
- ♡ J 9 5 2
- ◇ A K
- ♣ J 10 8

EAST
- ♠ K J 10 9 5
- ♡ 10 7 6
- ◇ 10 9 6 5
- ♣ 4

SOUTH
- ♠ 8 3
- ♡ A K Q
- ◇ J 8 7 3
- ♣ 9 7 6 3

WEST	NORTH	EAST	SOUTH
	1NT (1)	Pass	3NT
Pass	Pass	Pass	

Bidding : (1) Worth 16 points because of the 5th club. If North opened 1♣, the bidding might go 1♣ : 1◇, 1NT : Pass.

Lead : ♠ J. When holding 3 honors, lead top of the touching honors. This holding is known as an interior sequence and you lead top of where the sequence begins.

Correct play : After winning the ♠ A, play the ace, king and queen of clubs, *unblocking the 9-7-6 from dummy* and retaining dummy's 3 of clubs. Continue with the 5 of clubs, keeping the lead in your own hand as dummy has the 3 left, and then the 2 of clubs. This makes 5 clubs, 3 hearts and 1 spade.

Wrong Play : Playing the 3 of clubs from dummy on any of the first 3 rounds of clubs. This means the 4th round of clubs will be won in dummy and declarer's 5th club will be stranded.

A few bitter experiences will lead to the recognition that to make 5 club tricks the lead must stay in hand. Thus, the 5 of clubs must win a trick and to achieve that, dummy must not be left with a higher club.

Hand 2 : Staying with no-trumps when holding length in a minor — Avoiding a blockage

Dealer East : North-South vulnerable

NORTH
- ♠ K 7 5 4
- ♡ Q J 10 5 2
- ◇ Q 8
- ♣ 10 8

WEST
- ♠ 9 2
- ♡ 7 3
- ◇ K 7 6 4 3 2
- ♣ 6 4 2

EAST
- ♠ A J
- ♡ A 8 6 4
- ◇ A 9 5
- ♣ A K Q 3

SOUTH
- ♠ Q 10 8 6 3
- ♡ K 9
- ◇ J 10
- ♣ J 9 7 5

WEST	NORTH	EAST	SOUTH
		2NT	Pass
3NT (1)	Pass	Pass	Pass

Bidding : (1) With barely the values for a game, stick with partner's no-trumps and do not explore a minor suit game. Do not bid a minor suit unless you wish to play in that minor suit contract.

Lead : ♠ 6. It is normal to lead your long suit against no-trumps and 4th-highest is standard if no sequence is held.

Correct play : With only 7 top tricks and the spades wide open, you will need a 2-2 break in diamonds to succeed. After winning the ace of spades, play the ace of diamonds and then carefully *unblock the 9 of diamonds from hand* when leading to dummy's king on the second round of diamonds. After the 2-2 split, dummy's diamonds are high : again be careful to continue with the 7 or 6 from dummy (not a lower card) to ensure that the lead stays in dummy. If the diamonds happened to be 3-1, the contract was destined to fail on the spade lead.

Wrong play : It would be all right to lead the 9 of diamonds to the king on the first round, and then back to your ace, overtaking the ◇ 5 on the 3rd round. However, the contract will fail if you do not unblock the ◇ 9 on the 1st or 2nd round of diamonds The 3rd round of diamonds would be won in hand and 3 diamond winners would be stranded in dummy, leaving declarer with only 8 tricks.

EXERCISE

You opened 1◇ and partner responded 1♠. What is your rebid on each of these hands?

1.	2.	3.	4.	5.
♠ K 7	♠ A 7	♠ A	♠ A 7 2	♠ A 8 7 2
♡ 7 3	♡ A Q	♡ A K J	♡ A J	♡ 6
◇ A Q 9 6 4	◇ Q 9 7 6 4	◇ 8 7 6 4 3	◇ A K 8 6 2	◇ A K 9 4 3
♣ K J 7 3	♣ J 7 3 2	♣ J 8 5 4	♣ Q 9 7	♣ K Q J

Hand 3 : Creating an entry to a blocked suit — Not playing mechanically and carelessly

Dealer South : East-West vulnerable

NORTH
- ♠ 6 3
- ♡ 8 4
- ◇ Q J 10
- ♣ J 10 8 6 4 3

WEST
- ♠ K 9 8
- ♡ Q 7 6
- ◇ K 8 6 3 2
- ♣ 7 2

EAST
- ♠ Q 7 5 4 2
- ♡ A 10 9 2
- ◇ 5 4
- ♣ 9 5

SOUTH
- ♠ A J 10
- ♡ K J 5 3
- ◇ A 9 7
- ♣ A K Q

WEST	NORTH	EAST	SOUTH
			2NT
Pass	3NT (1)	Pass	All pass

Bidding: (1) With length in a minor but only 25-27 points in the combined hands, stick with no-trumps and do not look for the minor suit game.

Lead: ◇ 3. 4th-highest from your long suit is normal.

Correct play: When dummy's diamond holds the trick, there is a natural instinct to play low from hand. When dummy appears, a vital plan is to count your tricks and, if you have the tricks needed, check whether there is any problem in taking those tricks. Here South has 1 spade, 2 diamonds and 6 clubs, enough tricks, but the club suit is blocked. To use dummy's club winners, dummy needs an outside entry, and the only possible entry is in diamonds.

The solution is simple, though contrary to instinct : Win the lead with the *ace*, cash ♣ A-K-Q and then lead a diamond. North's diamonds ensure an entry to dummy later to cash the club winners.

Winning the 1st diamond "cheaply" in dummy is a fallacy. If you win the 1st diamond in dummy, you make 2 diamond tricks, but winning the 1st diamond with the ace also makes 2 diamond tricks! Keep a constant lookout for blocked suits and the entry needed to reach the winners after unblocking.

Hand 4 : Length points for no-trumps — Overtaking in order to set up a long suit

Dealer West : Both vulnerable

NORTH
- ♠ Q J 9 7 3
- ♡ J 8
- ◇ J 8 7 6 5
- ♣ 3

WEST
- ♠ A K 5
- ♡ 7 5 3 2
- ◇ A 9 4 3
- ♣ K Q

EAST
- ♠ 10 8
- ♡ A 10 6
- ◇ 10 2
- ♣ A 10 9 8 7 6

SOUTH
- ♠ 6 4 2
- ♡ K Q 9 4
- ◇ K Q
- ♣ J 5 4 2

WEST	NORTH	EAST	SOUTH
1NT	Pass	3NT (1)	All pass

Bidding: (1) East is worth 10 points, counting 2 Length Points for the clubs. With barely enough for game, stick with no-trumps and do not introduce a minor suit.

Lead: ♠ Q. Top of a near-sequence is the standard lead. Treat Q-J-9-x-x the same as Q-J-10-x-x. As it happens, a heart lead would knock out the vital entry to dummy, but there is no way that North could deduce that. The heart lead would fail far more often than it would succeed.

Correct play: There are 7 top tricks and the clubs are needed to provide the additional tricks. Mostly the clubs will divide 3-2 and mostly it would be adequate to play ♣ K-♣ Q, cross to the ♡ A and run the club winners. However, there is the possibility of a bad break and when North shows out on the 2nd club, declarer can cope with the bad split by overtaking with dummy's ace and continuing dummy's clubs, forcing South to take the jack sooner or later. When North shows out, it is clear that a club has to be lost anyway and the ♡ A is vital as an entry to dummy later. Declarer thus makes 2 spades, 1 heart, 1 diamond and 5 clubs. At teams or rubber bridge, it would be correct to overtake the 2nd club even if North follows, just in case *North* has ♣ J-x-x-x.

EXERCISE

Partner opened 1NT (16-18). What is your response on each of these hands?

1. ♠ 8 7	2. ♠ A 7	3. ♠ 7 6	4. ♠ K 8	5. ♠ 10 9
♡ 7 6	♡ 7 3	♡ 8 5	♡ 8 2	♡ 8 3
◇ Q 9 4 3	◇ K 9 8 6 4	◇ 4 3	◇ A J 10 6 4 3	◇ 7 6 4
♣ A K 7 4 2	♣ 7 6 4 3	♣ A K 9 6 4 3 2	♣ 9 7 6	♣ A Q 10 8 7 2

CHAPTER 2

WEAK RESPONDING HANDS AFTER A SUIT OPENING

VALUING YOUR HAND AS RESPONDER

No trump fit yet found : Count just your HCP (but allow 1 point for any long suit)

An 8-card or better trump fit has been found : Count HCP and add 5-3-1 Count

The 5-for-a-void, 3-for-a-singleton, 1-for-each-doubleton distributional count is used by both the responder and the opener after a trump fit has come to light. The shortage itself is not valuable. What is measured is the ability to ruff and score tricks with low trumps. All point count methods measure trick-taking potential and counting for shortages should not be used when opening. At that stage there is no certainty that you will end up in a trump contract or be able to agree with partner on a trump suit.

WHAT IS A WEAK RESPONDING HAND?

Hands in the 0-9 point range are considered weak. Any 4-3-3-3 with 10 HCP or any 4-4-3-2 with 10 HCP which has not located a trump fit should also be classified as a weak responding hand. 4-4-3-2 hands with 10 HCP which have located a trump fit and other patterns with 10 HCP should be classified as strong responding hands (see Chapter 3). The 0-9 framework will be used with the understanding that it does also include the above poor 10-counts. Responder should upgrade or downgrade 10-counts according to shape, trump fit, good features or poor features.

RESPONDER'S STRATEGY

0-5 Points : PASS. It is more dangerous to bid than to pass with a rotten hand, even with a misfit.

Pass is best because the chance for game is so remote and if we do respond, partner will assume we hold some values and may make a jump-response on the next round. Even if you do not hold support for partner's suit, it is better to pass with nothing than to reply and find the partnership much higher on the next round. Rather pass 1♣ than reply and hear 3♣ next time. If opener is weak, 4th player usually bids after you pass, while if opener is strong, the likely jump rebid after you respond puts you overboard.

6-9 Points : BID. Bid something, anything. Do not pass. It is more dangerous to pass than to bid.

It is correct to respond with 6 points or better ("keep the bidding alive") just in case opener has a huge hand and a game might be made. It is better to bid and risk failing in a partscore than to pass and risk missing a game. Responder is worth action even with 5 HCP plus a 5-card or longer suit.

CHOICE OF RESPONSES WITH 6-9 POINTS

● **Raise opener's suit** = 6-9 points (10) + support for opener's suit. Support is the number of trumps needed to make at least 8 trumps between you and partner. 3 cards is support for a 5-card suit, 4 cards is support for a possible 4-card suit, while opposite what could be a 3-card suit (commonly the 1♣ opening), 5-card support is needed to give a raise. Do not give a 3-card raise for a 4-card suit unless desperate.

● **Bid your own suit at the 1-level** = 6 or more points and at least a 4-card suit. The change of suit is forcing and the strength for a new suit bid includes hands with 10 or more points. This extra strength will be revealed later (see Chapter 3).

● **Bid 1NT as a last resort** = 6-9 points (10) and denies support for opener and denies a 4-card suit that could have been bid at the 1-level. 1◇ : 1NT, for example, denies 4 spades, 4 hearts or 4 diamonds. It is easy to deduce that the 1NT response to 1◇ must therefore include at least 4 clubs.

● **You must not bid a new suit at the 2-level if you have only 6-9 points** — *the 2-over-1 response promises 10 points or more.* This restriction is vital and as a result it is possible that the 1NT response may not be a balanced hand. If you hold 6-9 points, you must not pass but if your suit is lower-ranking than opener's, you are not permitted to bid it at the 2-level with such a weak hand. Bid 1NT as least of evils.

WHERE RESPONDER HAS A CHOICE OF ACTIONS

Where responder's hand fits more than one possible action, the order of priorities will depend on whether partner opened with a major suit or with a minor suit.

If the opening bid was in a major suit :

1. Raise opener's major.*

2. Over a 1♡ opening, bid 1♠ with 4+ spades if unable to support hearts.

3. Bid 1NT as a last resort.

If the opening bid was in a minor suit :

1. Bid a major suit at the 1-level.

2. Raise opener's minor suit.**

3. Bid 1NT as a last resort.

Basically, with a weak hand, major suit action comes first and 1NT is the last choice.

*The normal raise would be to the 2-level, but a pre-emptive raise (the "weak-freak") to the 4-level is also available. The 1♡ : 4♡ and 1♠ : 4♠ raises show less than 10 HCP, excellent trump support (at least 9 trumps together) and an unbalanced hand. The function of these shut-out raises is to keep 4th hand out of the bidding, to bid game and win the contract without promising a strong hand. If you have support for opener and a stronger hand, bid 1♡ : 3♡ or 1♠ : 3♠.

**Shut-out raises in the minors (1♣ : 4♣ *or* 1♣ : 5♣ *or* 1♢ : 4♢ *or* 1♢ : 5♢) are also available but are very rare since they bypass a possible 3NT contract. When used, however, they show the same sort of hand as the shut-out raise in the major suits, namely weak in high cards (usually 6-9 HCP, perhaps even weaker), 5-card or longer trump support and an unbalanced hand (must have a void or a singleton).

Where responder's action is to change suit and responder has a choice of new suits to bid, the order is :

● **Bid your longest suit first.**

● **With any 5-5 or 6-6 pattern, bid the higher-ranking suit first (bid "down-the-line").**

● **With two or three 4-card suits, bid the cheapest suit first (bid "up-the-line").**

It is important to bid your longer suit first, since the aim is to reach the partnership's best combined trump suit. If responder bids two suits, opener's choice with no clearcut preference will be to support the suit responder bid first. For example, after a 1♣ opening, if you hold 5 diamonds and 4 spades, respond 1♢ and not 1♠. Since the 1♢ bid is forcing, opener is obliged to bid again and you will have a chance to show the spades later if you think that is desirable. If you bid the spades first and the diamonds later, you suggest the spades are longer than the diamonds or at least that the suits are equal.

After a 1♣ opening, when responder holds 4 diamonds and a 4-card major, *it is best to respond 1♢* whether responder has a weak hand or a strong hand. This follows the up-the-line rule. Previously, the style with a weak responding hand was to bid the major, but this is no longer the case. Responding 1♢ enables a diamond fit to be found, allows opener to bid the major first and does not risk missing the major. If fourth player bids a major, either partner can use a takeout double to show the other major.

EXERCISE

A. Partner opened 1♣. What is your response on each of these hands?

1. ♠ K 7 4 3 2	2. ♠ A 7 4 2	3. ♠ 3	4. ♠ 8 7	5. ♠ A 8 7 2
♡ 2	♡ Q 6 5 3	♡ K J 6 5	♡ K 9 4 3	♡ 6 3
♢ A 9 6 4 2	♢ 6 4	♢ K 7 6 4 3 2	♢ K J 6 2	♢ 9 4
♣ 7 3	♣ 7 3 2	♣ 5 4	♣ 9 7 5	♣ K 6 4 3 2

B. What would your response be on the above hands if the opening had been 1♢?

C. What would your response be on the above hands if the opening had been 1♡?

D. What would your response be on the above hands if the opening had been 1♠?

OPENER'S REBIDS AFTER A WEAK RESPONSE

Opener's hand is generally divided into 3 ranges : 13-15 minimum, 16-18 strong, 19 up maximum.

Strategy : If the partnership may hold 26 points, keep on bidding since game is feasible. If the combined total is 25 points *at least* and there might be more, bid for a game. If the combined total is 25 points *at most* and there might be less, do not bid for a game. With 26 points together, game is a good bet; with 25 points together, game is a fair bet and with 24 points or less together, game is a poor bet. This bidding strategy is revealed in the approach taken by opener after a weak response from partner.

Opener's action after a raise to the 2-level (e.g. 1♡ : 2♡, . . . ?)

Opener applies the 5-3-1 count (void 5, singleton 3, doubleton 1). With 12-15 points, pass (responder has 6-10 = no 26 points); with 16-18, bid again (raise a major suit to the 3-level or change suit; if your suit is a minor, raise to the 3-level, change suit or try 2NT); with 19 up, bid game (if your suit is a major, raise it to the 4-level; if it is a minor, consider 3NT if your hand is balanced or semi-balanced).

After a 1NT response (e.g. 1◊ : 1NT, . . . ?)

If satisfied with no-trumps, pass with 12-15 points, raise to 2NT with 16-18 and bid 3NT with 19-20. If not happy with no-trumps: *with 12-15 points,* bid a new suit lower than your 1st suit *or* repeat your 1st suit with extra length; *with 16-18 points,* bid any new suit *or* with no 2nd suit, jump to 3-in-the-1st-suit with at least 6 cards in it; with 19 points up, jump to the 3-level in a new suit (jump-shift) *or* jump to game in your suit.

After a suit response at the 1-level (e.g. 1♣ : 1♡, . . . ?)

THE SKIP-OVER PRINCIPLE

Where opener's rebid skips over a suit, opener does not hold that suit. After 1◊ : 1♡, opener's 1NT or 2◊ rebid denies 4 spades. Similarly, after 1♣ : 1◊, opener's 2♣ denies 4 spades or 4 hearts, since the 1♠ and 1♡ rebids were bypassed. After 1♣ : 1♠, 2♣, however, opener may still hold 4 hearts or 4 diamonds, since the 1◊ and 1♡ rebids were not available. Similarly, if a 1NT rebid is available and opener bypasses 1NT (e.g. 1◊ : 1♠, 2◊), assume that opener does not hold a balanced hand. With a 5-3-3-2 minimum, opener should choose a 1NT rebid rather than rebid the 5-card suit.

THE BARRIER PRINCIPLE

Whichever suit is opened, the opener creates a barrier of 2-of-that-suit when making a rebid :

Any bid beyond that barrier (except raising partner) shows a strong hand, normally 16 point at least, and is forcing.

Suppose you have opened 1♣. Your barrier is 2♣ and all these rebids show a strong hand as the rebid is beyond the barrier :   1♣ : 1♡, 2◊   1♣ : 1♠, 2◊   1♣ : 1♠, 2♡   1♣ : 1♡, 2NT

These sequences do not promise a strong hand :   1♣ : 1◊, 1♡   1♣ : 1♠, 1NT   1♣ : 1♡, 2♡

Suppose you have opened 1◊. Your barrier is 2◊ and all these rebids show a strong hand as the rebid is beyond the barrier :   1◊ : 1♠, 2♡   1◊ : 2♣, 2♡   1◊ : 2♣, 2♠   1◊ : 1NT, 2♡

These sequences do not promise extra strength :   1◊ : 1♡, 1♠   1◊ : 1♠, 2♣   1◊ : 2♣, 3♣

Suppose you have opened 1♡. Your barrier is 2♡ and all these rebids show a strong hand as the rebid is beyond the barrier :   1♡ : 2◊, 2♠   1♡ : 2◊, 3♣   1♡ : 2♣, 3◊   1♡ : 2◊, 3♡

These sequences do not promise extra strength :   1♡ : 1♠, 2♣   1♡ : 2♣, 2◊   1♡ : 2♣, 3♣

The crux of making a natural rebid is this — **Opener should make a natural rebid unless that rebid goes beyond opener's barrier and opener has only a minimum opening.**

Within the framework of the above rules, opener chooses a rebid over a new suit response as follows :

(a) Opener has 12-15 points

With a minimum opening, make a minimum rebid. You must not make a jump rebid unless you have a strong opening. In order of preference, opener's possible rebids are :

● **Raise responder's suit.** This requires 4-card support since the suit bid by responder need not have more than four cards in it. The only time opener would not raise responder is when opener has a 4-card major as well as support for responder's minor. Show your major first rather than support partner's minor.

Bid a new suit at the 1-level. The new suit must have four cards in it, but any suit quality will do for a rebid. Prefer to bid a new suit at the 1-level to rebidding 1NT or repeating your 1st suit.

Rebid 1NT if your hand is balanced. You may also choose a 1NT rebid with a 5-4-2-2 pattern with most of your strength in the short suits, or even with a 5-4-3-1 pattern and a singleton in responder's suit, if your 5-card suit is too weak to rebid (less than two honors) and to bid your 4-card suit would take you beyond your barrier.

Bid a new suit at the 2-level lower than your 1st suit. With a minimum opening, you should not rebid higher than 2-of-your-1st-suit (your barrier) unless you are supporting responder's suit.

Rebid your 1st suit as a last resort. To rebid your 1st suit after a 1-level response, the suit must be at least 5 cards long and must have more length than the opening bid promised.

(b) Opener has 16-18 points

In order of preference, opener should :

Jump-raise responder's suit to the 3-level. Opener must have 4-card support for this action. If opener has support for responder, opener would decline to raise responder only if opener had an unbid major as well as support for responder's minor suit. In that case, show the major first.

Bid a new suit at the 1-level or 2-level.

As a last resort, jump to the 3-level in the suit opened with at least 6 cards in that suit.

(c) Opener has 19 points or more

In order of preference, opener should :

Jump to game in responder's suit. This requires 4-card support. With support, opener would decline to support responder only if opener has an unbid 4-card major as well as support for responder's minor. In that case, opener would jump-shift in the unbid major rather than support the minor yet. Majors come first.

Jump to 2NT, provided your hand is balanced. The jump to 2NT is played as forcing to game.

Jump-shift. The jump-shift denies a balanced hand but is forcing to game as it shows 19 points up.

As a last resort, if none of the above is available, jump to game in your first suit, provided that you have a very powerful 6-card suit (with at least four honours) or a very strong 7-card suit.

RESPONDER'S REBID WITH A WEAK RESPONDING HAND

If opener has made a minimum rebid, confirming a hand in the 12-15 point range, responder is allowed to pass. However, responder is not obliged to pass if opener's rebid is unsuitable, but responder with a weak hand must not make a strong rebid. Over opener's suit rebid, do not change suit or jump with a weak hand. Responder *is* entitled to bid again with a weak hand, provided that responder's rebid is :

A raise of opener's 2nd suit to the 2-level (e.g. 1♣ : 1♡, 1♠ : 2♠). This shows 6-9 points just as an immediate raise shows 6-9 points. *Four trumps are needed to raise opener's 2nd suit.*

A preference to opener's 1st suit (e.g. 1◇ : 1♡, 1♠ : 2◇). This also shows just 6-9 points in the same way that an immediate raise of opener's 1st suit (1◇ : 2◇) shows only 6-9 points.

A rebid of 1NT shows 6-9 points just as an initial response of 1NT shows 6-9 points.

As a last resort, rebid your own suit if it contains at least 6 cards or is a powerful 5-card suit.

If opener's rebid is a jump, showing 16-18 points, responder is permitted to pass with just 6-7 points but is expected to bid on with 8 points up since the partnership could then have 26 or more. With enough to bid, support opener's major suit as first priority; repeat your own 5-card suit as last choice.

If opener's rebid is a change of suit, opener may have up to 18 points (opener's range for a change of suit is 12-18 since 19 points or more are needed for a jump-shift rebid). Accordingly, responder strives to find a rebid with 8 points or better, since the partnership could have 26 points.

If opener's rebid is a jump showing 19 points or more (a jump-shift or a jump to 2NT or a jump to game), responder is obliged to bid again if game has not been reached, but is permitted to pass, of course, if opener's rebid is already a game (e.g. 1♡ : 1♠, 4♡).

EXERCISES

A. Partner opened 1♣. What is your response on each of these hands?

1. ♠ K 8 7 4 2	2. ♠ 8	3. ♠ J 8 7 5	4. ♠ A 9 8 3	5. ♠ 7
♡ Q 8 7 3	♡ K 7 5 4	♡ 5 2	♡ 6	♡ K 9 8 7 5
◊ J 2	◊ Q 7 6 3	◊ K 4 3 2	◊ Q 9 7 6 3	◊ Q J 7 6 2
♣ 7 2	♣ 8 6 3 2	♣ Q 5 4	♣ K 7 2	♣ 5 3

B. What would your response have been on the hands in A. if partner had opened 1♡?

C. You opened 1♣ and partner responded 1◊. What is your rebid on each of these hands?

1. ♠ K 7 6 4	2. ♠ A K 9 8	3. ♠ A 8	4. ♠ A Q 7 2	5. ♠ A 8 5
♡ Q 7 3 2	♡ A J 6 4	♡ K 6 3	♡ - - -	♡ 6 3
◊ J	◊ - - -	◊ A 7 6	◊ K 8 6 2	◊ K Q
♣ A K 9 7	♣ K 9 7 3 2	♣ Q J 8 5 4	♣ A Q 9 7 3	♣ A K J 9 5 2

D. What would your rebid be on the above hands in C. if partner's response had been 1♡?

E. You opened 1◊ and partner responded 1♡. What is your next action on each of these hands?

1. ♠ K 7 4 2	2. ♠ J 7 6 4	3. ♠ J 6 4	4. ♠ A 7	5. ♠ A 8 7
♡ 3	♡ K Q	♡ 5	♡ A J 8 6	♡ K 5
◊ K Q 9 8 7 3	◊ A K Q 3	◊ A K 4 3 2	◊ A Q 9 7 5	◊ A Q J 7 2
♣ A 2	♣ 6 3 2	♣ K Q 5 4	♣ 7 2	♣ 9 5 3

F. What would your next action be on the above hands if partner's response had been 1NT?

PARTNERSHIP BIDDING : How should the following hands be bid? West is the dealer on all hands.

SET 3 – WEST	SET 3 – EAST	SET 4 – WEST	SET 4 – EAST
1. ♠ A 8 5 2	1. ♠ 9 6 3	1. ♠ A 8 3	1. ♠ K 7 6
♡ A 7	♡ K 5 4	♡ A Q 8	♡ K 5 4
◊ Q 6 4	◊ 8 2	◊ K 8 6 4	◊ 9 5 2
♣ K 9 5 4	♣ Q J 7 6 2	♣ 9 4 3	♣ Q J 7 6
2. ♠ K 2	2. ♠ A J 10 3	2. ♠ Q 7 2	2. ♠ K 5 3
♡ 8 7 5	♡ K 6 2	♡ 8 6	♡ A K 7 4 3
◊ Q 6 3 2	◊ A K 9 4	◊ K 9 5	◊ A J 4
♣ K 8 5 3	♣ A 10	♣ Q 10 9 3 2	♣ K J
3. ♠ A Q 9 4	3. ♠ J 8	3. ♠ A J 8 6 5	3. ♠ 4 2
♡ K 8 7 6 2	♡ A 9 4 3	♡ K 4 3 2	♡ Q 8 6 5
◊ J 9	◊ K 7 5 2	◊ 7	◊ A 8 4 3
♣ K 4	♣ 8 7 2	♣ K Q 3	♣ 7 6 5
4. ♠ 9 6 4 3	4. ♠ A J 10 7 2	4. ♠ K 6 3	4. ♠ A J 8
♡ K 7	♡ A Q 10 4 3	♡ Q 7	♡ A J 10 5 4 2
◊ 7 6 2	◊ A Q	◊ A 8 4 2	◊ 3
♣ K 8 4 3	♣ 2	♣ 7 6 5 2	♣ K Q J
5. ♠ J 9 8 7 2	5. ♠ Q 10 6 5 4	5. ♠ A Q J 7 6 2	5. ♠ 4 3
♡ A K 3	♡ 8 6	♡ A K 3	♡ 8 7 5
◊ A J 4	◊ 3	◊ Q 4	◊ 9 6 5 2
♣ 8 2	♣ A 7 6 4 3	♣ 3 2	♣ A Q 6 4
6. ♠ K 5 4 3	6. ♠ A J 8 7 6 2	6. ♠ 3	6. ♠ A K 7 6 2
♡ Q 6 4 2	♡ J 7	♡ K 5 4 3	♡ A Q 9 8
◊ J 9 7	◊ 6 5	◊ K 7 5 3	◊ A Q 4
♣ 6 5	♣ A K Q	♣ 8 7 6 2	♣ 3

G. You opened 1♠ and partner responded 2♠. What is your next action on each of these hands?

1. ♠ A 8 7 5 3   2. ♠ A Q 7 6 4   3. ♠ K Q 8 6 4 3   4. ♠ Q J 7 5 3 2   5. ♠ A J 7 6 4
   ♡ K Q   ♡ A K   ♡ A K 4   ♡ A 2   ♡ J 9
   ◇ A 7 4   ◇ A Q 3   ◇ K J 3   ◇ A 4 3   ◇ 8 2
   ♣ 6 4 2   ♣ J 3 2   ♣ 5   ♣ J 6   ♣ A K 6 4

H. What would your next action be on the above hands in G. if partner's response had been 1NT?

I. Partner opened 1♣, you responded 1♡ and opener rebid 1♠. What is your next action on these hands?

1. ♠ K 8 4 3   2. ♠ K 9 8   3. ♠ 8 7   4. ♠ A 7   5. ♠ 10 6 3
   ♡ K 7 6 2   ♡ A 7 6 4   ♡ A 10 6 4   ♡ J 10 9 4 3 2   ♡ Q 9 7 4 2
   ◇ Q 3   ◇ Q 9 8   ◇ 8 3   ◇ J 8   ◇ K Q 3
   ♣ 8 7 6   ♣ 7 3 2   ♣ K 10 7 5 4   ♣ 6 4 2   ♣ 8 6

J. What would your next action be on the above hands in I. if partner's rebid had been 2♣?

K. Partner opened 1♡, you responded 1♠ and opener rebid 2♣. What is your next action on these hands?

1. ♠ A J 8 7   2. ♠ A J 7 6 4 2   3. ♠ Q 9 8 7 2   4. ♠ J 9 7 5 4   5. ♠ Q J 9 7 6 3
   ♡ 7 2   ♡ J   ♡ 9 7   ♡ 8   ♡ 10 5
   ◇ 9 8 4   ◇ J 4 3   ◇ Q 5 4 2   ◇ K Q 4 2   ◇ K 9 7
   ♣ J 7 5 2   ♣ 7 6 4   ♣ A 6   ♣ J 5 2   ♣ J 3

L. What would your next action be on the above hands in K. if opener's rebid had been 3♠?

PARTNERSHIP BIDDING : How should the following hands be bid? West is the dealer on all hands.

SET 5 – WEST	SET 5 – EAST	SET 6 – WEST	SET 6 – EAST
1. ♠ A J 3 ♡ K 7 4 ◇ K 3 ♣ K 9 7 3 2	1. ♠ K 6 5 ♡ Q 9 6 5 3 2 ◇ J 7 2 ♣ 5	1. ♠ A 7 6 4 ♡ A 7 2 ◇ 4 ♣ A K Q 7 6	1. ♠ K 9 5 3 2 ♡ K 6 ◇ J 8 5 2 ♣ 4 3
2. ♠ A 8 ♡ Q 7 4 3 2 ◇ K 6 5 ♣ 8 5 3	2. ♠ K 10 6 2 ♡ 9 8 ◇ A J 10 ♣ A J 9 4	2. ♠ K 7 3 ♡ A 10 3 2 ◇ 9 8 ♣ 10 7 6 5	2. ♠ A J 8 ♡ K Q 7 ◇ K J 7 3 ♣ A Q 4
3. ♠ A 8 ♡ 7 2 ◇ Q J 9 ♣ K Q J 6 4 3	3. ♠ K J 9 7 ♡ A 9 5 3 ◇ 6 5 ♣ 8 5 2	3. ♠ K Q 4 ♡ A Q 8 6 4 ◇ A K 9 8 ♣ Q	3. ♠ A J 8 7 3 2 ♡ 5 ◇ J 6 ♣ 8 6 3 2
4. ♠ Q 6 5 2 ♡ Q 9 5 3 ◇ 7 4 ♣ K 8 4	4. ♠ A 7 4 3 ♡ K 4 ◇ A Q 9 3 2 ♣ 7 6	4. ♠ 8 6 ♡ K 7 3 2 ◇ K 9 8 4 3 ♣ 7 5	4. ♠ A Q 7 3 ♡ A J 8 4 ◇ - - - ♣ K Q 6 3 2
5. ♠ 8 7 ♡ K Q ◇ A J 7 6 4 3 ♣ K 3 2	5. ♠ J 10 9 5 3 2 ♡ J 8 6 ◇ - - - ♣ A 7 5 4	5. ♠ A 9 6 2 ♡ K 6 2 ◇ - - - ♣ A K J 8 6 4	5. ♠ K Q ♡ J 10 9 7 5 3 ◇ 5 3 2 ♣ 7 3
6. ♠ K Q 8 7 ♡ K 5 4 3 ◇ 7 5 3 ♣ 6 4	6. ♠ 5 3 ♡ A 2 ◇ K Q 9 6 2 ♣ A J 7 2	6. ♠ K 9 5 3 ♡ 7 ◇ 8 7 4 3 ♣ K 7 6 2	6. ♠ Q 2 ♡ A Q J 10 6 4 3 ◇ K Q ♣ A 8

PLAY HANDS BASED ON WEAK RESPONDING HANDS

Hand 5 : Weak rebid by opener — Taking a discard before tackling trumps

Dealer North : North-South vulnerable

NORTH
- ♠ 10 7 6 4 2
- ♡ A 10
- ◇ 10 9 5
- ♣ A 9 8

WEST
- ♠ A K 8 3
- ♡ J 5
- ◇ 8 3 2
- ♣ 7 5 4 2

EAST
- ♠ Q
- ♡ K Q 9 8 6 2
- ◇ A 7 4
- ♣ Q 10 6

SOUTH
- ♠ J 9 5
- ♡ 7 4 3
- ◇ K Q J 6
- ♣ K J 3

WEST	NORTH	EAST	SOUTH
	Pass	1♡	Pass
1♠	Pass	2♡	All pass

Bidding: East's 2♡ rebid shows a long heart suit and a minimum opening and West has no cause to bid on since the partnership cannot have 25 points or more.

Lead : ◇ K. It is normal to lead an unbid suit and a sequence is the most attractive of leads against a trump contract.

Correct play : On most trump play hands, it is normal and best to draw trumps as soon as possible. However, there are also many cases where the drawing of trumps must be delayed. Counting losers, East can see that after taking the ◇ A, there are 2 diamond losers, possibly 3 club losers, 1 heart loser (on normal breaks) and 0 spade losers. This comes to 6 losers, but the spade suit allows 1 loser to be discarded. However, if declarer tackles trumps at trick 2, the opponents can take 2 diamonds and might be able to take 3 clubs : in practice, that is exactly what would happen.

If declarer wins the ◇ A and leads hearts, North would win and continue diamonds. After 2 diamond tricks, it is natural for South to switch to clubs, not spades. The ♣3 to North's ace and a club back gives the defence 3 club tricks. A greedy declarer might win the ◇ A, cash the ♠ Q and lead a heart, hoping the jack would be an entry. This fails when North has the ♡ A or when South has the ♡ A and rises with the ace on the first trump lead. As this play jeopardises the contract for a poor chance for an overtrick, it cannot be recommended.

Declarer should utilise the spade winners in dummy at once : win the ◇ A, lead the ♠ Q and overtake it in dummy, cash the other spade winner from dummy and discard a diamond. Then, and only then, lead the jack of hearts. Declarer loses only 1 heart, 1 diamond and 3 clubs.

Hand 6 : Strong opening hand — Delaying trumps until vital discards are taken

Dealer East : East-West vulnerable

NORTH
- ♠ 7 4 3
- ♡ 8 5 4 2
- ◇ A K Q
- ♣ 4 3 2

WEST
- ♠ K Q J 10 5
- ♡ A 9
- ◇ J 10 2
- ♣ 10 9 6

EAST
- ♠ 8 6
- ♡ 7
- ◇ 9 8 7 6 5 4
- ♣ A 8 7 5

SOUTH
- ♠ A 9 2
- ♡ K Q J 10 6 3
- ◇ 3
- ♣ K Q J

WEST	NORTH	EAST	SOUTH
		Pass	1♡
1♠ (1)	2♡	Pass	4♡ (2)
Pass	Pass	Pass	

Bidding: (1) An overcall at the 1-level is clearcut with a strong 5-card suit and 8-15 HCP. To pass is cowardly and poor strategy. (2) After the raise, opener's hand is worth 19 points, counting 3 for the singleton. That means the partnership has at least 25 points, and maybe more, so that game should be bid.

Lead : ♠K. Top of the sequence is normal.

Correct play : It is clear what would happen if declarer won the ace of spades and immediately set about trumps. West would take the ♡A and cash 2 more spades. The unavoidable club loser later would defeat the game. The folly of such a plan will be obvious to declarer upon counting losers : 2 spades, 1 heart and 1 club, all of which would be lost if trumps are led, since that gives the opponents the lead.

Declarer's solution is to delay trumps and utilise dummy's diamond winners first : win the ♠ A, lead a diamond to dummy, discard both spade losers on the next 2 diamonds from dummy, and then start trumps. This way declarer makes an overtrick instead of going down. Playing trumps first would be correct if South's trumps were winners so that playing trumps did not entail losing the lead.

Hand 7 : Strong opening hand — Setting up an extra winner in dummy to discard a loser

Dealer South : Both vulnerable

```
              NORTH
              ♠ A 5
              ♡ Q J 10
              ◇ 7 6 5 4
              ♣ A 10 3 2
WEST                      EAST
♠ K Q J 10 6             ♠ 9 8 4 3 2
♡ A 9 6                  ♡ K 4 3
◇ K 2                    ◇ Q J 8
♣ K Q 7                  ♣ 6 4
              SOUTH
              ♠ 7
              ♡ 8 7 5 2
              ◇ A 10 9 3
              ♣ J 9 8 5
```

WEST	NORTH	EAST	SOUTH
			Pass
1♠	Pass	2♠	Pass
4♠	Pass	Pass	Pass

Bidding: Despite the 5 trumps, East is worth only 2♠, because of the balanced nature of the hand. After the raise, West is worth 19 points and should therefore bid game.

Lead: ♡ Q. Top of sequence is the most attractive lead against trump contracts. You need a very powerful reason to choose something else when a 3-card or better sequence is available.

Correct play: It is instinctive to win the lead and start on trumps, but a check on the losers will prevent your playing too hastily. You have a loser in each suit. As nothing can be done about the 3 missing aces, is there anything you can do about the heart loser? Losers can be eliminated by ruffing (not applicable to hearts here) or by discarding.

There are no extra winners in dummy yet, but you can set up an extra diamond winner by knocking out the ◇ A. This must be done at once, before starting on the trumps, otherwise the opponents come to their heart trick before the extra diamond winner is set up. If you lead trumps at trick 2, North can win and lead a second heart and now you cannot escape the heart loser. The correct order is to win the opening lead with the ♡ A (not the king) and lead the ◇ K (if they duck this, play a second diamond). After they take ◇ A and play another heart, win ♡ K (your entry to dummy) and cash the diamond winners, discarding the losing heart. Then, and only then, start on the trumps.

Hand 8 : Weak freak raise to game — Setting up a winner in dummy for a discard

Dealer West : Nil vulnerable

```
              NORTH
              ♠ Q 7 6
              ♡ K 8 7 6 5
              ◇ A Q
              ♣ A 6 4
WEST                      EAST
♠ K J 5 4 3             ♠ A 10 8 2
♡ A                     ♡ 10
◇ 9 8 6 4               ◇ K 10 5 3
♣ Q 8 2                 ♣ J 10 9 3
              SOUTH
              ♠ 9
              ♡ Q J 9 4 3 2
              ◇ J 7 2
              ♣ K 7 5
```

WEST	NORTH	EAST	SOUTH
Pass	1♡	Pass	4♡ (1)
Pass	Pass	Pass	

Bidding : (1) South's jump to 4♡ is known as a "weak freak" raise because it is a hand weak in high cards and freakish in shape. It is also known as a pre-emptive or shut-out raise because one aim is to shut the 4th player out of the bidding.

Lead : ♣J. Top of a sequence is usually best.

Correct play : Declarer would fail by tackling trumps straight away : there are 4 possible losers, 1 in each suit. If declarer started trumps at once, West would win and a 2nd club lead would leave declarer with a club loser in addition to the inevitable losers in each major, so that when the diamond finesse failed, declarer would be one off. Nor would it help to win the ♣ K and take the diamond finesse at once. When that loses, the next club lead knocks out your ace and there is no quick entry to dummy's ◇ J after the ◇ A has been unblocked. Again, one off.

The diamond finesse looks appealing but is an illusion. You can eliminate the club loser by setting up the ◇ J as an extra winner in dummy. Forget the finesse in diamonds. The finesse is only a 50% chance — the right play is much better : Win the first trick with the ♣ A (not with the ♣ K which you need as an entry to dummy later), play your ◇ A and then the ◇ Q. Now the ◇ J is high and the ♣ K is the entry to reach it. If they refuse to take the ◇ Q with the ◇ K, you have no diamond loser. If they take the ◇ K and return a club, you win the ♣ K, discard your club loser on the established ◇ J and then, but no earlier, start trumps. Delay trumps if an early discard has to be found and a winner in dummy needs to be set up first.

CHAPTER 3

STRONG RESPONDING HANDS AFTER A SUIT OPENING

VALUING YOUR HAND AS RESPONDER

No trump fit yet found : Count just your HCP (but allow 1 point for any long suit)

An 8-card or better trump fit has been found : Count HCP and add 5-3-1 Count

WHAT IS A STRONG RESPONDING HAND?

Hands of 11 HCP or more are automatically considered strong, even with poor features. Hands with support for opener and 11 points up, counting distribution, are too strong for a single raise and are treated as strong responding hands. Unbalanced hands of 10 HCP and hands with 9 HCP plus a 6-card or longer suit are also in the strong category. Strong hands are usually worth a game bid (13 points or more) or at least a game invitation (10-12 points). Strong hands will be termed 10-up, with the understanding that 9 HCP plus a 6-card or longer suit qualifies and that flat hands of 10 HCP do not (see Chapter 2). It is vital for a strong responding hand to avoid clearly weak responses or weak rebids (such as 1NT or raising opener to the 2-level or rebidding your own suit at the 2-level).

RESPONDER'S STRATEGY FOR THE INITIAL RESPONSE

With the initial response, a strong hand is shown one of two ways :

CHANGING SUIT *or* MAKING A JUMP-BID

A change of suit at the 1-level (e.g. 1♣ : 1♠) is ambiguous : it could be 6-9 or it could be 10 or more, and responder will clarify the range on the next round, taking minimum action with the 6-9 range and strong action with the 10-up range. A change of suit to the 2-level (e.g. 1♡ : 2♣) is always strong and a jump-response is always strong, except for the pre-emptive jump to game (such as 1♠ : 4♠ — see Chapter 2). A change-of-suit response forces opener to bid again but if responder's action is not a change of suit or a jump, opener is permitted to pass. Bidding 1NT is not a change of suit.

Responder's most common action with a strong hand is to change suit, await further information from opener and then either make a decision as to the best contract or make a further descriptive bid to help partner decide the contract. When responder changes suit, the standard order of priorities applies :

● **Bid your longest suit first.**

● **With 5-5 or 6-6 patterns, bid the higher-ranking suit first.**

● **4-card suits are bid up-the-line, i.e, bidding the cheaper suit first.** You can decide later, on the basis of opener's rebid, whether to show the other suit or not. With 4 diamonds and a 4-card major, it is best to respond 1◇ with a weak responding hand (see Chapter 2). With 11-15 HCP, you may choose to respond in the major, intending to rebid 2NT (11-12) or 3NT (13-15). Slam is unlikely unless opener can rebid 2◇.

A weak responder may have to bid suits in abnormal order or to respond 1NT on an unsuitable hand because the hand is not strong enough for a natural 2-level response (see Chapter 2), but a strong responder has no need to make an unnatural response. When choosing a new suit response, the new suit is shown at the cheapest level and a suit response at the 1-level does not deny a strong hand. If responder combines both strong actions, jump *and* change suit, this is the strongest of all responses and is known as a "jump-shift" which shows 19 points or more in standard methods, is forcing to game and strongly suggests slam is likely. The jump-shift is normally based on a powerful 5-card or longer suit. Where the responder holds support for opener's major, a jump-shift in a 4-card (or even 3-card) minor is permissible, with the intention of supporting opener's major on the next round.

A new suit response is taken as a 4-card suit and opener needs 4-card support to raise. This is true for any 1-level response and for a 2-level response in a minor suit. However, a jump-shift is taken to be a strong 5-card or longer suit (see above) and opener should raise with 3 trumps in normal circumstances.

You should particularly note that in the sequence 1♠ : 2♡ (which is discussed fully in Chapter 4), responder guarantees 5 or more hearts and opener should raise hearts with 3 or more trumps.

Aside from changing suit, responder has three specific strong jump-responses, but the hand must fit the requirements before these bids are chosen :

- 2NT response — 13-15 points, balanced shape, stoppers in unbid suits.
- 3NT response — 16-18 points, balanced shape, stoppers in unbid suits.
- Jump-raise, e.g. 1♠ : 3♠ — 13 points or more and strong support (4 or more trumps).

The 2NT and 3NT responses are not all that common but if the hand fits, prefer that response to a change of suit. The minimum holdings which qualify as stoppers are A-x, K-x, Q-x-x or J-x-x-x.

RESPONDER'S GENERAL STRATEGY OF DEVELOPING A STRONG HAND

With 10-12 points : Respond with a change of suit initially and then bid again, inviting game. For example, 1♠ : 2♣, 2♢ : 3♢ ... or 1♠ : 2♣, 2♢ : 3♣ ... or 1♡ : 2♣ : 2♢ : 2♡ ... or 1♢ : 1♠, 1NT : 2NT ... Where responder wishes to support opener's suit and holds 11-12 points, counting distribution, the hand is too strong for a single raise and too weak for a jump-raise. With these in-between values, responder's best approach is to change suit first and support opener on the next round (e.g. 1♠ : 2♣, 2♢ : 2♠).

With 13-15 points : These hands are strong enough to bid for a game. If the hand fits 2NT or a jump-raise, choose that response. If not, change suit and bid game on the next round if you know the best spot *or* change suit again which will require the opener to bid once more *or* jump on the next round. For example, 1♢ : 1♠, 1NT : 4♠ ... *or* 1♡ : 2♣, 2♡ : 4♡... *or* 1♡ : 2♣, 2♡ : 2♠ ...

With 16-18 points : Choose the 3NT response or a jump-raise if the hand fits. If not, change suit initially and jump-rebid to insist on game. If opener has confirmed a minimum opening, be content with game but if opener has promised better than minimum, you should plan to look for a slam.

With 19 points or more : Jump-shift if possible, showing a powerful hand *and* a strong 5-card or longer suit, which opener should support with three trumps. If the hand is not suitable for a jump-shift, just change suit and judge which slam to attempt after further description from opener's rebid. If you need more information from opener, you can continue to force opener to bid by changing suit or making a jump-rebid below game.

An opening hand facing an opening hand should produce a game.

An opening hand facing an opener who jumps should produce a slam if a good trump fit is located.

A 19-up hand opposite an opening will usually produce a slam if a good trump fit is located.

WHERE RESPONDER HAS A CHOICE OF ACTIONS

Where responder's hand is strong and fits more than one possible action, the order of priorities will depend on whether partner opened with a major suit or with a minor suit.

After a 1♡ or a 1♠ opening

1. Jump-raise opener's major with 4-card or better support and 13+ points.

2. Use the 2NT or 3NT response if the hand fits the requirements.

3. Bid a new suit.

If the partnership is playing 5-card majors, prefer a 2NT response or a change of suit to a jump-raise of opener's major with only 3-card support. Since 2NT or the new suit will be forcing, you will still have the opportunity to show the 3-card support on the next round. It is quite all right to give a single raise (1♡ : 2♡ or 1♠ : 2♠) with 3-card support, but it is desirable to have 4-card or better trump support for the jump-raise, so that a good trump suit is assured if the partnership proceeds to a slam.

Where the opening was 1♡ and responder has the choice of a 1♠ response or a 2NT response, prefer the 2NT response if the 1♡ opening is guaranteed to be a 5-card suit (with 5 hearts and 4 spades, opener will rebid 3♠ over 2NT), but prefer the 1♠ response if playing 4-card majors.

Where the opening was 1♠ and responder has a hand suitable for 2NT and also has 4 hearts, choose the 2NT response. With 5 spades and 4 hearts, opener will rebid 3♡ over 2NT and the heart fit will be located.

After a 1♣ or a 1◇ opening

1. Bid a major suit (rather than 2NT or 3NT).

2. Use the 2NT or 3NT response if the hand fits the requirements.

3. Jump-raise opener's minor with 4-card or better support and 13+ points.

4. Change suit by bidding the other minor suit.

Basically, where responder has a strong hand, major suit action is first 1st, no-trumps is 2nd priority and minor suit action is the least attractive action (in contrast to a weak responding hand where the 1NT response is the last choice). This reflects the chance of success of game contracts : major suit games have the best chance of success, followed by 3NT with minor suit games as the least likely to succeed, all things being equal. The assumption here is that there is a genuine choice and that responder's hand does fit each of the possible actions. Often, of course, responder will not have a choice of actions. For example, after a 1♣ or a 1◇ opening, if responder has 11-12 points with no 4-card major and less than adequate support for opener, the only choice is to bid the other minor. The hand is too weak for 2NT or a jump-raise, too strong for 1NT or a single raise and there is no major to bid.

OPENER'S REBIDS AFTER A STRONG RESPONSE

After a suit response at the 1-level

A suit response at the 1-level can be weak or strong. See Chapter 2 for opener's rebids.

After a response of 2NT or 3NT or a jump-raise

A minimum opener should bid no higher than game, but explore slam possibilities with a powerful opening. Where the response was 2NT or 3NT, opener will stay with no-trumps with a balanced hand, but will try to play in a trump contract if the hand is unbalanced. For example, after 1♠ : 2NT, opener would rebid 3♡ to show 5 spades and 4 hearts and a desire to play in a major rather than no-trumps.

After a jump-shift response

Opener should support responder's suit with 3 or more trumps. Without support, make a natural rebid, bidding a 2nd suit if possible, or no-trumps if balanced, or rebidding the 1st suit as a last resort.

After a suit response at the 2-level (e.g. 1♡ : 2♣)

With a minimum opening, your order of priorities are :

● Support responder to the 3-level (e.g. 1♡ : 2♣, 3♣), but after 1♠ : 2♣ or 1♠ : 2◇, with support and also 4 hearts, rather bid 2♡ to show the other major than support responder's minor.

● Bid a new suit, lower-ranking than the 1st suit (e.g. 1♡ : 2♣, 2◇).

● Repeat the 1st suit with at least 5 cards in the suit (e.g. 1♡ : 2♣, 2♡). The suit need not be more than 5 cards long — after a 2-over-1 response, the rebid of opener's 1st suit is used to confirm a minimum opening with no cheaper suit to bid (see The Barrier Principle, Chapter 2, page 16).

With a strong opening, your order of priorities are :

● Jump-support responder's suit to the 4-level. If it is a minor suit, the sequence is forcing to game and inviting responder to explore slam possibilities.

● Jump to 3NT with 19-20 points and a balanced hand.

● Bid a new suit. With 19 points or more, you may jump-shift.

● Jump rebid the suit opened (e.g. 1♡ : 2♣, 3♡) which promises a good 6-card suit, 16 points or more and denies holding a 2nd suit (change of suit would receive priority).

Where opener's rebid is clearly a strong action (a jump-rebid or a new suit higher than the barrier), the auction is logically forcing to game, since opener's strong action shows 16 points or more and responder's 2-level response has promised 10+ points. Opener's change of suit to a lower suit (e.g. 1♠ : 2◇, 2♡) has a range of 13-18 points, since a jump-shift needs 19 points or more. It may thus be a minimum opening or a strong opening and change-of-suit after a 2-level response is forcing. A new suit by opener above 2-in-the-suit-opened (e.g. 1◇ : 2♣, 2♡) will promise better than a minimum opening (see The Barrier Principle, page 16). Strong rebids by opener include 1♡ : 2♣, 2♠ (above 2♡) *or* 1♠ : 2♡, 3♣ (above 2♠) and any jump rebid by opener.

Opener's 2NT rebid after a 2-level response can be played as strong or minimum, according to partnership agreement. In standard methods, 1 ◇ : 2♣, 2NT shows a minimum balanced hand, while after a major suit opening, the 2NT rebid (e.g. 1♡ : 2♣, 2NT... *or* 1♠ : 2◇, 2NT... *or* 1♠ : 2♡, 2NT...) is normally played as a better-than-minimum opening. It is usually about 15-18 HCP with a 5-card major and logically forcing to game opposite a 2-level response of 10 points or more. However, if the partnership chooses to open 1NT with all 5-3-3-2 hands (5-card major *or* minor) when holding 15-18 points, then the 2NT rebid after a major suit opening can be played as a minimum balanced opening. On the other hand, if the partnership does not wish to open 1NT when holding a 5-card major, then it is best to use the 2NT rebid as the 15-18 strongish range. With the minimum hands, rebid the major suit (e.g. 1♡ : 2♣, 2♡ is a minimum opening and may hold only 5 hearts, while 1♡ : 2♣, 2NT would show a 15-18 5-3-3-2 hand with 5 hearts).

RESPONDER'S REBIDS WITH A STRONG HAND

With the rebid, responder shows a strong hand in one of three ways :

CHANGING SUIT *or* A JUMP-REBID *or* REBIDDING 2NT

The change-of-suit rebid is forcing in normal circumstances and the jump-rebid is best played as forcing until the partnership is familiar with 4th-Suit-Forcing (see Chapter 17). The 2NT rebid will not be forcing if 1NT has been bid previously, but is best played as forcing in a suit auction, again until 4th-suit-forcing is part and parcel of the partnership methods. If responder's rebid is not a change of suit or a jump or 2NT, opener is permitted to pass — responder shows only 6-9 points for a weak rebid. *Do not make a weak rebid (such as 1NT, rebidding your suit at the 2-level or raising opener to the 2-level) with a strong hand.*

Responder's general strategy for rebidding :

10-12 points : Raise opener from 1NT to 2NT or raise opener's suit to the 3-level, inviting game. For example, 1◇ : 1♠, 1NT : 2NT... *or* 1♠ : 2♣, 2◇ : 3◇ ... *or* 1♡ : 1♠, 2♡ : 3♡ ... If the initial response was already at the 2-level, thus already promising at least 10 points, responder shows just 10-12 points by giving preference to opener's first suit at the 2-level (e.g. 1♡ : 2♣, 2◇ : 2♡ ...) or by rebidding responder's suit (e.g. 1♡ : 2♣, 2◇ : 3♣ ...). Repeating your own suit as responder after a 2-level response is taken as showing 9-11 HCP and a 6-card suit with no support for opener's suit(s).

13-15 points : If your initial response already promised 13-15 points (e.g. a 2NT response), all your rebids are forcing since your initial response created a force to game. If your initial response was a suit bid at the 1-level, you have to make sure that you do not make a rebid that could be dropped. If the correct game is obvious, bid it. If not, change suit or make a jump-rebid, but make sure you avoid the *encouraging but droppable* sequences which show 10-12 points in the paragraph above. In particular, you must not simply raise opener's 1-level suit bid to the 2-level or opener's 2-level suit bid to the 3-level, both of which are droppable. You must not give a simple preference to opener's 1st suit (droppable after a minimum rebid by opener) *or* rebid your own suit at the cheapest level (droppable after a minimum rebid by opener). If opener's rebid was 1NT, you will need to jump to force opener *or* bid a new suit higher than your initial response. After opener's 1NT rebid, a new suit at the 2-level is not forcing if it is lower-ranking than responder's 1st suit (e.g. 1◇ : 1♠, 1NT : 2♡ is *not* forcing). This is discussed in detail in Chapter 7.

16-18 points : Opposite a minimum rebid by opener, slam is unlikely if responder holds only 16-18 unless an exceptionally good trump fit has come to light. Where the trump fit is only 4-4 or 5-3, slam is usually not a good bet with 30 HCP or less together. Often a finesse to capture a critical card will be necessary and there is about a 1-in-3 chance of a bad trump break as well. Be satisfied to find the best game and opposite a minimum opening, you can either bid game or explore game in the same manner as with the 13-15 hand above.

However, with a particularly strong trump fit (9 or more trumps together), slam is likely to succeed if responder is in this point range, even opposite a minimum opening.

If opener has made a strong rebid, showing 16 points or more, head for a slam once the best fit is known. If opener's rebid is not clearcut, such as a change of suit (e.g. 1♡ : 2♣, 2◇), prefer to change suit again (4th-suit) to discover whether opener has a minimum hand or a strong opening.

19 points or more : Slam is likely even opposite a minimum opener if a trump fit is found. If the best fit is not yet known, change suit or make a jump-rebid below game and continue towards slam later.

EXERCISES

A. Partner opened 1♣. What is your response on each of these hands?

1. ♠ K 8 7 4 2	**2.** ♠ A K Q 8	**3.** ♠ A 8 7 5	**4.** ♠ A Q 9 8	**5.** ♠ A Q 7 3
♡ 3	♡ A Q 5 4	♡ A 2	♡ 6 2	♡ K 9
◇ A K J 5 2	◇ 7 6	◇ K Q 3 2	◇ Q 9	◇ Q J 7 6 2
♣ 7 2	♣ 8 6 3	♣ J 5 4	♣ K Q 7 4 2	♣ 5 3

B. Partner opened 1♡. What is your response on each of these hands?

1. ♠ 8 7	**2.** ♠ A K 9 8	**3.** ♠ A 8 2	**4.** ♠ Q J 7 2	**5.** ♠ 8 5
♡ Q	♡ 6 4	♡ 6 3	♡ 4	♡ Q 8 6 3
◇ K Q 7 6 3	◇ Q 2	◇ A 7 6 3	◇ A J 6 2	◇ 9 4 2
♣ A J 7 3 2	♣ K 9 7 3 2	♣ Q J 8 5	♣ A Q 9 7	♣ A K J 5

C. Partner opened 1♠. What is your response on each of these hands?

1. ♠ 4 2	**2.** ♠ J 7	**3.** ♠ K 6	**4.** ♠ A J 2	**5.** ♠ A 8 7 4
♡ A J 6 4 3	♡ K Q 4 2	♡ A Q 5 3	♡ 9 2	♡ K 5 3
◇ Q 9 8	◇ A J 8 3	◇ K 4 3	◇ A K 9 7	◇ 9 8 7
♣ A 6 2	♣ 6 3 2	♣ Q 9 5 4	♣ Q 9 7 2	♣ A 5 3

D. You opened 1♣ and partner responded 1◇. What is your next action on each of these hands?

1. ♠ K J 7 2	**2.** ♠ A J 4 3	**3.** ♠ A J	**4.** ♠ 8 4	**5.** ♠ 5 3 2
♡ Q J 4 3	♡ A 7 3 2	♡ 4 3	♡ K Q J	♡ A 6
◇ - - -	◇ 6	◇ A 8 3 2	◇ 4 3	◇ A J
♣ A K 9 6 2	♣ K 9 4 2	♣ A K 7 5 2	♣ A K 9 6 4 2	♣ A K J 7 5 3

PARTNERSHIP BIDDING : How should the following hands be bid? West is the dealer on all hands.

SET 7 – WEST	SET 7 – EAST	SET 8 – WEST	SET 8 – EAST
1. ♠ K 7 4 3	**1.** ♠ Q J 9 2	**1.** ♠ A J	**1.** ♠ K Q 9 7 6 3
♡ A 8	♡ K Q 4 3	♡ 7 2	♡ 4 3
◇ 6 4 2	◇ Q 3	◇ A Q 8 6 4	◇ J 3
♣ A K 7 3	♣ Q J 8	♣ K J 9 8	♣ A Q 3
2. ♠ A 8	**2.** ♠ K Q 9 2	**2.** ♠ A J	**2.** ♠ Q 5 3
♡ 7 4 3	♡ A K 5 2	♡ 6	♡ K Q 8 7 5 2
◇ A Q 8	◇ 7 4 3	◇ A 10 7 4 2	◇ K Q
♣ K 9 7 6 2	♣ Q 3	♣ K Q 10 6 3	♣ J 2
3. ♠ A 7 3	**3.** ♠ K Q 6 2	**3.** ♠ A 6 3	**3.** ♠ K Q 8 4 2
♡ K 9 7 2	♡ Q J 4 3	♡ 7 2	♡ K Q J 8
◇ 7 6	◇ A 4	◇ A Q 10 7 6 2	◇ 5 3
♣ A Q 5 4	♣ J 7 3	♣ K 3	♣ Q 4
4. ♠ Q J 6 2	**4.** ♠ K 7 5 4	**4.** ♠ 10 4 3	**4.** ♠ A J
♡ 2	♡ A Q 8 6 3	♡ A 9 8 6	♡ 7 2
◇ A 3	◇ K 9	◇ K 7	◇ A Q 9 6 4
♣ A Q 9 8 6 4	♣ 5 2	♣ A 9 8 3	♣ K J 5 2
5. ♠ Q J 6	**5.** ♠ K 7 5 4	**5.** ♠ A 2	**5.** ♠ K Q 7 4
♡ 4 3	♡ A Q 8 6	♡ 7	♡ K Q J 2
◇ A 3	◇ K J 8	◇ A K 8 7 4	◇ 9 5 3
♣ A Q 7 5 4 2	♣ 8 3	♣ A Q J 5 3	♣ 8 6
6. ♠ 8 2	**6.** ♠ K 7 3	**6.** ♠ A J 7	**6.** ♠ K 5
♡ J 4	♡ K Q 8 2	♡ K 4 3	♡ J 2
◇ A Q 8	◇ K 4 3	◇ A 9 8 4 3	◇ K Q 6 5 2
♣ A K Q 7 4 3	♣ 6 5 2	♣ Q 6	♣ A 9 8 3

EXERCISES

E. You opened 1♡ and partner responded 2♣. What is your next action on each of these hands?

1. ♠ A Q 7 3	2. ♠ A Q 7 3	3. ♠ 4	4. ♠ A 7 3	5. ♠ 7
♡ K Q 10 5 3	♡ A Q 8 5 4	♡ K 8 7 4 2	♡ A Q 7 6 4	♡ A Q J 7 4 2
◇ A J 2	◇ 7 4 2	◇ A 5 2	◇ 8	◇ A K 8
♣ 4	♣ 3	♣ A J 4 3	♣ A K 4 3	♣ Q 9 3

F. You opened 1♠ and partner responded 2◇. What is your next action on each of these hands?

1. ♠ A K 7 6 2	2. ♠ A K 7 6 3	3. ♠ A J 6 4 3	4. ♠ K Q J 7 4	5. ♠ A Q J 8 6 4 3
♡ K Q 4 3	♡ 7 3 2	♡ 7 2	♡ A Q	♡ K J 2
◇ 6	◇ 6	◇ A K 9 5	◇ A 8 3	◇ A J
♣ 7 3 2	♣ K Q 4 3	♣ 8 3	♣ K 5 2	♣ 2

G. Partner opened 1♣, you responded 1◇ and opener rebid 1♡. What is your next action on these hands?

1. ♠ K Q 4 2	2. ♠ J 7	3. ♠ 7 6	4. ♠ A Q J 2	5. ♠ A J 7
♡ A J	♡ Q 4	♡ A Q	♡ 9	♡ 6 5 3
◇ Q 9 8 6 4 3	◇ A J 8 3 2	◇ A K 9 7 4 3	◇ A K 9 7	◇ A Q 8 7
♣ 2	♣ K Q 9 2	♣ J 5 4	♣ Q 9 7 2	♣ A 5 3

H. Partner opened 1♡, you responded 2♣, and opener rebid 2♡. What is your next action on these hands?

1. ♠ K J 7 2	2. ♠ A 4 3	3. ♠ A J	4. ♠ J 8 4	5. ♠ 5 3
♡ 3	♡ A 7 3	♡ 4 3 2	♡ J	♡ 6
◇ 8 6 2	◇ 6 2	◇ 8 3 2	◇ 4 3 2	◇ A J 10 2
♣ A K J 6 2	♣ K Q 9 4 2	♣ K Q 7 5 2	♣ A K J 9 4 2	♣ A K J 7 5 3

PARTNERSHIP BIDDING : How should the following hands be bid? West is the dealer on all hands.

SET 9 – WEST	SET 9 – EAST	SET 10 – WEST	SET 10 – EAST
1. ♠ A J 8 7 2	1. ♠ 5 3	1. ♠ A 7 6	1. ♠ Q 3
♡ K 8 3	♡ A 6 4 2	♡ K 8 5 3	♡ A 6 4 2
◇ K Q	◇ J 10 4 2	◇ A Q 8 7 2	◇ 9 3
♣ 7 4 2	♣ A K Q	♣ 3	♣ K Q J 5 4
2. ♠ A 8 7 4 2	2. ♠ K 3	2. ♠ K Q	2. ♠ 4 3
♡ K Q 9 3	♡ A 10 4 2	♡ A J 8 6 4 2	♡ K 7 5
◇ K 7	◇ Q J 10 3	◇ K 4 3	◇ A 7 5 2
♣ 8 3	♣ Q J 7	♣ 6 2	♣ A 9 8 4
3. ♠ A J 10 9 2	3. ♠ 4 3	3. ♠ A 10 8 6 5 2	3. ♠ 3
♡ A Q J 2	♡ K 4 3	♡ A	♡ K Q 5 2
◇ J 7 4	◇ A K 6 2	◇ K J 3	◇ Q 10 7 4
♣ 8	♣ Q J 9 7	♣ 6 3 2	♣ K Q J 10
4. ♠ A 9 7 4 2	4. ♠ J 5 3	4. ♠ K Q 8 5 4	4. ♠ 6 3 2
♡ 8 3	♡ Q J 10	♡ A 6 3	♡ 7 2
◇ K J 6	◇ A Q 4	◇ 7	◇ A J 8 4
♣ A 9 4	♣ K Q J 2	♣ A 6 4 3	♣ K Q J 7
5. ♠ A Q 7 2	5. ♠ K 10 6	5. ♠ 7	5. ♠ K 3 2
♡ K 8 6 4 3	♡ A 5 2	♡ A Q J 6 4 3	♡ 5 2
◇ A 6 2	◇ K 7 4	◇ A Q 3	◇ K 7 5 2
♣ 7	♣ A 8 6 2	♣ 10 9 6	♣ A K 5 3
6. ♠ A 8 7 4 3	6. ♠ K 6 2	6. ♠ 7	6. ♠ A Q 6
♡ K Q	♡ A 9 8 2	♡ K Q 5 3 2	♡ 8
◇ K 7 6	◇ A Q 4 3	◇ J 4 3	◇ A 10 7 2
♣ J 5 3	♣ 9 2	♣ A Q 7 2	♣ K J 6 4 3

PLAY HANDS BASED ON STRONG RESPONDING HANDS

Hand 9 : Discarding a loser — Ruffing a loser in dummy

Dealer North : East-West vulnerable

NORTH
♠ A 10 5 4 3
♡ A K 7 6
◊ Q 6
♣ Q 4

WEST
♠ J 6
♡ J 8
◊ J 10 7 4 3
♣ A K 5 2

EAST
♠ Q 9 8
♡ Q 10 9 5 4
◊ 9
♣ J 10 9 6

SOUTH
♠ K 7 2
♡ 3 2
◊ A K 8 5 2
♣ 8 7 3

WEST	NORTH	EAST	SOUTH
	1♠	Pass	2◊
Pass	2♡	Pass	2♠
Pass	4♠	All pass	

Bidding : South is too strong for an immediate raise to 2♠. To cater for the 11-12 raise, change suit first and show support later.

Lead : ♣J. Top of a solid sequence. Prefer a sequence lead to a singleton lead, especially when you have a certain or probable trump trick anyway. Singleton leads are best when you can ruff with a worthless trump.

Correct play : West wins the king of clubs (it would be a serious error to duck) — a defender wins with the cheapest possible card — cashes the ace of clubs and North wins the 3rd trick. North should play ♠K, ♠A and leave the last trump out. Next comes the ◊ Q and another diamond — play the winner from the short hand first. If East discards, win ◊ A and discard a heart on the ◊ K. Later play ♡A, ♡K and ruff a heart, losing just 1 spade and 2 clubs.

Wrong play : (1) Playing a 3rd round of trumps. Now dummy cannot ruff a heart.
(2) Trying to ruff a heart before starting trumps. West can overruff dummy and the contract would fail.
(3) Ruffing a heart before starting the diamonds. This would be an unlucky way to fail, but taking the discard before going for the ruff is sound technique. If you ruff the third club, play ♠ K, ♠ A, ♡ A, ♡ K, ruff a heart and then play a diamond to the queen and another diamond, East could ruff the 2nd diamond and cash a heart before North obtains the discard. By going for the diamonds first, North's deep heart losers are not yet exposed.

Hand 10 : Setting up a winner for a discard before going for a ruff

Dealer East : Both vulnerable

NORTH
♠ A 10 6 4 2
♡ Q 10 9
◊ 9 4 3
♣ A 10

WEST
♠ 8
♡ K J 7 6 4
◊ A 5 2
♣ K J 8 6

EAST
♠ Q J 3
♡ A 8 5 3 2
◊ K 8 6
♣ Q 3

SOUTH
♠ K 9 7 5
♡ - - -
◊ Q J 10 7
♣ 9 7 5 4 2

WEST	NORTH	EAST	SOUTH
		1♡	Pass
3♡ (1)	Pass	4♡ (2)	All pass

Bidding : (1) Too strong for 1♡ : 4♡ which almost never has more than 9 HCP (see Chapter 2). With 10 HCP or more, good support and an unbalanced pattern, your hand would be worth 13 points at least.
(2) 3♡ is forcing to game and with an absolute minimum, East simply bids the game. Any other action would show extra values and suggest slam.

Lead : ◊ Q. Top of the sequence is normal.

Correct play : Win the ◊ K, cash the ♡ A and lead a heart to the king. Leave their top trump out. Continue with a low club to your queen. If North ducks this, win the ♣Q and play a 2nd club to dummy's jack, forcing out the ace. Win the ◊ A next and discard a diamond loser on the ♣K. If North wins the ♣A on the 1st round of clubs, and continues diamonds, win the ◊ A, play the ♣K to keep the lead in dummy (even though you have to play the ♣Q under your king), and then the ♣J, discarding a diamond and losing just 1 spade, 1 heart and 1 club.

Wrong play : (1) Giving up the lead in trumps too early. If you concede a trump to North on the 2nd or 3rd round of hearts, the ◊ A would be knocked out before the clubs were set up to discard the diamond loser.
(2) Playing either spades or diamonds after cashing the ace and king of hearts instead of knocking out the ace of clubs. If the defenders take a diamond trick, the contract can be defeated.

Hand 11 : Setting up your second suit by ruffing losers in dummy

Dealer South : Nil vulnerable

NORTH
♠ 3
♡ 9 8 6 4
◊ A J 4 3
♣ A Q 6 4

WEST
♠ K 10 7 5
♡ K Q J
◊ 8 5 2
♣ 10 8 7

EAST
♠ Q 9 8
♡ 10
◊ Q 10 9 6
♣ K J 9 5 3

SOUTH
♠ A J 6 4 2
♡ A 7 5 3 2
◊ K 7
♣ 2

WEST	NORTH	EAST	SOUTH
			1♠ (1)
Pass	2♣ (2)	Pass	2♡
Pass	4♡ (3)	All pass	

Bidding : (1) Open the higher-ranking suit with a 5-5 pattern.
(2) 4-card suits are bid up-the-line, cheapest first.
(3) Worth 14 points now, counting 3 points for the singleton after the heart fit is known.

Lead : ♡ K. The heart lead is safe and with strength in declarer's other suit (spades), trump leads may minimise dummy's capacity to ruff losing spades.

Correct play : Win the ♡ A. Do not lead another trump — leave the top trumps out if you need dummy's trumps for ruffing. Play the ♠ A, ruff a spade, play a diamond to the king, ruff a spade, cash the ♣ A, ruff a club and ruff another spade, setting up your 5th spade as a winner. Ruff another club and lead the 5th spade, losing just 2 heart tricks.

Wrong play : (1) Winning the ace of hearts at trick 1 and leading a heart back. This allows West to draw 3 rounds of trumps, preventing 3 spade ruffs in dummy and leading to 2 more losers later.
(2) Ducking the 1st heart. In other circumstances, this manoeuvre could be correct, but it is inappropriate here since it eliminates 1 possible spade ruff in dummy and reduces your trick-taking potential by 1 trick.
(3) Ruffing clubs or diamonds in your own hand, except as necessary entries. As your spades are longer than dummy's suits, you should play to set up your 2nd suit.

Hand 12 : Ruffing losers in dummy — Setting up a ruff before drawing trumps

Dealer West : North-South vulnerable

NORTH
♠ K J 9 7
♡ Q 10 6
◊ J 10 9 8
♣ Q 9

WEST
♠ Q 10 6
♡ A K 9 7 4 2
◊ A 7 6
♣ 8

EAST
♠ 3
♡ J 5 3
◊ K Q 4 2
♣ A J 7 5 2

SOUTH
♠ A 8 5 4 2
♡ 8
◊ 5 3
♣ K 10 6 4 3

WEST	NORTH	EAST	SOUTH
1♡	Pass	2♣ (1)	Pass
2♡ (2)	Pass	4♡ (3)	All pass

Bidding : (1) Prefer not to give a jump raise with only 3 trumps.
(2) Only worth a minimum rebid. 3♡ would confirm 6 hearts but would also promise more than minimum opening.
(3) Worth 14 points, counting 3 points for the singleton.

Lead : ◊ J. Top of sequence.

Correct play : Win the ◊ K and lead dummy's singleton spade at once. If South wins and leads a second diamond, win the ace, ruff a spade, play a heart to your ace and ruff a spade. Then cash the ace of clubs, ruff a club and cash the king of hearts. When the trumps are not 2-2, declarer loses just 1 spade and 1 heart. If South wins the ♠ A at trick 2 and leads a heart, win the ace, ruff a spade, cash the ♣ A, ruff a club, ruff a spade, cross to the ◊ A and play the ♡ K, leading to the same result. It is important to score 2 spade ruffs in dummy.

Wrong play : If West were to win the lead and play the ace and king of hearts first, the contract could be defeated. When West next leads a spade, North could win and cash the queen of hearts — it is good defensive strategy to cash your top trump and take out a trump from dummy and a trump from declarer whenever possible — you get 2 trumps for 1 and cut down declarer's ruffing potential. This would draw dummy's last trump and then the defense could take two more spade tricks. Even if this defense were not found, cashing the ace and king of hearts first is an error. Since you wish to ruff 2 spade losers in dummy, this leaves dummy with only 1 trump. When dummy is short in trumps and you need ruffs in dummy, take those ruffs before drawing trumps. Where dummy has plenty of trumps, you can afford to draw trumps first.

CHAPTER 4

RAISING PARTNER'S SUIT AND GIVING A PREFERENCE

AFTER RESPONDER HAS GIVEN OPENER A SINGLE RAISE

After 1♡ : 2♡ or 1♠ : 2♠ — Pass with a minimum opening, while with 19 points or more, counting short suits, bid game. Hands in the 16-18 zone are worth a game invitation and this can be a re-raise (e.g. 1♡ : 2♡, 3♡) or a change of suit (e.g. 1♡ : 2♡, 3♣), known as a trial bid. With a strong holding in the trial suit, responder should bid game in opener's major, but with a poor holding, sign off in 3-of-opener's-major. Trial bids are detailed in Chapter 24. Opener may also try 2NT with a balanced 16-18, offering partner a choice of games: with a minimum, responder should pass or sign off in 3-major, but with a maximum, bid 3NT or jump to 4-major.

After 1♣ : 2♣ or 1♢ : 2♢ — Pass with a minimum, but with 19 or more points, either bid game (3NT if balanced or 5-minor if unbalanced) or change suit. After a raise, change of suit is forcing, whether the raise is in a minor or a major. With 16-18 points, invite game, either by a re-raise (e.g. 1♣ : 2♣, 3♣) or by changing suit or by a 2NT rebid. A new suit shows a strong holding in that suit, indicating a stopper in the suit for no-trumps.

AFTER RESPONDER HAS GIVEN OPENER A JUMP-RAISE

After 1♡ : 3♡ or 1♠ : 3♠ — The sequence is forcing to game and with a minimum, opener simply bids game in the major. With more than a minimum, slam is a chance and any action other than bidding game in the major indicates slam possibilities. Bidding a new suit shows the ace or void in the suit bid and is known as a "cue bid".

After 1♡ : 4♡ or 1♠ : 4♠ — Responder's immediate game raise is a weak, pre-emptive raise and responder will rarely hold more than 9 HCP. Accordingly, slam prospects are remote and opener will pass except with a powerful, freakish hand. Opener's 4NT would be Blackwood while a new suit would be a cue bid.

After 1♣ : 3♣ or 1♢ : 3♢ — The response is forcing to game, but it is not compulsory to continue in the minor suit. With most minimum openings, prefer to try for the easier 3NT. With a balanced hand, opener may simply bid 3NT or may bid a new suit at the 3-level, promising a stopper in the suit bid and angling to play 3NT. Stopper-showing is covered in Chapter 21. With an unbalanced hand, opener may jump to 5-minor or, with slam prospects, can use 4NT or raise the minor to the 4-level (forcing and asking partner to start cue bidding).

After 1♣ : 4♣ or 1♣ : 5♣ or 1♢ : 4♢ or 1♢ : 5♢ — Normally pass, but with significant extra values, opener may bid on after the jump to the 4-level. After the weak-freak raise, a good slam will be very rare.

OPENER RAISES RESPONDER AFTER A 1♡ OR 1♠ RESPONSE

- ● **Raise to 2-level**   (e.g. 1♣ : 1♡, 2♡)   =   **Minimum opening, 12-15 points**
- ● **Jump raise to 3-level** (e.g. 1♣ : 1♡, 3♡)   =   **Strong opening, 16-18 points**
- ● **Jump raise to game**   (e.g. 1♣ : 1♡, 4♡)   =   **Maximum opening, 19 points up**

Do not mix up opener's game raise (e.g. 1♢ : 1♠, 4♠) with responder's game raise (e.g. 1♠ : 4♠). *Responder's* jump to game is weak and is intended as a shut-out raise, aimed at keeping 4th hand out of the auction. *Opener's jump-to-game rebid is never weak and is not a shut-out bid. There are no shut-out bids on the 2nd round of bidding. If the bidding has been* 1♢ : Pass : 1♠ : Pass, whom would you want to shut-out? Two opponents who could not bid on the 1st round? Opener's rebids show the value of the hand and opener's jumps to game in opener's suit or in responder's suit are stronger than jump rebids in these suits below game.

Opener should raise responder's suit only with 4 trumps since responder has promised no more than a 4-card suit. However, a single raise of responder's *first* bid suit (e.g. 1♢ : 1♠, 2♠) is permitted with just 3 trumps, provided that opener holds a shortage and has no better descriptive bid available.

After opener's raise to the 2-level : responder passes with 6-10 points, invites game with 11-12 points, bids game with 13 points up and should consider slam with 18 points or more.

After opener's jump-raise to the 3-level : responder passes with just 6-7 points, bids game with 8 points or more and should consider slam with 15 points or more.

After opener's jump-raise to game : responder passes unless slam is possible opposite opener's 19 points up.

OPENER RAISES RESPONDER AFTER A 2♣ OR 2♦ RESPONSE

Raise to 3-level   (e.g. 1♡ : 2♣, 3♣)=   **Minimum, 12-16 points**

Jump raise to 4-level (e.g. 1♡ : 2♣, 4♣)=   Strong, 17 points up, game force.

After opener's raise to the 3-level: responder passes with a minimum but should explore game with 12 or more points. A new suit at the 3-level (e.g. 1♡ : 2♣, 3♣ : 3♦) would show a stopper in the quest to reach 3NT.

After opener's jump raise to the 4-level: this is forcing to game and leaves it to responder to explore slam prospects. Unless the bidding has revealed that there is no chance for slam, do not jump raise a minor to game. 1♡ : 2♣, 5♣ would eliminate responder's slam investigation or the 4NT ask for aces, so opener has to be satisfied with the jump raise to the 4-level as a game-force. In most auctions, raising a minor to the 4-level is strong, forcing to game and suggesting slam.

Where responder used a 2♣ or 2♦ response with support for opener's major, then if opener raises the minor, responder will now support the major (e.g. 1♡ : 2♣, 3♣ : 3♡ or 1♡ : 2♣, 3♣ : 4♡ or 1♡ : 2♣, 4♣ : 4♡).

RAISING PARTNER'S SECOND SUIT

Since a new suit bid by opener or responder need be only 4 cards long, it is *vital* to have 4-card support to raise a 2nd suit. Until the partnership uses 4th-Suit-Forcing (see Chapter 17), it is best to treat responder's raises of opener's 2nd suit to have the same meaning as responder's raises of opener's 1st suit. For example, 1♦ : 1♡, 1♠ : 2♠ means the same as 1♠ : 2♠ and you can treat 1♦ : 1♡, 1♠ : 3♠ the same as 1♠ : 3♠.

GIVING PARTNER A PREFERENCE

When partner bids 2 suits, you are asked to give preference to the suit for which you have better support.

1. Prefer the suit in which you hold more cards.

2. With equal length in each suit, prefer partner's 1st bid suit, irrespective of the quality of the cards involved (e.g. with 6-4-2 in the 1st suit and A-K-5 in the 2nd, give preference to the 1st suit).

When you have the same number of cards in each of partner's suits, it is immaterial to you which suit is trumps. If partner also has equal length, it will not matter but if partner has unequal length, the 1st bid suit will be longer. As it pays to end up in the partnership suit which has greater length, you show preference for the 1st suit.

Where partner's last bid does not force you to bid again and you have no significant extra values, you may indicate your preference for the last bid suit by passing.

Simple preference means that you give support to partner's first bid suit at the cheapest possible level (e.g. 1♡ : 1♠, 2♦ : 2♡ or 1♦ : 1♡, 1♠ : 2♦ or 1♠ : 1NT, 2♡ : 2♠). Simple preference shows that you prefer partner's 1st suit *but you have no extra values* (i.e. no more than already promised). In the examples given above, responder would have 6-9 points.

Jump preference means that you still revert to the 1st suit bid by partner but skip one level in doing so (e.g. 1♡ : 1♠, 2♦ : 3♡ or 1♠ : 2♣, 2♡ : 3♠). Jump preference shows that you prefer partner's 1st suit and you have more strength than previously promised. After an initial 1-level response, jump preference to the 3-level implies 10-12 points. After an initial 2-level response which already promised 10 points at least, jump preference indicates 13 points up, since with 10-12 points, responder need give only simple preference.

False preference means that you give support for partner's first bid suit even though you have more cards in partner's 2nd suit. False preference is used in situations such as these:

1. Partner bids a major first and a minor next. With 3 cards in the major and 4 cards in the minor, give preference to the major if game is the limit of your aims. If a slam is feasible, however, prefer to give the 4-card support.

2. Partner's rebid is forcing and you do not have genuine support for either suit and no stopper in the missing suit for no-trumps. The following hands are examples:

♠ A K 4 3   Partner opens 1♡, you respond 1♠ and partner rebids with a jump shift to 3♦. What next?
♡ 9 3   The jump shift is forcing to game but you cannot rebid your spades with only 4 and you
♦ 8 4 3   have no club stopper for 3NT. Best is to give false preference to 3♡. Partner will be wary
♣ 5 4 3 2   since you did not support hearts initially.

♠ K 7
♡ K 8 3
◇ 7 4 2
♣ A 9 7 4 2

Partner opens 1♠, you respond 2♣ and partner rebids 2♡. What next? Change of suit after a 2-over-1 response is forcing but you should not rebid your clubs (3♣ would imply 6 clubs or a superb 5-card suit) and you have no diamond stopper for no-trumps. It is better to give false preference to 2♠ than to raise the hearts with just 3 trumps.

3. Partner's rebid is not forcing but you are at the upper end of your minimum range and do not wish to pass in case game is still available.

♠ K 7
♡ K 4 3
◇ 8 7 6 2
♣ K 9 4 3

Partner opens 1♠ and rebids 2♡ over your 1NT response. What next? With a minimum (take one of the kings away) you should pass, but with a maximum, you should bid again, in case opener has a 16-17-18 count, just short of a jump-shift. False preference to 2♠ is better than either passing or bidding 3♡. If partner is minimum, you will play a 5-2 fit rather than a 4-3, perhaps, but if partner has the extra strength, partner has another chance and your failure to raise spades at once will make partner suspicious of the degree of your support.

♠ Q 7 6 4 2
♡ 8 4 3
◇ A 9
♣ K 7 2

Partner opens 1◇, you respond 1♠ and partner rebids 2♣. This is not forcing, but as opener's range is 12-18, it is not appealing to pass, since there could be enough for game. You do not have enough to raise to 3♣, but 2◇, false preference, is superior to rebidding 2♠ on such a weak suit.

DELAYED SUPPORT

"Delayed support" is intrinsic to all systems. It is vital to grasp the concept and be able to apply its principles.

As opener is expected to raise responder's suit only with 4 trumps and responder is expected not to rebid a 5-card suit except as a last resort, the partnership has to be careful not to miss 5-3 trump fits where responder holds the 5-card suit. Since responder bids 4-card suits up-the-line, if responder bids higher suit, then lower new suit (e.g. 1◇ : 1♠, 2◇ : 2♡) responder will hold at least 5 cards in the first suit, because of the failure to bid up-the-line. With 4-4, you would have bid up-the-line; your actual sequence of bids was "down-the-line", and therefore your suits cannot be 4-4; they must be at least 5-4. In such a case, it is easy for opener to give 3-card support for the first bid suit, as it is known to contain at least 5-cards.

However, in many auctions, opener will not know whether responder's 1st suit has 5 cards, for example, if responder rebids in no-trumps, (e.g. 1◇ : 1♡, 1♠ : 2NT), raises opener's second suit (1◇ : 1♠, 2♣ : 3♣) or gives preference to opener's first suit (e.g. 1◇ : 1♠, 2♣ : 2◇). To cater for the *possibility* that responder holds a 5-card suit, opener should give "delayed support", i.e. support responder's first suit on a later round of bidding. Immediate support = 4 trumps normally. Delayed support = 3 trumps normally.

♠ K 7
♡ Q 8 4
◇ A K 8 7 6 4
♣ J 3

You open 1◇, partner replies 1♡, you rebid 2◇ and partner rebids 2♠. What now? You should give delayed support to 3♡. You do not know partner has 5 hearts but that is immaterial: *partner knows* you do not hold 4 hearts (or you would have bid 1◇ : 1♡, 2♡), so your delayed support shows 3 hearts and it is now up to partner to choose 4♡ or 3NT.

♠ K 7 2
♡ A Q 8 6 4
◇ A 8
♣ J 7 4

You open 1♡, partner replies 1♠, you rebid 1NT and partner invites game with 2NT. What next? As you have better than a minimum, you should accept the invitation to game, but bid 3♠, delayed support, not 3NT. Partner knows you do not have 4 spades (your 1NT rebid denied four spades) and over 3♠, partner can choose 4♠ *if* holding five spades or 3NT if holding only four spades.

♠ A Q 8 6
♡ Q 3 2
◇ A K 9 8 2
♣ 4

You open 1◇, partner replies 1♡, you rebid 1♠ and partner rebids 2NT. What next? Partner may or may not hold five hearts. Best is to give delayed support with 3♡ and leave it to partner to choose 4♡ or 3NT. Your failure to raise hearts at once means partner knows you hold only three hearts. With only four hearts, partner will revert to 3NT.

♠ A 8 6 4 3
♡ A K 7 2
◇ A 9 3
♣ 6

You open 1♠, partner replies 2◇, you rebid 2♡ and partner rebids 2NT. What next? Best is to give delayed support with 3◇. Where a player bids 2 suits and gives delayed support in a 3rd suit, clearly there cannot be much in the remaining suit. 3◇ here also warns partner about the need to have clubs well covered in order to try 3NT.

THE 1♠ : 2♡ AUCTION

The 2♡ response to 1♠ promises 5 hearts. This is useful in order to find support quickly without having to rebid the suit and also to eliminate problems at the 3-level (such as whether to try for 3NT or whether to repeat the heart suit). Since *five* hearts are promised, opener should raise the hearts with just 3-card support on all normal hands. In standard methods, 1♠ : 2♡, 3♡ would show support and a minimum hand while 1♠ : 2♡, 4♡ would show extra values, enough for game opposite a 10-count. It follows that 1♠ : 2♡, 2♠ would deny 3 hearts, as would 1♠ : 2♡, 2NT. If opener changes suit (e.g. 1♠ : 2♡, 3♣), responder should assume opener does not hold 3 hearts and responder would show 6 hearts by rebidding 3♡, asking for doubleton support.

MORE ON DELAYED SUPPORT

Where partner has had a chance to show 3-card support for a known 5-card suit but denied such support, then later delayed support will be doubleton support.

Delayed support for a possible 4-card suit = 3-card support.

Delayed support for a known 5-card suit = 2-card support.

♠ A Q 8 6 4 3 ♡ A 2 ◇ K 7 ♣ 4 3 2	You open 1♠, partner replies 2♡, you rebid 2♠ (denying 3 hearts) and partner now rebids 3◇. What next? Best is 3♡, delayed support. Since you previously denied 3 hearts, this delayed support can be no better than a doubleton and partner will recognise that you cannot hold 3 hearts because of your failure to support hearts at once.
♠ K 2 ♡ 7 2 ◇ A 8 3 ♣ A Q 8 6 4 2	You open 1♣, partner replies 1♠, you rebid 2♣, partner rebids 2♡, showing at least 5 spades–4 hearts. You rebid 2NT, showing the diamond stopper, denying 3 spades and denying 4 hearts. Partner rebids 3♡, showing at least 5-5 in the majors. What now? Best is 3♠, delayed support, showing only a doubleton since 2NT had denied 3 spades.
♠ K 2 ♡ 4 3 ◇ A 10 9 4 2 ♣ A 7 3 2	Partner opens 1♠, you reply 2◇, partner rebids 2♡ and you rebid 2NT, denying 3 spades. Partner now produces 3◇. What next? Partner is very likely to hold a 5-4-3-1 pattern with a singleton club and this makes 3NT very unappealing with only one stopper and the marked club lead. You could stay with the diamonds but 3♠, delayed doubleton support (as 2NT denied 3 spades) may locate a cheaper and higher-scoring

game. Partner knows that you have only *two* spades and if partner does not wish to stay with the spades, partner can revert to diamonds or no-trumps. If you held a singleton spade and K-x-x in hearts, you could have produced delayed heart support with 3♡.

BIDDING FALSE SUITS TO OBTAIN PREFERENCE OR DELAYED SUPPORT

The Skip-Over Principle was mentioned in Chapter 2 (see page 16) so that where opener bypasses a suit that could have been bid conveniently, opener denies holding that suit. For example, 1♣ : 1◇, 1♠ denies 4 hearts and 1♣ : 1♡, 1NT denies 4 spades. Similarly a jump-rebid in the suit opened will deny any 2nd suit (e.g. 1◇ : 1♠, 3◇ denies 4 hearts). Responder can harness this principle to solve many bidding problems.

It is safe for responder to bid a suit that opener has denied, *even with only 2 or 3 cards in that suit,* **since opener needs 4 cards to raise responder's 2nd suit and opener has denied 4 cards in that suit.**

♠ A K ♡ A Q 8 3 2 ◇ 7 4 2 ♣ 6 4 3	Partner opens 1◇, you respond 1♡ and partner rebids 2◇. You have enough for game, but 3◇ is not forcing, 3♡ would show *six* hearts and the absence of a club stopper makes a no-trump bid unappealing. What do you do? A rebid of 2♠ is best *and is safe*. Partner's 2◇ denied 4 spades, so that you will not hear 3♠ or 4♠. (If you do(!), bid 5◇.) If partner gives delayed support via 3♡, bid 4♡, while if partner bids 2NT, promising clubs stopped,

bid 3NT. If partner rebids 3◇, either pass (enough is enough) or make one more effort with 4◇ (our choice).

♠ A Q 8 7 3 ♡ K Q 4 ◇ 7 3 2 ♣ 6 4	Partner opens 1◇, you reply 1♠ and partner rebids 3◇. What next? The 3◇ rebid denied 4 hearts — partner would have rebid 2♡, introducing a major, rather than 3◇ — so that 3♡ is now safe. If partner bids 3♠, go to 4♠ and if partner has the clubs stopped, partner will rebid 3NT. Bidding a suit which partner has denied is more in the nature of a stopper bid than a real suit, although it can, of course, be a genuine suit.

BIDDING BY A PASSED HAND

Once you have passed initially, the meaning of some of your bids will be affected, since it is no longer possible for you to hold 13 points, else you would have opened. Your weak responses are not affected: a raise of opener's suit to the 2-level is still 6-10 points and the 1NT response is also still 6-10 points. A change of suit at the 1-level has a range of 6-12 points as opposed to the unlimited nature of the 6 or more points attached to the response of a new suit at the 1-level normally.

The responses with changed meanings are the jump responses and the change of suit to the 2-level. Since a passed hand cannot hold 13 points, a jump response now shows exactly 11-12 points. The specific meanings:

● Jump to 2NT by a passed hand (e.g. Pass : 1♡, 2NT) shows 11-12 points, balanced shape and denies support for opener's suit.

● Jump-raise by a passed hand (e.g. Pass : 1♠, 3♠) shows 11-12 points and support for opener's suit. The shape need not be balanced.

● Jump-shift by a passed hand (e.g. Pass : 1◇, 2♠) shows 11-12 points and a strong 5-card suit. If the suit is only four cards long or if the suit is not strong, bid the suit at the cheapest level without a jump.

The most important rule about bidding by a passed hand is this :

A BID BY A PASSED HAND IS NOT FORCING

This applies whether it is a jump bid or a change of suit so that the normal rules about change-of-suit-forcing or jump responses forcing to game do not apply when the responder is a passed hand. Because any bid by a passed hand is not forcing, it is vital to make a response which gives partner the most important message in one bid — there might be no second chance. Therefore, raise a major suit as first priority. Do not bid a new suit when you have a major suit raise available.

The change of suit to the 2-level still requires 10 points, but the range is 10-12 points rather than the normal 10 points or more, and a very significant difference is that a 5-card or longer suit is promised (since it may be passed by opener). With only 4-card suits, bid a suit at the 1-level (a new suit at the 1-level does not promise more than 4 cards) or respond 1NT or 2NT.

EXERCISES

A. Partner opened 1◇. You responded 1♡ and partner rebid 1♠. What is your next action on these hands?

1. ♠ K 8 2	2. ♠ A 9 8 3	3. ♠ A 7	4. ♠ Q 7	5. ♠ 9 2
♡ Q 9 8 2	♡ K 7 6 4	♡ K J 8 6 4 3	♡ K J 8 4	♡ A K 7 6 4 3
◇ 7 6 4	◇ 7	◇ 7 6	◇ Q 7 5 2	◇ A J
♣ K 7 6	♣ A 7 4 3	♣ 4 3 2	♣ 8 4 3	♣ J 3 2

B. Partner opened 1◇ and rebid 2♣ over your 1♡ response. What is your next action on these hands?

1. ♠ K 7	2. ♠ 8 6	3. ♠ A J 8 3	4. ♠ 8 7 3	5. ♠ 6 4
♡ Q 7 5 3	♡ A 9 3 2	♡ K J 9 2	♡ A Q J 6	♡ A K 7 6 2
◇ 9 6 4	◇ 9 7 6 2	◇ A J 7	◇ J 8	◇ Q J 10 4
♣ Q 8 7 2	♣ K 7 3	♣ 5 2	♣ K 9 7 4	♣ 8 7

C. Partner opened 1♡ and rebid 2◇ over your 1♠ response. What action do you take on these hands now?

1. ♠ K J 7 4 3	2. ♠ A Q J 5	3. ♠ K 8 7 5	4. ♠ J 7 4 3 2	5. ♠ K Q 3 2
♡ 7 4 2	♡ K 7 4	♡ 2	♡ Q 8	♡ K J
◇ 8 6 2	◇ 3 2	◇ K 8 4 3	◇ K 6	◇ J 4 2
♣ A 3	♣ J 8 3 2	♣ 9 8 5 3	♣ 8 6 5 2	♣ 9 7 3 2

D. You opened 1♣ and rebid 2♣ over partner's 1♠ response. Partner now rebids 2♡. What action do you take on these hands now?

1. ♠ Q 7 2	2. ♠ Q 7	3. ♠ K	4. ♠ J 2	5. ♠ 7 3 2
♡ 8 3	♡ 8 3 2	♡ 7 4 2	♡ K 3	♡ 8
◇ A 7	◇ A 7	◇ A J 9	◇ 7 4 2	◇ A Q 8
♣ A K 8 6 3 2	♣ A K 8 6 3 2	♣ A Q 8 5 4 2	♣ A K J 9 7 4	♣ A Q 8 7 4 3

E. You opened 1♠ and partner responded 2♡. What is your next action on these hands?

1. ♠ A K 9 8 2
   ♡ Q 9 8
   ◊ Q J 4
   ♣ 7 6

2. ♠ A Q 8 3 2
   ♡ K 7 6
   ◊ A 4 3 2
   ♣ 2

3. ♠ A K 8 7 5 3
   ♡ K J 6
   ◊ A 6
   ♣ 4 3

4. ♠ A Q 7 4 3
   ♡ 4
   ◊ K Q 7 5 2
   ♣ J 3

5. ♠ Q J 8 7 2
   ♡ A 7
   ◊ A K Q 7
   ♣ 3 2

F. Partner opened 1♠ and rebid 3◊ over your 2♡ response. What action do you take on these hands now?

1. ♠ K J
   ♡ A Q 9 7 4 3
   ◊ 8 6
   ♣ 6 3 2

2. ♠ Q 7
   ♡ K 9 5 4 2
   ◊ J 2
   ♣ A Q 3 2

3. ♠ K J
   ♡ A J 9 5 2
   ◊ Q 8
   ♣ 6 4 3 2

4. ♠ 7
   ♡ A Q 8 5 4
   ◊ K Q 7 2
   ♣ Q J 2

5. ♠ 4 2
   ♡ K Q J 8 6 5 3
   ◊ 9 8
   ♣ A 3

G. You passed as dealer and partner opened the bidding 1♡. What action do you take on these hands?

1. ♠ K 7 2
   ♡ A 3
   ◊ Q 7 5 2
   ♣ 7 6 5 3

2. ♠ Q 7 5 2
   ♡ 3 2
   ◊ A K 9
   ♣ J 6 3 2

3. ♠ K Q 2
   ♡ 7 4 2
   ◊ J 9 6 4
   ♣ A J 7

4. ♠ A 2
   ♡ K 9 5 3
   ◊ K 4 2
   ♣ 8 7 3 2

5. ♠ K 2
   ♡ A J 6 5 2
   ◊ 9 8 6 4 3
   ♣ 2

H. Partner passes as dealer. You open 1♡ and partner responds 2◊. What is your next action on these hands?

1. ♠ K Q 6
   ♡ Q 9 7 3 2
   ◊ J 9 6
   ♣ A 8

2. ♠ Q 9 7 2
   ♡ A J 8 5 2
   ◊ 9 7
   ♣ K Q

3. ♠ A Q 8 5
   ♡ A J 8 6 2
   ◊ A J
   ♣ 6 3

4. ♠ K Q
   ♡ A J 6 5 2
   ◊ 2
   ♣ A Q 7 3 2

5. ♠ 3
   ♡ A 9 7 6 2
   ◊ A Q 6 4
   ♣ A 8 4

PARTNERSHIP BIDDING : How should the following hands be bid? West is the dealer on all hands.

SET 11 − WEST	SET 11 − EAST	SET 12 − WEST	SET 12 − EAST
1. ♠ A 9 7 3 ♡ K Q ◊ Q 7 6 4 ♣ 8 3 2	1. ♠ K 6 5 4 2 ♡ A 9 3 ◊ K 3 ♣ A 7 4	1. ♠ A Q 7 5 4 ♡ K 3 2 ◊ K 6 2 ♣ 4 3	1. ♠ 2 ♡ A 9 8 6 5 ◊ A Q 5 4 ♣ Q 7 2
2. ♠ K 7 3 ♡ A 9 ◊ 6 4 ♣ A Q 7 6 4 2	2. ♠ Q J 5 4 2 ♡ K Q 6 2 ◊ A 3 2 ♣ 3	2. ♠ K Q 8 6 4 3 ♡ K 2 ◊ K Q ♣ 7 6 4	2. ♠ 2 ♡ A Q J 6 5 ◊ A J 8 4 3 ♣ 3 2
3. ♠ 8 3 ♡ Q 6 ◊ A Q 8 ♣ A J 9 7 6 4	3. ♠ A K 7 4 2 ♡ A K 9 3 ◊ 4 3 ♣ 5 2	3. ♠ A Q 8 7 6 ♡ K 2 ◊ 4 ♣ A K 7 3 2	3. ♠ K ♡ A J 8 7 4 3 ◊ Q 7 3 ♣ 8 6 4
4. ♠ A Q 9 4 ♡ 7 2 ◊ A K 7 6 2 ♣ Q 8	4. ♠ 6 3 ♡ K Q 8 6 5 ◊ 9 8 5 3 ♣ J 6	4. ♠ A J 8 6 4 2 ♡ 7 ◊ K 7 6 ♣ K J 8	4. ♠ 3 ♡ A K 9 4 2 ◊ A Q 5 ♣ Q 10 7 2
5. ♠ A 8 3 ♡ A Q 7 6 4 ◊ 7 6 4 ♣ A 8	5. ♠ K 9 6 5 4 ♡ J 2 ◊ A Q J ♣ 7 3 2	5. ♠ 7 ♡ J 8 2 ◊ A Q 7 6 4 ♣ A K 4 3	5. ♠ K 9 6 5 4 ♡ Q 7 6 3 ◊ J 5 ♣ Q 2
6. ♠ A 2 ♡ K 3 2 ◊ A K 8 6 4 2 ♣ 8 4	6. ♠ K Q 8 4 ♡ Q J 8 6 5 ◊ Q 3 ♣ 7 2	6. ♠ K 4 3 ♡ 7 ◊ A K 8 6 2 ♣ A Q 9 8	6. ♠ A 8 7 5 2 ♡ 9 8 3 ◊ Q 5 4 ♣ K 4

PLAY HANDS BASED ON PREFERENCES & DELAYED SUPPORT

Hand 13 : Giving a preference — Discarding a loser to create a ruff in dummy

Dealer North : Both vulnerable

	NORTH		
	♠ A 9 6		
	♡ 10 4 3		
	◇ K J 8 7 5		
	♣ J 8		

WEST		EAST	
♠ K J 5 4 2		♠ Q 7 3	
♡ K Q 6 2		♡ A 9	
◇ A 3 2		◇ 6 4	
♣ 3		♣ A K 7 6 4 2	

	SOUTH		
	♠ 10 8		
	♡ J 8 7 5		
	◇ Q 10 9		
	♣ Q 10 9 5		

WEST	NORTH	EAST	SOUTH
	Pass	1♣	Pass
1♠	Pass	2♣	Pass
2♡ (1)	Pass	2♠ (2)	Pass
4♠ (3)	Pass	Pass	Pass

Bidding : (1) New suit is forcing. 1♠ followed by 2♡, bidding down-the-line, promises 5+ spades and 4+ hearts.
(2) Delayed support = 3 trumps. It is far superior to show the secondary spade support than to rebid the clubs.
(3) Note how badly 3NT would fare on a diamond lead.

Lead : ◇7. Where 3 suits have been bid, the unbid suit is the normal lead.

Correct play : Best is to win the ace of diamonds, play a heart to the ace and back to the king of hearts, followed by the queen of hearts on which you discard a diamond from dummy. Continue with a diamond ruff, cash the ace of clubs, ruff a club, ruff a diamond and play the king of clubs to discard the heart loser.

However, this is ruffed by North and only 11 tricks are made.

As the cards lie, it would work to lead trumps at trick 2, but this could fail, for if trumps were 4-1, declarer might lose 2 spades and 2 tricks in the red suits. Where you can discard a loser and you hold 6 cards or fewer in the suit which provides the discard (the hearts in the above hand), it is unlikely that the opposition will be able to ruff that suit on the first 3 rounds.

Hand 14 : Delayed support — Ruffing losers in dummy

Dealer East : Nil vulnerable

	NORTH		
	♠ K Q 5 2		
	♡ Q 10 8 4 2		
	◇ 5		
	♣ A J 3		

WEST		EAST	
♠ J 9 8 6		♠ 10 7	
♡ A J 9		♡ 5 3	
◇ J 8		◇ K 10 9 7	
♣ Q 9 5 2		♣ K 10 8 7 6	

	SOUTH		
	♠ A 4 3		
	♡ K 7 6		
	◇ A Q 6 4 3 2		
	♣ 4		

WEST	NORTH	EAST	SOUTH
		Pass	1◇
Pass	1♡	Pass	2◇ (1)
Pass	2♠ (2)	Pass	3♡ (3)
Pass	4♡ (4)	All pass	

Bidding : (1) Do not raise responder's possible 4-card suit with only 3 trumps unless there is no attractive alternative.
(2) Although South has denied spades, North uses the 2♠ rebid (new suit forcing) to obtain more information to locate the best game contract. North's plan is to play in 4♡ if partner can show 3-card heart support and to end in 3NT if South cannot support the hearts.
(3) Delayed support = 3 trumps. North cannot be misled since South did not raise the hearts on the previous round.
(4) Note that 3NT would be easily defeated on a club lead.

Lead : ♣7. Leading the unbid suit is best unless you have a strong reason for a different choice.

Play : Win the ace of clubs, ruff a club, play a spade to the king, ruff the 3rd club, then lead the king of hearts. With normal breaks, you lose only 2 hearts and perhaps a spade. If West wins the ace of hearts and plays a 4th club, you ruff, cash the queen of hearts and take the diamond finesse while dummy still has the ace of spades as an entry. Whether the finesse wins or loses, you can discard a spade on the ace of diamonds later. As it happens, the diamond finesse works and declarer can make 11 tricks.

Wrong play : It would be an error to lead trumps at trick 2. Where dummy is able to ruff and has few trumps, it is best to start ruffing early and delay drawing trumps till the ruffs have been taken.

Hand 15 : The 1♠ : 2♡ auction — Unblocking and discarding losers from hand

Dealer South : North-South vulnerable

NORTH
- ♠ 10 5 3
- ♡ 8
- ◇ K Q 8 7 5
- ♣ Q 10 5 4

WEST
- ♠ A K 8 6 2
- ♡ Q 6
- ◇ 6 4
- ♣ A K J 2

EAST
- ♠ Q
- ♡ K J 9 7 5 3
- ◇ A 9 3
- ♣ 9 7 3

SOUTH
- ♠ J 9 7 4
- ♡ A 10 4 2
- ◇ J 10 2
- ♣ 8 6

WEST	NORTH	EAST	SOUTH
			Pass
1♠ (1)	Pass (2)	2♡ (3)	Pass
3♣ (4)	Pass	3♡ (5)	Pass
4♡ (6)	Pass	Pass	Pass

Bidding: (1) With most of your points in the long suits, bid your suits rather than no-trumps.
(2) Too weak to overcall 2◇.
(3) Shows 5+ hearts, 10+ points.
(4) Strong rebid as it bypasses the 2♠ barrier.
(5) Shows 6 hearts since 2♡ already showed 5. The auction is forcing since West has shown 16 or more points (with the 3♣ rebid) and East has shown 10 or more points (with the 2♡ response).
(6) Note how poor a contract 3NT is on the diamond lead, marked by the bidding.

Lead : ◇ J. From J-10-x, the jack is standard (top of touching honors from a 3-card suit).

Correct play : Win the ◇ A, cash the ♠ Q (unblocking), lead a club to the ace and discard your diamond losers on the ♠ A and ♠ K. There is only one spade now missing and quite a good plan is to continue with another spade. If North ruffs, overruff — you have now set up dummy's last spade as a winner. Lead a trump now, but later when you win dummy's ♣ K, you can discard your club loser on the 5th spade. This is better than taking the club finesse. You lose just 2 trumps and make 11 tricks.

Hand 16 : The 1♠ : 2♡ auction — Delayed support — Unblocking a second suit before drawing trumps

Dealer West : East-West vulnerable

NORTH
- ♠ K Q 8 6 4 3
- ♡ K 2
- ◇ K Q
- ♣ 7 6 4

WEST
- ♠ 10 7 5
- ♡ 10 9 4 3
- ◇ 10 7
- ♣ A K 10 8

EAST
- ♠ A J 9
- ♡ 8 7
- ◇ 9 6 5 2
- ♣ Q J 9 5

SOUTH
- ♠ 2
- ♡ A Q J 6 5
- ◇ A J 8 4 3
- ♣ 3 2

WEST	NORTH	EAST	SOUTH
Pass	1♠	Pass	2♡ (1)
Pass	2♠ (2)	Pass	3◇ (3)
Pass	3♡ (4)	Pass	4♡ (5)
Pass	Pass	Pass	

Bidding: (1) With a 5-5 pattern, bid the higher suit first. The 2♡ response shows 5+ hearts and 10+ points.
(2) Failure to support hearts denies 3-card support.
(3) New suit forcing.
(4) Delayed support here = 2 trumps only since 2♠ denied 3-card support. With no club stopper, 3NT is out and 3♡ is superior to repeating the spades again.
(5) South knows it is only a 5-2 fit, but cannot bid 3NT with no cover in clubs. Note how poor the 3NT and 4♠ contracts are.

Lead : ♣ K. King from ace-king is standard, although some pairs lead ace from ace-king suits. It matters little as long as you are consistent and partner knows which you do.

Correct Play : East should encourage the club lead and South ruffs the 3rd round. Lead a heart to king, cash the king and queen of diamonds, and then continue with a heart to the ace, followed by the queen and jack of hearts, drawing trumps. Finally cash the ace of diamonds, jack of diamonds and the 5th diamond. Making 5 hearts and 5 diamonds.

Wrong Play : (1) Drawing trumps before unblocking the ◇ K, ◇ Q. As long as East does not discard a diamond, declarer would fail, as South is out of trumps and has no entry after playing ◇ K and ◇ Q, while if South plays ◇ K and overtakes the ◇ Q, East's ◇ 9 becomes high on the 4th round of diamonds. East should retain all 4 diamonds, following the principle "Keep length in declarer's known 2nd suit".
(3) Failing to draw all the trumps before cashing your other winners or losing count in trumps.

CHAPTER 5

SUIT RESPONSES TO 1NT AND 2NT

Bidding after balanced 1NT and 2NT openings is considered easiest of all since partner's point range is closely limited and partner's hand pattern is also known within closely defined limits. As opener has no singleton or void and a major suit game is the No. 1 priority, responder with a 6-card major and sufficient values for game can simply bid 4♡ or 4♠, knowing that the partnership has at least 8 trumps.

A suit response to a no-trump opening promises at least a 5-card suit.

Exception : 1NT : 2♣ Stayman and 2NT : 3♣ Stayman — see Chapter 6.

The standard approach to suit responses to 1NT and 2NT is :

1NT : 2♢ **1NT : 2♡** **1NT : 2♠**	Weakness takeout, 5-card or longer suit, no chance for game. Opener must pass (but see text below for one other option for opener after these signoffs). 1NT : 2♣ is not used to show a genuine suit but is the Stayman Convention (see Chapter 6).
1NT : 3♣ **1NT : 3♢** **2NT : 3♢**	Game-force, 5-card or longer suit, no 4-card major, suggests slam possibilities. Most hands with a 5-card or longer minor, no 4-card major and no prospects beyond game should bid 1NT : 3NT or 2NT : 3NT and not introduce the minor suit, even with a singleton.
1NT : 3♡ **2NT : 3♡** **1NT : 3♠** **2NT : 3♠**	Game force, 5-card or longer suit, denies 4 cards in the other major. Opener must reply and should show support for responder's major with 3-card or better support. Weak support or strong support can be shown — see opposite page. The 2NT opening is not forcing but if responder does reply, it is forcing to game : there is no weakness takeout over 2NT.
1NT : 4♡ **2NT : 4♡** **1NT : 4♠** **2NT : 4♠**	6-card or longer suit, no prospects for slam, opener is obliged to pass. Responder's game bid after 1NT or 2NT is an absolute sign-off, no ifs, no buts. If there were a chance for slam, responder should have bid 1NT : 3♡ or 1NT : 3♠. Responder knows opener's range and after 1NT or 2NT, it is responder's duty to investigate slams, not opener's.

A 1NT or 2NT bidder (opener or responder) has no right to bid beyond game.

After 1NT : 2♢ *or* **1NT : 2♡** *or* **1NT : 2♠** — **the weakness takeout:** Although the rule is that opener *must* pass and novices should be trained early to pass regularly and to pass quickly, opener is permitted *one* further action: you may raise responder's suit with excellent support, a maximum 1NT and a doubleton outside (ruffing value). You may raise only to the 3-level and if you choose not to raise, you MUST pass.

After 1NT : 3♣ *or* **1NT : 3♢** *or* **2NT : 3♢** : Responder should not hold a 4-card major in addition to the long minor, since it is better to use the Stayman Convention when holding 4-major—5-minor hands (see Chapter 6) to explore the possibility of playing in a superior major suit game.

With a doubleton or 3 rags in responder's suit, opener should rebid 3NT over 3♣ or 3♢. With better support for the minor, opener should cue bid (bid your cheapest ace, e.g. 1NT : 3♢, 3♠ ...) as responder usually has at least mild slam interest when making the 3♣ or 3♢ response. Since responder is prepared to play in 5-of-the-minor opposite moderate support and a minimum no-trump, there must be slam chances if opener has excellent support and a maximum no-trump. If opener holds support but no ace, raise the minor suit to the 4-level (e.g. 1NT : 3♢, 4♢). Responder can sign off in game with no further slam interest or, with hopes for slam, cue bid an ace or use 4NT.

After 1NT : 3♡ *or* **2NT : 3♡** *or* **1NT : 3♠** *or* **2NT : 3♠** : Responder is showing a 5-card suit and opener should support with any 3 trumps. Opener has two basic choices :

DENY SUPPORT with any doubleton : Bid 3NT (e.g. 2NT : 3♡, 3NT *or* 1NT : 3♠, 3NT), *or*

SHOW SUPPORT with any 3 trumps. Opener may give weak support or strong support :

WEAK SUPPORT : Raise responder's major (e.g. 2NT : 3♡, 4♡ *or* 1NT : 3♠, 4♠)

STRONG SUPPORT : Cue bid your cheapest ace (e.g. 2NT : 3♡, 3♠ *or* 1NT : 3♠, 4♢)

The NT bidder is not permitted to bid beyond game but when holding support for partner's suit, you can indicate how suitable the hand is for slam purposes. With the weaker type of supporting hand, raise the major to the 4-level. The features which make up the weak type of raise are : 3 trumps rather than 4 + minimum HCP + any 4-3-3-3 pattern. The features which indicate strong support are : 4 trumps rather than 3 + maximum HCP + an outside doubleton (ruffing value). Two out of the three strong features justify the cue bid indicating the strong raise, e.g. 1NT : 3♠, 4♢ = spade support, maximum values, ♢ A (cue), no ♣ A (4♣ was bypassed). If you have no ace to cue, raise the major. Absence of outside aces is itself a poor feature.

The above approach also applies in comparable NT auctions. For example, it would apply when you have made a 2NT response, e.g. after 1♠ : 2NT, 3♠ or 1♠ : 2NT, 3♡ — raising the major to game is weak support, while a cue bid is strong support of the last suit bid. Also, 1♠ : 2NT, 3♡ : 3♠ is stronger than 1♠ : 2NT, 3♡ : 4♠.

Responder uses the 1NT : 3♡ and 1NT : 3♠ responses on two types of hands :

(a) Game-going hands without slam prospects with *exactly* five cards in the major suit bid.

(b) Hands which have slam possibilities with five *or more* cards in the major suit bid.

If opener rebids 3NT (no support), responder will pass with type (a). If responder rebids the major over 3NT (e.g. 1NT : 3♡, 3NT : 4♡), responder is showing type (b), a mild slam invitation with 6 or more trumps.

If opener raises responder's major, responder passes with type (a) and may also pass with type (b) if opener's weak supporting raise has dampened responder's hopes for slam. If responder is still interested in slam despite opener's weak supporting raise, responder may use 4NT or make a cue bid.

If opener shows strong support via a cue bid, type-a responder simply bids game (e.g. 1NT : 3♠, 4♣ : 4♠) but with slam interest, type-b responder can continue with a cue bid or with 4NT, asking for aces.

PARTNERSHIP BIDDING : How should the following hands be bid? West is the dealer on all hands.

SET 13 — WEST	SET 13 — EAST	SET 14 — WEST	SET 14 — EAST
1. ♠ A Q ♡ K 6 3 ♢ A K 8 7 ♣ 7 6 5 4	1. ♠ K 4 2 ♡ A 9 8 7 2 ♢ Q J 9 ♣ 9 3	1. ♠ Q J 7 6 3 2 ♡ 4 3 ♢ 7 5 2 ♣ 7 4	1. ♠ A K ♡ K Q J ♢ K Q 8 3 ♣ A 8 6 2
2. ♠ K 7 6 4 2 ♡ A 3 ♢ 8 7 4 3 ♣ K 8	2. ♠ J 3 ♡ K 6 5 2 ♢ A K 9 5 ♣ A Q 9	2. ♠ A 8 6 ♡ A 7 ♢ A K J 3 ♣ K Q J 9	2. ♠ - - - ♡ J 8 6 5 4 3 2 ♢ 6 5 2 ♣ 8 6 3
3. ♠ K 7 ♡ A 4 2 ♢ A K 7 2 ♣ Q 9 8 6	3. ♠ A 8 6 5 3 2 ♡ 7 6 ♢ 6 5 ♣ A J 3	3. ♠ K 8 7 5 4 ♡ 7 ♢ J 9 3 ♣ 6 5 4 2	3. ♠ Q J 2 ♡ A 6 3 ♢ K Q 8 ♣ A K Q J
4. ♠ J 8 6 5 4 2 ♡ 9 6 ♢ J 4 3 ♣ 6 2	4. ♠ A 9 ♡ A K 8 2 ♢ 9 8 5 ♣ A Q 4 3	4. ♠ K Q J 2 ♡ K 5 ♢ A 9 7 ♣ A K Q 10	4. ♠ A 3 ♡ Q 7 6 4 3 ♢ 6 4 2 ♣ 8 7 6
5. ♠ A 9 4 ♡ 8 7 5 ♢ A Q J ♣ K Q J 4	5. ♠ 6 ♡ A J 9 6 4 3 2 ♢ 7 4 ♣ 8 3 2	5. ♠ A 5 3 ♡ Q 8 6 4 3 ♢ 8 6 4 ♣ 5 4	5. ♠ K Q 2 ♡ K 5 2 ♢ A K Q J ♣ A 9 8
6. ♠ A 8 7 2 ♡ A 8 ♢ A K Q 2 ♣ 8 7 3	6. ♠ 5 4 ♡ Q J 10 7 2 ♢ 6 4 ♣ 9 6 5 2	6. ♠ A J 8 ♡ K 3 ♢ A 9 5 4 2 ♣ A K Q	6. ♠ 4 ♡ J 5 2 ♢ K 8 6 ♣ 9 8 7 5 3 2

PLAY HANDS BASED ON SUIT RESPONSES TO NO-TRUMP OPENINGS

Hand 17 : Weakness takeout — Drawing trumps — Discarding losers

Dealer North : Nil vulnerable

NORTH
♠ A 2
♡ 7 6 5 4
♦ A 8 3
♣ A K Q 9

WEST
♠ Q J 8
♡ K
♦ K Q J
♣ 10 8 7 6 3 2

EAST
♠ 10 9
♡ A Q J 9 2
♦ 9 7 6 2
♣ J 5

SOUTH
♠ K 7 6 5 4 3
♡ 10 8 3
♦ 10 5 4
♣ 4

WEST	NORTH	EAST	SOUTH
	1NT	Pass (1)	2♠ (2)
Pass	Pass (3)	Pass	

Bidding : (1) Too weak to call over the 1NT opening, but with one more heart and a singleton, 2♡ would be reasonable.
(2) The weakness takeout, a rescue from 1NT. With a weak hand, a long suit and no entries in the other suits, it is much safer to play in your long trump suit. It is clearly better to end in 2♠ making 8 or 9 tricks than to play 1NT, one off.
(3) Opener must pass (except with support and a maximum, when opener can raise responder's suit to the 3-level).

Lead : ♦ K. Top of sequence.

Correct play: Win the ♦ A and cash the ♠ A and ♠ K. Then play 3 rounds of clubs, discarding either diamond or heart losers on the club winners. Making 9 tricks. On the ♦ K, East should play the 2, the lowest card, as a discouraging signal. With the strong clubs in dummy, West can deduce that East likes hearts.

Wrong play: (1) Failing to draw 2 rounds of trumps after winning the ♦ A. If you play A-K-Q of clubs first, East ruffs the 3rd club and if you discard, you make only 8 tricks, while if you overruff, you go down.
(2) Playing ♠ A, ♠ K and a 3rd spade after taking the ♦ A. When West wins the 3rd round of trumps, the defense can cash 5 red tricks to defeat 2♠ by 1 trick. On most hands, it is best to leave the top trump out.

If North plays 1NT, East leads the ♡ Q (interior sequence), West wins the ♡ K and switches to the ♦ K and declarer has no more than 6 tricks available.

Hand 18 : Suit bidding after 2NT opening — Ruffing finesse to discard losers

Dealer East: North-South vulnerable

NORTH
♠ J 10
♡ 9 8 2
♦ A 9 7 4 2
♣ K Q 5

WEST
♠ A K 7 3
♡ K Q
♦ K Q J 6
♣ A 8 6

EAST
♠ 8 6 5
♡ J 10 7 6 5 4 3
♦ - - -
♣ 9 3 2

SOUTH
♠ Q 9 4 2
♡ A
♦ 10 8 5 3
♣ J 10 7 4

WEST	NORTH	EAST	SOUTH
		Pass	Pass
2NT	Pass	4♡ (1)	Pass
Pass (2)	Pass		

Bidding: (1) East knows that the partnership holds at least 9 hearts and can thus count shortage points. 5 for the void makes the East hand worth 6 points, easily enough for game opposite 2NT. Note how poor it would be to pass 2NT (or try 3NT!): West would find it almost impossible to make more than 6 tricks in no-trumps, yet 10 tricks in hearts are relatively comfortable. Again, with a long trump suit and no outside entries, it is clearly superior to play with the long suit as trumps.
(2) A no-trump bidder is not permitted to bid beyond game unless responder indicates slam values. West has already revealed a powerful hand with the 2NT opening and any slam bidding is up to responder. If partner chooses game, a NT bidder may not overrule that decision and bid higher.

Lead : ♣4. Better to lead from a suit with 2 honors than from a suit with only 1 honor.

Correct play: Win the ♣A and lead the ♦ K. If North plays low, discard a club, but when North plays the ace, ruff and cross to the ♠ A in order to play the ♦ Q and ♦ J on which you discard 2 club losers. Then start the trumps. Making 11 tricks, losing 1 spade and 1 heart. You could start on the trumps at once and play the ruffing finesse in diamonds later, but then you would make only 10 tricks as the defence could cash 2 clubs upon winning the ♡ A. Playing on diamonds first cannot harm you.

Hand 19 : Ducking the opening lead in dummy — Nullifying the danger of a ruff

Dealer South : East-West vulnerable

NORTH
♠ K Q J 10 9 8
♡ 9 6 4
◇ A
♣ 9 6 5

WEST
♠ A 7 6
♡ A 7
◇ 10 9 6 5 2
♣ 10 7 2

EAST
♠ 3
♡ Q J 10 3 2
◇ J 8 7
♣ J 8 4 3

SOUTH
♠ 5 4 2
♡ K 8 5
◇ K Q 4 3
♣ A K Q

WEST	NORTH	EAST	SOUTH
			1NT
Pass	4♠ (1)	All pass	

Bidding: (1) North knows that the partnership has at least 8 spades and, counting the singleton, North is worth 13 points, enough for a game but not quite enough for a slam, even opposite a maximum 1NT. North's 4♠ is an absolute signoff — opener must pass. Note that 3NT could be defeated on a diamond lead and repeated diamond leads later. The diamond lead knocks out the entry to the North hand and if the defense held off with the ♠A till the 3rd round, declarer could score only 2 spade tricks in no-trumps.

Lead: ♡Q. Top of sequence.

Correct play: Play low in dummy — do not play the king. If East plays a 2nd heart, play low from dummy again — playing the king will lose to the ace. West wins ♡A on the 2nd round and should lead a diamond. Win your ace, play a club to dummy and cash a top diamond, discarding your last heart. Only then lead trumps.

Wrong play: (1) Playing the ♡K on the opening lead: West is marked with the ace and you will just lose your king. Playing low is not certain to win, but playing the king is sure to lose. West would win the ♡A and return a heart and you would lose 3 hearts and 1 spade.

(2) Playing trumps when in with the ◇A. As the cards lie, this does not cost, but if East held the ♠A, East could win and lead a third heart for West to ruff. You would then lose the ♠A and *three* hearts. By discarding your last heart on a diamond winner, you can overruff if West does ruff the ♡K. If you do lead a trump from hand at trick 4, lead the 8, not the king. If East has A-x, East may play low and then your 2nd round of trumps will draw the missing trumps. If you wish to sneak a round of trumps, lead the lowest of equal trumps.

Hand 20 : Suit bidding over 2NT — The double finesse

Dealer West : Both vulnerable

NORTH
♠ 8 6 5
♡ Q 9 5
◇ K Q 10 9
♣ 10 7 5

WEST
♠ K 2
♡ 8 7 6 4 2
◇ 7 5
♣ 8 6 4 3

EAST
♠ A Q J 4
♡ A J 10
◇ J 4 2
♣ A K Q

SOUTH
♠ 10 9 7 3
♡ K 3
◇ A 8 6 3
♣ J 9 2

WEST	NORTH	EAST	SOUTH
Pass	Pass	2NT (1)	Pass
3♡ (2)	Pass	4♡ (3)	All pass

Bidding: (1) The diamond holding is a drawback but 2NT is still the only sensible opening. To open with a 1-bid risks being left there (West would pass a 1-opening) and a 2-opening does not solve the diamond problem. It is reasonable to take a risk with one unguarded suit and open 2NT as long as the hand is balanced. (2) Promises 5 hearts (need not be strong hearts) and is forcing to game. It is better to explore the major suit contract than bid 3NT. (3) Shows support for hearts but a relatively weak hand. The weak features are minimum HCP and the 4-3-3-3 pattern. Even if East had a hand suitable for a cue bid, West would sign off in 4♡. It would be an error to choose 3NT: not only might you lose the first 5 or 6 diamond tricks but, in no-trumps, West does not have a 2nd entry for the double finesse in hearts. In no-trumps, East has only 8 tricks even though the defence can take only 4 diamonds.

Lead: ◇K. Top from K-Q holdings is standard in suit contracts.

Correct Play: South encourages the diamond lead and West ruffs the 3rd round. Lead a heart to the 10 and king (first finesse). Regain the lead (ruff a diamond continuation in *your* hand or come to hand via the ♠K) and lead another heart: 9 — J — the 2nd finesse wins. Cash the ♡A and the rest of the tricks are yours. The double finesse is the best chance for success with low cards opposite A-J-10. If dummy had only 2 diamonds, you could come to hand twice for the double finesse via the ♠K and by ruffing a spade winner.

CHAPTER 6

STAYMAN OVER 1NT AND 2NT

After a 1NT or 2NT opening, the partnership may have a 4-4 fit in a major suit which would be superior to no-trumps. However, we saw in Chapter 5 that a suit bid after a 1NT or 2NT opening shows a 5-card or longer suit, so that it is not possible to locate such a 4-4 fit by bidding your suit. Partner would be misled about the length of your suit and may support you with only 3 trumps, landing you in an inferior 4-3 trump fit.

The solution is the Stayman Convention, a 2♣ response to 1NT and a 3♣ response to 2NT, each of which is a question to opener: "Do you hold a 4-card major?" Opener replies by bidding a major suit held (e.g. 1NT : 2♣, 2♡ *or* 2NT : 3♣, 3♠) or by bidding diamonds to deny holding either major (D.D. = "Diamonds Deny", e.g. 1NT : 2♣, 2♢ *or* 2NT : 3♣, 3♢). If opener is 4-4 in the majors, show the hearts first, following the normal rule that 4-card suits are bid up-the-line. In other words, 1NT : 2♣, 2♡ *or* 2NT : 3♣, 3♡ does not deny holding 4 spades, but 1NT : 2♣, 2♠ and 2NT : 3♣, 3♠ does deny holding 4 hearts. In the standard version of Stayman, opener has only 3 possible replies to the enquiry (spades, hearts or diamonds). There are extended versions of the Stayman Convention but at this stage it is not recommended that you adopt any version of Extended Stayman.

BASIC REQUIREMENTS FOR THE USE OF STAYMAN

● **At least one 4-card major,**

● **A shortage somewhere, at least a doubleton, and**

● **Enough points to be able at least to invite game.**

These are the requirements when you are looking to find the best game contract. The use of Stayman for weakness rescue is covered in Chapter 22. For now, the use of Stayman is confined to game-possible hands.

WHEN SHOULD YOU USE STAYMAN?

If you have enough points to make game a possibility, you should use Stayman in each of these situations:

1. Your hand pattern is 4-4-4-1 (so that you must hold at least one 4-card major).

2. Your hand pattern is 4-4-3-2 including at least one 4-card major.

3. You hold both majors in a 4-4, 5-4, 6-4, 5-5 or 6-5 pattern. Any hand with both majors is suitable.

4. You hold a 5-card or longer minor but a 4-card major as well. Use Stayman to search for the major fit.

It is preferable not to use Stayman if your hand pattern is 4-3-3-3, as you have no ruffing ability. If you cannot ruff, why play in trumps? Stick with no-trumps. The principle is "no shortage − no Stayman".

♠ A Q 8 6 ♡ A J 7 4 ♢ 9 8 6 5 ♣ 7	If partner opens 1NT, bid 2♣. If partner bids 2♡, raise to 4♡, while if partner replies 2♠, you should raise to 4♠. If partner bids 2♢ (no 4-card major), rebid 3NT. While the singleton club is a risk, 3NT is now the best chance and if partner has no 4-card major, partner has length in the minors and is likely to have the clubs under control.
♠ A 7 ♡ K J 7 3 ♢ Q J 6 3 ♣ 7 5 2	If partner opens 1NT, bid 2♣. Many players would wrongly jump to 3NT at once. You have the values for game but should explore the possibility of 4♡. If partner bids 2♡, raise to 4♡, while if partner replies 2♢ or 2♠, each denying holding 4 hearts, rebid 3NT. You have found there is no 4-4 fit in hearts, so 3NT figures to be best.

SUBSEQUENT BIDDING AFTER STAYMAN HAS BEEN USED

A 2NT rebid by responder or raising opener's major shows the values to invite game.

♠ 7 5 3 ♡ A J 8 3 ♢ K 9 7 2 ♣ 9 4	If partner opens 1NT, bid 2♣. Then if opener replies 2♡, raise to 3♡ − opener will pass with a minimum or bid 4♡ with a maximum. However, if opener bids 2♢ or 2♠, rebid 2NT, inviting game. Opener will pass with a minimum or bid 3NT if maximum. The 2NT rebid after Stayman is the same as the 1NT : 2NT response without Stayman.

A change of suit by the Stayman bidder promises a 5-card suit.

♠ A Q 8 6 4   If partner opens 1NT, bid 2♣. You have the values for game, but it is not clear yet
♡ A J 8 3   whether to play 3NT, 4♡ or 4♠. Whenever you hold both majors, investigation via
◇ 7   2♣ Stayman works best. After 2♣, if opener bids 2♡ or 2♠, raise the major suit to
♣ 8 7 5   game. If, however, opener replies 2◇ — no major — you can dismiss game in hearts but
a spade game might still be on. Jump to 3♠, showing a strong hand (you jumped) and
five spades (change of suit). Opener will raise to 4♠ with 3 spades and will rebid 3NT with a doubleton spade.
The jump to 3-major after using Stayman has the same meaning as the jump to 3-major without Stayman
(e.g. 1NT : 3♠), i.e. game force, 5+ suit.

If opener bids hearts in reply to Stayman, a no-trump rebid by responder promises 4 spades.

Thus, 1NT : 2♣, 2♡ : 2NT *or* 1NT : 2♣, 2♡ : 3NT shows responder holds 4 spades and likewise,
2NT : 3♣, 3♡ : 3NT also shows responder has 4 spades.

♠ K 7 4 2   If partner opens 2NT, bid 3♣. If opener replies 3♠, raise to 4♠, while if opener bids
♡ J 8   3◇, no major, you should rebid 3NT. However, if opener replies 3♡, opener may still
◇ 7 4 2   hold 4 spades, but responder should still rebid 3NT, not 3♠. The 3♠ rebid would show
♣ 9 6 5 2   *five* spades (change of suit after Stayman) and even if it did not, it would be inferior to
reach 4♠ with the weaker hand as declarer. Bidding 3NT over 3♡ promises 4 spades.
Therefore, if opener does not hold spades, opener will pass 3NT, while if opener does have 4 spades as well
as 4 hearts, opener will rebid 4♠ over 3NT. Thus the strong hand will be declarer in each game contract.
It is perfectly logical that responder's no-trump rebid promises spades after opener shows hearts, since 2♣
was looking for a major suit fit. If the bidding has been 1NT : 2♣, 2♡ : 3NT, responder's 2♣ said "I am
interested in a major suit" and 3NT said, "Hearts was not the major suit I wanted". Clearly it was spades.

PARTNERSHIP BIDDING : How should the following hands be bid? West is the dealer on all hands.

SET 15 — WEST	SET 15 — EAST	SET 16 — WEST	SET 16 — EAST
1. ♠ K Q 6 ♡ K 9 7 3 ◇ A 3 ♣ A 7 6 4	1. ♠ A 3 ♡ Q J 10 2 ◇ 8 4 ♣ K 8 5 3 2	1. ♠ K 6 ♡ A K 5 2 ◇ A Q J 6 ♣ A J 10	1. ♠ 8 5 2 ♡ 8 7 6 3 ◇ K 7 4 3 2 ♣ 6
2. ♠ 9 8 4 2 ♡ A 3 2 ◇ K Q 9 4 ♣ J 8	2. ♠ A K 6 3 ♡ K Q 5 ◇ A J 6 ♣ 6 3 2	2. ♠ A Q 6 5 ♡ K J 9 7 ◇ K 8 ♣ A K Q	2. ♠ K 7 3 2 ♡ A 4 ◇ 6 4 2 ♣ 9 8 5 3
3. ♠ K Q 6 ♡ A J 10 4 ◇ A J 8 ♣ Q 10 2	3. ♠ J 10 3 2 ♡ K 6 ◇ K 10 3 ♣ J 8 7 6	3. ♠ J 8 7 3 ♡ K 6 5 2 ◇ J 8 ♣ 9 8 3	3. ♠ A K 2 ♡ A Q 3 ◇ K Q 6 ♣ A 7 5 4
4. ♠ A J 6 2 ♡ A 7 ◇ 9 6 5 4 ♣ J 8 2	4. ♠ 8 5 4 ♡ K 9 ◇ A K 3 ♣ K Q 10 7 6	4. ♠ K 8 7 6 3 ♡ K 7 6 4 ◇ 5 4 ♣ 6 2	4. ♠ A 2 ♡ A 9 3 2 ◇ A K J ♣ K Q J 4
5. ♠ K 6 5 4 ♡ K Q 6 4 ◇ A K 6 ♣ Q 6	5. ♠ A 8 7 3 ♡ A 2 ◇ Q 7 4 ♣ 8 7 3 2	5. ♠ Q 7 5 4 ♡ A 9 4 3 2 ◇ 7 ♣ 4 3 2	5. ♠ A 8 3 ♡ Q J 6 ◇ A K Q ♣ K Q J 6
6. ♠ K Q 8 6 2 ♡ A 7 4 2 ◇ 6 3 2 ♣ 5	6. ♠ A 3 ♡ K 9 8 3 ◇ A K 4 ♣ Q 7 3 2	6. ♠ K J 3 ♡ K Q 5 4 ◇ A K ♣ A Q 7 6	6. ♠ Q 8 7 6 2 ♡ J 7 6 3 2 ◇ 8 ♣ 4 2

PLAY HANDS ON STAYMAN

Hand 21 : Stayman over 1NT — Technique in drawing trumps — Marked finesse

Dealer North : North-South vulnerable

NORTH
♠ 9 3
♡ K 5 4 2
♢ A Q 3
♣ Q 7 5 4

WEST
♠ A J 8 4 2
♡ Q
♢ J 10 8 6
♣ 9 6 2

EAST
♠ K 7 6
♡ 10 8 6 3
♢ 9 7 5 2
♣ 10 8

SOUTH
♠ Q 10 5
♡ A J 9 7
♢ K 4
♣ A K J 3

WEST	NORTH	EAST	SOUTH
	Pass	Pass	1NT
Pass	2♣ (1)	Pass	2♡
Pass	4♡	All pass	

Bidding : (1) A common error would be to raise to 3NT which would fail on West's ♠4 lead. East would win the ♠K and return the ♠7 (top from a remaining doubleton), allowing the defense to take the first five tricks, despite South's respectable stopper in spades. After a 1NT or 2NT opening, you have not done your duty if you fail to explore the possibility of a major suit game, in the same way that you would respond with a major suit over a suit opening bid rather than respond in no-trumps. North's approach is to find out whether South holds four hearts and the 2♣ enquiry enables North to discover the relevant information. If South shows hearts, North intends to play in 4♡ but to rebid 3NT over any other reply.

Lead : ♢ J. Top of a near-sequence.

Correct play : With 8 trumps including the ace, king and jack, it is correct to finesse for the queen, but this finesse is normally taken on the 2nd round of the suit. First cash a top honor in case the queen is singleton. So, win the ♢ K and lead a low heart to the king. When West plays the queen it is clearly a singleton. Win the ♡ K and lead a heart, finessing the 9 if East plays low. Draw the remaining trumps and then cash the clubs and the diamonds, discarding a spade loser on the 3rd diamond. Making 11 tricks.

Wrong play : Taking a 1st round finesse in trumps, losing a trick unnecessarily to the singleton queen.

Hand 22 : Stayman with 4-major—5-minor — Establishing winners before cashing long suit

Dealer East : East-West vulnerable

NORTH
♠ 9 5 4 2
♡ K Q 10 6
♢ J 8 4
♣ J 10

WEST
♠ J 10 7 6
♡ 4 2
♢ Q 7
♣ K Q 8 4 3

EAST
♠ K Q
♡ A J 7 3
♢ K 10 3
♣ A 9 5 2

SOUTH
♠ A 8 3
♡ 9 8 5
♢ A 9 6 5 2
♣ 7 6

WEST	NORTH	EAST	SOUTH
		1NT	Pass
2♣ (1)	Pass	2♡ (2)	Pass
2NT (3)	Pass	3NT (4)	All pass

Bidding : (1) With a 4-card major as well as a 5-card minor, it is better to explore the major suit game possibility as first priority.
(2) Shows 4 hearts but does not deny 4 spades as 4-card suits are shown up-the-line.
(3) West should not bid 2♠, since that would show *five* spades and if a spade contract is available, it is normally preferable for the strong hand to be declarer. Stayman followed by a no-trump rebid after opener shows hearts promises 4 spades, otherwise why did you bother to use Stayman? Prefer 2NT (8-9 points, invitational) to 3♣ which would be a weakness signoff.
(4) East should accept the invitation. East has 17 points, not a minimum, and the ♠ K-Q should be useful opposite West's spades.

Lead : ♢ 5. 4th-highest of the long suit is normal.

Correct play : Play low from dummy and let the lead come to your K-10-x. This guarantees you 2 tricks in diamonds. Play the ♠ K and if they duck, continue with the ♠ Q, before starting on the clubs. You need to set up dummy's spade winners while you still have an entry to dummy and the only entries are in clubs. If they take the 1st spade and knock out your diamond stopper, unblock the ♠ Q before crossing to dummy. If they duck the first two spades, cross to dummy and lead the ♠ J. Take care when playing the clubs : ace first, then the 9, unblocking, so that you cannot be stuck in your own hand later.

Hand 23 : Stayman when holding both majors — Setting up an extra winner

Dealer South : Both vulnerable

NORTH
♠ 3 2
♡ 10 9 4
♢ Q 9 6 2
♣ K Q 6 5

WEST
♠ 9 5
♡ K Q 5 2
♢ A K 10 3
♣ A 8 7

EAST
♠ K Q 8 6 4
♡ A 8 7 3
♢ J 7
♣ 4 2

SOUTH
♠ A J 10 7
♡ J 6
♢ 8 5 4
♣ J 10 9 3

WEST	NORTH	EAST	SOUTH
			Pass
1NT (1)	Pass	2♣ (2)	Pass
2♡	Pass	4♡ (3)	All pass

Bidding : (1) Do not worry about a worthless doubleton if the rest of the hand fits the no-trump opening. Partner will be anxious to explore a major suit contract if possible, and partner usually has length and strength where you are weak and short.
(2) With both majors, Stayman is best. 3NT, a very poor choice, could be defeated on a club lead. 3♠ is also an inferior choice : if partner bids 3NT, denying spade support, there could be a heart fit but 4♡ is not a safe rebid since opener could have 2 spades and 3 hearts when 3NT could be the best spot. 2♣ allows you to discover whether there is a fit in hearts; if not, you can then rebid 3♠ to find out whether a 5-3 spade fit exists.
(3) Having found the 4-4 fit, stick with hearts. It is possible to rebid 3♠ over 2♡, showing 5 spades, but if opener has 3 spades and raises the spades, you would be in a 5-3 fit instead of the superior 4-4 fit.

Lead : A spade, a trump or the ♣K is possible. A diamond from just one honor would be the least attractive.

Correct play : On say the ♣K lead, declarer should take the ace, draw trumps ending in dummy and lead the ♢ J. When South plays low, let the jack go. North wins the ♢ Q, but your ♢ 10 is now high. Thus you lose 1 spade, 1 diamond and 1 club, the other club loser being ruffed in dummy. It would be an error to draw 3 rounds of trumps and then play ♢ A, ♢ K and ruff a diamond, as dummy has only one trump left, which is not enough to take care of 2 diamonds and 1 club ruff.

Hand 24 : Stayman over 2NT — Marked finesse — Discarding losers and ruffing in dummy

Dealer West : Nil vulnerable

NORTH
♠ Q 10 8 6
♡ K Q J 10
♢ A K J
♣ A Q

WEST
♠ J 9 7 2
♡ A 9 5
♢ 10 5 3
♣ J 10 5

EAST
♠ K
♡ 8 7 4 3
♢ Q 9 6 4
♣ K 9 4 3

SOUTH
♠ A 5 4 3
♡ 6 2
♢ 8 7 2
♣ 8 7 6 2

WEST	NORTH	EAST	SOUTH
Pass	2NT	Pass	3♣ (1)
Pass	3♡ (2)	Pass	3NT (3)
Pass	4♠ (4)	All pass	

Bidding : (1) South has enough for a game but as North might also have 4 spades, South should explore the possibility of the spade game via the Stayman 3♣.
(2) With both majors, show the hearts first in reply to Stayman.
(3) South could bid 3♠ but then South would be declarer in 4♠. Where possible, prefer to have the strong hand as declarer, since the opening lead into strength is an advantage. Here, if North is declarer, a club or a diamond lead gives North a trick, while the same lead if South is declarer is no help at all.
(4) Stayman followed by a NT rebid over opener's heart reply always promises spades : why else would responder ask for a major? Therefore, where opener has both majors, opener will bid spades over partner's no-trumps rebid.

Lead : ♡7. It is very risky to lead a suit with just one honor (or two split honors) into a 2NT opener.

Correct Play : When North gains the lead, play a low spade to the ace. When East plays the king, lead a spade back and finesse the 8 if West plays the 7. Next play hearts and discard a diamond on the 3rd heart, followed by ♢ A, ♢ K and a diamond ruff. Next comes another spade, finessing the 10 when West plays the 9 (it does not help West to play a higher card at any stage). Draw West's last trump. Making 11 tricks. (An initial club lead gives declarer 12 tricks on this line : win the club, spade to ace, spade finesse, ♡ K to force out the ace, later discard a diamond and ruff a diamond to reach dummy for the 2nd spade finesse).

CHAPTER 7

BIDDING OVER OPENER'S 1NT AND 2NT REBIDS

AFTER OPENER'S 1NT REBID (e.g. 1♣ : 1♡, 1NT . . .)

Opener's 1NT rebid normally shows a balanced hand below the strength of the 1NT opening, generally about 12-15 points. It also denies a 4-card major that could have been bid at the 1-level (e.g. 1♣ : 1♡, 1NT denies 4 spades). On the odd occasion, opener may hold a singleton in responder's suit. However, opener would not rebid 1NT with a singleton anywhere else. A 3-card raise to the 2-level with minimum values and an outside singleton is quite normal if no other action is clearly indicated.

With two exceptions, bidding over the 1NT rebid is exactly the same as bidding over a 1NT opening (see Chapter 5). Bids at the 2-level are weak, looking for the best partscore, the raise to 2NT is invitational, jumps to game are signoffs while jumps to the 3-level are forcing to game. If responder jumps to the 3-level in the suit first bid (e.g. 1♣ : 1♠, 1NT : 3♠), this is exactly the same as a jump to the 3-level over a 1NT opening (e.g. 1NT : 3♠) and shows a 5-card suit, asking for 3-card support. If responder has a 6-card major and no ambitions beyond game, responder can jump straight to game over 1NT (e.g. 1♣ : 1♠, 1NT : 4♠).

Exception 1 : There is no Stayman after a 1NT rebid. Stayman does not apply after suits have been bid genuinely. Thus, 1◇ : 1♡, 1NT : 2♣ really shows clubs and is a weak rebid (because it is at the 2-level), asking partner to choose hearts or clubs. There is no point asking for spades — the 1NT rebid denied 4 spades.

Exception 2 : A new suit by responder at the 2-level higher-ranking than responder's first suit is forcing. For example, 1◇ : 1♡, 1NT : 2♣ is not forcing but 1◇ : 1♡, 1NT : 2♠ is forcing (2nd suit higher ranking).

AFTER OPENER'S 2NT REBID TO A 1-LEVEL RESPONSE (e.g. 1◇ : 1♠, 2NT . . .)

Opener is showing a balanced hand too strong for a 1NT opening but too weak for 2NT, in other words, around 19-20 points and therefore forcing to game opposite a responder showing 6 points or more. Rebids by responder at the 3-level are natural (3♣ is not Stayman, but shows at least 4 clubs) and jumps to game are signoffs. Responder should rebid a 5-card major to show the 5-card suit and change of suit by responder would normally show at least a 5-4 pattern, seeking a suit contract rather than no-trumps.

With 19-20 points balanced and a 4-card major, should opener rebid to show the major or jump to 2NT to show the points? If the partnership elects to show the major, you must then treat auctions like 1♣ : 1♡, 1♠ as forcing. That is no hardship, since if responder can reply to 1♣, responder would have enough to reply to 1♠ and can therefore rebid over 1♠. A 1NT rebid over 1♠ is no stronger than a 1NT response to a 1♠ opening.

However, the 2NT rebid has a benefit since more often there will be no spade fit and it is superior to have the stronger hand as declarer if you end in 3NT. If the auction begins 1-minor : 1♡, 2NT . . . how should responder check back on a possible spade fit? With 4 spades - 4 hearts, rebid 3♠, while with 4 spades - 5+ hearts, rebid 3♡ (to show the 5-card suit) : then, over 3♡, with 4 spades, opener bids 3♠, but without 4 spades, opener may support hearts or rebid 3NT without support for either major. With 4 spades *and* support for hearts, opener shows the spades first and if not supported, opener can show support for the hearts on the next round.

After 1-minor : 1♠, 2NT : 3♡ (5 spades - 4 hearts at least), opener may support spades (4♠ weak support, 3♠ strong support), support hearts (4♡ weak support, cue bid 4♣ or 4◇ = strong support for hearts) or rebid 3NT (no support for either major). After 1-minor : 1♡, 2NT : 3♠, a cue bid of 4♣ or 4◇ shows strong support for spades (the cue bid always shows support for the last suit bid) while 4♠ would be the weaker raise. After a cue bid showing strong support, responder signs off in game in the agreed major with no slam ambitions.

After 1-minor : 1-major, 2NT : 3-minor, responder may have only a 4-card major with a longer minor. Opener shows 3-card support for the major as first priority (e.g. 1♣ : 1♠, 2NT : 3◇, 3♠) and this does not indicate weak or strong support. If opener gives 3-card support and responder continues with 3NT, responder has only 4 cards in the major and has 5 or more in the minor bid. Even if responder's 3-minor is in opener's suit (e.g. 1♣ : 1♠, 2NT : 3♣) opener still gives delayed support for the major as first priority. Without 3-card support for the major, opener may rebid 3NT or support the minor (cue bid any new suit or raise the minor).

THE 1♡ : 1♠, 2NT AUCTION

In standard methods, this sequence shows opener with about 16-18 points and a 5-card heart suit, a 1NT opening except for the 5-card major. The sequence is not forcing and 3♡ or 3♠ by responder is also not forcing. Any change of suit would be forcing. You can show 4 or 5 hearts with 19-20 points via 1♡ : 1♠, 3NT. However, if the partnership systemically opens 1NT with 5-3-3-2 hands including a 5-card major, then the sequence 1♡ : 1♠, 2NT is not needed for 16-18 points and would then show 19-20 points, forcing to game (just as the 2NT rebid does after a minor suit opening, with subsequent bidding along the same lines, too).

OPENER'S 2NT REBID AFTER A JUMP-SHIFT

The jump-shift is forcing to game and opener's 2NT shows a balanced hand and denies 3-card support for responder's suit. All further bidding is natural and the auction will proceed to at least game. An auction like 1♢ : 2♡, 2NT is similar to 1♢ : 1♡, 1NT except that the auction is game-forcing and one level higher.

OPENER'S 2NT REBID AFTER A 2-OVER-1 RESPONSE

In standard methods, 1♢ : 2♣, 2NT shows a minimum balanced hand and is not forcing. However, the 1-major : 2-minor, 2NT sequence is taken as showing extra values, normally 15-18 points, and is forcing to game. With fewer points and a 5-3-3-2 pattern, repeat the 5-card major. Where the partnership opens 1NT with 5-3-3-2 hands including a 5-card major, then this use of the 2NT rebid is not required and one may use the 2NT rebid for minimum balanced hands, not forcing. There are drawbacks to both methods and the partnership has to elect which approach to adopt.

Change of suit over 2NT is forcing and if responder rebids the minor suit (e.g. 1♡ : 2♣, 2NT: 3♣), this shows a 6-card suit. It would be forcing if opener's 2NT showed 15-18 points, but if the partnership rebids 2NT on 12-14 points, rebidding the minor shows about 9-11 points, a 6-card minor and is not forcing.

PARTNERSHIP BIDDING : How should the following hands be bid? West is the dealer on all hands.

SET 17 – WEST	SET 17 – EAST	SET 18 – WEST	SET 18 – EAST
1. ♠ 8 3 ♡ Q 9 8 5 2 ♢ K 9 6 4 ♣ J 3	1. ♠ A J 6 ♡ J 4 ♢ A Q 7 2 ♣ Q 8 7 2	1. ♠ A J 6 ♡ A Q 8 ♢ K 8 4 3 2 ♣ K Q	1. ♠ K 8 5 4 2 ♡ K 9 7 3 ♢ 7 ♣ J 4 3
2. ♠ K 7 4 ♡ Q 9 ♢ K Q 7 3 ♣ A 8 4 2	2. ♠ A Q 8 ♡ K J 10 8 6 3 ♢ 9 8 2 ♣ 5	2. ♠ K 8 6 3 ♡ K 9 5 2 ♢ 7 2 ♣ Q 8 3	2. ♠ A J 5 2 ♡ A Q ♢ K 8 3 ♣ A J 10 4
3. ♠ A J 3 ♡ K 9 5 2 ♢ A 2 ♣ J 8 4 3	3. ♠ K 9 6 4 2 ♡ A 4 3 ♢ 9 8 ♣ K Q 2	3. ♠ Q 7 ♡ A 8 4 2 ♢ A 8 5 ♣ A K Q 2	3. ♠ J 10 8 6 5 4 ♡ - - - ♢ K 9 6 2 ♣ J 4 3
4. ♠ 10 9 7 6 4 3 ♡ 4 ♢ A K 3 ♣ 8 4 3	4. ♠ A 2 ♡ A 7 6 5 ♢ 9 8 2 ♣ K Q 7 5	4. ♠ K 5 2 ♡ J 10 6 4 3 ♢ 6 2 ♣ K 4 3	4. ♠ A Q 6 ♡ K Q 2 ♢ A 8 ♣ A 9 6 5 2
5. ♠ 8 7 3 ♡ A 8 6 ♢ K Q 3 ♣ A 6 4 2	5. ♠ A K Q 5 ♡ K 9 5 4 3 ♢ 6 2 ♣ 9 5	5. ♠ A 6 ♡ Q 4 2 ♢ A Q J ♣ K Q J 8 4	5. ♠ K J 5 4 2 ♡ K 9 7 3 ♢ 8 4 ♣ 7 6
6. ♠ K 9 7 ♡ A 7 2 ♢ K 9 4 ♣ A 8 6 2	6. ♠ Q J 6 5 2 ♡ K Q 4 3 ♢ 7 ♣ K Q 9	6. ♠ J 2 ♡ K 10 6 4 3 ♢ Q J 10 3 2 ♣ 5	6. ♠ A K ♡ Q J 2 ♢ K 5 4 ♣ K Q J 7 6

PLAY HANDS ON OPENER'S 1NT AND 2NT REBIDS

Hand 25 : Unblocking a long suit — Card-reading — High cards from shortage first

Dealer North : East-West vulnerable

NORTH
♠ K Q
♡ A 8 3
♢ Q 9 6 4 2
♣ Q 10 7

WEST
♠ A
♡ K J 5 4
♢ 10 8 7 5
♣ J 6 4 3

EAST
♠ 9 8 5 3 2
♡ 10 7
♢ J
♣ A 9 8 5 2

SOUTH
♠ J 10 7 6 4
♡ Q 9 6 2
♢ A K 3
♣ K

WEST	NORTH	EAST	SOUTH
	1◇	Pass	1♠
Pass	1NT (1)	Pass	3♡ (2)
Pass	3NT (3)	All pass	

Bidding : (1) It would be very poor to rebid 2◇.
(2) The jump is forcing to game and 3♡ shows 4+ hearts and therefore at least 5 spades, as spades were bid first.
(3) No support for hearts and no delayed support for spades.

Lead : ♣5. The unbid suit is the normal lead.

Correct play : The ♣K wins, South encouraging with the 6, and declarer should tackle spades next, as some spade tricks are needed to make 3NT. West wins and leads a low club. As the ♣A is marked with East at trick 1, finesse the ♣10 which luckily forces out the ace. Later, unblock your spade winner, play a diamond to the ace (noting the fall of East's jack); cash 2 spades, discarding 2 hearts, and then continue with dummy's top diamond. When East shows out, finesse the ◇9 on the next round. Making 11 tricks.

Hand 26 : Locating the 5-3 fit — Correct technique with an 8-card suit missing the queen

Dealer East : Both vulnerable

NORTH
♠ 9 7 5 4 3 2
♡ 3
♢ A 8 5 3
♣ 9 4

WEST
♠ Q J 6
♡ A J 8 4 2
♢ J 10 6
♣ A 5

EAST
♠ A K
♡ K 10 6
♢ K 9 4
♣ 8 7 6 3 2

SOUTH
♠ 10 8
♡ Q 9 7 5
♢ Q 7 2
♣ K Q J 10

WEST	NORTH	EAST	SOUTH
		1♣	Pass
1♡	Pass	1NT	Pass
3♡ (1)	Pass	4♡ (2)	All pass

Bidding : (1) The jump to 3♡ is forcing to game and promises 5 hearts, asking for 3-card support. Without support, opener would rebid 3NT.
(2) A cue bid of 3♠, showing heart support, maximum values and the ♠A, would be reasonable. Although East has only 13 points, they are all in primary values, aces and kings.

Lead : ♠4. A singleton trump is a poor choice, as is a suit headed by the ace (diamonds). A doubleton club is unlikely to gain a ruff when only one trump is held. By elimination, lead a spade.

Correct play : Win the ♠A and start on the trumps. Cash the ♡K (in case the queen is singleton) and then lead the ♡10. If South plays low, let the 10 run and repeat the finesse on the next round. If South covers with the queen, North shows out, so that South is known to have 9-x left : cross to the ♠K and lead another heart from dummy, finessing the 8. With 8 trumps missing the queen, it is normal to finesse for the queen on the 2nd round. When the trump length includes the 8, you can pick up Q-9-x-x under the trump length and that is why the ♡10 is led from dummy on the 2nd round of trumps. After trumps are drawn, lead the ◇J and let it run. This finesse loses to South's queen but declarer makes 10 tricks, losing 2 diamonds and 1 club.

EXERCISE

Partner opened 1◇, you responded 1♠ and partner rebid 1NT. What is your rebid on each of these hands?

1. ♠ K J 9 7 2	2. ♠ A 8 6 3	3. ♠ A 9 4 3	4. ♠ A 9 6 4 3	5. ♠ A J 8 7 4 2
♡ 3	♡ 7 2	♡ J	♡ K Q	♡ Q J 9 7 6
◇ A Q 9 6 4	◇ Q 9 7 6 4	◇ 8 7	◇ Q 8 3	◇ 3
♣ Q 7	♣ 10 7	♣ Q 9 6 4 3 2	♣ 9 7 2	♣ J

Hand 27 : Rebidding after opener's 2NT rebid — Not leading an honor card for a finesse

Dealer South : Nil vulnerable

NORTH
- ♠ A 9 3
- ♡ A K 5
- ◇ K 8 3
- ♣ K Q 8 6

WEST
- ♠ Q
- ♡ 10 7 6 4 3
- ◇ Q J 9 6
- ♣ 9 4 3

EAST
- ♠ K 8 7 6
- ♡ J 8
- ◇ 10 7 5 2
- ♣ A J 10

SOUTH
- ♠ J 10 5 4 2
- ♡ Q 9 2
- ◇ A 4
- ♣ 7 5 2

WEST	NORTH	EAST	SOUTH
			Pass
Pass	1♣	Pass	1♠
Pass	2NT (1)	Pass	3♠ (2)
Pass	4♠ (3)	All pass	

Bidding : (1) Shows around 19-20 points + a balanced hand and is forcing to game.
(2) Worth showing the 5 spades, even though they are not strong.
(3) Not worth a cue bid of 4♡ (minimum and no ruffing value).

Lead : ◇ Q. Top of a near sequence.

Correct play : Win the lead with the ◇ A and lead a *low* spade, planning to finesse the 9 if West plays low, and later to lead the jack for a 2nd finesse. As it happens, the ♠ Q is singleton with West, so take it with the ace and continue spades, making sure to draw all East's trumps after forcing out the king. Later lead a club to dummy's king. As East has the ♣ A, 2 clubs have to be lost in addition to the ♠ K. Trap to avoid : Do not lead the ♠ J or ♠ 10 on the 1st round of spades : if you do, East will score 2 spade tricks and 4♠ can then be defeated.

Hand 28 : Rebidding over opener's 2NT rebid — Play at trick 1 — Double finesse

Dealer West : North-South vulnerable

NORTH
- ♠ K Q J 10
- ♡ 9 4
- ◇ A 7 6 5
- ♣ 8 5 3

WEST
- ♠ 9 5 3
- ♡ A Q 10 6
- ◇ K 3
- ♣ A K Q J

EAST
- ♠ A 8 7 4 2
- ♡ 8 7 3 2
- ◇ Q 2
- ♣ 6 2

SOUTH
- ♠ 6
- ♡ K J 5
- ◇ J 10 9 8 4
- ♣ 10 9 7 4

WEST	NORTH	EAST	SOUTH
1♣	Pass (1)	1♠	Pass
2NT	Pass	3♡ (2)	Pass
4♡ (3)	Pass	Pass	Pass

Bidding : (1) Not good enough for a vulnerable overcall, although the spades are very strong. A powerful 4-card suit may justify a 1-level overcall to indicate a good lead.
(2) Show the other major, even though it is very weak, rather than rebid the 1st suit. There is no suit quality requirement for responder. 3♡ promises a 4-card heart suit — any 4 cards will do — and implies 5 spades, as spades were bid first.
(3) West has support for spades and for hearts. Prefer the 4-4 fit.

Lead : ◇ J, top of sequence.

Correct play : Play low in dummy — if North also plays low, you win the ◇ Q and can discard the other diamond on the third round of clubs. North should also realise the danger: the ◇ J lead denies the queen and with 5 spades and 4 hearts on the bidding, East cannot hold more than 4 minor suit cards. North can deduce that East would win the ◇ Q and discard the other diamond(s) if North plays low. Therefore, North should take the ace at trick 1, followed by a switch to the ♠ K. One trick has been lost and 2 spade losers are unavoidable. Declarer must avoid losing a trump trick and the only chance with this holding is a double finesse : win the ♠ A and lead a heart, playing the 10 if South plays low. When the 10 wins, play ♣ A, ♣ K and ruff a club in order to regain the lead. Next comes another heart : jack — queen, wins. Cash the ♡ A and the game has been made. You should note the necessity of ruffing a club winner to reach your hand in order to take the 2nd heart finesse.

EXERCISE

Partner opened 1 ◇ , you responded 1♠ and partner rebid 2NT. What is your rebid on each of these hands?

1.	2.	3.	4.	5.
♠ K 7 6 4 3 2	♠ A 7 6 2	♠ Q J 7 3 2	♠ A 9 7 4 2	♠ A Q 8 7 5
♡ 3	♡ A Q	♡ K J 7 2	♡ J	♡ 2
◇ 6 4	◇ 6 4 3	◇ 8 7	◇ 8 6	◇ 9 4 3
♣ K 9 7 3	♣ 8 7 3 2	♣ 8 5	♣ K 9 7 3 2	♣ 8 6 4 3

CHAPTER 8

DEMAND OPENINGS AND SLAM BIDDING

Almost every bidding system has one or more opening bids for the super-strong hands. The actual bids chosen will vary from system to system. A demand opening may be a "1 round force" (responder must reply to the opening but may pass on the next round) or "a game-force" (the partnership must keep bidding until game is reached, with very rare exceptions).

Demand bids are based either on a specified minimum point count or on a specific number of "playing tricks". Playing tricks = the number of tricks you can expect to win on normal breaks if your long suit is trumps.

How to count your playing tricks: *In 3-card or longer suits:* count the ace and king as winners, count the queen as a winner if the suit has another honor and count every card after the third card as a winner. If the suit has the queen but no other honor, count the queen as a ½-winner. *In a doubleton:* count A = 1, K = 1, A-K = 2 and A-Q = 1½, but lower holdings are losers. *In a singleton:* count the ace as a winner and all others as losers. A void is counted as no losers.

GOREN TWOS — **All 2-openings in a suit are game-forcing.** The opening bid of 2NT may be passed but 2-in-a-suit demands an answer. The 2♣/2◇/2♡/2♠ openings are based on unbalanced or semi-balanced hands with 22 HCP or more *or* a hand with fewer points but at least 10 playing tricks (3 losers or fewer). With a choice of suits, use the same rules as for opening with a 1-bid.

The Goren 2-opening is forcing to game and the 2-opening in a major promises at least a 5-card suit. A 2-opening in a minor could be a 4-card suit with a super-strong 4-4-4-1 pattern or an exceptionally strong balanced hand, say about 28 HCP or more.

The weakest possible response to a 2-opening is 2NT, showing 0-7 points and any shape. As opener's hand is not balanced, the final contract will rarely be no-trumps, so that it is all right for the weak hand to respond in no-trumps. After the 2NT response, opener may rebid in a new suit (promises 5 cards in the first suit bid and 4 cards in the second suit) or rebid the first suit (denies a second suit and promises at least 6 cards in the suit bid). If responder bids a new suit after the initial 2NT response, such a suit will be at least 5 cards long.

The other negative response is to raise 2♡ to 4♡ or 2♠ to 4♠. The game raise of a 2-major opening shows trump support (at least 3 trumps), but *no ace, no king, no void, no singleton,* in other words, no first and no second round controls and so a hand very poor for slam purposes.

All other replies are positive responses, promising 8 points or more, or, if less than 8 points, an ace + a king or an A-Q holding (i.e. 1½ quick tricks) will justify a positive response. You may raise a 2-opening with just 3 trumps or bid a suit (same rules as for responding to a 1-opening) or bid 3NT (balanced, 8-10 points). All subsequent bidding is natural.

If right-hand opponent interferes over the 2-opening, pass shows a negative response, while any bid promises a positive response and double would be for penalties. It is quite safe to pass over interference when you hold a weak hand since the opponent's bid will give partner a chance to bid again and the bidding can then proceed to game at least.

It is important to distinguish between negative responses and positive responses. The function of these replies is not to reach a game, since the 2-opening commits you to game anyway, but to indicate how suitable responder's hand is for slam purposes. As a 2-opening is worth around 10 tricks at least, it does not take too much to reach a slam. A negative response indicates that the responder's hand is unlikely to have enough values for a slam if opener has only 10 winners, while a positive reply (8 points or better or 1½ tricks or more) indicates that responder is likely to have enough for a small slam at least.

However, Goren Twos are not popular except in some rubber bridge games and in social games. One reason is that such bids arise infrequently and it is not desirable to use four opening bids for something that occurs very rarely. In addition, Goren Twos do not cope well with the hands too strong for a 1-opening but not quite strong enough to insist on game, hands in the 21-22 point zone with about 9 playing tricks. With Goren Twos, there is no middle road: either you open with a 1-bid and risk being passed or you have to insist on game on a hand where game may be hopeless if partner has no values at all. These drawbacks have led players to search for methods that are more accurate and can cope with a greater variety of hand strengths.

STRONG TWOS: In this method, the opening bids of 2♠ /2♡ /2♢ are forcing for 1 round. They promise at least 5 cards in the suit bid and a hand just short of a force to game, usually around 21-22 HCP and 8-9 playing tricks. There is no available action for an equivalent hand where the long suit is clubs, but the system does cope well with the hands about one trick short of game where the long suit is spades, hearts or diamonds.

The negative reply is 2NT and responder may pass on the next round unless opener jumps in a new suit below game. All other replies are positive and are forcing to game. Responder may bid again after a negative response. All stronger hands worth a force to game are opened 2♣.

If right-hand opponent (RHO) interferes over partner's Strong Two opening, the principles are the same as for Goren Twos. Pass shows a negative response, bids are based on a positive response and double is for penalties. Because the opening 2-bid is so strong it is not common to encounter an intervening bid.

THE 2♣ GAME-DEMAND: When using this method, the 2♣ opening shows hands of about 23 HCP or stronger, or if fewer HCP, then it will be a hand with 3 losers or fewer. The negative response to 2♣ is 2♢ and all other responses are positive, either 8 HCP or more, or a hand with an ace + a king, or an A-Q suit. Players using the 2♣ demand frequently also play a 2NT opening with a balanced hand of 21-22 points, while balanced hands of 23-24 points are opened 2♣, followed by a 2NT rebid. The sequence 2♣ : 2♢ , 2NT showing the balanced 23-24 is the only sequence that can be passed (but with 2 or more points, responder would bid on to game anyway). All other sequences are game-forcing. Balanced hands with 25 HCP or more are also opened 2♣, but after a 2♢ negative, opener will bid 3NT (25-28 points) or higher.

Positive responses to 2♣ : A suit bid other than 2♢ is taken as a 5-card or longer suit and 2NT is used for a positive reply without a 5-card suit. If your long suit is clubs or diamonds, the response will be 3♣ or 3♢ . If you have a positive reply with a 4-4-4-1 pattern, bid 2♡ or, if your singleton is hearts, 2♠. After a positive reply, a suit bid by opener is at least a 5-card suit and further bidding is natural. A positive reply to the 2♣ demand frequently leads to a slam (23 HCP opposite 8 HCP or more, or 10 tricks opposite 1½ tricks or better). After 2♣ : 2NT, 3♣ by opener is Stayman; other suit bids show at least 5-card suits and ask for 3-card or better support. After 2♣ : 2NT, opener with 23-24 points balanced should not bid beyond game. 2♣ already promised at least 23 HCP. With a balanced 25 HCP or more, opener has enough to push on to a small slam.

After 2♣ : 2♢ negative: A suit bid by opener will be at least a 5-card suit and responder should support a major suit at once with 3-card or better support. Where responder raises opener's suit, a jump to game is weaker than a raise below game (e.g. 2♣ : 2♢ , 2♠ : 4♠ is weaker than 2♣ : 2♢ , 2♠ : 3♠). The jump to game says, "I have support for your suit, but no ace, king, singleton or void" while the raise below game says, "I have support for your suit and some additional values as well. My hand is not utterly hopeless for a slam."

If responder changes suit after opener's suit bid, responder is also showing at least a 5-card suit (for example, 2♣ : 2♢ , 2♠ : 3♢ promises 5 or more diamonds). If responder cannot support opener's suit and does not have a 5-card suit to bid, bid no-trumps at the cheapest level (e.g. 2♣ : 2♢ , 2♠ : 2NT or 2♣ : 2♢ , 3♢ : 3NT). After 2♣ : 2♢ , 2NT responder can bid 3♣ Stayman or other suits at the 3-level to promise at least a 5-card suit. Any reply to opener's 2NT rebid is a game-force.

If right-hand opponent intervenes over the 2♣ opening, the standard approach applies: Pass confirms a negative response, bids show a positive response and double is for penalties.

SLAM BIDDING

Where the hands are balanced, either partner can bid 6NT direct if the partnership holds at least 33 HCP and 7NT direct if the partnership has 37 HCP or more. A slam can also be bid direct (e.g. 1♠ : 3♠ , 6♠) if there are sufficient values for a slam, the trump suit is adequate and the bidder can see that the opponents cannot cash the first two tricks. The slam bidder would need to holds first round control in all suits or first round control in three suits and second round control in the other suit. A first round control is an ace or a void; a second round control is a king or a singleton.

Most slams, however, cannot be bid directly. After it is apparent that the values for slam are present and a trump suit has been agreed (or you hold a self-sufficient trump suit, one which needs no support from partner), it is normal to ask for aces using 4NT Blackwood. A small slam needs about 33 points and a grand slam about 37 points or more. As these points need not all be high card points, you may hold 33 points but have two aces missing or 37 points and an ace, a key king or a key queen missing. If you are in any doubt, settle for a good small slam rather than take a risk for a grand slam. Some good guides for slams include :

An opening hand opposite an opening hand is worth a game — an opening hand opposite an opener who can make a jump rebid is worth a slam if a decent trump fit can be found.

A positive reply to a game-force opening indicates slam values are present.

A small slam is a good bet if you have a strong trump fit, a secondary solid suit and cannot lose the first two tricks. A 5-card or longer side suit which is headed by the A-K-Q is so valuable because it provides discards for losers in partner's hand.

A grand slam is a good bet it you have a strong trump fit and are not missing any aces or the K-Q of trumps and there are no losers in the first three rounds of any suit.

If you can count 13 sure winners, play in 7NT.

Before you use Blackwood, you should be confident of two things. Firstly, you need enough points for a slam. Having enough aces will not cure a deficiency in points — even all 4 aces will produce only 4 tricks, while 4 aces and 4 kings add up to only eight tricks. Secondly, you need to know your final destination. Perhaps you are confident of a strong trump fit, or you have a powerful self-sufficient trump suit, or you know that no-trumps is all right. If you are not sure of the correct denomination for the slam, keep making forcing bids until you learn enough about partner's hand. Then and only then should you embark on Blackwood.

BLACKWOOD 4NT AND 5NT — ASKING FOR ACES AND KINGS

A JUMP TO 4NT AFTER A SUIT BID ASKS PARTNER : "HOW MANY ACES DO YOU HAVE?" THE REPLIES ARE :	AFTER THE ANSWER TO 4NT, 5NT ASKS PARTNER : "HOW MANY KINGS DO YOU HOLD?" THE REPLIES ARE :
5♣ = 0 or 4 5♢ = 1 5♡ = 2 5♠ = 3	6♣ = 0 6♢ = 1 6♡ = 2 6♠ = 3 6NT = 4

A bid of 4NT is usually Blackwood asking for aces. However, if 4NT is used as an immediate response to an opening bid of no-trumps (e.g. 1NT : 4NT *or* 2NT : 4NT) this is not Blackwood but is an invitation to 6NT. Opener is asked to pass with a minimum opening and to bid on with more than minimum points. Pass with the absolute minimum, bid 5NT with one extra point and 6NT if absolutely maximum. If you wish to check on aces after a no-trump opening, you have to bid a suit first (e.g. 1NT : 3♡ *or* 2NT : 3♢) and then bid 4NT later. It is an ask for aces if there has been a suit bid in the auction.

4NT can be used at any time, but it is most commonly used immediately after suit agreement when you know the values for slam are present. It can also be used later after either partner has made a cue bid. The answer to 4NT includes only aces, not voids. 5NT without using 4NT first is a **Trump Ask for the A-K-Q of trumps** : the simplest answers are 6♣ = no trump honor, 6♢ = 1, 6♡ = 2 and 6♠ = the top 3 honors.

In order to use the 5NT ask for kings after the answer to 4NT, you should have ambitions for a grand slam. The partnership should have the values for a grand slam, a strong trump suit and there should not be any aces missing. In other words, the use of 5NT asking for kings promises that the partnership holds all the aces.

The Blackwood 4NT bidder is in control of the final decision whether to stop at the 5-level if 2 aces are missing, whether to bid 6, whether to try for 7, whether to play in a suit or in no-trumps and partner should accept that decision in normal circumstances. If you have the values for a slam and find one ace is missing, bid the small slam — do not give up at the 5-level.

EXERCISES

A. How many playing tricks are each of these suits worth?

1. A K Q x x x x	**4.** A K Q x x x x x	**7.** Q J 10 x x x x	**10.** K x x x x x x	**13.** Q J x x x x x x
2. K Q J x x x x x	**5.** A Q J x x x x	**8.** A K x x x x x x	**11.** K Q J x x x x	**14.** A Q J x x x x x
3. A K x x x x x	**6.** A x x x x x	**9.** A J x x x x x	**12.** K J x x x x	**15.** J x x x x x x x

B. Partner opened 2♣, an artificial game demand. What is your response on these hands?

1. ♠ 9 7	**2.** ♠ K Q 5 4 2	**3.** ♠ 8 6	**4.** ♠ A 7 2	**5.** ♠ Q 8 7
♡ 7 3	♡ 4 3	♡ Q 7 6 3 2	♡ A J	♡ 6
◇ 9 7 4 3 2	◇ 7 6 4	◇ A Q 8 7 6	◇ K 8 6 2	◇ A Q 9 4 3
♣ 9 7 6 3	♣ 7 3 2	♣ 4	♣ 9 7 4 3	♣ J 10 5 2

C. You opened 2♣ and partner responded 2◇, the negative response. What is your rebid on these hands?

1. ♠ K Q	**2.** ♠ 7	**3.** ♠ A J 5 2	**4.** ♠ A Q J 2	**5.** ♠ A K J 2
♡ A K J 10 6 2	♡ A K Q	♡ A K J	♡ A	♡ 6
◇ A K	◇ A K Q J 4	◇ K Q 6 4	◇ A 8	◇ A K Q 4
♣ Q J 3	♣ Q J 3 2	♣ A Q	♣ A K J 8 4 3	♣ K Q J 10

D. Partner opened a 2♣ demand and rebid 2♠ over your 2◇. What is your rebid on each of these hands?

1. ♠ 9 7	**2.** ♠ A 7 2	**3.** ♠ 5	**4.** ♠ Q 7 6 2	**5.** ♠ - - -
♡ 8 7 3	♡ 6	♡ Q 8 7 6 3 2	♡ J 2	♡ 6 2
◇ 10 6 5 2	◇ 9 7 6 4	◇ 8 7 6	◇ 9 6 2	◇ J 9 8 6 3 2
♣ 9 7 5 3	♣ 8 7 5 3 2	♣ J 8 5	♣ Q 9 7 2	♣ 8 7 5 3 2

PARTNERSHIP BIDDING : How should these hands be bid, using the 2♣ demand. West is dealer.

SET 19 – WEST	**SET 19 – EAST**	**SET 20 – WEST**	**SET 20– EAST**
1. ♠ J 10 7 6	**1.** ♠ A K	**1.** ♠ J 8	**1.** ♠ K Q
♡ 8 5 4 2	♡ A K 6	♡ 10 9 5 2	♡ A Q J 8 6 3
◇ A Q 3	◇ K J 6 4	◇ 6 4 3	◇ A K Q J
♣ A 4	♣ K Q 5 3	♣ Q 7 4 3	♣ J
2. ♠ J 7 5 4 3 2	**2.** ♠ A 9	**2.** ♠ Q 8 7	**2.** ♠ A K J 9 5 2
♡ 7	♡ A K 5 4	♡ A J 8 6 3	♡ Q
◇ 7 4 2	◇ A K Q	◇ K 7 4	◇ A Q J
♣ 8 6 2	♣ A 9 4 3	♣ 3 2	♣ K Q J
3. ♠ K Q 10 3	**3.** ♠ J 7 6 4	**3.** ♠ K Q 9 7 4 2	**3.** ♠ 8
♡ A J 10	♡ Q 8 3 2	♡ A 8 6	♡ Q 9 5 4 3 2
◇ K 4	◇ 8 7	◇ A K	◇ 7 6 3
♣ A K Q J	♣ 9 5 3	♣ A K	♣ 8 5 4
4. ♠ 9 6 5 3 2	**4.** ♠ K 8	**4.** ♠ A K Q J	**4.** ♠ 8
♡ Q J 3 2	♡ A K 5 4	♡ 3	♡ A K 4
◇ 8	◇ K Q 6 3	◇ K Q 4 3 2	◇ A 9 7 6 5
♣ 7 3 2	♣ A K J	♣ A K J	♣ 9 7 4 3
5. ♠ K 6 5	**5.** ♠ A Q 2	**5.** ♠ - - -	**5.** ♠ A K Q 7 3 2
♡ A K 5 2	♡ 4 3	♡ A 9 8 4 2	♡ K Q 7 6 5
◇ A K Q 4	◇ 10 2	◇ 7 4 3 2	◇ A
♣ A 7	♣ K Q J 10 4 2	♣ 9 6 4 2	♣ A
6. ♠ J 8 7 6 4	**6.** ♠ A K 3	**6.** ♠ A Q J 7 6	**6.** ♠ K 9 3
♡ J 8 7 5 2	♡ A 9 4 3	♡ A K	♡ 7 6 5 3
◇ 6 2	◇ A K Q 7	◇ A Q J 5	◇ K 6 2
♣ 3	♣ A 6	♣ A 9	♣ K 8 2

PLAY HANDS ON DEMAND OPENINGS AND SLAM BIDDING

Hand 29 : Slam bidding — Unblocking your winners — Protecting an entry to dummy

Dealer North : Both vulnerable

WEST	NORTH	EAST	SOUTH
	2♣ (1)	Pass	2♡ (2)
Pass	2♠	Pass	3♢
Pass	4NT (3)	Pass	5♣ (4)
Pass	6NT (5)	All pass	

NORTH
♠ A K J 4 2
♡ J 4
♢ A K
♣ A K Q 2

WEST
♠ 8 7 5
♡ A 10 9 8
♢ 10 7 2
♣ 5 4 3

EAST
♠ Q 9 3
♡ 7 6
♢ 9 8 6 5
♣ 10 9 8 7

SOUTH
♠ 10 6
♡ K Q 5 3 2
♢ Q J 4 3
♣ J 6

Bidding : (1) Artificial game force
(2) Positive response, 8+ points and a 5-card or longer suit.
(3) It is clear that there is no trump fit but the values are there for a slam as South has shown at least 8 points. The slam should be played in no-trumps but North plans to ask for aces and if South has the ♡ A, North intends to continue with 5NT, confirming that all the aces are held and looking for a grand slam if East happens to have significantly extra values.
(4) Shows 0 or 4 aces, clearly zero.
(5) If the values are present for a small slam, do not sign off just because one ace is missing. Take the plunge and bid the small slam.

Lead : ♣10. Top of sequence in the unbid suit is best.

Correct play : There are 10 instant winners (2 spades, 4 diamonds, 4 clubs) and 2 extra tricks can be set up in hearts, but the A-K of diamonds must be unblocked and dummy needs an entry to the diamonds. In addition, the heart tricks need to be established and if the defence ducks the 1st heart, again dummy needs an entry to the 2nd heart trick. It would be an error to win the ♣ J, cash the ♢ A-K and then lead a heart : if West ducks this, declarer cannot enjoy 2 heart tricks and have an entry to dummy. Correct is to leave the ♣ J in dummy as an entry : win the ♣ A, cash ♢ A-K and then lead the ♡ J. If this is ducked, play another heart. Later, lead the ♣ 2 to dummy's jack to score your red suit winners and use the spade entries to hand for your black suit winners.

Hand 30 : 2NT response to 2♣ — Use of Stayman — Finessing and safety plays

Dealer East : Nil vulnerable

WEST	NORTH	EAST	SOUTH
		2♣	Pass
2NT (1)	Pass	3♣ (2)	Pass
3♠ (3)	Pass	4NT (4)	Pass
5♢	Pass	5NT (5)	Pass
6♣	Pass	6♠ (6)	All pass

NORTH
♠ Q 10 6 5
♡ 10 9 8 4
♢ 7 6
♣ K 8 7

WEST
♠ A J 7 2
♡ J 6 2
♢ 9 4 3
♣ Q J 10

EAST
♠ K 9 4 3
♡ A K Q 5
♢ A K Q
♣ A 6

SOUTH
♠ 8
♡ 7 3
♢ J 10 8 5 2
♣ 9 5 4 3 2

Bidding : (1) Positive reply with a balanced hand, no 5-card suit.
(2) Stayman, asking for a 4-card major.
(3) Shows 4 spades, denies 4 hearts.
(4) Enough for a small slam at least opposite a positive response.
(5) Confirms all aces are held and is looking for a grand slam.
(6) With a king missing, and the ♠ Q also possibly missing, a grand slam is too risky. 6NT would be a reasonable choice, but it may be necessary to ruff a heart or a club for the 12th trick. On the actual cards, the play in 6♠ or 6NT would be the same.

North should not tip off the bad break by doubling.

Lead : ♡10. Top of sequence is normal.

Correct play : The play of the spade suit varies according to whether 3 or 4 tricks are needed and so West should take the club finesse first : win the ♡ J, lead the ♣ Q (North should play low) and the ♣ Q wins. Now only 3 spade tricks are needed. To guard against a bad break, cash the ♠ A and lead low towards K-9-4, playing the 9 if North plays low : if South wins, the ♠ K will draw the last spade, but as the cards lie, the 9 wins. If North inserts the ♠ 10, win the ♠ K and force out the queen. Had the club finesse lost, play ♠ K and finesse ♠ J.

Hand 31 : Assessing grand slam prospects − Ruffing a loser − Coping with a bad trump break

Dealer South : North-South vulnerable

NORTH
♠ A K Q 4
♡ K Q J 9
♢ A K Q
♣ A 8

WEST
♠ 9 2
♡ 10 8 7 6
♢ 7 5 3 2
♣ J 10 9

EAST
♠ J 10 7 5 3
♡ 4
♢ 10 9 8
♣ Q 6 4 3

SOUTH
♠ 8 6
♡ A 5 3 2
♢ J 6 4
♣ K 7 5 2

WEST	NORTH	EAST	SOUTH
			Pass
Pass	2♣	Pass	2NT
Pass	3♣ (1)	Pass	3♡
Pass	4NT	Pass	5♢
Pass	5NT (2)	Pass	6♢
Pass	7♡ (3)	All pass	

Bidding : (1) Stayman. If a 4-4 major fit exists, this may produce one trick more than if the hands are played in no-trumps. If no major fit is found, you can still bid at least 6NT later.
(2) If partner can produce the ♣K as well, North has enough to bid the grand slam : a strong trump fit and no loser in the first three rounds of any suit.
(3) North can count on 3 spade winners, 4 hearts, 3 diamonds and 2 clubs and there is no guarantee of a 13th trick for 7NT (which would be a very poor contract and should be defeated easily, as long as East retains 4 spades, following the discarding principle "Keep length with dummy"). Played in hearts, the 13th trick can come from a ruff, either a spade ruff in the South hand or a club ruff in the North hand.

Lead : ♣J. Top of sequence.

Correct play : Win the lead and start on the trumps ♡K, ♡Q. If trumps were 3-2, it would be correct to draw the last trump. When trumps are 4-1, you must take one ruff before drawing all the trumps. Best is to switch to ♠A, ♠K and ruff the ♠4 with the *ace* of hearts : if you can afford it, ruff high. Next lead your last heart and finesse dummy's ♡9 and then draw West's last trump. It would be an error to ruff a club in dummy because the South hand has no convenient entry to draw West's trumps.

Hand 32 : Slam prospects after a negative response − Finding the best fit − Marked finesse

Dealer West : East-West vulnerable

NORTH
♠ - - -
♡ J 10 7
♢ K Q 8 6
♣ Q 9 6 5 4 3

WEST
♠ A K Q 10
♡ A K Q 8 6 4 2
♢ 4
♣ A

EAST
♠ 8 6 5 4 3
♡ 5
♢ A 7 3 2
♣ J 7 2

SOUTH
♠ J 9 7 2
♡ 9 3
♢ J 10 9 5
♣ K 10 8

WEST	NORTH	EAST	SOUTH
2♣ (1)	Pass	2♢	Pass
2♡ (2)	Pass	2♠ (3)	Pass
4NT (4)	Pass	5♢	Pass
7♠ (5)	Pass	Pass	Pass

Bidding : (1) There is a temptation on freak hands like this to open 6♡, but not only does this risk missing a grand slam, but you may also be in the wrong trump suit. As you have only 1 loser, you are worth 6♡, but you can still bid 6♡ later if nothing better turns up.
(2) Again it is quite enough to bid 2♡ as this is forcing to game. The jump to 3♡ would be suitable with a solid 1-suiter, but not here when a 2nd suit is held.
(3) Shows 5 or more spades and denies support for hearts. Without support and with only 4 spades, East would rebid 2NT.
(4) West knows that a 9-card fit exists in spades and checks whether East holds the missing ace. If not, West would rebid 6♠.
(5) West should not rebid 7♡ or 7NT, both of which could be defeated on a diamond lead as that removes the only entry to East before the bad spade break is revealed.

Lead : ♢ J, top of sequence.

Correct play : Win the ♢ A and lead a spade to the ace. If both opponents had followed, you would draw the remaining trumps and then run the heart suit. When North shows out, you need to return to hand to finesse the 10 of spades. The only entry is via a heart ruff, so cash ♡ A, ruff a low heart next and then lead a spade, finessing dummy's 10 when South plays low. Draw South's last two trumps with the K-Q and claim the rest.

REVISION TEST ON PART 1

The answers to all these questions can be found in Chapters 1-8. Give yourself 1 mark for each correct answer. If you score less than 40, it will profit you to revise the relevant sections.

A. You opened 1◇ and partner responded 1♠. What is your rebid on each of these hands?

1. ♠ K Q 2	2. ♠ A 7	3. ♠ - - -	4. ♠ A 7	5. ♠ A 8 7 2
♡ A J	♡ K 8 6 3	♡ A K 8 2	♡ A J 3 2	♡ - - -
◇ A Q 9 6 4	◇ J 9 7 6 4	◇ K 7 6 4 3	◇ A K 9 8 6 2	◇ A K 10 9 4 3
♣ K J 7	♣ A Q	♣ K 8 5 4	♣ 7	♣ K J 6

6. ♠ K 7 2	7. ♠ 7	8. ♠ 7	9. ♠ J 7	10. ♠ A 8 7 2
♡ K 9 7 3	♡ K 8 3 2	♡ A K J	♡ 2	♡ J 2
◇ A Q 9 6 4	◇ Q 9 7 6 4	◇ K Q J 8 7 6 4	◇ A K 8 6 2	◇ A Q 9 4 3
♣ 3	♣ A K Q	♣ J 8	♣ A K Q J 7	♣ K Q

B. Partner opened 1♣ and rebid 1♠ over your 1♡ response. What is your rebid on each of these hands?

1. ♠ K 7 3	2. ♠ A 7	3. ♠ A	4. ♠ J 3 2	5. ♠ A 8 7 2
♡ Q 8 7 3 2	♡ Q 8 6 3 2	♡ K J 10 9 8 6 4	♡ A Q 7 6	♡ A K 9 6 2
◇ J 7 3	◇ 7 6	◇ 8 7	◇ 2	◇ 4 3
♣ Q 9	♣ J 9 7 3	♣ K 8 5	♣ A K 8 4 2	♣ Q 2

6. ♠ 8 7 3 2	7. ♠ A 7	8. ♠ K Q J 5 2	9. ♠ A 7 2	10. ♠ A 2
♡ K Q 8 6 5	♡ A Q 8 6 3 2	♡ A K Q 6 3 2	♡ J 10 7 6 3 2	♡ Q J 7 5 2
◇ 6 4	◇ Q 9 7	◇ 3	◇ 2	◇ K 7 6
♣ Q 7	♣ 3 2	♣ 6	♣ J 9 7	♣ K 8 5

C. Partner opened 1NT. What is your response on each of these hands?

1. ♠ A J 8 7	2. ♠ J	3. ♠ A J 5 3 2	4. ♠ J 8 2	5. ♠ J 8 7 5 4 2
♡ 7 3	♡ A Q 6 5 4 3	♡ K J 6 2	♡ A J 7 3	♡ 6
◇ A Q 9 2	◇ 7 6 4	◇ J 7 6	◇ 8 6 5 2	◇ Q 9 4 3
♣ 10 5 2	♣ K 7 3	♣ 4	♣ 9 7	♣ 7 2

D. What would your answer be on the hands in C. if partner had opened 2NT?

E. Partner opened 1NT and replied 2◇ to your 2♣ Stayman. What is your rebid on each of these hands?

1. ♠ K 7 4 2	2. ♠ A 7	3. ♠ A 5 3	4. ♠ A 7 3 2	5. ♠ A 9 8 7 2
♡ A Q 7 3	♡ A Q 3 2	♡ Q J 7 2	♡ A J 5 4 3	♡ K J 8 4 2
◇ A J 9	◇ J 10 4	◇ 8 7	◇ 2	◇ J 2
♣ A 2	♣ 9 7 3 2	♣ J 8 5 4	♣ Q 9 7	♣ 5

F. Partner opened 2NT. What would response be on the hands in E. above?

G. Partner opened 1♣, you responded 1♠ and partner rebid 1NT. What is your rebid on these hands?

1. ♠ K 7 6 4 3	2. ♠ A J 7 5 2	3. ♠ A 8 6 3 2	4. ♠ K J 9 7 2	5. ♠ Q J 10 9 3 2
♡ Q J 7 3	♡ A Q 3 2	♡ J 2	♡ A J	♡ - - -
◇ J 6 4	◇ Q 9 7	◇ 4 3	◇ 8 6 2	◇ A 9 4 3
♣ 3	♣ 3	♣ J 8 5 4	♣ A 9 7	♣ K J 2

H. Partner opened 1♣, you responded 1♡ and partner rebid 2NT. What is your rebid on these hands?

1. ♠ K 7	2. ♠ K 7 5 2	3. ♠ A 9 7 2	4. ♠ A 7 2	5. ♠ A 8 7
♡ J 10 8 6 3	♡ A 9 6 4	♡ K J 6 4 3	♡ A J 3 2	♡ Q 10 9 4 3 2
◇ 9 6 4	◇ Q 9	◇ 8	◇ A Q 8	◇ 3
♣ K 3 2	♣ 7 3 2	♣ 9 5 4	♣ 10 9 7	♣ 8 5 2

PART 2

CONSOLIDATE YOUR
DEFENSIVE & DESTRUCTIVE BIDDING

Unless you are exceptionally lucky, your side will open the bidding only 50% of the time. It is vital to be able to enter the auction with suitable values in order to contest the partscores, locate a possible game for your side, indicate a sound lead to partner and interfere in their auctions. This part describes the actions available after the opponents have opened the bidding, the requirements for such actions and the subsequent bidding. It also shows how to shut out the opposition safely but effectively when you have a weak hand and how to cope with these shut-outs when you are on the receiving end.

Chapter 9 deals with overcalls; when to overcall and when to pass, when to overcall with a suit and when to overcall 1NT; actions available in reply to an overcall.

Chapter 10 is concerned with jump overcalls; the standard strong jump overcall and also the weak and the intermediate jump overcalls; partner's responding strategy in each case.

Chapter 11 examines the unusual 2NT for the minor suits; when to use it; partner's actions after you use it; when to sacrifice and when to defend; defenses against the unusual 2NT.

Chapter 12 covers pre-emptive openings and pre-emptive overcalls; when to pre-empt and when to make a simple overcall; how high to pre-empt; when to pre-empt with a good hand; using the gambling 3NT overcall.

Chapters 13, 14 and 15 deal with takeout doubles; when to make a takeout double and when to prefer a simple overcall or a jump overcall; how to respond to partner's takeout double with hopelessly weak hands (Chapter 13), with moderate hands (Chapter 14) and with strongish hands (Chapter 15); each chapter includes strategy for replying to the double when third player has redoubled or taken some other action.

Chapter 16 outlines defensive methods against their weak two-openings and higher pre-empts; when to overcall and when to make a takeout double; responding to these actions; how to deal with 4-level pre-empts; defending against the gambling 3NT.

CHAPTER 9

STANDARD OVERCALLS & RESPONSES

THE SIMPLE SUIT OVERCALL

The functions of a simple suit overcall ("simple" = at the cheapest level) are :

- To indicate a sound lead to partner
- To compete for the partscore
- To rob the opponents of bidding space
- To lay a basis for reaching a game

Note : You do not require as many points to overcall as you do to open the bidding. An opener needs about 12 points or better, but you may overcall at the 1-level with 8 points or more or at the 2-level with 10 points or more. The emphasis when opening is on strength, the number of points held, and length of suit, but the quality of the suit opened is immaterial. For overcalling, the quality of the suit is the paramount consideration; the length of the suit is also important but the points held are not the deciding factor. You may overcall on a weak hand if your long suit is strong, but you would not overcall a suit with a strong hand if the suit is weak. Where your long suit is weak, you may be able to enter the auction with a double or with a 1NT overcall, but if these are also unsuitable, you should pass at first and you may be able to enter the auction later. With length and strength in the opposition's suit(s), it is usually best to pass initially and plan to defend unless the hand is worth a 1NT overcall (see later) or you hold 19 points or more (strong enough to double first and bid no-trumps later).

Under normal circumstances, the overcall suit should be at least 5 cards long and should contain at least 2 honors, including the A, K or Q.

At the 1-level, the strength is about 8-15 HCP.

At the 2-level, the strength is about 10-15 HCP.

At the 3-level, the strength is about 12-16 HCP.

Some players feel that they must double whenever they hold 13 HCP or more. This approach is not sound since if you double with a 1-suited hand, partner will almost never bid your long suit and the bidding may climb too high to show your long suit later. It is quite safe to overcall on hands up to 15 HCP, since partner should reply to the overcall when holding 9 HCP or more, and may reply with even less with support for your suit or with something useful to bid. Thus, you cannot miss a game if you overcall and it is not necessary to double with the 1-suited hand in the 12-15 range. Takeout doubles are suitable for 2-suited or 3-suited hands and are also used for 1-suited hands with 16 HCP or more, too strong for the simple overcall.

OVERCALLING WITH A 4-CARD SUIT : This is permitted only at the 1-level and the suit must contain 3 of the top 4 honors. Suits such as A-K-Q-x, A-K-J-x, A-Q-J-x and K-Q-J-x have such a strong lead-directing element that they justify misleading partner as to length of the suit held. At the worst, partner may raise you with just 3 trumps and if so, your suit is so powerful that you should be able to handle it. The benefits of these 4-card overcalls are that partner makes the best lead and the opponents may forego 3NT.

THE SUIT QUALITY TEST : How strong a suit must you have to justify an overcall? A sound guide is the Suit Quality Test which measures your suit strength. The hand may be strong enough for an overcall but if the suit quality is below par, you should be very wary of overcalling in that suit

COUNT THE CARDS IN THE SUIT YOU WISH TO BID.

ADD THE HONOR CARDS IN THE SUIT YOU WISH TO BID.

IF THE TOTAL EQUALS OR EXCEEDS THE NUMBER OF TRICKS BID, OVERCALL.

IF THE TOTAL IS LESS THAN THAT, DO NOT OVERCALL IN THAT SUIT.

In other words, Length + Honors should equal (or exceed) Tricks to be bid. When counting your honor cards for this test, count the jack or ten only if the suit also contains a higher honor. Thus, the suit quality of K-10-x-x-x is 7, and the suit quality of Q-J-x-x-x-x is 8, but J-x-x-x-x measures only 5 — the jack is not counted with no higher honor in the suit.

If you intend to overcall at the 1-level, your suit's quality should be 7 or more. If you wish to overcall at the 2-level, your suit's quality should be 8 or more, and if you propose to overcall at the 3-level, your suit's quality should be 9 or better. Of course, if the suit quality total is more than the tricks for which you intend to bid, that is quite all right and you would not make a jump overcall just because your suit is exceptionally good. Jump overcalls are covered in Chapter 10.

RESPONDING TO THE SUIT OVERCALL

There is less urgency to reply to an overcall than to an opening. As opener may have 20 points or so, it is vital to reply with 5-6 points or better. A simple overcall has a top limit of around 15 HCP, so that hands in the 5-7 HCP range are rarely worth a response without good support for the overcalled suit.

0-4 HCP : Pass, even with good support for partner.

5-7 HCP : Normally pass unless you have good support for partner, either 4 trumps or a singleton plus Q-x-x or better 3-card support. Do not support with such a poor hand if balanced or with a weak 3-card holding as your support.

8 HCP : Bid with support for partner's suit or with something worthwhile to say, otherwise pass. Game chances are remote.

9 HCP up : Find some bid. Support partner, bid no-trumps or bid your own 5-card or longer suit.

If you intend to support partner, a single raise = 8-11 and a jump raise = 12-15, whether partner's overcall was at the 1-level or 2-level. Raising a 1-level major suit overcall to game is based on a hand worth 16 points or more, counting shortages as well as HCP. With a 4-3-3-3 pattern, prefer a no-trump response to a raise, provided that you hold at least one stopper in their suit.

If you do not have a hand suitable for a raise, you may respond to a 1-level overcall with 1NT on 8-11 points, 2NT on 12-14 and 3NT on 15-17. In each case, you must have at least one stopper in the enemy suit, and if their suit is known to be at least a 5-card suit, it is desirable to hold a second stopper or at least a potential second stopper. Single stoppers are A-x, K-x, Q-x-x, J-x-x-x or better. Double stoppers are A-Q, A-J-10, K-Q-10, Q-10-9-x or better. Potential double stoppers include A-J-x, K-Q-x, K-J-x, Q-10-x-x or better, and these become full double stoppers if an extra card is held, e.g. K-J-x-x can be considered a double stopper. A 2NT response to a 2-level overcall is about 11-13 HCP and a jump to 3NT is justified with about 14 HCP or better. In each case, you must again hold at least 1 stopper in the enemy suit.

If you respond with a new suit at the 1-level, this is at least a 5-card suit with 8-15 points. A new suit at the 2-level would be a good 5-card suit and 10-15 points. A change-of-suit response to an overcall is not forcing and a jump response is also not forcing (in contrast to these actions in reply to an opening bid when they are forcing). If you wish to force the overcaller to bid again, you must either jump-shift (showing a hand of 16 HCP or more) or bid the enemy suit (indicating enough for game, but no strong suit of your own).

After partner's reply to your overcall, you may pass if your overcall was minimum and you have nothing worthwhile to add, but keep on bidding if :

● Partner's reply was forcing, *or*

● You have more than a minimum overcall (e.g. you are in the 12-15 HCP zone), *or*

● You are minimum but you have something extra which is worth showing.

EXERCISE

Your right-hand opponent opened 1 ◊ . What action should you take on these hands?

1. ♠ K J 9 4 2
   ♡ 7 3
   ◊ A Q 9
   ♣ J 8 7

2. ♠ A 9
   ♡ Q 7 3 2
   ◊ A J 9
   ♣ 8 6 3 2

3. ♠ 5
   ♡ A K J 10 2
   ◊ 8 7 6
   ♣ 9 8 5 4

4. ♠ K Q 2
   ♡ A J
   ◊ 7 6 3
   ♣ Q 9 7 6 2

5. ♠ 9 8 7 2
   ♡ 6
   ◊ Q J 8 4 3 2
   ♣ A K

6. ♠ A K Q J
   ♡ 7 3
   ◊ Q 9
   ♣ 8 7 5 3 2

7. ♠ J 8 6 5 4 2
   ♡ A Q
   ◊ Q 7 6
   ♣ 9 2

8. ♠ A
   ♡ K Q J 10 2
   ◊ 8 7 6
   ♣ K 8 5 4

9. ♠ K 7
   ♡ 5 4
   ◊ 10 6 2
   ♣ A Q J 7 4 2

10. ♠ J 7 2
    ♡ 6
    ◊ A K 9 4 3
    ♣ K Q J 2

TREATMENT OF BALANCED HANDS AFTER THEY OPEN :

0-11 HCP : Always pass.

12-15 HCP : Usually pass, unless your hand is suitable for a takeout double.

16-18 HCP : Overcall 1NT with a stopper in their suit; without a stopper in their suit, double if you have the other requirements for a takeout double (see Chapter 13).

19 HCP up : Make a takeout double initially and bid again later.

The above strategy applies only if your hand is balanced and may not apply for unbalanced hands. If you hold a balanced hand after they open the bidding, it is risky to enter the bidding, because it is very easy for them to double your side for penalties. If you do not have a strong suit or a good trump fit, the penalties can be very severe. Even with opening values in the 13-15 range, it is better to pass than to intervene with a balanced hand unless the hand qualifies for a takeout double (see Chapter 13). In general, if your main strength is in the enemy suit, prefer to pass unless your hand qualifies for a 1NT overcall or if you hold 19 HCP with which you could double and rebid no-trumps with a suitable hand and their suit covered.

THE 1NT OVERCALL : 16-18 points, balanced shape and at least one stopper in their suit.

With a double stopper, you may overcall 1NT with just 15 points, as your points are well placed over the opening bidder. If suitable for no-trumps, it is better to overcall 1NT with 15 points than to pass.

If your hand is suitable for a 1NT overcall, nevertheless prefer to double if they opened with 1 ◇ or 1 ♣ *and* your pattern is 4-4-3-2 *and* you hold two 4-card majors. As always, a major suit trump fit is more attractive than no-trumps and if you have 4-4 in the majors, the chance of finding a major suit fit is very high. If you overcall 1NT, partner will normally pass with 0-7 points, but if you double, partner is forced to reply and any major suit fit will come to light. Also, with 16 HCP or more and a strong 5-card major in a 5-3-3-2 pattern, it is better to double first and bid your suit later than to overcall 1NT.

BIDDING AFTER THE 1NT OVERCALL

The preferred approach is for all responder's actions and opener's rebids to be the same as if your side had opened 1NT. Thus, 2NT would be invitational (8-9 points), a 2♣ response is Stayman and other suit bids would have their normal meaning. The advantage of this method is that you do not have to remember 2 sets of bids, one when your side has opened 1NT and another when your side has overcalled 1NT.

Some pairs prefer to vary their approach after a 1NT overcall, where bidding the enemy suit replaces Stayman and 2♣ is a natural, weak bid (unless they opened 1♣) showing a long club suit. The logic of this approach is that if the opponents have opened and partner has overcalled 1NT, there is a greater need than usual to make a weak takeout bid, so that 2♣ would be more useful more often for the weak hand with long clubs. Each partnership needs to settle which approach is to be used, preferably *before* a disaster occurs.

EXERCISES

A. Your right-hand opponent has opened 1 ◇ . What action do you take on each of these hands?

1. ♠ K J 4 2	2. ♠ A K Q 2	3. ♠ A 9	4. ♠ A Q 6	5. ♠ K 7 4 2
♡ A 3	♡ Q 2	♡ K Q 9 2	♡ K Q 9 3	♡ Q 4
◇ Q 9 6	◇ 7 6 4	◇ A 7 6	◇ 6 5	◇ A K 8
♣ J 8 4 3	♣ 9 7 3 2	♣ K J 8 4	♣ A Q 5 3	♣ Q 6 3 2

6. ♠ K 7 2	7. ♠ A 7 3 2	8. ♠ A 9 8	9. ♠ K Q	10. ♠ A K J
♡ A K 2	♡ A Q 4 3	♡ K 9 2	♡ A J 2	♡ A K
◇ 9 6 4	◇ Q 9 7	◇ A Q 4	◇ A K 8 6	◇ K J 7 4
♣ A Q 7 3	♣ A J	♣ Q 10 5 4	♣ K 9 7 5	♣ A 7 3 2

B. Your right-hand opponent opened 1♠. What action would you take on each of these hands?

1. ♠ Q J 3	2. ♠ 9 7	3. ♠ A Q 2	4. ♠ A J 2	5. ♠ A J 10 8 7 2
♡ 7	♡ A 2	♡ J	♡ K J	♡ - - -
◇ A K 9 6	◇ A Q J 9 7 6	◇ 8 7 6 4 3	◇ A K 8 6	◇ A K 9 4
♣ Q 8 5 4 2	♣ 7 5 2	♣ A K 5 4	♣ Q J 7 2	♣ J 4 2

C. Left-hand opponent opened 1♣, partner overcalled 1♡ and right-hand opponent passed. What **action** would you take on each of these hands?

1. ♠ K 8 4 3 ♡ 7 6 ♢ K 7 6 3 ♣ 9 4 3	**2.** ♠ 8 7 5 ♡ Q 9 6 3 2 ♢ 6 4 ♣ Q 7 5	**3.** ♠ 6 4 ♡ K 9 3 2 ♢ A 7 6 4 ♣ 9 3 2	**4.** ♠ A 7 2 ♡ 8 3 2 ♢ Q J 2 ♣ 9 8 5 2	**5.** ♠ A K 7 ♡ K 6 3 ♢ Q J 6 5 3 ♣ 8 2
6. ♠ A K 7 5 2 ♡ 7 3 ♢ A J 8 6 4 ♣ 3	**7.** ♠ A K 7 5 2 ♡ A J 8 6 4 ♢ 7 3 ♣ 2	**8.** ♠ A 9 6 ♡ J 2 ♢ J 9 6 2 ♣ K 8 5 4	**9.** ♠ A J 2 ♡ Q 4 2 ♢ J 10 7 3 ♣ K Q 10	**10.** ♠ A Q 7 ♡ 6 ♢ K Q 8 4 3 ♣ J 8 3 2
11. ♠ A Q 2 ♡ K 3 ♢ Q J 10 4 ♣ K Q 9 3	**12.** ♠ A 7 4 ♡ 8 3 2 ♢ J 9 7 6 ♣ K 7 3	**13.** ♠ A J 10 6 2 ♡ K 2 ♢ A K Q 4 ♣ 5 4	**14.** ♠ Q 7 2 ♡ A J ♢ A K Q J 2 ♣ 9 7 3	**15.** ♠ A K J ♡ 6 3 2 ♢ A K Q 3 ♣ 8 6 2

D. Right-hand opponent opened 1♣, you overcalled 1♠, left-hand opponent passed and your **partner** responded 1 NT. Right-hand opponent has passed. What action would you take now on each of these hands?

1. ♠ K Q 10 4 2 ♡ A 3 ♢ J 7 3 2 ♣ 6 2	**2.** ♠ A J 9 6 3 2 ♡ 4 2 ♢ K Q J ♣ 3 2	**3.** ♠ A Q J 9 2 ♡ J 9 8 ♢ A 4 ♣ K 8 5	**4.** ♠ A J 8 7 2 ♡ J ♢ A Q 8 6 2 ♣ 9 7	**5.** ♠ A K Q 2 ♡ 6 2 ♢ K 9 4 3 ♣ 8 7 3

PARTNERSHIP BIDDING : How should the following hands be bid? South is the dealer and there is no North-South bidding other than that indicated for each hand.

SET 21 — WEST	SET 21 — EAST	SET 22 — WEST	SET 22 — EAST
1. South opens 1♣. ♠ K Q J 8 6 ♡ A 8 7 ♢ 4 3 ♣ 9 8 5	**1. South opens 1♣.** ♠ A 7 4 ♡ 9 6 ♢ K Q 8 6 5 ♣ J 4 2	**1. South opens 1♢.** ♠ A Q J 7 2 ♡ 8 6 2 ♢ 7 2 ♣ Q J 3	**1. South opens 1♢.** ♠ K 5 ♡ K Q 7 3 ♢ A J 8 ♣ 10 6 4 2
2. South opens 1♡. ♠ A Q 10 5 4 ♡ 5 3 2 ♢ 7 5 ♣ K J 8	**2. South opens 1♡.** ♠ K 9 8 7 6 ♡ 7 ♢ A K 8 3 2 ♣ 9 5	**2. South opens 1♠.** ♠ 6 2 ♡ K 7 3 ♢ A 4 ♣ A Q 8 6 4 2	**2. South opens 1♠.** ♠ 9 5 3 ♡ A Q 9 6 5 ♢ K Q 8 ♣ 7 3
3. South opens 1♢. ♠ A J 10 8 6 ♡ Q J 2 ♢ 7 3 ♣ K J 9	**3. South opens 1♢.** ♠ K 7 5 2 ♡ K 8 6 ♢ J 9 ♣ A Q 3 2	**3. South opens 1♢.** ♠ A J 10 7 2 ♡ K Q 9 ♢ 7 ♣ A 8 4 3	**3. South opens 1♢.** ♠ K 9 8 3 ♡ A 7 ♢ 9 8 5 3 ♣ Q 5 2
4. South opens 1♣. ♠ 7 2 ♡ A K Q 8 2 ♢ 7 6 4 ♣ 8 3 2	**4. South opens 1♣.** ♠ K Q J ♡ J 9 5 4 ♢ A J 10 3 ♣ Q 6	**4. South opens 1♠.** ♠ A K 8 ♡ J 10 3 ♢ K 4 ♣ A J 10 7 2	**4. South opens 1♠.** ♠ 6 4 2 ♡ A Q 2 ♢ A 8 5 ♣ 9 6 4 3
5. South opens 1♡. ♠ 4 3 ♡ 6 3 2 ♢ A 8 ♣ A K Q 7 4 3	**5. South opens 1♡.** ♠ K 9 7 ♡ A Q 7 ♢ K 6 3 ♣ 8 6 5 2	**5. South opens 1♡.** ♠ A Q J ♡ A 9 8 ♢ K Q 3 ♣ Q 7 5 4	**5. South opens 1♡.** ♠ 8 6 5 4 2 ♡ 7 ♢ A J 8 ♣ K J 6 2

PLAY HANDS ON OVERCALLING THEIR SUIT OPENING

Hand 33 : 1NT overcall — Stayman — Card combination and compulsory duck — Card reading

Dealer North : Nil vulnerable

NORTH
- ♠ Q 7 6 2
- ♡ 7
- ◇ A 8 4 3 2
- ♣ Q 9 7

WEST
- ♠ J 9 4
- ♡ 6 5 3 2
- ◇ 10 7
- ♣ 8 4 3 2

EAST
- ♠ A 10
- ♡ K J 10 9 4
- ◇ K Q J
- ♣ 10 6 5

SOUTH
- ♠ K 8 5 3
- ♡ A Q 8
- ◇ 9 6 5
- ♣ A K J

WEST	NORTH	EAST	SOUTH
	Pass	1♡	1NT (1)
Pass	2♣ (2)	Pass	2♠
Pass	4♠	All pass	

Bidding : (1) 16-18, balanced, stopper in their suit.
(2) Stayman, as though partner had opened 1NT. (If the partnership is using 2♣ over a 1NT overcall as a weak hand with long clubs, North would bid 2♡, the enemy suit, as Stayman, and the rest of the auction would be the same.)

Lead : ♡5. It is normal to lead partner's suit unless you have a very strong reason to choose another lead. From 3 or 4 rags, lead second top (middle-up-down).

Correct play : Declarer is bound to lose 2 diamonds, so that it is vital to hold the trump losers to just the trump ace. With Q-x-x-x opposite K-x-x-x, to lose just one trick, you must lead towards one of your honors and hope 2nd player holds ace-doubleton : no other holding allows you just one loser. If 2nd player plays the ace, your king and queen are high; if 2nd player plays low, play your honor which will win, and then duck the next round of the suit, praying that the ace will fall. If it does, your remaining honor is high and can capture the remaining card in that suit. To succeed, you must make the player with the ace play second to the trick. As there are 25 HCP between declarer and dummy, and only 15 HCP are missing, the ♠ A should be with East for the opening bid. You must play East for the ace, so win the heart, ruff a heart and lead a low spade to your king. When it wins, duck the next spade — do not play dummy's queen! Once the ace has dropped, you will be able to play the ♠ Q later to draw West's last trump.

Hand 34 : 1NT overcall — Suit response — Card reading — Avoiding a futile finesse

Dealer East : North-South vulnerable

NORTH
- ♠ 9 7
- ♡ 8 7 6 5
- ◇ 9 8 6 3
- ♣ J 10 9

WEST
- ♠ A Q J
- ♡ A K
- ◇ Q J 10
- ♣ 8 7 5 4 2

EAST
- ♠ K 5 4 3 2
- ♡ J 2
- ◇ 7 5 2
- ♣ A Q 3

SOUTH
- ♠ 10 8 6
- ♡ Q 10 9 4 3
- ◇ A K 4
- ♣ K 6

WEST	NORTH	EAST	SOUTH
		Pass	1♡
1NT (1)	Pass	3♠ (2)	Pass
4♠ (3)	Pass	Pass	Pass

Bidding : (1) 16-18 points, balanced, stopper in hearts.
(2) Promises 5 spades and is forcing to game.
(3) Shows 3+ spade support. A cue bid of 4♡ showing spade support, a maximum 1NT overcall + ♡A would be reasonable. If so, East would sign off in 4♠ as East has no ambitions for slam.

Lead : ◇ K. To lead from a suit headed by A-K is highly attractive, as you win the trick, retain the lead and can judge from seeing dummy and partner's signal whether to continue that suit or whether to switch. Only a strong sequence like K-Q-J or Q-J-10 has the same appeal.

Correct play : South might cash the diamonds and continue with a 3rd diamond or switch to spades or hearts. South should not switch to clubs as this is far too risky.

When East gains the lead, East should draw trumps and then tackle the clubs. The 2 diamond losers are inevitable and declarer cannot afford 2 club losers. The normal club play is to finesse the queen, but here that play is bound to fail. Declarer and dummy hold 27 HCP. With 13 HCP missing, the ♣ K will be with South because of the opening bid. *When the finesse cannot win, play for the drop.* After trumps have been drawn, play a club to the ace and then a low club. When the king falls doubleton, the ♣ Q is high.

Hand 35 : Raising partner's suit overcall − Card combination − Card reading

Dealer South : East-West vulnerable

NORTH
- ♠ 5
- ♡ 10 8 6 5
- ◇ 10 9 2
- ♣ 8 7 6 5 3

WEST
- ♠ A J 10 6 2
- ♡ K 7 2
- ◇ J 7
- ♣ A J 4

EAST
- ♠ K 9 7 3
- ♡ Q J 4 3
- ◇ K 3
- ♣ K Q 9

SOUTH
- ♠ Q 8 4
- ♡ A 9
- ◇ A Q 8 6 5 4
- ♣ 10 2

WEST	NORTH	EAST	SOUTH
			1◇
1♠	Pass	3♠ (1)	Pass
4♠ (2)	Pass	Pass	Pass

Bidding : (1) Shows values equivalent to an opening hand plus support for the overcalled suit. The jump raise of an overcall is not forcing but is highly encouraging.
(2) With 12 or more HCP (or with 13 points or more counting shortages), the overcaller should accept the invitation.

Lead : ◇ 10. It is normal to lead partner's suit and from K-Q-x, Q-J-x, J-10-x and 10-9-x, the top card is led. From 3-card suits headed by an honor *plus a touching card,* lead top.

Correct play : Declarer should play low from dummy, but South wins the ◇ Q and cashes the ◇ A. South's best switch then is to the ♡ A and another heart, hoping that North might hold the ♡ K.

Having lost the first 3 tricks, declarer must avoid a trump loser. The normal play with 9 trumps missing the queen is to play the ace and king, hoping that the queen drops singleton or doubleton. However, you may be able to deduce the location of the queen and if that is possible, you may be able to capture the queen via a finesse. The best guide is to count dummy's points and add your own. Deduct the total from 40 to determine the missing HCP. Here dummy has 14 HCP and declarer has 14 HCP, so that 12 HCP are missing. As South opened the bidding, it is a virtual certainty that the ♠ Q is with South. Therefore, do not play for the drop but play South to hold the queen. When you gain the lead, play a spade to dummy's king and a spade back, finessing when South plays low. Draw South's trump and claim.

Hand 36 : Bidding over a suit overcall − Card combination − Card reading for a passed hand

Dealer West : Both vulnerable

NORTH
- ♠ 6 5 4 3 2
- ♡ A J 10 9 5
- ◇ J
- ♣ A 2

WEST
- ♠ A K Q J 8
- ♡ 6 4 2
- ◇ 10 8 6 3
- ♣ 5

EAST
- ♠ 7
- ♡ K
- ◇ Q 9 7 5 4 2
- ♣ 10 7 6 4 3

SOUTH
- ♠ 10 9
- ♡ Q 8 7 3
- ◇ A K
- ♣ K Q J 9 8

WEST	NORTH	EAST	SOUTH
Pass	Pass	Pass	1♣
1♠ (1)	2♡ (2)	Pass	4♡ (3)
Pass	Pass	Pass	

Bidding : (1) Even though neither West nor East could open, West should overcall, as spades is the only lead West wants.
(2) Shows at least 5 hearts and 10-12 points, not more since North passed initially.
(3) The South hand is worth 17 points. It would be a serious error to rebid clubs when support for partner's major is present, and 3♡ would not do the South hand justice.

Lead : ♠7. A singleton in partner's suit is very attractive.

Correct play : West should win with the ♠ J (a defender wins with the cheapest card possible) and cash another spade. The best chance to defeat the contract is for West to switch to a club, hoping for a club ruff if East has the ♣ A or can win the lead before trumps have been drawn. It is true that a 3rd spade would guarantee that East makes the ♡ K, but that would not allow the contract to be defeated.

The normal way to play the heart suit is to finesse for the king but if declarer does that here, East would win and the club return ruffed by West would defeat the game. *When a finesse is sure to fail, play for the drop.* When East shows out on the second round of spades, declarer can work out that West began with A-K-Q-J-x, a total of 10 HCP. As West passed as dealer, West cannot hold the ♡ K also for that would make 13 HCP and with that, West would have opened. Thus, East has the ♡ K, the finesse is futile, so play the ♡ A first. Even if the ♡ K location were unknown, playing the ♡ A is a sound precaution against a possible club ruff.

CHAPTER 10
SINGLE JUMP OVERCALLS & RESPONSES

A jump overcall skips at least one level over a bid made by an opponent who has opened or responded to an opening bid. When writing the order of bidding, a useful convention is to write bids by the opponents in brackets. Thus, (1♠) : 2♣ would indicate that an opponent opened 1♠ and our side made an overcall of 2♣. A single jump overcall is an overcall one above the minimum permissible. For example, (1♢) : 1♠ is a simple overcall, while (1♢) : 2♠ is a single jump overcall. Likewise, (1♠) : 2♡ is a simple overcall, while (1♠) : 3♡ is a single jump overcall. Double and triple jump overcalls are pre-emptive and are covered in Chapter 12 on Pre-empts.

Regardless of the system you play for your opening bids, the partnership may stipulate which variety of single jump overcalls shall be played. A bidding system (Standard, Precision, Acol, Goren, and so on) refers to the rules and agreements governing the bidding when your side opens the bidding. It need not restrict the approach you adopt when the opponents open the bidding. There are 3 basic types of single jump overcalls : Weak Jump Overcalls, Intermediate Jump Overcalls and Strong Jump Overcalls. Naturally you can play only one method at a time and the partnership will have agreed which to use before play commences.

WEAK JUMP OVERCALLS : 6-10 HCP AND A 6-CARD OR LONGER SUIT

Where the jump is to the 3-level, such as (1♡) : 3♣, the suit is often a 7-card suit. Weak jump overcalls are popular at duplicate because they occur more frequently than other kinds of jump overcalls. They are designed to shut the opponents out of the auction or at least impede their auction, and partner needs a strong opening hand to bid on. With no fit for the overcalled suit, partner should have at least 16 points to bid (since the maximum opposite is 10), but with a fit, a hand with 4 winners or better should bid. Change of suit is forcing.

If the partnership plays weak jump overcalls, then when the hand is too strong for a weak jump overcall, a simple overcall is made up to 15 HCP. When holding 16 HCP or more with a strong suit, double first and bid the long suit on the next round.

INTERMEDIATE JUMP OVERCALLS : 11-15 HCP AND A 6-CARD OR LONGER SUIT

The intermediate jump overcall is equivalent to a minimum opening bid with at least a 6-card suit, the sort of hand which would open 1♠ and rebid 2♠ over a 1NT response, for example. These are constructive and allow the overcaller to show a goodish hand and a good suit with one bid. Players not using intermediate jumps will often just overcall and rebid the long suit, provided that the bidding has not climbed too high.

Partner is expected to respond to an intermediate jump overcall with 9 HCP or better and may bid with less when holding support for the overcaller's suit. Support plus 3 winners or better would be enough to raise an intermediate jump in a major suit to game.

Players using intermediate jump overcalls will make a simple overcall when holding a long, strong suit and about 7-10 HCP, and with a long, strong suit and 16 HCP or better, double first and bid the long suit later.

STRONG JUMP OVERCALLS : 16-19 HCP AND A STRONG 5-CARD OR LONGER SUIT

The strong jump overcall is what most players learn initially and it is most commonly used in rubber bridge games. It is not popular at duplicate because it occurs too rarely and this kind of hand can be shown by doubling first and bidding the long suit later. Partnerships using strong jump overcalls will make simple overcalls with a long, strong suit and weaker values.

The strong jump overcall is not forcing but partner is expected to reply with 6 HCP or more. Raising a major suit would be first priority. Support and 2 winners would be enough to raise a strong jump in a major suit to game. If the strong jump is in a minor suit, 3NT takes precedence over a minor suit raise, but any no-trump bid promises at least 1 stopper in the enemy suit. Change of suit is forcing and promises at least a 5-card suit.

In response to any kind of single jump overcall, a bid of the enemy suit is artificial, forcing, looking for game and usually asking partner for a stopper in the enemy suit. This action is covered in detail in Chapter 25.

EXERCISES

A. Right-hand opponent opened 1♣. What action would take on these hands using Weak Jump Overcalls?

1. ♠ KQ8432	2. ♠ 75	3. ♠ 64	4. ♠ AK2	5. ♠ J7
♡ AK	♡ AQJ32	♡ AQJ852	♡ KQJ932	♡ K6
◇ 763	◇ 64	◇ 9764	◇ AJ2	◇ AJ10972
♣ 94	♣ Q752	♣ 2	♣ 2	♣ 842

B. What would your answer be for the hands in Question A if the partnership is using :

(1) Intermediate Jump Overcalls?   **(2)** Strong Jump Overcalls?

C. Left-hand opponent opened 1◇, partner overcalled 2♠, a weak jump overcall, and your right-hand opponent bid 3◇. What action would you take now on each of these hands?

1. ♠ KQ10 42	2. ♠ 62	3. ♠ 2	4. ♠ AJ8	5. ♠ 9
♡ A63	♡ KQJ2	♡ AJ984	♡ AQ102	♡ KQJ9752
◇ J732	◇ J52	◇ A4	◇ 862	◇ AQ
♣ A	♣ A832	♣ J8532	♣ QJ7	♣ KQJ

PARTNERSHIP BIDDING : South is the dealer and there is no North-South bidding other than indicated. You and partner are playing weak jump overcalls on Set 23 and intermediate jump overcalls on Set 24.

SET 23 – WEST	SET 23 – EAST	SET 24 – WEST	SET 24 – EAST
1. South opens 1♣.	**1. South opens 1♣.**	**1. South opens 1◇.**	**1. South opens 1◇.**
♠ KQJ862	♠ 3	♠ AQJ874	♠ K95
♡ K87	♡ 962	♡ KQ3	♡ A7
◇ 4	◇ KJ8632	◇ 76	◇ 9842
♣ 985	♣ AK6	♣ 42	♣ QJ103
2. South opens 1♠.	**2. South opens 1♠.**	**2. South opens 1♣.**	**2. South opens 1♣.**
♠ 7	♠ AQ62	♠ K43	♠ AQ985
♡ AQJ8643	♡ 1072	♡ AJ9872	♡ 6
◇ J103	◇ A2	◇ KQJ	◇ 962
♣ 62	♣ KQ54	♣ 4	♣ A873
3. South opens 1♡.	**3. South opens 1♡.**	**3. South opens 1◇.**	**3. South opens 1◇.**
♠ 106	♠ A95	♠ AK7542	♠ - - -
♡ 43	♡ A762	♡ 98	♡ J7632
◇ 82	◇ A943	◇ AJ	◇ 9874
♣ AK98742	♣ Q3	♣ 632	♣ KQJ5
4. South opens 1♠.	**4. South opens 1♠.**	**4. South opens 1♡.**	**4. South opens 1♡.**
♠ 4	♠ 9732	♠ 86	♠ K94
♡ KQJ875	♡ A93	♡ 43	♡ AJ5
◇ AK3	◇ QJ54	◇ AK2	◇ J1043
♣ 842	♣ A7	♣ AQ9864	♣ K32
5. South opens 1♣.	**5. South opens 1♣.**	**5. South opens 1◇.**	**5. South opens 1◇.**
♠ 863	♠ A92	♠ 5	♠ AQ732
♡ 7	♡ QJ8652	♡ J82	♡ Q953
◇ KQ10864	◇ 72	◇ K94	◇ 832
♣ A93	♣ 86	♣ AKQ872	♣ 6
6. South opens 1♡.	**6. South opens 1♡.**	**6. South opens 1♣.**	**6. South opens 1♣.**
♠ 862	♠ K943	♠ AKQ	♠ 96
♡ 7	♡ KQ10	♡ QJ9642	♡ AK7
◇ KQJ864	◇ A93	◇ 72	◇ AQ1093
♣ K93	♣ A52	♣ 93	♣ 864

PLAY HANDS ON WEAK JUMP OVERCALLS

Note the dealer on hands 39 and 40 in particular.

Hand 37 : Weak jump overcall — Coping with a bad break

Dealer North : North-South vulnerable

```
                    NORTH
                    ♠ A K 4
                    ♡ K J 10 9 4
                    ◇ J
                    ♣ J 10 9 8
WEST                                EAST
♠ Q 8 5 3                           ♠ J 6
♡ A Q 8                             ♡ 7 3
◇ A K Q                             ◇ 10 8 3
♣ 5 3 2                             ♣ A K Q 7 6 4
                    SOUTH
                    ♠ 10 9 7 2
                    ♡ 6 5 2
                    ◇ 9 7 6 5 4 2
                    ♣ - - -
```

WEST	NORTH	EAST	SOUTH
	1♡	3♣ (1)	Pass (2)
3NT (3)	Pass	Pass	Pass

Bidding : (1) Weak jump overcall, 6-10 HCP, good 6-card suit. If not using weak jump overcalls, North would make a simple overcall of 2♣ and South would still reply 3NT.
(2) Much too weak to compete.
(3) All suits covered and a powerful hand. Partner's clubs should provide the tricks and West provides the stoppers. It is desirable to have all outside suits stopped, but if the values are there for a game, it is permissible to have one suit unguarded, provided that you do have any suit bid by the opposition stopped and that you do not have a shortage (singleton or void) in the suit unguarded.

Lead : ♡J. Top from an interior sequence. You hope to set up the hearts before declarer can utilise the clubs. A top spade first is also a sound choice, but when partner discourages, you should switch back to hearts.

Correct play : On most days, declarer would have an easy road to 11 tricks, 6 clubs, 3 diamonds and 2 hearts. Here, declarer wins the heart lead and leads a club to the ace, but receives a nasty shock when South shows out. It would be an error to continue with the K-Q of clubs and a fourth club. This sets up 2 club winners in dummy but with no entry to reach them. *If you must give up a trick to set up winners, give up the necessary loser early.* After the ♣A reveals the break, duck one round of clubs (i.e. play a low club from both hands). When you regain the lead, the K-Q of clubs will draw the remaining clubs and allow you to cash the other two club winners.

Hand 38 : Weak jump overcall — Ducking to set up a long suit in dummy

Dealer East : East-West vulnerable

```
                    NORTH
                    ♠ A 9 8 3
                    ♡ A J 3 2
                    ◇ 5 4
                    ♣ A Q J
WEST                                EAST
♠ 10 7 5 4                          ♠ K Q 2
♡ 9 8 6 5                           ♡ K Q 7
◇ Q 10 9                            ◇ J 3
♣ 9 8                              ♣ K 10 5 4 3
                    SOUTH
                    ♠ J 6
                    ♡ 10 4
                    ◇ A K 8 7 6 2
                    ♣ 7 6 2
```

WEST	NORTH	EAST	SOUTH
		1♣	2◇ (1)
Pass	3NT (2)	All pass	

Bidding : (1) Worth a weak jump overcall only if not vulnerable. If vulnerable, the South hand does not have sufficient playing tricks to justify a weak jump overcall and would either make a simple overcall or pass. If not using weak jump overcalls, South is worth a simple overcall of 1◇ and again North-South should reach 3NT.
(2) 16 HCP is worth a shot at game opposite a simple overcall or a weak jump overcall. Here North has the stoppers and hopes to use South's diamond suit for most of the tricks.

Lead : ♣4. The long suit is normal but as North clearly has the clubs covered, it would not be unreasonable to lead the king from one of the major suits, hoping to hit a long suit with partner. As it happens, none of these leads proves successful.

Correct play : North should win the first club with the *queen*. It is sound technique for declarer to *win with the higher of equal winners.* Declarer needs to set up diamond winners in order to come to 9 tricks, but it would be an error to play ace, king and a third diamond as dummy has no entry to the established winners. As a trick has to be lost anyway to set up the diamonds, give up the inevitable loser early. Duck a round of diamonds at once and when you regain the lead, continue with the ◇ A-K, which draw the remaining diamonds. Cash the other diamond winners. Had the diamonds been 4-1, the contract would have failed. Just grin and bear it.

Hand 39 : Raising partner's weak jump overcall — Ducking to keep control

Dealer NORTH : N-S vulnerable

NORTH
- ♠ 10 9
- ♡ K J 10 9 7
- ◇ 10 5
- ♣ A K Q J

WEST
- ♠ 7 2
- ♡ A Q 3
- ◇ A K Q J 4 3
- ♣ 8 6

EAST
- ♠ A K 8 6 4 3
- ♡ 6
- ◇ 7 6 2
- ♣ 10 5 2

SOUTH
- ♠ Q J 5
- ♡ 8 5 4 2
- ◇ 9 8
- ♣ 9 7 4 3

WEST	NORTH	EAST	SOUTH
	1♡	2♠ (1)	Pass (2)
4♠ (3)	Pass	Pass	Pass

Bidding: (1) Worth a weak jump overcall only if not vulnerable. When vulnerable, a weak jump overcall should have potential for 6 tricks at the 2-level and 7 tricks at the 3-level. If not playing weak jump overcalls, East is worth a simple overcall of 1♠ and would rebid 3♠ over West's 3◇, enabling West to raise to 4♠.
(2) Much to weak to warrant a raise to 3♡.
(3) Partner should have a decent 6-card spade suit and around 5-6 playing tricks. As West has at least 5 winners a raise to game is reasonable. As the cards lie, 3NT would succeed but with the weakness in clubs, this is not sure and it is better to stick with the known 8-card major fit.

Lead: ♡5. It is normal to lead partner's suit and from 3 or 4 rags, prefer 2nd highest (middle-up-down). Leading the 4th-highest from a 4-card suit implies at least one honor card in the suit.

Correct play: Declarer should win the ♡A and lead a spade, ducking in hand. On regaining the lead, cash the ♠ A-K, drawing the missing trumps and then run the diamonds. This way the opponents can score only 1 spade and 2 clubs. The danger is to play A-K of spades first. Then if a 3rd spade is played, the opponents can cash 3 clubs, or if you start on the diamonds, an opponent will ruff and again 3 clubs can be cashed. By ducking a round of spades at once, dummy is left with a spade to cater for the 3rd round of clubs. You could win the lead and play a club, hoping to ruff a club in dummy, but the opponents can counter that by switching to a trump and again it will be vital to duck the 1st spade in order to prevent 3 clubs being cashed before trumps have been drawn and you can run the diamonds.

Hand 40 : Raising partner's weak jump overcall — Ducking to set up an extra trick —Timing

Dealer EAST : Nil vulnerable

NORTH
- ♠ A K 4 2
- ♡ A 5
- ◇ Q 3
- ♣ 8 7 6 4 2

WEST
- ♠ 10 8 6
- ♡ J 8 3
- ◇ 10 7 5
- ♣ K J 10 3

EAST
- ♠ Q J 9
- ♡ 7 4
- ◇ A K J 9 4
- ♣ Q 9 5

SOUTH
- ♠ 7 5 3
- ♡ K Q 10 9 6 2
- ◇ 8 6 2
- ♣ A

WEST	NORTH	EAST	SOUTH
		1◇	2♡ (1)
Pass (2)	3♡ (3)	Pass	4♡ (4)
Pass	Pass	Pass	

Bidding: (1) This hand has potential for 6 tricks and would also be worth a weak jump overcall if vulnerable.
(2) Not strong enough to take any action.
(3) Just worth a raise. With support and more than 3 winners, an invitation to game is justified and the potential for a diamond ruff provides the extra chance needed to warrant inviting game.
(4) 9-10 HCP is a maximum for a weak jump overcall and so South accepts the invitation.

Lead : ◇ 5. Partner's suit is the normal lead and with 3 cards including an honor, the lowest card is the standard lead. The 10 is an honor, so from 10-x-x, lead the bottom card.

Correct play: East should win the 1st diamond and switch to a trump. If East wrongly plays a 2nd diamond, declarer can easily ruff the 3rd diamond low in dummy and make 2 spades, 6 hearts, 1 diamond ruff and 1 club. Likewise, if East switches to a club, South wins and leads a 2nd diamond and will score the diamond ruff. If East switches to a trump at trick 2, South should see that the diamond ruff will vanish : win the ♡ A and duck a spade, hoping for a 3-3 spade break so that the 13th spade will be your 10th trick. Most texts recommend that you count your losers, but a count of winners helps, too. There are only 9 tricks and without a diamond ruff, the 10th trick can come only from spades. Note that the spade must be ducked before trumps have been drawn.

CHAPTER 11

THE UNUSUAL 2NT OVERCALL FOR THE MINORS

It is rare to pick up a huge hand after an opponent has opened and thus there would be little scope for a jump overcall of 2NT, such as (1♡) : 2NT, to show a balanced hand around 21-22 points. Such a hand, when it does arise, can be quite adequately shown by a takeout double, followed by a jump in no-trumps later. Accordingly, most partnerships have harnessed the jump overcall to 2NT after a major suit opening to show a weakish hand with both minor suits.

(1♡) : 2NT or (1♠) : 2NT = About 8-12 HCP and at least 5-5 in the minors.

Each minor suit should contain at least 2 honor cards if the pattern is 5-5. The strength may be less than 8 HCP when the pattern is 6-5 or more extreme, *or* at favourable vulnerability. Likewise you may take greater liberties with the suit quality when the pattern is at least 6-5. Each of these hands would be worth an overcall of 2NT after an opening bid of (1♡) or (1♠) :

♠ 7 2	♠ 9	♠ 8 3 2	♠ 6	♠ - - -
♡ 9	♡ J 2	♡ - - -	♡ 7	♡ 2
◇ K Q J 6 3	◇ Q J 10 7 2	◇ J 10 7 5 2	◇ Q J 8 6 4 2	◇ K 10 9 6 5 3
♣ K J 9 7 2	♣ A J 7 6 5	♣ A Q J 9 4	♣ Q J 10 5 2	♣ 10 9 8 5 3 2

The function of the unusual 2NT overcall is to suggest a sacrifice to partner if the opponents bid to a game. Accordingly, the 2NT overcall should not be too strong. If you hold 13 HCP or more, it is not too likely that the opponents will bid to a game, and if they do, you will have reasonable defensive prospects. Similarly, the 2NT overcall should not have strong defensive prospects against their game. A hand with 3 likely winners, such as suits headed by A-K and A, is too strong in defense for a 2NT overcall. With 5-5 in the minors and too much strength for the unusual 2NT, content yourself with a simple overcall first and compete again later. With 16 HCP or more, you could double first and show the suits later.

If the bidding starts, say, (1♠) : 2NT : (4♠) ... 4th player is in a good position to judge whether to defend against 4♠ or whether to save ("to save" = "to sacrifice") in 5♣ or 5◇. The advantages of sacrificing are that if the opponents allow you to play in 5♣ doubled or 5◇ doubled, the cost of the sacrifice may be less than the value of their game, or if the opponents decide to bid 5-in-their-major, that contract may fail. If they are unable to take more than 10 tricks, it obviously pays to push them one higher where they can be defeated.

PARTNER'S STRATEGY IF 3RD PLAYER PASSES 2NT

With a weak hand, bid 3♣ or 3◇, whichever minor suit holding is longer. It is almost always wrong to pass 2NT and if you have equal length in the minors, bid 3♣. With a strong hand and game chances, you may jump to 4♣ or 4◇ or even 5♣ or 5◇. You may choose 3NT with a very strong hand and double or triple stoppers in the majors. Remember that partner will have to play the hand in no-trumps and partner will have next to nothing in the majors. A bid of the other major, e.g. (1♡) : 2NT : (Pass) : 3♠, would be a strong hand with a strong 6-card or longer suit and partner should raise with doubleton support.

PARTNER'S STRATEGY IF 3RD PLAYER DOUBLES 2NT

The same strategy applies as though 3rd player had passed, except that with an equal holding in the minor suits, you should pass and allow the 2NT bidder to choose a suit. If you have a clear preference, bid your longer minor. With equal length, *you* have no preference, so that if one of partner's minors is longer, it will be better to have that suit as trumps. Pass and let partner choose. (This is also a situation where the Murray Principle applies : "If the contract looks like a disaster, let partner play the hand!")

PARTNER'S STRATEGY IF THIRD PLAYER BIDS 3-MAJOR

Pass with a weak hand, but bid 4♣ or 4◇ as an invitation to game or jump straight to 5♣ or 5◇ with good chances for game or if you expect not to go more than one off. It is not attractive to sacrifice yet. They may not even bid their game. However, if you are close to game values or if you are sure that they are going to bid their game anyway, a jump to 5-minor puts maximum pressure on opener.

PARTNER'S STRATEGY IF 3RD PLAYER BIDS 4-MAJOR

If they cannot make even 10 tricks, it does not pay to sacrifice at all. Why should you lose points when they are about to lose points in their contract? Accordingly, the first question is whether you have reasonable defensive prospects. If you have a fair chance of defeating their game, do not sacrifice. In making this assessment, do not count on the 2NT bidder for more than one defensive trick.

It also does not pay to sacrifice if they double you and the penalties cost more than the value of their game. Vulnerability is one factor and the degree of fit with partner's minors is the other. Do not sacrifice on balanced hands — the cost is usually too high. Do not sacrifice if you are vulnerable and they are not, unless you have some hope of making the contract — otherwise, the cost is usually too high. The best holdings for sacrificing are a 4-card or longer holding in one minor and a doubleton or less in the other minor, with very little in the way of defensive tricks. The more balanced your hand, the more you should choose to defend rather than bid on.

ACTION BY 3RD PLAYER AFTER AN OPPONENT'S 2NT OVERCALL

Pass indicates a weak hand. Double says you are angling for penalties and shows a strong 4-card holding in one of the minors, so that if 4th player bids the other minor and opener has a strong holding in that suit, opener is able to double for penalties. A bid of 3-of-opener's-major has the same value as a raise to the 2-level. With support for opener's suit and enough for game, bid 4-in-opener's-major. Bidding 3-of-the-other-major is forcing and shows a good 5-card or longer suit. Bidding 3-of-either-minor cannot be natural and may be used as an ask for a stopper for 3NT. Other systems of defense are possible but if you have no specific agreements, the above suggestions can be used.

THE UNUSUAL 2NT OVER A MINOR SUIT OPENING

These days opening bids of 1♣ or 1♢ are very often artificial or can be such short suits that it is reasonable to use the unusual 2NT overcall for the minor suits even if they open with a minor suit. That is the arrangement in many regular partnerships. However, another possible arrangement is for the unusual 2NT to show the two cheapest unbid suits, so that (1♣) : 2NT shows diamonds and hearts, while (1♢) : 2NT would show clubs and hearts. The strength would still be weakish, normally less than 13 HCP, and the suit texture would be good. Naturally, the partnership will stipulate before play starts which approach is to be used.

WHEN IS 2NT NOT FOR THE MINORS?

In most auctions, a bid of 2NT is not for the minors. 2NT normally indicates a balanced hand of a specific strength. The strength varies according to the auction but if 2NT can have a natural meaning showing a balanced hand, then that meaning is preferred. For example, 1♠ : (2♡) : 2NT would show a heart stopper and about 10-12 points. Likewise, 2NT over their weak 2-opening, e.g. (2♠) : 2NT, shows a balanced hand of about 16-18 points and does not ask for the minors. After (1♡) : Pass : (2♡) : Double, (Pass) . . . a bid of 2NT in answer to the double would be a natural bid, showing at least 1 stopper in the enemy suit.

OTHER SITUATIONS WHERE NO-TRUMP BIDS ARE USED TO SHOW THE MINORS

In general, if a no-trump bid *cannot* have a sensible natural meaning in a competitive auction, it is used to show the minor suits. In each of these auctions the final no-trump bid is commonly used for the minors.

WEST	NORTH	EAST	SOUTH
Pass	1♡	Pass	1♠
1NT			

West's 1NT should not be used in a natural sense. It would be lunacy to compete against two bidding opponents with a balanced hand containing less than 13 points. The 1NT overcall by a passed hand shows the minors, but not as freakish as 2NT which in this auction would also show the minors. 2NT suggests at least 5-5, while 1NT might be 5-4.

WEST	NORTH	EAST	SOUTH
Pass	1♡	Pass	2♡
2NT			

Again, since the 2NT bid here as a passed hand makes no sense as a balanced hand, it should be taken as showing both minors.

WEST	NORTH	EAST	SOUTH
1♠	Pass	2♠	Pass
Pass	2NT		

North's delayed 2NT shows the minors. It cannot be a huge balanced hand. With that, North would have bid immediately over 1♠. North is likely to be only 5-4 in the minors — with 5-5, 2NT could have been bid at once.

WEST	NORTH	EAST	SOUTH
1♠	Pass	3♠	3NT

It is wildly unlikely that 3NT would be needed in a natural sense (i.e. to play in 3NT) after a powerful raise to 3♠. Accordingly, most partnerships treat 3NT in such auctions as unusual for the minors, strongly suggesting a sacrifice as the opponents are clearly heading for at least a game.

WEST	NORTH	EAST	SOUTH
1♡	1♠	Pass	2♠
Pass	Pass	2NT	

East's 2NT figures to be for the minors, even by responder, something like ♠ 6   ♡ 43   ◇ J10943   ♣ K7642, perhaps. It cannot be a natural bid showing a spade stopper since East failed to bid 1NT or 2NT over 1♠.

WEST	NORTH	EAST	SOUTH
2♣*	2♡	Pass	3♡
Pass	Pass	3NT	

*Artificial, strong and forcing

This situation is arguable but many pairs would utilise the 3NT in this situation by such a weak hand as showing the minors rather than as a stopper in the enemy suit.

WEST	NORTH	EAST	SOUTH
3♠	4NT		

WEST	NORTH	EAST	SOUTH
4♡	4NT		

Many pairs play that a jump to 4NT over a pre-emptive opening shows both minors. Likewise, a 4NT bid over an opening bid of 4♡ or 4♠ is for takeout, not an ask for aces. However, this would always be based on a very strong hand and 5-5 in the minors at least. Clearly, such agreements need to be settled by your partnership in advance.

WEST	NORTH	EAST	SOUTH
1♡	2♣	4♡	Pass
Pass	4NT		

North's 4NT is again a takeout for the minors but the failure to bid 2NT over 1♡ marks North with longer clubs than diamonds, 6 or 7 clubs and perhaps only 4 diamonds. However, North is anxious to sacrifice and without clear preference for diamonds, South should choose clubs.

EXERCISES

A. Neither side is vulnerable. Your right-hand opponent opened 1♠. What action do you take on these hands?

1. ♠ 9 5	2. ♠ A	3. ♠ 2	4. ♠ 7 2	5. ♠ - - -
♡ 7 3	♡ A Q	♡ J 3	♡ - - -	♡ J 6 3
◇ A Q 10 6 4	◇ J 9 7 6 4	◇ A K 6 4 3	◇ K Q 8 6 2	◇ A Q J 4 3
♣ K Q 7 3	♣ 9 7 5 3 2	♣ A Q 9 5 4	♣ Q J 9 7 5 2	♣ Q J 8 3 2

6. ♠ A 6 5	7. ♠ - - -	8. ♠ - - -	9. ♠ 7 2	10. ♠ J 2
♡ - - -	♡ K	♡ J 6 2	♡ J	♡ 6
◇ A K Q 6 4	◇ Q 9 7 6 4 2	◇ A K 6 4 3	◇ K Q J 6 2	◇ Q J 10 3
♣ K Q 9 7 3	♣ J 9 8 6 3 2	♣ 8 7 5 4 2	♣ Q J 10 8 3	♣ K Q J 9 7 4

B. Partner opened 1♡ and right-hand opponent overcalled 2NT. What action do you take on these hands?

1. ♠ K 7 6 4 2	2. ♠ A 7	3. ♠ 9 8 3 2	4. ♠ A 7 2	5. ♠ A K 7 2
♡ 7 3	♡ 2	♡ A K J 2	♡ Q J 7 2	♡ K Q 6 3 2
◇ A J 9	◇ Q 9 8 6 4 2	◇ A 7 6 4	◇ K 8 6	◇ 2
♣ 9 7 3	♣ A 7 5 2	♣ 5	♣ 7 5 2	♣ K Q J

C. Left-hand opponent opened 1♡, partner overcalled 2NT and right-hand opponent passed. Your action?

1. ♠ K 8 7 5 4	2. ♠ A 8 7	3. ♠ Q 8 7 4 3	4. ♠ A 7 6 4 3 2	5. ♠ A 8 7 2
♡ 7 6 3	♡ A 9 5 3	♡ K J	♡ J	♡ 6 5 4 3 2
◇ 9 6 4	◇ Q 9	◇ 9 7 6	◇ A K 8 6 2	◇ Q 4
♣ J 7	♣ J 7 3 2	♣ 8 5 4	♣ 7	♣ J 2

6. ♠ A	7. ♠ Q J 10 9 2	8. ♠ A 8 6 3 2	9. ♠ A Q J 8 7 2	10. ♠ A Q 10 9
♡ 9 7 6 3	♡ K Q J 9 3	♡ K Q	♡ J 7 3	♡ A K J 9
◇ A Q 9	◇ 4	◇ A K	◇ A K 8	◇ J 3
♣ K Q J 3 2	♣ 7 2	♣ J 8 5 4	♣ 7	♣ K 3 2

D. What would your answers be in C. if right-hand opponent had raised to 3♡ over 2NT?

PLAY HANDS ON THE UNUSUAL NT FOR THE MINORS

Hand 41 : The 2NT overcall for the minors — Taking a sacrifice at unfavourable vulnerability

Dealer North : East-West vulnerable

WEST	NORTH	EAST	SOUTH
	1♡	2NT (1)	4♡ (2)
5♣ (3)	Pass (4)	Pass	Dble (5)
Pass	Pass (6)	Pass	

```
            NORTH
         ♠ J 9
         ♡ K Q 6 4 3 2
         ◇ A K 10 3
         ♣ 7
WEST              EAST
♠ A Q 8 7 2       ♠ 6
♡ 8 5             ♡ 7
◇ 5               ◇ Q J 9 6 4 2
♣ 9 8 6 4 2       ♣ A Q J 10 5
            SOUTH
         ♠ K 10 5 4 3
         ♡ A J 10 9
         ◇ 8 7
         ♣ K 3
```

Bidding : (1) Ideal for 2NT with excellent playing strength and very little defense. Clearly worth 2NT even at this vulnerability.
(2) Much too strong for just 3♡. Worth 13 points for hearts.
(3) Ideal for a sacrifice. Great support for one minor and shortage in the other minor. Such hands make many more tricks than the point count suggests. 5♣ might actually succeed (as 2NT will not be light at the vulnerability) and should not be more than one off.
(4) Very tough decision. The ◇ A-K suggest defending, but 5♡ could be on because of the good shape. 5♡ can be beaten, losing 2 spades and 1 club, but the defense could slip. Say East leads the ♠6 to West's Q and declarer drops the J : if West does not cash the ♠ A now (West can work out the ♠ J cannot be a singleton), declarer can later discard the spade loser on the ♣ K and make 5♡!

(5) Another tough decision. The absence of a shortage and the likely trump trick with the ♣ K suggest defending.
(6) If you pass the decision to partner and partner elects to double, abide by partner's decision.

Lead : ♡K. On the ♠J lead, West can succeed, discarding the heart loser on the second spade. On a trump lead, usually attractive against a sacrifice, declarer could make by winning the ♣ A and having the courage to finesse the ♠ Q, again discarding the heart loser. The ◇ K, dummy's second suit, is not an attractive lead.

Correct play : When West wins the lead, West should lead the singleton diamond. Later West should ruff 3 rounds of diamonds in hand, setting up dummy's diamonds. Declarer has to take care not to squander dummy's trumps. If dummy's trumps are used too early, dummy will not have an entry later to the diamonds. Going 2 down will cost 500. −200 is reasonable as 4♡ is on, but −500 is too expensive.

Hand 42 : Bidding over the 2NT overcall — Beware the finesse at trick 1

Dealer East : Both vulnerable

WEST	NORTH	EAST	SOUTH
		1♡	2NT (1)
4♡ (2)	Pass (3)	Pass	Pass (4)

```
            NORTH
         ♠ K 10 9 6 4
         ♡ K J
         ◇ 6 5
         ♣ 7 6 3 2
WEST              EAST
♠ A Q J 8         ♠ 7 3 2
♡ Q 7 5 3 2       ♡ A 9 8 6 4
◇ 7 4             ◇ A K 10
♣ K 4             ♣ Q 8
            SOUTH
         ♠ 5
         ♡ 10
         ◇ Q J 9 8 3 2
         ♣ A J 10 9 5
```

Bidding : (1) Again an excellent vulnerable 2NT overcall. Note especially the superb suit texture in each minor.
(2) Clearly enough values for game.
(3) Do not sacrifice on balanced hands or when all your strength is in the opponents' suits and therefore best for defence. 5♣ can be defeated by 3 tricks, −800, too expensive.
(4) If partner does not wish to sacrifice, neither should you, unless you have exceptional extra values, such as a 6-6 pattern.

Lead : ◇ Q or ♠5. The top of the near sequence is the solid lead, the singleton is the gambling lead which could work.

Correct play : On the ◇ Q lead, East should win and cash the ♡ A. If hearts are 3-0, there is nothing you can do if the void is with South, as expected. When trumps are 2-1, if the ♡K fell, you would draw the last trump. When the ♡ K does not drop, leave it out and take the spade finesse. Losing 1 spade, 1 heart and 1 club. On the ♠5 lead, declarer must not finesse. North would win the ♠ K and give South a spade ruff. Now 4♡ will go off. As South is 5-5 in the minors, beware of that spade lead. Do not fall for the finesse-at-trick-1 trap. Win the ♠ A and cash the ♡A.

Hand 43 : Bidding over the 2NT overcall — Card combination and card reading

Dealer South : Nil vulnerable

NORTH
- ♠ K 6 5 4
- ♡ K Q 5
- ◇ 7 6 3
- ♣ J 7 3

WEST
- ♠ 7
- ♡ J 10
- ◇ Q 10 9 8 2
- ♣ K Q 9 6 5

EAST
- ♠ Q 10 9
- ♡ A 9 8 7
- ◇ 5 4
- ♣ 10 8 4 2

SOUTH
- ♠ A J 8 3 2
- ♡ 6 4 3 2
- ◇ A K J
- ♣ A

WEST	NORTH	EAST	SOUTH
			1♠
2NT	3♠ (1)	Pass (2)	4♠ (3)
Pass	Pass	Pass (4)	

Bidding : (1) Not a good hand but it is vital to show support in case opener has a very strong hand. The raise to 3-major over 2NT shows a sound 1-major : 2-major raise, around 7-10 points.
(2) There are no prospects of making 5♣ and the bidding may die at the 3-level. Do not sacrifice if they may not bid the game.
(3) Worth 20 points because of the singleton.
(4) Not worth a sacrifice at equal vulnerability since the hand is balanced and all the strength is in the opposition's suits.

Lead : ♡J or ♣K. Leading Q-x, J-x or 10-x is not attractive, but these holdings are all right if you have the card below, i.e. Q-J, J-10 or 10-9. With the touching card as well, you are unlikely to damage your side and may help to build up tricks in partner's hand. The ♣K is a sound alternative and better than the ◇10.

Correct play : The normal play in spades with 9 trumps is king and ace, hoping that the queen will drop. However, in view of West's 2NT, the 2-2 break in spades is less likely and you should play a 2NT overcaller to be short in your trump suit. If the ♡J is led to the king and ace and a heart is returned to the queen, West is now known to hold 5 clubs, 5 diamonds and 2 hearts and so cannot hold more than 1 spade. Therefore, cash the ♠K and lead a spade to the jack. If you play for the drop, you are highly likely to fail. If the lead was the ♣K, you should play the same way. Firstly, with at least 10 cards in the minors, West figures to be short in spades. Secondly, West is likely to hold 2 hearts, and so at most 1 spade, as West may well have led a singleton heart.

Hand 44 : Using 4NT as a minor suit takeout — Competitive decisions

Dealer West : North-South vulnerable

NORTH
- ♠ 8 7 6 5
- ♡ - - -
- ◇ Q 9 8 4
- ♣ A 10 4 3 2

WEST
- ♠ A J 9 2
- ♡ K Q 6 5 4
- ◇ A J 6
- ♣ J

EAST
- ♠ K Q 10 4 3
- ♡ 10 9 8 7 2
- ◇ 7
- ♣ 9 7

SOUTH
- ♠ - - -
- ♡ A J 3
- ◇ K 10 5 3 2
- ♣ K Q 8 6 5

WEST	NORTH	EAST	SOUTH
1♡	Pass	4♡ (1)	4NT (2)
Dble (3)	5♣ (4)	Pass	Pass
Dble (5)	Pass	Pass	Pass

Bidding : (1) Standard gambling game raise (see page 15).
(2) In a competitive auction, 4NT as Blackwood is not as valuable as showing a 2-suiter. Locating the best game is more important than aces when nothing is yet known about either partner's hand. 4NT must show a good hand at this vulnerability, but knowing from the auction that North is very short in hearts, South is very confident of locating a fit in one of the minors.
(3) Looking for penalties, mainly because of the diamonds.
(4) Choosing the longer minor suit naturally. With equal length and strength, North could pass and let South make the choice.
(5) This is a common failing. Looking at 16 HCP and having heard partner bid game, West hopes that 5♣ will fail. Yet if the vulnerable opponents are bidding game with so many points missing, they must have excellent shape as compensation. Points do not take tricks when the opponents have voids and singletons. A good guide when you are in doubt in such situations : *If you cannot tell who can make what, bid one more.* If West had bid 5♡, this could be defeated by 2 tricks if North leads a spade or by 1 trick if North does not lead a spade, but the defense still finds the spade ruff. However, if declarer can draw trumps without the defense finding the ruff, 5♡ will make. Any of these results is better than 5♣ doubled which is unbeatable.

Lead : ◇7. From a very weak hand, it is sensible to look for a ruff.

Correct play : ◇A and another diamond gives the defense its ruff, but declarer easily makes the rest.

CHAPTER 12

PRE-EMPTIVE OPENINGS AND OVERCALLS

The function of pre-emptive openings is to get in the first blow and make it tough for the opposition to gauge their combined assets because you have taken away their bidding space. Pre-emptive overcalls also aim to force the opponents to guess at the correct contract by robbing them of the space needed to describe their values. Experts fear pre-empts more than any other action because it forces them to guess and they may well go wrong because they lack the information to make an informed judgment. When forced to guess, players may end in the wrong suit, may play in a suit when they should be in no-trumps, play in game when they should be in slam, double you for a small penalty when they could score more by bidding to their best contract. If your hand meets the requirements for a pre-empt, you should bid as high as the guidelines permit at your earliest opportunity. Pre-emptive action almost always occurs only on the first round of bidding and having made a pre-empt, the pre-emptor does *not* bid again unless forced by partner. Having made your pre-empt, let the opponents struggle to find their best fit. They will err often enough.

A pre-emptive opening is based on playing tricks rather than on points, but the hand should not be strong. The normal range is 6-10 HCP and a 7-card or longer suit, but in rare cases, a powerful 6-card suit may be suitable if the required number of tricks is present. There may be fewer than 6 points provided that the playing strength is correct, but only in rare situations should there be more than 10 HCP. If you hold a strong hand, there is less incentive to pre-empt since you may well have more strength than the opponents. The time to pre-empt is when you expect them to hold more points and possibly have a game or slam on. Furthermore, if you pre-empt when holding a strong hand, partner may play you for a weak hand and you may miss a slam. Also, *avoid pre-empting when you hold a side 4-card major.* There may be a better contract in the major suit.

WHEN MAY YOU PRE-EMPT WITH A STRONG HAND?

If slam prospects do not exist, you are permitted to pre-empt with a bid of $4\heartsuit$ or $4\spadesuit$ with a strong hand, up to about 15 HCP. One situation is when partner is a passed hand (as partner could not be expected to provide more than 3 tricks for you if partner could not open the bidding). Another situation is after the opponents have opened. It is highly unlikely that you can make a slam, given they have the values for an opening bid. However, when pre-empting with a strong hand, do not pre-empt just to the 3-level, since partner may pass and you may miss a game. With a good hand, either pre-empt to game at once or overcall at a cheaper level to see whether partner has any worthwhile values.

How to count your playing tricks: *In your long suit:* count the ace, king and queen as winners (if the queen is the only honor card in the suit, count it as a ½-trick), and every card beyond the 3rd card as a winner. *In your short suits:* Count the ace as a trick, count the king as a trick unless it is singleton and count the queen as a trick if it is supported by another honor in a 3-card suit. Count A-Q as 1½ tricks and K-Q as 1 trick.

THE RULE OF THREE AND TWO

When pre-empting, your playing tricks should be 3 less than your bid when not vulnerable and 2 less than your bid when vulnerable. The idea of the Rule of 3 and 2 is that if they double and partner produces no tricks at all, the cost will −500, down 3 doubled not vulnerable or down 2 doubled vulnerable. This will usually not be too bad since if partner has no tricks at all, they will often be able to make a slam, not just a game, and −500 is a bargain compared with your loss if they can make a slam. If you have a holding which includes a ½-trick, treat it as the next higher number if not vulnerable, but the lower number if vulnerable.

A pre-empt skips 2 levels or more in the bidding, but you should not pre-empt higher than game. If the Rule of 3 and 2 indicates you should open $5\heartsuit$ or $5\spadesuit$, choose to open only $4\heartsuit$ or $4\spadesuit$ — do not pre-empt beyond game. The pre-emptive suit openings are $3\clubsuit$, $3\diamondsuit$, $3\heartsuit$, $3\spadesuit$, $4\clubsuit$, $4\diamondsuit$, $4\heartsuit$, $4\spadesuit$, $5\clubsuit$ and $5\diamondsuit$.

OPENING $3\clubsuit/3\diamondsuit/3\heartsuit/3\spadesuit$ = 6 TRICKS NOT VULNERABLE, 7 TRICKS VULNERABLE.

OPENING $4\clubsuit/4\diamondsuit/4\heartsuit/4\spadesuit$ = 7 TRICKS NOT VULNERABLE, 8 TRICKS VULNERABLE.

OPENING $5\clubsuit$ OR $5\diamondsuit$ = 8 TRICKS NOT VULNERABLE, 9 TRICKS VULNERABLE.

In other words, given that you hold a long, strong suit and a weakish hand :

WITH 6 PLAYING TRICKS, OPEN 3 IF NOT VULNERABLE, PASS IF VULNERABLE.

WITH 7 PLAYING TRICKS, OPEN 4 IF NOT VULNERABLE, OPEN 3 IF VULNERABLE.

WITH 8 PLAYING TRICKS AND NOT VULNERABLE, OPEN 4 IF YOUR SUIT IS A MAJOR BUT OPEN 5 IF YOUR SUIT IS A MINOR. IF VULNERABLE, OPEN 4 IN EITHER CASE.

WITH 9 PLAYING TRICKS, OPEN 4 IF YOUR SUIT IS A MAJOR AND 5 IF IT IS A MINOR.

If not vulnerable against vulnerable opponents, you may shade your pre-emptive openings by a ½-trick.

PRE-EMPTIVE OVERCALLS

A pre-emptive overcall skips at least 2 levels of bidding. (1◇) : 3♡ is a pre-empt (you have skipped over 1♡ and 2♡), but (1◇) : 3♣ is not a pre-empt — in bridge jargon, it is a jump overcall. Still, a jump overcall may be a weak bid in the partnership methods — see Chapter 10 for weak jump overcalls. A pre-emptive overcall is not as efficient as a pre-emptive opening, since 3rd player has the advantage of knowing about the opening hand, but pre-emptive overcalls may still make it hard for the opponents to judge their combined values and if your hand is worth a pre-empt, do not lose your nerve. Pre-empt as high as you dare, following the Rule of 3 and 2 which applies to pre-emptive overcalls just as it applies to pre-emptive openings.

RESPONDING TO PARTNER'S PRE-EMPTIVE OPENING OR OVERCALL

1. Assess how many tricks your partner's bid has shown by deducting 3 if your side is not vulnerable or 2 if your side is vulnerable.

2. Add to this your own 'quick tricks' : Count the A, K or Q of partner's suit as 1 trick each. In other suits, count A-K as 2, A-Q as 1½, A as 1, K-Q as 1, and K as ½. If you have support for opener's suit, count an outside singleton as one trick and an outside void as 2 tricks, since opener will usually have some length, a doubleton at least, where you hold a shortage.

3. If the total is less than partner's bid or just enough for the contract, pass.

4. If the total is more than partner's bid, you should bid on to game (but if partner's bid is already a game, you would pass). If the total is 12 or more, bid on to a slam, provided that you are not missing 2 aces. If you are not sure, use Blackwood over partner's pre-empt to check on aces and, if relevant, kings.

5. Over an opening bid of 3♣ or 3◇, you may try 3NT with a strong balanced hand and at least 1 stopper in each of the outside suits.

6. Over other opening pre-empts, prefer to stick with partner's suit unless you have a strong hand and a long, powerful suit of your own. A change-of-suit in response to a pre-empt is forcing.

7. Do not 'rescue' partner from a pre-empt. With a weak hand, pass. Let partner suffer.

THE GAMBLING 3NT OPENING

The 3NT opening on a balanced hand of 25-27 points is not used by strong players because it occurs so rarely and there is little room for exploration after the bidding starts so high. It is better to open such powerful hands with a demand opening such as 2♣ (see Chapter 8) and follow up with a no-trump rebid.

As a result, the 3NT opening becomes available for pre-emptive purposes and one possibility is the Gambling 3NT Opening which shows a solid 7-card or longer minor (the suit must be A-K-Q-x-x-x-x or better) and no significant values outside the long suit. Partner is expected to pass with stoppers in the other suits and the theory is that the solid minor will provide 7 tricks while partner will provide at least 2 tricks and simultaneously prevent the opposition cashing a long suit.

It is important that opener does not hold any ace, king or Q-J-x outside the long suit, since this would provide a stopper of which partner would be unaware and partner would find it very difficult to gauge when to pass 3NT and when to run. If responder cannot provide 2 tricks or if responder has no stopper in one of the outside suits, responder will bid opener's minor at the 4-level, which opener must pass. If responder cannot tell which minor opener has, responder bids 4♣. If opener has clubs, opener passes, while if opener holds diamonds, opener bids 4◇ which responder can pass. If responder bids 4◇, and opener actually has clubs, opener will correct this to 5♣.

Responder may have the values to play in 5-of-opener's-minor rather than 3NT. If so, bid opener's minor suit at the 5-level or if unable to tell which minor opener has, bid 5♣. Opener will pass with clubs or correct to 5♢. Similarly, responder may have values for a slam and may bid opener's suit at the 6-level or 7-level. Opener will always pass if holding the suit bid or convert to the other minor if not.

THE GAMBLING 3NT OVERCALL

The Gambling 3NT is also used as an overcall, e.g. (1♡) : 3NT, but there is a significant difference. As the opponents have opened the bidding, the 3NT overcall not only contains a solid 7-card minor, but also has a stopper in the suit opened and one outside suit stopped. A typical hand for (1♠) : 3NT might look like this :

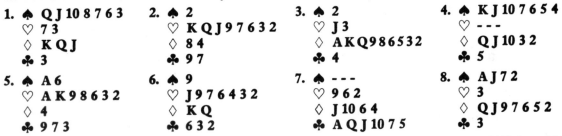

♠ K 7
♡ A
♢ A K Q 8 7 6 2
♣ 9 5 2

Thus, there is an expectancy of making 9 tricks on most occasions, particularly if the lead is the suit opened. Partner of the 3NT overcaller is expected not to run except in absolute desperation. If the opening bidder doubles the 3NT overcall, this requests partner to lead the suit opened despite the 3NT overcall.

EXERCISES

A. You are the dealer. What action do you take on these hands : (a) Not vulnerable?   (b) Vulnerable?

1. ♠ Q J 10 8 7 6 3	2. ♠ 2	3. ♠ 2	4. ♠ K J 10 7 6 5 4
♡ 7 3	♡ K Q J 9 7 6 3 2	♡ J 3	♡ - - -
♢ K Q J	♢ 8 4	♢ A K Q 9 8 6 5 3 2	♢ Q J 10 3 2
♣ 3	♣ 9 7	♣ 4	♣ 5

5. ♠ A 6	6. ♠ 9	7. ♠ - - -	8. ♠ A J 7 2
♡ A K 9 8 6 3 2	♡ J 9 7 6 4 3 2	♡ 9 6 2	♡ 3
♢ 4	♢ K Q	♢ J 10 6 4	♢ Q J 9 7 6 5 2
♣ 9 7 3	♣ 6 3 2	♣ A Q J 10 7 5	♣ 3

B. Partner opened 3♡, pass on your right. What action do you take : (a) Not vulnerable? (b) Vulnerable?

1. ♠ A J 9 5 2	2. ♠ A J 9 7 5 2	3. ♠ 2	4. ♠ A 7 2	5. ♠ A K 7 5 2
♡ 7	♡ - - -	♡ K 8 3	♡ 9 3	♡ 9
♢ A Q 10 6 4	♢ Q J 7	♢ A K 6 4 3	♢ K Q 8 6	♢ A K 9 3 2
♣ 6 2	♣ 9 7 3 2	♣ 10 9 5 4	♣ A 9 7 3	♣ 8 3

6. ♠ A K J 9 8 3	7. ♠ - - -	8. ♠ A	9. ♠ K Q J 9 8	10. ♠ A K Q 2
♡ 7	♡ K 8 7 3 2	♡ K J 6 2	♡ K 3	♡ - - -
♢ A Q J	♢ A K 9 8 6 2	♢ A K Q J	♢ K Q	♢ A K 8 3
♣ K 9 6	♣ K Q	♣ A 7 5 4	♣ K Q J 2	♣ Q J 7 4 2

PARTNERSHIP BIDDING : How should these hands be bid? West is the dealer and no one is vulnerable.

SET 25 — WEST	SET 25 — EAST	SET 26 — WEST	SET 26 — EAST
1. ♠ 7 3	1. ♠ A 9 6	1. ♠ 7 2	1. ♠ A K 3
♡ A Q J 7 6 4 3	♡ K 10 8 2	♡ 4 3	♡ K 10 8 2
♢ 9 2	♢ A K Q J 3	♢ 9 5	♢ Q 10 6 4
♣ 9 8	♣ A	♣ A K Q 8 6 4 3	♣ 7 5
2. ♠ 7	2. ♠ A Q 8 3	2. ♠ A K Q 2	2. ♠ 4
♡ 4 2	♡ K Q 10 3	♡ 8 6 4	♡ 9 3
♢ Q J 10 8 6 4 3	♢ K 7	♢ 8 5 3	♢ A K Q J 7 6 2
♣ K 8 3	♣ A J 9	♣ 9 8 3	♣ 7 6 4
3. ♠ 7 2	3. ♠ A K Q J 6 4 3	3. ♠ 7 3 2	3. ♠ 6
♡ 10 9 7 5 3	♡ 2	♡ 4	♡ A K Q 3
♢ K Q J	♢ 6 5 4	♢ 8 7	♢ K Q 6 4 2
♣ K 7 4	♣ Q 6	♣ A K Q 7 6 4 2	♣ 8 5 3
4. ♠ 7	4. ♠ A Q 3 2	4. ♠ 9 2	4. ♠ K 8
♡ 4	♡ A 8 6 5 3	♡ 4 3	♡ A Q 7 2
♢ 6 2	♢ 9	♢ A K Q 8 7 4 2	♢ 9 5 3
♣ A Q J 8 7 5 4 3 2	♣ K 10 6	♣ 6 4	♣ A K Q J

PLAY HANDS ON PRE-EMPTIVE BIDDING

Hand 45 : Pre-emptive opening — Card combination— Eliminating a loser — Card reading

Dealer North : Nil vulnerable

WEST	NORTH	EAST	SOUTH
	Pass	Pass	3♠ (1)
Pass (2)	Pass (3)	Pass (4)	

NORTH
- ♠ 9 8
- ♡ 6 5 3
- ◇ A 6 4 2
- ♣ A Q 7 4

WEST
- ♠ Q J 7
- ♡ J 10 9 8
- ◇ K 8 3
- ♣ K J 6

EAST
- ♠ 4
- ♡ A K Q
- ◇ J 10 9 5
- ♣ 10 8 5 3 2

SOUTH
- ♠ A K 10 6 5 3 2
- ♡ 7 4 2
- ◇ Q 7
- ♣ 9

Bidding : (1) Worth about 6 playing tricks not vulnerable. Not enough for a 4♠ pre-empt.

(2) Much too weak to bid, especially opposite a passed hand.

(3) Worth 2½ tricks in support of spades, not enough to raise. As a non-vulnerable pre-empt is 3 tricks short of the bid made, partner needs more than 3 tricks before bidding higher.

(4) Not suitable for any action. For competing over a pre-empt, see Chapter 16.

Lead : ♡J. Easy top of sequence.

Correct play : East should win with the ♡Q (a defender wins with the cheapest card possible) and cash the other top hearts, followed by a switch to the ◇ J, top of sequence. Declarer plays low and the jack is taken by dummy's ace. Declarer should tackle trumps and with 9 trumps missing Q and J, cashing the A and K is normal.

Only if left-hand opponent dropped the Q or J might this approach change. When trumps do not break, declarer is faced with 5 losers and to eliminate the diamond loser, declarer leads a club and finesses dummy's queen. When this holds, the ♣A allows the ◇ 7 to be discarded and 3♠ is just made.

Even if trumps had been 2-2, declarer should finesse the ♣Q and score an overtrick by eliminating the diamond loser. To make the overtrick would be vital at duplicate. Normally the club finesse when you hold just a singleton might be risky, but here East has shown up with A-K-Q in hearts and the ◇ J. East cannot hold the ♣K as well, for that would make 13 HCP : East passed and would have opened even with 12 HCP.

Hand 46 : Raising partner's pre-empt — Setting up a long suit in dummy

Dealer East : Nil vulnerable

WEST	NORTH	EAST	SOUTH
		3♠ (1)	Pass (2)
4♠ (3)	Pass	Pass	Pass

NORTH
- ♠ 4 2
- ♡ K Q 10
- ◇ K 10 8 2
- ♣ Q 7 6 3

WEST
- ♠ K 10 8
- ♡ A J 8 4 3
- ◇ A 5 4
- ♣ J 9

EAST
- ♠ A Q J 9 7 6 5
- ♡ 7
- ◇ 7 6 3
- ♣ 10 4

SOUTH
- ♠ 3
- ♡ 9 6 5 2
- ◇ Q J 9
- ♣ A K 8 5 2

Bidding : (1) 6 playing tricks. First-in-hand is the best time to pre-empt, when the opponents know least about each other's hand.

(2) Much too weak to enter the bidding at the 4-level.

(3) There are 3 sure tricks in the king of trumps and 2 aces. You need more than 3 tricks to raise a non-vulnerable pre-empt, but West has potential for a 4th trick, either via a club ruff if East has 3 or more clubs or by utilising the heart suit for extra tricks.

Lead : ♣K. An A-K suit is more attractive than a near sequence.

Correct play : South cashes ♣K and ♣A and should then switch to the ◇ Q. Declarer wins the ◇ A and needs to eliminate at least 1 diamond loser. Counting winners, East has 7 spades and 2 aces. The extra trick can come only from hearts, but it is vital to start setting the hearts up before drawing trumps, because dummy's trumps are needed as entries. The correct order is : win the ◇ A; cash the ♡ A; ruff a low heart; play a trump to dummy's 8 (all of dummy's trumps are winners); ruff a low heart. As it happens, the ♡K and ♡Q have now fallen, so dummy's ♡J is high. Cross to dummy's ♠ 10 and cash the ♡J and the 5th heart, discarding both diamonds and making an overtrick. If North held ♡ K-Q-x-x, declarer would have played ♡A; heart ruff; spade to the 8; heart ruff; spade to the 10; heart ruff; spade to the king and the last heart in dummy would be high, allowing 1 diamond to be discarded and making just 10 tricks.

Hand 47 : Responding to partner's pre-empt — Play at trick 1 — Change of plan

Dealer South : East-West vulnerable

NORTH
♠ A 8 3
♡ A J 10
♢ A Q J 10
♣ 8 5 3

WEST
♠ J 9
♡ Q 7 5 4 3
♢ K 4 2
♣ A 9 6

EAST
♠ K 10 6 5 4 2
♡ K 9 2
♢ 8 7 6 5
♣ - - -

SOUTH
♠ Q 7
♡ 8 6
♢ 9 3
♣ K Q J 10 7 4 2

WEST	NORTH	EAST	SOUTH
			3♣ (1)
Pass	3NT (2)	All pass	

Bidding : (1) Worth only 3♣. One of the drawbacks of opening 4-minor is that you bypass 3NT which might be the best spot. (2) With a strong balanced hand and all outside suits stopped, 3NT is a better shot than 5-minor.

Lead : ♠5. It is normal to lead the long suit.

Correct play : Declarer should play dummy's ♠Q at trick 1. With Q-x opposite A-x-x or K-x-x, it is best to rise with dummy's queen. You have 1 spade trick already; playing the queen is the best chance for a 2nd spade trick. Second-hand-low is a rule for defenders but not for declarer who can see the total values of the two hands. After the ♠Q wins, declarer should lead a top club, intending to set up the club suit. If clubs were 2-1, declarer would force out the ace and utilise dummy's 6 club winners. If West takes the ♣A early, declarer can likewise use the club winners.

However, West should duck the 1st club and when East shows out, marking declarer also with 3 clubs, West should plan not to take the ♣A until the 3rd round of clubs. If declarer does continue clubs and West wins the 3rd round, West would return a spade and dummy's clubs are useless as dummy has no entry. Declarer can give up a diamond but can be held to 8 tricks. After the 1st club is ducked and East shows out, declarer should realise that the club suit can be neutralised. Declarer should switch plans: win ♠Q; win ♣K; now take the diamond finesse, which wins; play another club to dummy which West must still duck; repeat the diamond finesse; cash the ♢A and when the ♢K drops, the last diamond is high. North wins 2 spades, 1 heart, 4 diamonds and 2 clubs, just making the contract.

Hand 48 : Responding to partner's pre-empt — Setting up a long suit rather than taking a finesse

Dealer West : North-South vulnerable

NORTH
♠ A Q 9
♡ 6 3
♢ 10 9 8
♣ J 9 7 5 3

WEST
♠ 2
♡ K Q J 9 8 7 4
♢ 6 5 4
♣ 8 4

EAST
♠ 8 7 6 5 4
♡ A 2
♢ A K J 2
♣ A K

SOUTH
♠ K J 10 3
♡ 10 5
♢ Q 7 3
♣ Q 10 6 2

WEST	NORTH	EAST	SOUTH
3♡	Pass	6♡ (1)	All pass

Bidding : (1) West should have strong hearts and 6 tricks, and East can see 5 certain winners, plus potential for an extra trick, making slam a reasonable chance. The extra trick could come from a club ruff if West started with 3 clubs, from finessing the ♢J or by utilising the spade suit. If slam is better than 50%, it is worth bidding. The ♢J finesse on its own is a 50% chance, so that the other chances justify trying for the slam. The spade suit is a risk, but partner might be short in spades (partner is usually short where you are long), or may have a spade winner or may be able to discard spade losers if the opponents do not lead a spade.

Lead : ♢10. Choose the sequence.

Correct play : The ♢10 lead makes it less likely that North has the ♢Q. Declarer should spurn the diamond finesse and aim to set up the spade suit: win ♢A (South signals encouragement with the ♢7); lead a spade; North will probably win and play a 2nd diamond; win the ♢K; ruff a spade; cash ♡K and lead a heart to dummy's ace; ruff a spade; club to the king and ruff another spade. Dummy's remaining spade is now high. Cross to the ♣A and play the spade winner, discarding the diamond loser. It is vital to start the spade suit early, before drawing trumps. All of dummy's entries, including the ♡A, are vital. You need to be able to cross to dummy 4 times, 3 times to ruff the spades and once to cash the 5th spade. When setting up a long suit, use the trump entries first and keep the entries in the side suits for later. It is vital that trumps are drawn before you attempt to cash an established winner.

CHAPTER 13

TAKEOUT DOUBLES (1)

If the opponents have opened the bidding and you have a strong hand, you will have a natural desire to enter the bidding. Yet if you lack a long, strong suit to overcall and the hand is not suitable for a 1NT overcall, you should pass even with 13 HCP or more unless your hand meets *all* the requirements for a takeout double. Two basic types of doubles are commonly used: The Penalty Double *which asks partner to pass* (and aims to collect large penalties by defeating the opponents' contract) and the Takeout Double *which asks partner to bid* (and aims to find a the best contract for your side). As the message of these two doubles is opposite, it is clearly vital to know when partner's double is for takeout and when it is for penalties.

WHEN IS A DOUBLE FOR TAKEOUT?

In standard methods, a double is for *penalties* if:

(a) It is a double of a no-trump bid, *or*

(b) It is a double at the 3-level or higher, *or*

(c) It is a double after partner has made a bid.

Some partnerships change these conditions, but unless you and your partner have some specific agreement to the contrary, a double in any of the above situations is intended as a penalty double.

Based on the above, **a double is for takeout if it is a double of a suit bid at the 1-level or the 2-level and partner has not made a bid yet.** However, in the modern style, most partnerships have expanded the range of the takeout double to include the following situations:

(a) Doubles of a suit at the 1-level or 2-level if partner has not yet bid. The doubler may have bid previously.

(b) A double of a 3-opening is generally played for takeout at duplicate.

(c) A double of a raise to the 3-level, e.g. (1◇): Pass: (3◇): Double, is usually played for takeout.

(d) A double of a 1NT or 2NT opening is played *for penalties*, but most duplicate players play that a double of a 1NT response is for takout. The double is for takeout of the suit opened. (1♠): Pass: (1NT): Double, for example, is played as a takeout double of 1♠ and is equivalent to (1♠): Double.

(e) A double of a suit overcall at the 1-level or 2-level, e.g. 1♠: (2◇): Double, is played *for takeout* by partnerships using negative doubles (see Chapters 30 and 31), while according to the standard rules such a double would be for penalties since partner has already bid. If the partnership has not stipulated that negative doubles are to be used, doubles of an overcall would be for penalties.

(f) Many partnerships have extended the concept of negative doubles to all doubles of suit bids at the 1-level or 2-level. Although not yet standard, such doubles are becoming more and more popular at duplicate since they are so valuable in competitive auctions. Do not adopt such doubles without discussion with your partner, but if these doubles are used, then all doubles whether by opener, responder or an overcaller, of a suit bid at the 1-level or 2-level are for takeout *unless specifically stated to be for penalties.*

A takeout double is usually made at first opportunity, but this need not be so. It is certainly possible to open the bidding and make a takeout double on the 2nd round or to make an overcall initially and follow with a takeout double on the next round, provided that the above conditions for a takeout double are met.

WHAT DOES A TAKEOUT DOUBLE SHOW?

Partner of the doubler can expect the doubler to hold:

● **High card values equivalent to at least an opening bid, generally 12 HCP or more,** *and*

● **Support (4 cards) or tolerance (3 cards) for any unbid suit.**

Where the doubler is a passed hand, the strength will be 9-11 HCP plus support for the unbid suits.

Where the opponents have bid 2 suits, a double promises 4-card or better support for the unbid suits.

WHAT DO YOU NEED TO MAKE A TAKEOUT DOUBLE?

A takeout double has point count requirements *and* shape requirements. The more strength, the more you may depart from the shape requirements, but if minimum, the shape factors are vital. In valuing your hand for a takeout double, count HCP and add 3 for a void, 2 for a singleton and 1 for a doubleton *in the opposition's suit(s)*. This is one of the few areas where counting shortages for your initial action is useful, but because it is highly likely that you will locate a trump fit, counting shortage potential is reasonable. If on this basis your hand has 13 points or more, you have the minimum needed for a double. The correct shape may still be necessary.

DOUBLING ON HANDS IN THE 12-15 ZONE

To double with the minimum high card content, the hand shape should contain :

(a) A void, a singleton or at most a doubleton in the enemy suit, *and*

(b) Not less than *three* cards in any unbid major.

If your hand does not meet these requirements, *do not double* with just 12-15 HCP. Either overcall in a strong 5-card suit, upgrade a balanced 15-count to a 1NT overcall or, if neither of these are available, **PASS**. There is no obligation to bid after they have opened the bidding. For example, suppose you have picked up :

♠ **Q 6**   If right-hand opponent opens 1◇, you should PASS despite your 14 points, because you
♡ **A 9 7 5**   do not have support or tolerance for spades. If they opened 1♣ or 1♡, you should PASS for
◇ **A K 7**   the same reason. Only if their opening bid was 1♠ should you double. You should open the
♣ **J 8 7 4**   bidding with 12 HCP or more, but there is no obligation to enter the bidding with 12-15 HCP
after they have opened the bidding if your hand is unsuitable for a double and unsuitable for an overcall. There is no such concept as "opening for your side". On many hands it is better to defend than to play as declarer, particularly balanced hands and those hands which have length and strength in the enemy suit(s).

WHEN TO DOUBLE & WHEN TO OVERCALL IN THE 12-15 ZONE

Just because you have enough points to double does not mean you must double. A suit overcall can be made on hands in the 8-15 points zone (1-level overcall) or 10-15 points zone (2-level overcall), so that there is an overlap in the 12-15 range between doubles and overcalls.

If they have opened with a minor suit and you are in the 12-15 zone :

● With equal length in the majors (4-4 or 5-5), Double.

● With almost equal length in the majors, no more than 1 card difference, (4-3 or 5-4 or 6-5), Double.

● With greater difference in length, 2 cards difference or more (5-3 or 6-4), overcall in the long major if that suit is strong enough — if it meets the Suit Quality Test — but double if the long major is weak.

If they have opened with a major suit and you are in the 12-15 zone : Overcall with a strong 5-card or longer holding in the other major — Overcall with a strong 5-card or longer holding in a minor *and* 3 cards or fewer in the other major — Double with a strong 5-card minor *and* 4 cards in the other major.

DOUBLING ON HANDS IN THE 16-18 ZONE

Do not double if your hand fits a 1NT overcall. The balanced 16-18 point hand with their suit stopped is best described in one bid by 1NT (see Chapter 9). However, with 16-18 balanced but no stopper in their suit, you may double, but be prepared to pass any minimum reply from partner. With no stopper in their suit, you will not be able to bid no-trumps later unless partner bids no-trumps first and thus indicates a stopper in their suit.

With 16-18 points, not balanced, and a 2-suiter or 3-suiter, you may double, but if partner bids a suit for which you do not have tolerance, remove this to a long suit of your own. Pairs who use weak jump overcalls or intermediate jump overcalls utilise the takeout double also for 1-suited overcall-type hands of 16 HCP or more. After a weak reply to a double, the doubler shows extra strength by bidding again, so that the 16-up overcall is shown by doubling and then changing suit, which confirms 16 points or more (by doubling and bidding again) and a 5-card or longer suit (by doubling and changing suit). For example :

WEST	NORTH	EAST	SOUTH	
1♡	**Double**	Pass	2◇	North is showing 5 or more spades and 16 points at least. Double followed by a new suit = 5-card suit or longer,
Pass	**2♠** . . .			16 points or more, and no support for partner's suit. With

support and more than 1 trick, South should raise to 3♠ and with 2 tricks, South should raise to 4♠.

DOUBLING ON HANDS IN THE 19-21 ZONE

With 19 HCP or more, you should start with a double and then :

1. If your hand is balanced and you have a stopper in their suit, bid no-trumps at the cheapest available level if unable to support a major suit bid by partner in reply to your double. For example, suppose you hold :

♠ Q 5 4   If your right-hand opponent has opened 1♦, you should start by doubling and then :
♡ A K J 7   If partner replies 1♡, you should raise this to 3♡.
♦ A Q   If partner replies 1♠, you should rebid 1NT.
♣ K J 4 2   If partner replies 2♣, you should rebid 2NT.

2. If your hand is not balanced, make a jump rebid, either by raising partner's suit with a jump or making a jump-rebid in your own long suit. Suppose you hold :

♠ A Q J 6 5   If your right-hand opponent has opened 1♦, you should double initially and then :
♡ K Q 5 2   If partner replies 1♡, you should give a jump-raise to 3♡.
♦ 3 2   If partner replies 2♣, jump-rebid your long suit to 3♠.
♣ A K   If partner happens to reply 1♠, take a shot at 4♠. The jump to game with a 4-loser hand is used only when you hold exceptional support for partner's suit.

ACTION ON HANDS WITH 22 POINTS OR MORE

With 22-24 points balanced, double first and then jump in no-trumps (a very rare situation). With 22 points or more and unbalanced shape, or with fewer points but no more than 3 losers, in other words, with a hand worth a 2♣ demand opening, the standard approach is to start by cue bidding the enemy suit, e.g. (1♡): 2♡ ... This shows a huge hand worth game on its own. However, if the partnership uses the immediate cue bid for some other convention, then double first and bid the enemy suit on the next round is used as a force to game, e.g. (1♡) : Double : (Pass) : 2♣, (Pass) : 2♡ ... is artificial and forcing to game.

RESPONDING TO PARTNER'S TAKEOUT DOUBLE

Since the doubler can be expected to have support or tolerance for any unbid major, the doubler's partner, when responding in a major, should count HCP plus 5/3/1 shortage points. If the doubler does not have tolerance for the suit chosen, the doubler will be very strong and will bid again to remove an unsuitable reply. If holding a decent 5-card minor, also use the 5/3/1 shortage count when valuing your hand and deciding at which level to show your suit. The doubler will either have tolerance for your suit or will have a strong hand with which further action can be taken.

GENERAL APPROACH WHEN REPLYING TO PARTNER'S DOUBLE

Responder holds	Responder's action if 3rd player passes
0-5 points	Bid a suit — No other choice.
6-9 points	Bid a suit *or* Bid 1NT.
10-12 points	Jump bid a suit *or* Bid 2NT.
13 points or more	Bid game in a major suit *or* Bid 3NT *or* Bid the enemy suit to force to game.

STRATEGY WHEN REPLYING TO THE DOUBLE WITH 0-5 POINTS

For practical purposes, you *must* reply to partner's takeout double when you hold 0-5 points and right-hand opponent passes. (Perhaps once in a lifetime you might pass a takeout double for penalties with 0-5 points. A long and powerful holding in their suit, such as Q-J-10-x-x-x-x, would be acceptable.) *The only reply permitted with 0-5 points is a suit bid. You may not bid 1NT with such a weak hand.*

When you have a choice of suits to bid :

● With a major and a minor, always choose the major even if the minor is longer or better or both.

● With 2 majors or 2 minors, bid the longer. With 5-5 in the suits, bid the higher-ranking suit, and with 4-4 in the suits, bid the cheaper suit.

● If your only 4-card or longer suit is the opposition suit, bid your cheapest 3-card suit. Do not bid a 3-card suit if you hold a 4-card or longer suit elsewhere that you could bid (excluding their suit, of course).

Replying to partner's double with 6-9 points and 10-12 points is covered in Chapters 14 and 15 respectively.

STRATEGY WITH 0-5 POINTS WHEN THIRD PLAYER DOES NOT PASS THE DOUBLE

(A) THIRD PLAYER REDOUBLES (e.g. 1♠ : Double : Redouble : ?)

Over the redouble, take the same action as though 3rd player had passed. The bidding is no higher, the redoubler has not robbed you of any bidding space and so your task in replying to the double is no tougher. When it is said that your obligation to reply to the double ceases if 3rd player bids, this does not include a redouble.

One of the reasons you should act over the redouble is that the doubler is usually unsure of the best spot (that is why the double was chosen, to ask you for your best suit) and if you pass it back to the doubler, the doubler may not have a clearcut choice or even an easy choice. You take the pressure off partner by making your normal reply. Another important reason is that with the redouble showing 10 HCP or more, your side is in considerable jeopardy and a penalty double is quite feasible. To bid immediately over the double is a show of confidence (even if you feel anything but confident) and the opponents may think twice about doubling a confident bidder. However, if you pass, you are advertising grave weakness and the opponents will be only too pleased to double you or partner now wherever you run.

Bidding over the redouble is a psychologically sound show of strength, passing over the redouble gives away your abject weakness. Partner will not be misled by your action. With an opening bid, a takeout double and a redouble, how much can there be left for you?

(B) THIRD PLAYER BIDS A NEW SUIT OR RAISES OPENER

Now you should pass with all hands in the 0-5 range. To bid over intervention promises 6 points or more. However, partner may take further action, including another double, and you may be required to bid later.

SOUTH		1. WEST	NORTH	EAST	SOUTH		2. WEST	NORTH	EAST	SOUTH
♠ 7 2		1♠	Double	Pass	?		1♠	Double	Rdble	?
♡ Q 8 6 4										
◊ 9 4 3 2		3. WEST	NORTH	EAST	SOUTH		4. WEST	NORTH	EAST	SOUTH
♣ 7 6 2		1♠	Double	2♣	?		1♠	Double	2♠	?

In auctions 1 and 2, South should bid 2♡ but in 3 and 4, South should pass. In 4, the bidding might continue:

WEST	NORTH	EAST	SOUTH	
1♠	Double	2♠	Pass	North's 2nd double is still for takeout (double of a suit
Pass	Double	Pass	?	at the 2-level when partner has not bid) and South is obliged

to reply. South should bid 3♡ (prefer a major to a minor).

FURTHER ACTION BY THE DOUBLER AFTER A MINIMUM SUIT REPLY

12-15 points, 6-7 losers	:	Pass. Do not bid again with a minimum double after a weak reply.
16-18 points, 5 losers	:	Bid again. Raise partner's suit or bid your own 5-card or longer suit.
19 points up, 4 losers	:	Make a jump rebid. Jump raise partner's suit or jump bid your own long suit.
19-21 points, balanced	:	Bid no-trumps at cheapest level unless able to jump raise partner's major suit.
22-24 points, balanced	:	Jump rebid in no-trumps unless able to raise partner's major suit to game.

Because the doubler is expected to pass any weak suit reply with a minimum double, the doubler has to be prepared for any reply. If doubling with minimum points, the doubler must have support or tolerance for any suit partner might bid. To double and bid again shows a strong doubling hand, at least 16 points or more.

FURTHER ACTION BY THE DOUBLER'S PARTNER

If the doubler raised your suit reply, you can bid again with prospects for 2 tricks. By bidding again, the doubler indicates a hand of about 5 losers. If you have 2 winners, that will reduce the losers to 3, enough for game in a major. Similarly if the doubler jump-raised your suit, e.g. (1♣) : Double : (Pass) : 1♡, (Pass) : 3♡, you should bid on with 1 sure winner. The doubler's jump indicates a 4-loser hand, 1 trick short of game, and if you have a winner, that should be enough to produce game in a major. With a minor, you would need a little bit more. If the doubler did not have 4 losers or the equivalent, the doubler should not be bidding for 9 tricks opposite a hand which could be worthless. If 1 trick is not enough for game, the doubler should not follow up with a jump-rebid. That is why with a balanced hand of 19-21 points, the doubler rebids no-trumps at the cheapest level and not with a jump rebid. A balanced hand has too many losers and makes few tricks opposite a worthless or almost worthless hand. Balanced hands need the full point count quota for game.

EXERCISES

A. Right-hand opponent opened 1◇. What action do you take on each of these hands?

1. ♠ K862	2. ♠ AJ74	3. ♠ AJ7	4. ♠ A72	5. ♠ A872
♡ AQ73	♡ AQ983	♡ AQ983	♡ J2	♡ Q6
◇ 4	◇ 7	◇ 7	◇ AK862	◇ AK94
♣ KJ73	♣ Q72	♣ Q752	♣ Q97	♣ KJ8

B. Partner doubled left-hand opponent's 1◇ opening. Right-hand opponent passed. Your action on these hands?

1. ♠ 9543	2. ♠ 98732	3. ♠ 8742	4. ♠ J872	5. ♠ 652
♡ 83	♡ K952	♡ 83	♡ J872	♡ 963
◇ 10642	◇ 64	◇ 64	◇ Q8	◇ A43
♣ 973	♣ 53	♣ K8643	♣ 752	♣ 9853

6. ♠ 742	7. ♠ 87532	8. ♠ J32	9. ♠ 872	10. ♠ 742
♡ 973	♡ J6542	♡ 2	♡ J2	♡ 63
◇ Q853	◇ 97	◇ 875432	◇ QJ62	◇ AJ108
♣ 652	♣ 6	♣ J75	♣ 8532	♣ 9742

C. You doubled their 1◇ opening and partner replied 1♠. The opener passes. Your next action on these hands?

1. ♠ KQ95	2. ♠ KQ84	3. ♠ 3	4. ♠ AQ72	5. ♠ AK3
♡ A873	♡ AK76	♡ AKJ93	♡ KQJ2	♡ AQJ2
◇ J4	◇ 3	◇ AK6	◇ 2	◇ 64
♣ KJ7	♣ AQJ3	♣ AQ95	♣ AJ52	♣ J873

PARTNERSHIP BIDDING : How should the following hands be bid? South is the dealer on all hands and there is no North-South bidding other than indicated.

SET 27 — WEST	SET 27 — EAST	SET 28 — WEST	SET 28 — EAST
1. South opens 1◇.	**1. South opens 1◇.**	**1. South opens 1◇.**	**1. South opens 1◇.**
♠ AKJ8	♠ 64	♠ AJ43	♠ 82
♡ AJ5	♡ Q7432	♡ KQ72	♡ J983
◇ Q8	◇ 973	◇ A3	◇ 862
♣ 8743	♣ 652	♣ K72	♣ QJ54
2. North opens 1♣.	**2. North opens 1♣.**	**2. North opens 1♡.**	**2. North opens 1♡.**
♠ J732	♠ KQ64	♠ 8742	♠ KQJ5
♡ 83	♡ A972	♡ J63	♡ 9
◇ Q9864	◇ A32	◇ 852	◇ AK7
♣ 73	♣ 84	♣ 984	♣ AK632
3. North opens 1♠.	**3. North opens 1♠.**	**3. South opens 1◇.**	**3. South opens 1◇.**
♠ 8532	♠ Q4	♠ AK7	♠ 9632
♡ 7643	♡ AJ98	♡ KQJ5	♡ A643
◇ 98	◇ KQ72	◇ 9	◇ 43
♣ 843	♣ A97	♣ AK632	♣ 854
4. South opens 1♡.	**4. South opens 1♡.**	**4. North opens 1♣.**	**4. North opens 1♣.**
♠ KQJ6	♠ 1082	♠ 7642	♠ AQ98
♡ 7	♡ 65432	♡ A2	♡ QJ973
◇ AK98	◇ 73	◇ 765	◇ AK
♣ QJ94	♣ K75	♣ 9842	♣ 73
5. South opens 1♠,	**5. South opens 1♠,**	**5. South opens 1◇,**	**5. South opens 1◇,**
North raises to 2♠.	**North raises to 2♠.**	**North responds 1♠.**	**North responds 1♠.**
♠ 863	♠ 72	♠ J87	♠ 63
♡ Q753	♡ AKJ4	♡ 62	♡ AKJ5
◇ 72	◇ AQ83	◇ 9742	◇ A63
♣ J743	♣ K65	♣ 8643	♣ AQJ7

PLAY HANDS ON TAKEOUT DOUBLES (1)

Hand 49 : Bidding over a takeout double — Card combinations and card reading

Dealer North : Nil vulnerable

NORTH
- ♠ A 7 4 2
- ♡ A K 6
- ◇ A 10 7 3 2
- ♣ 6

WEST
- ♠ 5
- ♡ 8 5 4 3
- ◇ Q 8 4
- ♣ J 10 5 4 2

EAST
- ♠ Q 10 8
- ♡ Q J 10 9
- ◇ 6 5
- ♣ A K Q 9

SOUTH
- ♠ K J 9 6 3
- ♡ 7 2
- ◇ K J 9
- ♣ 8 7 3

WEST	NORTH	EAST	SOUTH
	1◇	Dble (1)	1♠ (2)
Pass (3)	3♠ (4)	Pass	4♠ (5)
Pass	Pass	Pass	

Bidding: (1) Worth a double. 14 HCP, short in the suit opened, support for hearts and clubs, tolerance for spades.
(2) The modern style is to make your normal bid over the double.
(3) If 3rd hand bids over the double, pass with 0-5 HCP.
(4) Too strong for just 2♠. Worth 18 points counting the singleton.
(5) With 8 points or more, accept opener's game invitation.

Lead : ♣4 or ♡5. The club holding is the stronger, so that the ♣4 is slightly preferable. A singleton trump lead is usually very poor and so is a suit bid by dummy, hence diamonds are out.

Correct play: East would win the club lead with the Q and switch to the ♡Q. After winning, declarer should play ♠A, followed by a spade to the jack when East follows with the 10. Normally with 9 cards missing the queen, the best chance is to cash the A and K and hope for the Q to drop, but here East's double implies tolerance for spades and declarer should play East to hold 3 spades, not 2. After the ♠J wins, draw the last trump and switch to diamonds. Here the best play is to cash the ◇K and then lead the jack, letting it run if West plays low (it cannot gain West to cover with the Q). When the J scores, diamonds are continued, and via two working finesses, declarer makes a lucky 12 tricks. The diamond finesse could have been taken the other way, cash the A and then finesse the J. However, because of the double, East is more likely to be shortish in diamonds and while East could have Q-x, the odds favour playing the non-doubler for a missing honour in the suit doubled. It is normally best to finesse for a Q on the 2nd round of the suit, so that the ◇K is cashed first, just in case the Q happens to be singleton.

Hand 50 : Responding to a double — Doubler's rebid — Card combination and card reading

Dealer East : North-South vulnerable

NORTH
- ♠ J 3
- ♡ K J 4 2
- ◇ 9 8 6 3
- ♣ 10 7 5

WEST
- ♠ 10 9 4
- ♡ 10 8 6
- ◇ Q J 10 2
- ♣ Q 9 2

EAST
- ♠ 8 7 6 2
- ♡ Q 9
- ◇ K 7 5
- ♣ A K J 6

SOUTH
- ♠ A K Q 5
- ♡ A 7 5 3
- ◇ A 4
- ♣ 8 4 3

WEST	NORTH	EAST	SOUTH
		1♣	Dble (1)
Pass	1♡ (2)	Pass	2♡ (3)
Pass	Pass (4)	Pass	

Bidding: (1) Not ideal for the double because of the shortage in diamonds, but with both majors and better than minimum values, it is better to double than to pass or overcall 1NT.
(2) Show the major, not the minor, in response to a double.
(3) Just OK to raise to 2♡. Worth 18 points for hearts.
(4) With 8 points or with 2 tricks, North would bid on.

Lead : ♣K. An A-K suit is very attractive.

Correct play: West encourages with the ♣9. East continues with the ♣A and a third club to West who then switches to the ◇Q. Declarer should win the ◇A and start on trumps. The normal play with 8 trumps missing the queen is to finesse the jack on the 2nd round. Here, however, the ♡Q is marked with East. Dummy has 17 HCP, you have 5 HCP, 18 HCP are missing. As West has shown up with the ♣Q, the ◇Q and presumably the ◇J because of the ◇Q lead, virtually all the remaining points will be with East who opened. Thus, East figures to hold the ♡Q (otherwise East would have opened with only 11 HCP, possible but unlikely) and the heart finesse is not going to work. Therefore, reject the normal heart finesse. Cash the ♡A and ♡K and when the queen drops, lucky you, draw the last trump and run the spades, playing the jack first. 9 tricks. If the ♡Q had not dropped, you would still make 8 tricks.

Hand 51 : Desperation response to a takeout double — Scrambling for tricks with a poor trump fit

Dealer South : East-West vulnerable

NORTH
♠ A 9 5
♡ A K J 9 3
◇ K 8 5 3
♣ Q

WEST
♠ 10 7 2
♡ 8 6 5 4 2
◇ 9 6
♣ K 4 3

EAST
♠ K Q J 8
♡ 7
◇ A Q 7 2
♣ A 9 8 6

SOUTH
♠ 6 4 3
♡ Q 10
◇ J 10 4
♣ J 10 7 5 2

WEST	NORTH	EAST	SOUTH
			Pass
Pass	1♡	Dble	Pass
1♠ (1)	2◇ (2)	2♠ (3)	Pass
Pass (4)	Pass (5)		

Bidding : (1) With 0-5 points and no 4-card suit other than the opposition's, bid your cheapest 3-card suit. 2♣ would be sensible because of the ♣ K, but the drawback is that if East raises, you are in *three* clubs, but if East raises spades, you can stop in *two*.
(2) Certainly worth a 2nd bid. Best to show your 2nd suit.
(3) Even over an intervening bid, the doubler's raise promises more than minimum values. It is a mild invitation for game, showing 16 points or more and about a 5-loser hand.
(4) Do not panic when raised. Pass and do your best.
(5) If partner cannot raise an effort when you have bid twice, do not persevere without about 19 points up or excellent shape.

Lead : ♡ K. An initial trump lead would also be very sensible.

Correct play: North should switch to ace and another trump. When dummy has ruffing potential but no long suit, a trump lead or trump shift is very attractive. Declarer could unblock dummy's ♠ J under the ace so that the next spade can be won by the 10. The entry is desirable but, as it happens, not critical, as the ♣ K is also an entry. Declarer should come to hand and finesse the ◇ Q, cash the ◇ A and ruff a diamond. Then, cross to the ♣ A and draw the trumps. If North switches to the ♣ Q at trick 2, win ♣ K, finesse ◇ Q, cash ◇ A, ruff a diamond, ruff a heart, ruff a diamond and then lead a trump or a club. When you are short of trumps, do not draw trumps early, but try to scramble ruffs in both hands.

Hand 52 : Doubler's strong rebid — Ruffing high when you can afford to

Dealer West : Both vulnerable

NORTH
♠ A J 6
♡ 9 8 3
◇ A 10
♣ K Q 6 4 2

WEST
♠ 8 5 4 3 2
♡ K 7 5
◇ 6 2
♣ J 5 3

EAST
♠ K
♡ A Q J 10 6 2
◇ K Q J 7
♣ A 7

SOUTH
♠ Q 10 9 7
♡ 4
◇ 9 8 5 4 3
♣ 10 9 8

WEST	NORTH	EAST	SOUTH
Pass	1♣	Dble (1)	Pass (2)
1♠	Pass (3)	3♡ (4)	Pass
4♡ (5)	Pass	Pass	Pass

Bidding : (1) Hands with only 4 losers are too strong for a simple overcall or a strong jump overcall, and should start by doubling.
(2) With too little to reply normally, do not bid over a double.
(3) Opener should not bid again in the direct seat with only minimum values.
(4) The 4-loser hand is shown by doubling first and a jump rebid later. 3♡ shows 5 or more hearts, a huge hand worth 4 losers in hearts and no fit for spades. It is not forcing but partner should bid on with a sure trick or a likely trick.
(5) The ♡ K counts as a winner in this auction, as partner would be counting its absence as a loser. If the doubler can bid for 9 tricks opposite nothing, the king of trumps is worth one trick more.

Lead : ♣ 10. Partner's suit and a sequence.

Correct play: Declarer should win the ♣ A, cash the ♡ A and then lead the ◇ K. North wins and continues clubs. East should ruff the 3rd club high, just in case South is void, cash the ◇ Q and then ruff the ◇ 7 with dummy's ♡ K. When you can afford to, ruff high. A heart from dummy allows trumps to be drawn and East loses 1 spade, 1 diamond and 1 club. The traps to avoid are drawing 3 rounds of trumps (dummy will be without a trump to ruff the diamond), drawing 2 rounds of trumps (North can lead a 3rd trump when in with the ◇ A and again dummy has no trump to ruff the diamond loser), playing the ♡ K early (then North can overruff dummy on the 3rd diamond) or failing to ruff with the ♡ K (again North can overruff dummy).

CHAPTER 14

TAKEOUT DOUBLES (2)

STRATEGY WHEN REPLYING TO THE DOUBLE WITH 6-9 POINTS

With 6-9 points, you may reply with a suit bid at the cheapest level, but you may also reply with 1NT, which shows 6-9 points and a stopper in the opposition's suit. With a choice of actions, your priorities are:

● Major suit as first choice ● 1NT as second choice ● Minor suit as the last choice

A 1NT reply denies a 4-card major (other than in their suit, of course). A minor suit bid denies an available major and also denies the ability to reply 1NT (inadequate strength or no stopper or shape too unbalanced). Exceptionally, with 5+ trumps including 3 honors, you may pass and convert the takeout double to penalties.

With 6-9 points, you are strong enough to bid twice. You can bid quite safely up to the 2-level, and you may bid to the 3-level if necessary to compete against their 2-level contract. Thus, if the auction does become competitive, the doubler with a minimum double can let the bidding come to back to you, safe in the knowledge that with 6-9 points, you will not allow the opponents to buy the contract at the 2-level. The basic principle is *"Do not sell out at the 2-level if you have a trump fit or if they have a trump fit."*

CHOICE OF SUITS WHEN REPLYING WITH BOTH MAJORS OR BOTH MINORS

When replying to partner's takeout double and obliged to choose between two suits of the same rank: Bid your longer suit first and with 5-5, bid the higher-ranking first. However, with 6-9 points and 4-4 in suits of the same rank, it is better to bid the higher-ranking suit first in reply to a double. You may have to bid twice in a competitive auction and rebidding in the lower-ranking suit next time allows partner a cheaper preference.

STRATEGY WITH 6-9 POINTS WHEN 3RD PLAYER DOES NOT PASS THE DOUBLE

(A) 3RD PLAYER REDOUBLES (e.g. 1◊ : Double : Redouble : ?)

Over the redouble, take the same action as though 3rd player had passed. You will not be faced with this problem very often with 6-9 points, since if the opening, the double and the redouble are all genuine, you will rarely have 6 points. Still, the opposition's bidding is not always trustworthy and particularly when the opening bid was in 3rd seat, you can find yourself in this situation. The reasons for taking the same action as if 3rd player had passed are exactly the same as when you had 0-5 points (see Chapter 13, page 81). Do not be reluctant to reply 1NT over the redouble if that is your normal action. The advantage of 1NT is that it guarantees some values while a suit bid might be 0-5 points or 6-9 points. The 1NT reply gives the doubler a better picture of the values held and if you have enough to bid 1NT, the hand will often belong to you.

(B) 3RD PLAYER BIDS A NEW SUIT OR RAISES OPENER

With 6-9 points, you are strong to bid despite the interference. If your normal reply is still available, make that reply. Bidding over interference will show 6-9 points. You would pass with 0-5 points and you would jump with 10-12 (see Chapter 15). If 3rd player bids a major suit at the 1-level, your 1NT need have a stopper only in the suit opened: you can rely on the doubler for a stopper in the suit bid by 3rd player. If 3rd player changes suit, double for penalties with a strong 4-card holding in that suit. As the doubler should also have tolerance for that suit, your side figures to have more trumps than the bidder. Even players using negative doubles or competitive doubles treat (Suit Opening) : Double : (New Suit) : Double as a penalty double. It is vital to do so, since this is an area where it is common for 3rd player to psyche ("to psyche" = to make a bluff bid) and they will rob you of your suits if you cannot double for penalties. To expose a psyche, double for penalties and if they run back to opener's suit, you can then bid your suit at the appropriate level.

FURTHER ACTION BY THE DOUBLER AFTER A 1NT REPLY

The doubler's action over a minimum suit reply was covered in Chapter 13, page 81. Over 1NT, the doubler passes with a minimum hand with no 5-card suit. A suit bid at the 2-level will promise a 5-card suit but it is not forcing: Pass with a doubleton or with a minimum and 3-card support, but with a maximum and 3 trumps, raise to the 3-level. A raise to 2NT is invitational (17-18 points) while a jump to the 3-level in a suit is forcing and promises a 5-card suit. The 1NT bidder raises with 3-card support or bids 3NT with only a doubleton.

EXERCISES

A. The bidding has been (1 ◇) : Double : (Pass) : ? What do you reply to partner's double with these hands?

1. ♠ K 8 6 4	2. ♠ 8 4 3	3. ♠ 8 4 3	4. ♠ 8 2	5. ♠ K 8 7 2
♡ Q 7	♡ Q 7	♡ K Q	♡ 9 2	♡ K 9 4 2
◇ K 9 7 3	◇ K 9 7 3	◇ 7 6 4 3	◇ K Q J 10 8	◇ 7 3 2
♣ 8 4 3	♣ K 8 6 4	♣ K 8 6 4	♣ Q J 7 4	♣ Q 7

B. The bidding has been (1♠) : Double : (Pass) : ? What do you reply to partner's double with these hands?

1. ♠ 4 2	2. ♠ A J 6	3. ♠ A J 6	4. ♠ A J 6 2	5. ♠ 6 4 3
♡ Q J 6 4	♡ K 9 7 2	♡ 8 4 3 2	♡ 7 6	♡ 9 7
◇ J 3	◇ 8 4 3 2	◇ K 9 7 2	◇ K 9 7 2	◇ A 9 8 3
♣ K 8 7 3 2	♣ 7 5	♣ 7 5	♣ 8 4 3	♣ A 8 7 4

C. After (1♡) : Double : (2♡) : ? what action do you take on these hands in reply to the double?

1. ♠ K 7 6 4	2. ♠ Q J 7 3 2	3. ♠ A 6	4. ♠ 9 7 2	5. ♠ 9 8 7 2
♡ A 3	♡ 7 4 3	♡ 9 6 3	♡ 8 7 2	♡ 6 2
◇ 8 6 2	◇ 6 4	◇ J 7 6 4 3	◇ 8 6 2	◇ Q 8 6 4 3
♣ 9 6 4 3	♣ 8 3 2	♣ K 8 5	♣ A K 9 7	♣ K Q

D. You doubled 1 ◇ and partner responded 1NT. What is your rebid on each of these hands?

1. ♠ K Q 6 2	2. ♠ A J 7 2	3. ♠ A 9 4 2	4. ♠ A 7 3 2	5. ♠ A Q 8 7 2
♡ A Q 7 3	♡ A Q 4	♡ A K J	♡ A J 9 7 5	♡ K Q J 6
◇ 4	◇ Q 9 7	◇ 8 7 6	◇ 2	◇ A K
♣ K 9 7 3	♣ A K 3	♣ K Q 5	♣ K 9 7	♣ 4 3

PARTNERSHIP BIDDING : There is no North-South bidding other than indicated.

SET 29 — WEST	SET 29 — EAST	SET 30 — WEST	SET 30 — EAST
1. South opens 1 ◇.	**1. South opens 1 ◇.**	**1. North opens 1♠.**	**1. North opens 1♠.**
♠ A Q 9 2	♠ K 5	♠ K 9 6 2	♠ 10 3
♡ A 8 7 3	♡ J 6	♡ 7 3	♡ A J 8 4
◇ A 8	◇ 6 4 3 2	◇ A J 7 4	◇ K Q 9
♣ J 4 3	♣ K 8 7 5 2	♣ 7 4 2	♣ A 9 8 6
2. North opens 1♣.	**2. North opens 1♣.**	**2. South opens 1♣.**	**2. South opens 1♣.**
♠ K 7 4	♠ A Q 5 2	♠ K 6 5	♠ A 8 7 3
♡ A 8 3 2	♡ K Q 6 5	♡ A Q 7 2	♡ K 9 6 4
◇ 9 5	◇ A J 7 3	◇ A 7 5 4	◇ J 2
♣ J 9 3 2	♣ 6	♣ 9 6	♣ 7 4 2
3. South opens 1♠.	**3. South opens 1♠.**	**3. North opens 1♣.**	**3. North opens 1♣.**
♠ 7	♠ 8 6 4 3 2	♠ A 8 3 2	♠ K 6 5 4
♡ A J 9 7	♡ K Q 4 3	♡ K 6 5 2	♡ A Q 7
◇ K J 8 3	◇ 7 6	◇ 9 8	◇ A 7 5 4
♣ A 9 6 2	♣ Q 4	♣ 7 5 3	♣ 6 2
4. North opens 1♡.	**4. North opens 1♡.**	**4. South opens 1 ◇.**	**4. South opens 1 ◇.**
♠ K 8 2	♠ Q J 6 3	♠ A K 7	♠ 9 5 2
♡ 7 6 4 2	♡ 8	♡ K 9 4 2	♡ A Q 3
◇ Q J 4	◇ K 9 5 2	◇ 7 5 3	◇ K 6 4
♣ Q 8 2	♣ A K 7 5	♣ A K J	♣ 10 6 3 2
5. South opens 1 ◇,	**5. South opens 1 ◇,**	**5. North opens 1♠,**	**5. North opens 1♠,**
South rebids 2 ◇.	**South rebids 2 ◇.**	**North rebids 2♠.**	**North rebids 2♠.**
♠ K J 8 3	♠ 9 7 6 5 4	♠ 6 5 3	♠ 7 2
♡ K 9 7	♡ A Q 3 2	♡ 8 3	♡ K Q 9 7
◇ A 2	◇ 8 6	◇ K 7 5 2	◇ A 8 4 3
♣ Q 7 4 3	♣ 9 8	♣ A Q 6 4	♣ K J 2

PLAY HANDS ON TAKEOUT DOUBLES (2)

Hand 53 : NT response to a takeout double — Card reading for two-way finesse

Dealer North : North-South vulnerable

NORTH
♠ 6 4 2
♡ 8 6 2
♢ K 9 4
♣ K J 10 3

WEST
♠ 10 9 8 5
♡ 10 7 5 4 3
♢ 7 5
♣ 9 6

EAST
♠ K J 7
♡ A 9
♢ Q J 10 8 6
♣ Q 8 5

SOUTH
♠ A Q 3
♡ K Q J
♢ A 3 2
♣ A 7 4 2

WEST	NORTH	EAST	SOUTH
	Pass	1♢	Dble (1)
Pass	1NT (2)	Pass (3)	3NT (4)
Pass	Pass	Pass	

Bidding: (1) If too strong for a 1NT overcall, start by doubling. If no major fit is discovered, rebid in no-trumps. Double and no-trumps later is stronger than 1NT at once.
(2) 1NT is superior to 2♣. If the opening bid had been in a major, 2♣ would be correct.
(3) Unless you have freakish shape, a minimum opener should not bid again if partner is too weak to find a response.
(4) As the 1NT shows 6-9 points, South has enough to raise to game. Had North replied 2♣, which has a range of 0-9, South could not afford to bid 3NT opposite perhaps zero or 1 or 2 points. Over 2♣, South would rebid only 2NT.

Lead: ♢ Q. Even though the opponents have a stopper, a long suit headed by a sequence is your best start.

Correct play: Counting dummy's and declarer's points, only 13 HCP are missing, almost all of which must be with East for the opening bid. Knock out the ♡ A first. East wins the ♡ A and continues with the ♢ J. Now tackle the clubs. Without any clues about the location of the high cards, cashing A and then finessing the J is the best play, but here the ♣ Q figures to be with East, so cash the ♣ K can lead the ♣ J. If East covers, capture the Q; if East plays low, let the J run. Even if this lost to West (when East opened with just 11 HCP), West would be out of diamonds and East would have no entry because you carefully knocked out the ♡ A first. Using a club entry, you can finesse the ♠ Q and make 10 tricks (2 spades, 2 hearts, 2 diamonds, 4 clubs).

Hand 54 : Penalty pass of a takeout double — Opening lead after a penalty pass

Dealer East : Nil vulnerable

NORTH
♠ A 8 6 5
♡ 7 5 3 2
♢ 9
♣ 9 7 4 3

WEST
♠ K Q 9 3
♡ A Q 9 4
♢ 3
♣ A 10 6 2

EAST
♠ 10 7
♡ J 10
♢ K Q J 10 8 6
♣ J 8 5

SOUTH
♠ J 4 2
♡ K 8 6
♢ A 7 5 4 2
♣ K Q

WEST	NORTH	EAST	SOUTH
		Pass	1♢
Double	Pass (1)	Pass (2)	Pass (3)

Bidding: (1) Do not bid. Usually East will reply to the double and North-South are off the hook, while bidding on a weak misfit is asking for trouble. It is far riskier for North to bid than to pass.
(2) A very rare creature, the penalty pass of a takeout double at the 1-level. To justify passing out a 1-level double, your trumps should be better than declarer's, normally 5 or more trumps with at least 3 honors. This is logical since to beat 1♢, you have to take 7 tricks or more with diamonds as trumps and as partner is likely to be short in diamonds, your diamonds must be superb. You never pass a takeout double out of weakness or out of fear. Converting a takeout double to penalties by passing is always based on a deliberate intention of massacring their contract.
(3) If South had an escape suit, South would bid it, but West would double any escape attempt, including 1NT.

Lead: ♢ 3. When partner passes out your takeout double, a trump lead is expected. Since partner's trumps are better than declarer's, this helps partner draw declarer's trumps.

Correct play: South wins ♢ A and should lead ♣ K. West wins and should switch to ♠ K. South might duck this, hoping to keep the ♠ A in dummy as an entry for a club ruff. West continues with the ♠ Q and when East gets in, East draws South's trumps and switches to the ♡ J. Best defense can score 1 spade, 3 hearts, 5 diamonds and 1 club, defeating 1♢ doubled by 4 tricks. South does well to score a club ruff and go only 3 off. Only?

Hand 55 : Doubler's rebid after a 1NT response — Leading towards honors to set up a long suit

Dealer South : Both vulnerable

NORTH
♠ 10 5 2
♡ 10 9 6 2
◇ Q 9
♣ 10 9 5 4

WEST
♠ K Q 7 6 4
♡ A Q 8 3
◇ 7 2
♣ A K

EAST
♠ 9 3
♡ K 5 4
◇ A 10 5 3
♣ 8 7 3 2

SOUTH
♠ A J 8
♡ J 7
◇ K J 8 6 4
♣ Q J 6

WEST	NORTH	EAST	SOUTH
			1◇
Dble (1)	Pass (2)	1NT (3)	Pass (4)
3♠ (5)	Pass	3NT (6)	All pass

Bidding : (1) Much too strong for an overcall or even a strong jump overcall. With both majors and opening values, choose the double.
(2) Pass with a poor hand over the double.
(3) Shows 6-9 points, a stopper in diamonds and no 4-card major.
(4) Do not bid twice with a modest opening if partner cannot reply.
(5) Forcing, showing 5 spades. The 1NT denial of a 4-card major means a heart fit does not exist, but East could still hold 3 spades.
(6) Denies 3 spades.

Lead : ◇ 6. The long suit is normal, but the ♣ Q is a sensible choice, hoping to hit partner's suit, as declarer has indicated that the diamonds are stopped.

Correct play : On the ◇ 6 lead, North plays the Q and East should win the ace. With only 6 top winners, spades must be tackled.
Lead a spade towards dummy, playing the K if South plays low. Return to hand with a heart to the K and lead another spade, playing the Q if South plays low. Play a 3rd spade, drawing the remaining spades and setting up 2 spade winners. If South plays the ace earlier, declarer's task is simplified. The defense can cash 2 more diamonds, but the 10 is a stopper on the 4th round. With 15 HCP missing + North's ◇ Q at trick 1, virtually all the remaining points will be with South, including the ♠ A and the diamond honors. On the ♣ Q lead, win ♣ A, come to the ♡ K and lead a spade to the K, return to the ◇ A and lead another spade. If North hangs on to all the hearts ("keep length with dummy"), East scores 10 tricks : 4 spades, 3 hearts, 1 diamond and 2 clubs.

Hand 56 : Competitive bidding after a takeout double —Setting up a winner for a discard

Dealer West : Nil vulnerable

NORTH
♠ K 3
♡ A 8 7 3 2
◇ J 6 4
♣ K Q 4

WEST
♠ J 10 7 4 2
♡ Q J 10
◇ 10 9 2
♣ A 10

EAST
♠ A Q 9 8
♡ 9
◇ A K 7 5 3
♣ J 8 7

SOUTH
♠ 6 5
♡ K 6 5 4
◇ Q 8
♣ 9 6 5 3 2

WEST	NORTH	EAST	SOUTH
Pass	1♡	Dble (1)	2♡ (2)
2♠ (3)	Pass (4)	3♠ (5)	Pass
4♠ (6)	Pass	Pass	Pass

Bidding : (1) With 4 cards in the other major and opening values, double rather than overcall in a 5-card or longer minor.
(2) Worth 7 points in hearts because of the 2 doubletons.
(3) It would be very timid to pass. You are not obliged to bid over 2♡, but you are also not obliged to pass. 2♠ shows 4+ spades and 6-9 points. Had partner opened 1♠ you would support to the 2-level — your 2♠ bid here is a similar supporting bid.
(4) In the direct seat, do not bid again with a minimum hand. If East also passes 2♠, partner can compete to 3♡, following the precept "Do not sell out at the 2-level if a trump fit exists".
(5) 14 HCP plus 3 for the singleton justifies an invitation to game.
(6) With 9 points (1 for the doubleton), West is maximum and should accept the game invitation.

Lead : ♣ K. Spades are out. It is not attractive to lead from an ace-high suit without the king as well, even if partner has supported, so hearts are out (although the ♡ A lead here would not cost). Prefer clubs with the 2 honors to diamonds with only 1 honor.

Correct play : Win the ♣ K with the ace, lead the ♠ J for a finesse and draw trumps. A club to the 10 forces out the Q. You later discard a diamond loser on the ♣ J and play ◇ A, ◇ K and ruff a diamond, setting up dummy's diamonds. On ♡ A lead and another heart, ruff in dummy, play ◇ A, ◇ K and give up a diamond. Later, cross to the ♣ A, take the spade finesse, draw trumps and again dummy's diamonds have been set up. 11 tricks.

CHAPTER 15
TAKEOUT DOUBLES (3)

STRATEGY WHEN REPLYING TO THE DOUBLE WITH 10-12 POINTS

With 10-12 points, make a *jump reply* in a suit or in no-trumps. With a choice of actions, the priorities are:

- Major suit as first choice
- 2NT as second choice
- Minor suit as the last choice

With 10-12 points, including shortage points when bidding a major or a good 5-card minor, you have almost enough for a game, but not quite. To show how close you are, a jump bid is made to encourage the doubler to push on to game. The jump bid in a suit is not forcing and does not promise a 5-card suit. If you intend to bid a suit in reply to a double, any quality 4-card suit will do (and we have seen that in desperation you may have to bid a 3-card suit). Likewise, any 4-card suit is good enough for a jump response to a double.

A 2NT reply denies a 4-card major (other than in their suit, of course). A minor suit bid denies an available major and also denies the ability to reply 2NT (incorrect strength or no stopper or shape too unbalanced). Exceptionally, with 5+ trumps including 3 honors, you may pass and convert the takeout double to penalties.

A reply showing 10-12 points is a strong answer and if the doubler bids a new suit, that shows at least a 5-card suit and is forcing for 1 round. If the doubler bids the enemy suit over a jump in a suit, this asks for a stopper in their suit. With a stopper, bid no-trumps; with no stopper, make the most descriptive bid available.

CHOICE OF SUITS WHEN REPLYING WITH BOTH MAJORS OR BOTH MINORS

If you are worth a jump reply and have to choose between two suits of the same rank: Bid your longer suit first and with 5-5, bid the higher-ranking first. With 4-4 in the suits, it is standard to jump in the cheaper 4-card suit. (Some pairs use a bid of the enemy suit to cater for this problem and play that a cue bid of their suit is forcing to suit agreement. They bid the enemy suit and then, with a fit, raise the suit bid by the doubler but not to game, e.g. (1◇) : Double : (Pass) : 2◇, (Pass) : 2♠ : (Pass) : 3♠ . . . This raise is encouraging but not forcing.)

STRATEGY WITH 10-12 POINTS WHEN 3RD PLAYER DOES NOT PASS THE DOUBLE
(A) 3RD PLAYER REDOUBLES (e.g. 1◇ : Double : Redouble : ?)

Over the redouble, give a jump reply just as though 3rd player had passed. Someone does not have their bid, but you cannot be sure who is foxing, the opener or the redoubler. Trust partner to have the values for the double and give your normal reply. If you bid but do not jump, partner will place you with 0-9 points (see Chapters 13 and 14) and not with 10-12.

(B) 3RD PLAYER BIDS A NEW SUIT OR RAISES OPENER
1. The bidding is still at the 1-level, e.g. (1◇) : Double : (1♠) : ?

Give your normal reply with a jump, either in a suit or to 2NT. For a 2NT reply, it is more important to have a stopper in the suit opened (since the doubler is usually weak in the suit opened) than a stopper in the suit bid by 3rd player (since opener has support or tolerance for that suit). With a strong 4-card or better holding in the suit bid by 3rd player, double for penalties. There is a strong chance that 3rd player is psyching.

2. The bidding has reached the 2-level, e.g. (1◇) : Double : (2◇) : ?

With 10-12 points and a major, jump to 3♡ or 3♠. With a no-trump bid, reply 2NT which still shows 10-12 points. If your suit is a minor, it is not attractive to jump to the 4-level with only 10-12 points, firstly because you do not have the values for the 4-level and secondly, you thereby pass 3NT. Be prepared with 10-12 points over interference to bid just 3-minor if no other action is available. Jump to 4-minor only with a very good suit and no prospects for 3NT.

3. The bidding has reached the 3-level, e.g. (1◇) : Double : (3◇) : ?

The opponents will often try to make things difficult and their jump raise does make it much tougher for you. With 8-10 points, bid a suit at the 3-level and with 11-12, be prepared to make a mild overbid by jumping a major suit to the 4-level. With 10-12 and a no-trumps hand, including a double stopper, you may try 3NT. With a good minor suit and 10-12, it is better to compete with 4-minor than to pass.

FURTHER ACTION BY THE DOUBLER AFTER A JUMP REPLY

The jump is not forcing. Pass with the bare minimum of 12-13 points. With 14-15, invite game by raising partner's suit *or* change suit *or* raise 2NT to 3NT. With 16 or more, make sure you reach a game, either by bidding it *or* by changing suit (which is forcing over a strong reply) and bidding game next round. A change of suit by the doubler shows a 5-card or longer suit and partner should support with 3 trumps. It is logical that a major suit bid by the doubler over a NT reply or a minor suit reply shows a 5-card suit. Partner's reply to the double denied a 4-card major and so the doubler would not bother showing a 4-card major later.

ACTION ON HANDS OF 13 POINTS OR MORE IN REPLY TO THE DOUBLE

With such strength you have enough for game. See Chapters 25 and 26.

EXERCISES

A. The bidding has been (1 ◇) : Double : (Pass) : ? What do you reply to partner's double with these hands?

	1.	2.	3.	4.	5.
♠	K 8 6 4	8 4 3	A 4	8 2	8 6 5 2
♡	Q 7	Q 7 6 4 3	K 2	A 2	A K
◇	A J 7 3	A K 7	7 6 4 3	K Q J 8	7 3 2
♣	8 4 3	6 4	K 8 6 3 4	J 6 4 3 2	Q J 8 7

B. You doubled 1 ◇ and partner responded 2 ♡. What is your rebid on each of these hands?

	1.	2.	3.	4.	5.
♠	K Q 6 2	A J 7	A Q J 4 2	A Q 3 2	A 8 4 2
♡	A Q 7 3	K 8 4 2	A J	7 5	K 6 5 3
◇	4	9 7	8 7	A K J	K 2
♣	K 9 7 3	A 9 6 3	K Q 5 2	K Q 7 2	K 10 7

PARTNERSHIP BIDDING : There is no North-South bidding other than indicated.

SET 31 — WEST	SET 31 — EAST	SET 32 — WEST	SET 32 — EAST
1. South opens 1 ◇ .	**1. South opens 1 ◇ .**	**1. North opens 1 ♣ .**	**1. North opens 1 ♣ .**
♠ A Q 8 7	♠ K 9 6 4	♠ K 9 5	♠ A 8 3 2
♡ A 8 7 2	♡ 6 3	♡ Q J 9	♡ K 7 6 5
◇ J 9	◇ Q 3 2	◇ Q 4 3	◇ K J 5
♣ K 3 2	♣ A Q 9 8	♣ K 9 3 2	♣ Q 4
2. North opens 1 ◇ .	**2. North opens 1 ◇ .**	**2. South opens 1 ♠ .**	**2. South opens 1 ♠ .**
♠ K 2	♠ A J 6 5 4	♠ 4	♠ A 9 3 2
♡ 8 7 3 2	♡ A K 6 5	♡ A K 6 2	♡ Q 7
◇ A J 8	◇ 9 2	◇ A Q J 9	◇ 8 7 5
♣ Q 7 6 5	♣ K 3	♣ K 7 6 4	♣ A 9 5 3
3. South opens 1 ♡ .	**3. South opens 1 ♡ .**	**3. North opens 1 ◇ .**	**3. North opens 1 ◇ .**
♠ A 9 7 4	♠ K 8 5 3	♠ J 7 2	♠ K Q 8 6 3
♡ J 6	♡ Q 2	♡ K Q	♡ A 9 7 2
◇ A K 9	◇ Q 6 4 2	◇ 9 8 2	◇ 7 6
♣ J 7 5 3	♣ A 8 6	♣ K Q 6 4 3	♣ A J
4. North opens 1 ♣ .	**4. North opens 1 ♣ .**	**4. South opens 1 ♣ .**	**4. South opens 1 ♣ .**
♠ 5 4 3	♠ K Q 7 6	♠ A 8 6 5	♠ K 9 4
♡ J 5	♡ A K 3 2	♡ K 9 7 4 2	♡ A 6 5
◇ A K Q 4 3	◇ J 7 6	◇ A K 2	◇ J 8 6 3
♣ 7 6 2	♣ 4 3	♣ 8	♣ K 9 7
5. South opens 1 ♠ ,	**5. South opens 1 ♠ ,**	**5. North opens 1 ♡ ,**	**5. North opens 1 ♡ ,**
North raises to 2 ♠ .	**North raises to 2 ♠ .**	**South raises to 2 ♡ .**	**South raises to 2 ♡ .**
♠ 7	♠ J 3 2	♠ K 9 7 3	♠ A 8 6 4
♡ A 7 3 2	♡ K Q 5 4	♡ 7 4 3	♡ 6
◇ K Q 8 7 6	◇ 4	◇ A Q	◇ K 6 5 3
♣ A J 9	♣ K 7 5 3 2	♣ J 6 5 2	♣ A Q 8 4

PLAY HANDS ON TAKEOUT DOUBLES (3)

Hand 57 : Jump reply to a double — Leading towards honors — Ruffing finesse

Dealer North : East-West vulnerable

NORTH
- ♠ 9
- ♡ A J 10
- ◇ Q 10 7 2
- ♣ A K 9 8 7

WEST
- ♠ K 2
- ♡ 8 7 6 3 2
- ◇ K 3
- ♣ Q J 10 2

EAST
- ♠ A J 8 7
- ♡ K Q 5 4
- ◇ A 9 6 4
- ♣ 4

SOUTH
- ♠ Q 10 6 5 4 3
- ♡ 9
- ◇ J 8 5
- ♣ 6 5 3

WEST	NORTH	EAST	SOUTH
	1♣	Double	Pass (1)
2♡ (2)	Pass (3)	4♡ (4)	All pass

Bidding : (1) With a very weak hand, pass.

(2) Decide first what you intend to bid and then how high to bid it. West is clearly going to bid hearts rather than no-trumps and in hearts, the hand is worth 11 points, counting 1 for each doubleton. With 10-12 points, give a jump reply to the double. If South had unwisely bid 1♠, West should jump to 3♡.

(3) Do not bid again with a minimum opposite a passing partner.

(4) Worth 17 points in hearts, counting 3 for the singleton, and thus enough for game opposite 10-12 points.

Lead : ♣K. There is no urgency to lead the singleton spade. Firstly, you have trump control and can lead the singleton later if that seems best. Secondly, with such strong trumps, you are usually not looking for a ruff. After the ♣K, the switch to the ♠9 looks the best continuation.

Correct play: Declarer should win the spade lead in hand with the K and lead a trump towards dummy's K-Q. Without a solid sequence, lead towards honors rather than lead the honors themselves. If North plays low, play the K. When it wins, do not lead another heart from dummy. That will cost you an extra loser. Come to hand with the ◇ K and lead a 2nd heart from hand towards the Q. If North plays low and the Q wins, abandon trumps. If North takes the A, win any switch and draw North's last trump. Cross to hand via a spade ruff or diamond ruff and lead the ♣ Q. The ace is marked with North on the lead. If North plays low, let the Q run. If North covers with the A, ruff it and your remaining clubs are high.

Hand 58 : No-trumps reply to a takeout double — Card combinations and card reading

Dealer East : Both vulnerable

NORTH
- ♠ 7 4 3
- ♡ A 9 3 2
- ◇ A Q 8 4
- ♣ J 8

WEST
- ♠ 9 5
- ♡ 8 6 5
- ◇ J 7 6 3
- ♣ 9 6 4 3

EAST
- ♠ K 8 6 2
- ♡ K Q J 10 7
- ◇ 10
- ♣ A 10 5

SOUTH
- ♠ A Q J 10
- ♡ 4
- ◇ K 9 5 2
- ♣ K Q 7 2

WEST	NORTH	EAST	SOUTH
		1♡	Double
Pass	2NT (1)	Pass (2)	3NT (3)
Pass	Pass	Pass (4)	

Bidding: (1) The first decision is that you intend to bid no-trumps rather than diamonds. Next, with 11 points, you have enough for a jump reply. 2NT shows a balanced hand of 10-12 points with hearts covered and denies 4 spades.

(2) Not worth any action with minimum values. East is happy to defend NT with an excellent suit to lead and the ♣ A entry.

(3) With 15 HCP opposite 10-12, game is likely. If your side could hold 26 points, keep bidding. With no long suit and relying on partner to have a stopper in hearts, South's best bid is 3NT. 5◇ is a good contract but most pairs would reach 3NT.

(4) Tempting to double 3NT with 5 probable winners, but it is not sure that you have 4 heart winners (North might have A-9-x-x-x) and they might make their 9 tricks before you can make your 5.

Lead : ♡K. May all your leads be so easy.

Correct play: Win the ♡ A. There is no point holding up as East's opening bid must include the ♣ A which will always be an entry. Do not tackle clubs (instant demise). The missing points indicate the ♠ K is with East. Finesse the ♠ Q; play the ◇ K and a diamond to the A; repeat the spade finesse; as East showed out on the 2nd diamond, finesse the ◇ 8; repeat the spade finesse. Making 9 tricks via 4 spades, 1 heart and 4 diamonds. You must start on the spades while you still have diamond entries and you must note the fall of East's ◇ 10.

Hand 59 : Doubler's rebid after a jump response — Holdup and avoidance play

Dealer South : Nil vulnerable

NORTH
- ♠ K Q J
- ♡ 10 9 5 4
- ◇ K Q J 10 8
- ♣ 7

WEST
- ♠ 8 4
- ♡ A Q
- ◇ 9 4 3 2
- ♣ K 10 8 5 4

EAST
- ♠ A 10 9 3
- ♡ K J 8 2
- ◇ A 6
- ♣ A J 2

SOUTH
- ♠ 7 6 5 2
- ♡ 7 6 3
- ◇ 7 5
- ♣ Q 9 6 3

WEST	NORTH	EAST	SOUTH
			Pass
Pass	1◇	Dble (1)	Pass
3♣ (2)	Pass	3NT (3)	All pass

Bidding : (1) East has the values for a 1NT overcall, but with both majors and only 1 stopper in diamonds, double is a better initial action. If partner bids a major, you can raise to 2-major, and if partner is unable to make a jump reply, game is not very likely. If East does overcall 1NT, West is worth a raise to 3NT.
(2) West has no major to call and no stopper in diamonds, so that leaves only a reply in clubs. West is worth 11 points for clubs, counting the 2 doubletons, as West has a decent 5-card minor.
(3) As 3♣ denies a 4-card major, there is no point introducing hearts or spades. East's 17 points are enough to take shot at game and with a stopper in diamonds, 3NT is the best chance. Even with just 1 stopper, prefer 3NT to 5-of-a-minor.

Lead : ◇ 7. Partner's suit is normal. Top from a doubleton.

Correct play : Duck the first diamond. With A-x or A-x-x, it is best not to take the ace early if all the other suits are well covered. After winning the ◇ A at trick 2, East should tackle the clubs. Normal is ♣ A first, followed by the ♣ J, intending to let it go if South plays low. However, North is likely to hold the ♣ Q on the bidding and you do not want to give the lead to North to cash the other diamond winners. Cross to the ♡ A and lead a low club to your J. If the J wins, cash the ♣ A. If they break, you have 11 tricks, while if South shows out, you have 9 tricks. As it happens, South wins the ♣ Q but has no more diamonds. (If South had another diamond, the suit would be 4-3 and you would lose at most 3 diamonds and 1 club.) If South switches to a spade, win the ♠ A, cross to ♡ Q, back to ♣ A, cash the ♡ K and ♡ J, followed by the rest of the clubs. 10 tricks.

Hand 60 : Competitive bidding after a double — Card combination and Rule of Restricted Choice

Dealer West : North-South vulnerable

NORTH
- ♠ A K 9 5
- ♡ 7 2
- ◇ K Q 8
- ♣ Q 10 7 4

WEST
- ♠ J 8 5
- ♡ A Q J 10 6
- ◇ A 10 7
- ♣ 8 5

EAST
- ♠ Q
- ♡ K 8 5 4
- ◇ 9 6 5 4 3
- ♣ 9 3 2

SOUTH
- ♠ 10 7 4 3 2
- ♡ 9 3
- ◇ J 2
- ♣ A K J 6

WEST	NORTH	EAST	SOUTH
1♡	Double	2♡ (1)	3♠ (2)
Pass (3)	4♠ (4)	All pass	

Bidding : (1) With support and the values for a raise, give a normal raise over a double.
(2) Spades is the suit to bid, not clubs. Worth the jump because of the doubletons. If you are worth a jump reply, make that jump even over a bid by 3rd player. 2♠ here would show only 6-9 points.
(3) Not worth any further action in the direct seat.
(4) Worth 15 points and as partner's range is 10-12, there could be 26 points between you. If that is possible, keep bidding. To pass is risky, to bid 4♠ is risky. If both actions are risky, choose the action which yields the greater reward if successful. Clearly, it is more valuable to bid a game than a partscore.

Lead : ♣8. Spades are out. It is not attractive to lead from an ace-high suit without the king as well, so that excludes the red suits and leaves only clubs. Lead top from a doubleton.

Correct play : Win the ♣ A and lead a spade to the A. East's Q could be from Q-J doubleton or Q-singleton. When an honour drops, the odds favour it to be a singleton (Rule of Restricted Choice). In addition, as West failed to lead a heart, West would not have A-K or K-Q in hearts. That marks East with at least the ♡ K. With only 17 HCP missing, virtually all the remaining points must be with West. Without the ♠ J, West would have opened with 11 HCP, possible but not likely. Lead a diamond to your J (if they fail to cash their hearts now, you can discard one). When you regain the lead, play a spade to dummy's 9. Making 4♠ when the 9 wins.

CHAPTER 16

DEFENDING AGAINST PRE-EMPTS

1. OVER THEIR WEAK TWOS

Weak two openings, used normally only in the majors, are based on a strong 6-card suit and 6-10 HCP. You are less likely to meet weak twos in rubber bridge but they are very popular and common at duplicate. The recommended defense is to treat a weak two as a 1-opening and to use the same style of defense. Thus:

2NT = 16-18 points, balanced, with at least 1 stopper in their suit (same as a 1NT overcall over a 1-opening). With a double stopper, the strength may be shaded to 15 points. After 2NT, partner's new suit at the 3-level is droppable. Bidding the suit opened, e.g. $(2\heartsuit) : 2NT : (Pass) : 3\heartsuit = $ Stayman.

Suit bid = Strong 5-card or longer suit and opening hand values at least, up to a maximum of about 16 points. With more than 16 points, double first and bid the suit later or jump bid your suit later with a 4-loser hand. Jump overcalls, e.g. $(2\heartsuit) : 3\spadesuit$, are strong, even if the partnership uses weak jump overcalls over 1-openings.

Double = For takeout. The double promises a sound opening with 4 cards in the other major. Treat it like the double of a 1-opening, e.g. $(2\spadesuit)$: Double is equivalent to $(1\spadesuit)$: Double *or* $(1\spadesuit)$: Pass: $(2\spadesuit)$: Double. In reply to the double, bid a suit at the cheapest level with 0-5 points. With 6-9 points, bid your suit at the cheapest level or bid 2NT with a stopper in their suit and no 4 cards in the other major. With 10-12 points, make a jump reply and with 13 points or more, bid game or, if uncertain of the best game, bid their suit.

Bidding their suit, e.g. $(2\heartsuit) : 3\heartsuit = $ An artificial game force, equivalent to a demand 2♣ opening.

2. OVER THEIR 3-OPENINGS

When you hold a good hand, a sound working approach is to bid on the assumption that partner has about 6-8 points. Since the pre-emptor has a weak hand, it is unlikely, although possible, that partner has a worthless hand. Say you hold 20 HCP; assume the pre-emptor has about 8; it is reasonable to place partner with 6 HCP, half of the points missing. If about 6-8 points is enough for game, bid the game. If you need more than 8 points for game, bid a suit below game or make a takeout double. While this will not always work out, it is dangerous to be too conservative over a pre-empt, as you may easily miss a game. Pre-empts work well since they force you to guess, but the following guidelines will assist you in guessing correctly more often than not.

3NT = 18 or more points, balanced, stopper in their suit. With a double stopper, shade this to 17 points.

Suit at the 3-level = About 14-17 points, strong 5-card or 6-card suit, around 6 losers.

Minor at the 4-level = Strong, 17-20 points, excellent suit, around 5 losers.

Jump to 4-major = Strong, 17-20 points, excellent suit, around 5 losers. A 4-loser hand with a strong suit can be shown by doubling first and bidding game in your suit on the next round.

Jump to 4NT over $3\heartsuit$ or $3\spadesuit$ = Takout for the minors, not Blackwood. See Chapter 11, page 70.

Bid their suit, e.g. $(3\heartsuit) : 4\heartsuit = $ Artificial game force. Equivalent to a 2♣ demand, around 3-losers.

DOUBLE = For takeout is the recommended approach, although many other methods exist. Using the double for takeout over a 3-level pre-empt includes these benefits: partner's reply can be at the 3-level *or* at the 4-level; partner can choose 3NT as a contract; partner can pass the double for penalties with a strong holding in their suit; it frees all other actions for natural bidding, so that you do not lose 3NT or some suit bids. The only immediate loss when using double for takeout is the inability to make a penalty double. Even so, you will still collect penalties a lot of the time when they are available, since after a takeout double, partner may pass for penalties. If you have the penalty double type hand, you should either bid 3NT and forego the penalties if your hand justifies 3NT, or pass and hope that partner might be able to rake up a takeout double in 4th seat, so that you can then pass and convert the double to penalties. Even if you do occasionally miss doubled penalties, the advantages of using the double for takeout far outweigh the disadvantages. Part of the superiority of the takeout double is its greater frequency. If they pre-empt, which do you pick up more often, a strong holding in their suit or a shortage in their suit? Catering for the shortage makes more sense.

WHEN SHOULD YOU DOUBLE FOR TAKEOUT?

With a good hand with support or tolerance for the missing suits, it is highly likely that a trump fit exists for your side, and so you may anticipate this fit and value your hand by counting HCP plus shortage in their suit at once, using 3 for a void, 2 for a singleton and 1 for a doubleton. Count nothing for an unsupported Q or J in their suit or for a singleton K in their suit. There is also a distinction between bidding in the direct seat (2nd seat) and bidding in the pass out seat (4th seat). It is riskier to take action in 2nd seat since 3rd player may have a very strong hand and you may be caught by a penalty double, but if it has gone (Pre-empt) : Pass : (Pass) to you, 3rd player is not that strong. You can reduce the requirements for action in 4th seat by about 3 points.

A takeout double in 2nd seat should be worth 17 points, calculated as above, while a double in 4th seat should be worth 14 points. If you find this too limiting and want to be more daring, shade the requirements by 1 point only. The double should include support for any unbid major unless you have a safe haven if partner makes an unwelcome reply. In 4th seat, you should be quick to double with modest values and any reasonable excuse, because partner may have a penalty double type hand and may be delighted to pass out your takeout double for penalties. Be wary of taking action in 4th seat, however, when 3rd player trances for some time, thus indicating strength but uncertainty about what to bid. Do not protect on moderate values against a trancer.

RESPONDING TO A SUIT OVERCALL AT THE 3-LEVEL

With 9 HCP or more, you are worth some action, but with less than 9 HCP or less than 3 winners, pass. With 3 winners or more, bid on. You should support partner's major as first priority or try 3NT as second choice.

RESPONDING TO THE TAKEOUT DOUBLE

With 0-8/9 points and 9 losers or worse, bid a suit at the cheapest level. Prefer a major to a minor. With 9/10 points or more and either 3 winners or 8 losers, or better, bid game in a major or bid 3NT if you have a stopper in their suit and no major to bid. With a 2-suited hand and not certain of the best game, you can bid the enemy suit, e.g. (3 $\diamondsuit$) : Double : (Pass) : 4 $\diamondsuit$ asks partner to choose the contract. Slam is possible with a strong trump fit and either 5 winners or a 6-loser hand, or better. After a pre-empt, however, it pays to be conservative about slam bidding. In view of the pre-empt, bad breaks in the other suits are quite likely.

REBIDS BY THE DOUBLER

After a weak reply to the double, the doubler should normally pass unless holding a total of about 20 points or more, or 5 losers or better. Do not bid the same values twice. In answer to a double or in answer to a suit overcall, partner is expected to bid game on about 9 HCP or more or equivalent distributional values. If partner has not bid game, you should not have to bid partner's cards as well as your own.

3. OVER THEIR 4-LEVEL PRE-EMPTS

There are no ideal methods for coping with high level pre-empts. Most pairs prefer to use Double as "Co-operative", suggesting a very strong, balanced type of hand. Others prefer to use Double for takeout (and that use is recommended for duplicate). Partner is always entitled to pass a co-operative double or a takeout double for penalties with values in the opener's suit. Over a 4 $\heartsuit$ or 4 $\spadesuit$ pre-empt, many pairs like to use 4NT as a takeout bid, but you should settle with partner whether it is a 3-suited takeout or a 2-suited takeout. For duplicate, a sensible approach is to use Double as a 3-suited takeout and 4NT as a 2-suited takeout, although most pairs do use Double of a 4-major opening for penalties. Suit bids over a 4-level pre-empt are natural and very strong hands. Bidding the enemy suit is a gigantic takeout bid, looking for a slam.

4. OVER THE GAMBLING 3NT (see Chapter 12, page 74)

If you pass a gambling 3NT, lead an ace or a K-Q combination to take a look at dummy and then decide on the best way to continue the defense. Once they obtain the lead, they usually have at least 9 tricks available. If you wish to bid over their 3NT, a sensible method is :

Double = Strong balanced hand, looking for penalties. A double of 3NT followed by a double of their run to 4 $\clubsuit$ or 4 $\diamondsuit$ is also for penalties.

4 $\clubsuit$ = Takeout for the major suits, equal suits or hearts are preferred.

4 $\diamondsuit$ = Takeout for the major suits, emphasis on spades which will be the longer suit or the stronger suit.

4 $\heartsuit$ or 4 $\spadesuit$ = 1-suited hands, no interest in the other major.

If you wish to bid in 4th seat after the bidding has started (3NT) : Pass : (4 $\clubsuit$ or 4 $\diamondsuit$) . . . use the same methods that the partnership uses over a 4 $\clubsuit$ or 4 $\diamondsuit$ opening bid.

EXERCISES

A. Neither side is vulnerable. Your right-hand opponent opens 3♢. What action do you take on these hands?

1. ♠ K 5	2. ♠ A 9 8 2	3. ♠ A Q J 7 6 2	4. ♠ A 2	5. ♠ A 2
♡ 7 3	♡ A Q 4 3	♡ J 3	♡ K 4 3	♡ Q J 3
♢ A Q 10 6 4	♢ 9	♢ 4 3	♢ 8 6 2	♢ A Q 2
♣ K Q 7 3	♣ A J 3 2	♣ K Q 9	♣ K Q J 7 5	♣ K Q J 3 2

6. ♠ A K 5	7. ♠ K Q J 2	8. ♠ A Q 8 2	9. ♠ A J 8 7	10. ♠ K Q J 9
♡ A J 2	♡ A Q J 8 3	♡ J 6 2	♡ A K 8	♡ A K Q J
♢ A K 4	♢ 9	♢ Q J 9 7	♢ 6 2	♢ 3
♣ A J 9 7	♣ A K 6	♣ A 9	♣ A Q 5 2	♣ A K J 9

B. Neither side is vulnerable. The bidding has been (3♡) : Double : (Pass) to you. Your action on these hands?

1. ♠ 9 5 3 2	2. ♠ 6	3. ♠ K Q 7 2	4. ♠ A Q 9 7 4 2	5. ♠ 8 2
♡ 7 3	♡ 4 3 2	♡ J 3	♡ 8	♡ K 6 3
♢ Q 10 6 4	♢ J 9 7 6 4	♢ A 9 6 4	♢ Q 8 6 2	♢ A Q J 4
♣ Q 7 3	♣ 9 7 5 3	♣ J 9 5	♣ 5 2	♣ Q 9 8 3

C. Neither side is vulnerable. The bidding has been (3♣) : Double : (Pass) to you. Your action on these hands?

1. ♠ 9 6 4 3 2	2. ♠ 4	3. ♠ 9 5 2	4. ♠ Q 8 7 2	5. ♠ A Q 7 2
♡ Q J 7 3	♡ A Q 2	♡ J 3	♡ Q 9 5 3	♡ K Q 6 3
♢ 6 4	♢ J 9 7 6 4	♢ A K 6 4 3	♢ Q 8 2	♢ J 4 3
♣ 7 3	♣ Q J 9 3	♣ A 8 4	♣ 4 3	♣ 3 2

PARTNERSHIP BIDDING : There is no North-South bidding other than indicated.

SET 33 — WEST	SET 33 — EAST	SET 34 — WEST	SET 34 — EAST
1. North opens 2♠.	**1. North opens 2♠.**	**1. South opens 3♣.**	**1. South opens 3♣.**
♠ J 4 2	♠ 7 6	♠ K J 9 7	♠ 8 5
♡ K 8 5 3	♡ A 9 7 4	♡ A Q 9 6	♡ J 7 5 3 2
♢ 6 4	♢ A Q 9 8	♢ A J 8 3	♢ 7 6 5 2
♣ 7 6 5 2	♣ K Q J	♣ 7	♣ Q 5
2. South opens 2♠.	**2. South opens 2♠.**	**2. North opens 3♣.**	**2. North opens 3♣.**
♠ 3	♠ 7 6 4	♠ K 9 8 3 2	♠ 7 6
♡ Q 8 6 2	♡ A J 10 3	♡ K 4 3	♡ A Q J 8 6 2
♢ A K Q 9 3	♢ 8 5	♢ A 7 5	♢ K Q J
♣ K 8 5	♣ A Q 4 2	♣ 8 5	♣ Q 4
3. North opens 2♡.	**3. North opens 2♡.**	**3. South opens 3♢.**	**3. South opens 3♢.**
♠ K 7 4	♠ A Q	♠ A Q 6 4	♠ 5 3
♡ 7 3	♡ K Q 9	♡ K Q 8 3	♡ A 7 6 5 4
♢ J 5 3	♢ A K 7 6	♢ 7	♢ J 8 3
♣ A Q 9 7 5	♣ 6 4 3 2	♣ A 9 8 3	♣ K Q 5
4. South opens 2♡.	**4. South opens 2♡.**	**4. North opens 3♡.**	**4. North opens 3♡.**
♠ A K	♠ 8 5 4	♠ A K 8 3	♠ 7 6
♡ 8 6	♡ A 7	♡ 7	♡ K Q 9 3
♢ A Q J 7 6 2	♢ K 4 3	♢ K 5 4 3	♢ A Q 2
♣ 7 4 3	♣ A J 10 8 5	♣ A 9 6 2	♣ 8 7 4 3
5. North opens 2♠.	**5. North opens 2♠.**	**5. North opens 3♢.**	**5. North opens 3♢.**
♠ Q 5 4	♠ 3	♠ A Q 8 4	♠ K 9 7 2
♡ 7 3 2	♡ K Q J 8 6 4	♡ A 7 4 2	♡ K Q 6
♢ 8 7 5	♢ A K Q	♢ 8 6	♢ J 2
♣ Q 9 6 5	♣ K J 2	♣ Q 9 8	♣ A K J 3

PLAY HANDS ON DEFENDING AGAINST PRE-EMPTS

Hand 61 : Jump reply to a double of a pre-empt — Signalling — Defensive technique

Dealer North : Nil vulnerable

NORTH
- ♠ A K 10 4 2
- ♡ 10 8
- ◇ Q 10 3
- ♣ J 10 6

WEST
- ♠ Q 5
- ♡ K J 9 7 5 2
- ◇ J
- ♣ 9 8 7 4

EAST
- ♠ 7 3
- ♡ 6
- ◇ A K 9 8 5 4 2
- ♣ 5 3 2

SOUTH
- ♠ J 9 8 6
- ♡ A Q 4 3
- ◇ 7 6
- ♣ A K Q

WEST	NORTH	EAST	SOUTH
	Pass	3◇	Dble (1)
Pass (2)	4♠ (3)	All pass	

Bidding : (1) All right for a takeout double, although minimum. Support for both majors and shortage in their suit are vital when you compete at the 3-level on minimum values. The double allows partner to bid 3-major or 4-major, while inferior takeout methods (such as 3NT or cheaper minor 4♣) commit you to the 4-level.
(2) Do not consider "rescuing" a pre-empt with a weak hand.
(3) Too strong for just 3♠ with an excellent 5-card major and better than 2 winners. Even allowing for the doubtful value of the ◇ Q, the hand is too good for just 3♠.

Lead : ◇ K. Routine.

Correct play : After West drops the ◇ J, East should continue with the ◇ A. An honor card signal denies the next honour up (if West had ◇ Q-J, West would drop the Q under the K, not the J). West shows out on the second diamond and West should discard the 2 of hearts, discouraging a switch to hearts. A signal does not show or deny high cards; it is meant to tell partner what to do. West may want a heart switch now and a high heart would ask for a heart *now*. As West wants another diamond, West should discourage hearts. On the 3rd diamond, declarer ruffs high in dummy but West overruffs and exits in a black suit. Ultimately West scores the ♡ K for one down. If East leads a heart or switches to a heart at trick 2 or trick 3, North should win with dummy's ace. It would be an error to play the queen, as a lead or a shift by a pre-emptor is so likely to be a singleton. If the ♡ Q were played, West would win and give East a heart ruff, but if you win ♡ A and draw trumps, the contract is home.

Hand 62 : Takeout double after a pre-empt — Penalty pass — Signalling and defensive technique

Dealer East : Nil vulnerable

NORTH
- ♠ A Q J 3
- ♡ A J 7 6 2
- ◇ 10
- ♣ J 8 2

WEST
- ♠ K 10 9 4 2
- ♡ K Q 10 8
- ◇ 5
- ♣ 7 6 5

EAST
- ♠ 7 5
- ♡ 5
- ◇ A K 8 7 4 3 2
- ♣ Q 9 4

SOUTH
- ♠ 8 6
- ♡ 9 4 3
- ◇ Q J 9 6
- ♣ A K 10 3

WEST	NORTH	EAST	SOUTH
		3◇	Pass (1)
Pass (2)	Dble (3)	Pass	Pass (4)
Pass			

Bidding : (1) Much too weak to take any action here.
(2) Do not bid with a weak hand after partner's pre-empt.
(3) In the direct seat, these values would be too skimpy for action, but in 4th seat, you have enough. With both majors, choose the takeout double.
(4) South could choose 3NT, but to pass the double is superior. 3NT may or may not make but with excellent trumps, playing for penalties is bound to score a plus result. You may score penalties when 3NT was failing, while if 3NT is on, you may find that the penalties you score are greater than the value of the game.

Lead : ♣ K. An A-K suit lead is highly attractive.

Correct play : 3◇ doubled should fail by 4 or 5 tricks. On the ♣ A, North discourages with the ♣ 2. South should switch to the ♠ 8, as North is marked with strength in the majors. (It would be an error to cash the ♣ A at trick 2, as North would not discourage clubs if North held the Q. Cashing the ♣ A sets up declarer's Q.) North wins the ♠ 9 with the J and returns the ♣ J. South cashes a 3rd club and switches back to spades : 10, Q, 7. North should cash the ♡ A next (otherwise East would discard a heart on the ♠ A) and then play the ♠ A. East ruffs and South overruffs. South exits with the 13th club, North ruffs with the ◇ 10, an "uppercut" (so called because it knocks out a high trump), which sets up an extra trump trick for South. That defense beats 3◇ by 5 tricks.

Hand 63 : Action after a pre-empt — Defensive technique — Card reading and countermeasures

Dealer South : North-South vulnerable

NORTH
- ♠ 5
- ♡ A 7
- ◇ 8 4 3
- ♣ K Q 10 9 8 7 3

WEST
- ♠ K J 9 7 6
- ♡ J
- ◇ K 10 9 7
- ♣ J 6 5

EAST
- ♠ A 10 4 2
- ♡ K Q 10 8
- ◇ A Q J
- ♣ 4 2

SOUTH
- ♠ Q 8 3
- ♡ 9 6 5 4 3 2
- ◇ 6 5 2
- ♣ A

WEST	NORTH	EAST	SOUTH
			Pass
Pass	3♣ (1)	Dble (2)	Pass
4♠ (3)	Pass	Pass	Pass

Bidding : (1) The clubs are worth 6 tricks, the ace makes it 7, which is what is needed for a vulnerable 3-opening.

(2) Just enough for a takeout double.

(3) Even discounting the ♡ J and ♣ J completely, the hand is worth 10 points for spades. Count the singleton as 3, since a spade fit is known because of the takeout double. 3♠ would be a very timid effort, which East would pass and a game could be missed.

Lead : ♣ K. Far more likely to be productive than the ♡ A, hoping for a ruff. The ♡ K is almost certainly going to turn up in dummy because of the double.

Correct play : South is obliged to win the ♣ A and returns a heart. North wins the ♡ A and cashes the ♣ Q, noting that South shows out and that West holds another club. North's best defense is to play a third club, particularly when South discourages diamonds with the ◇ 2. The best chance to avoid a trump loser with K-J-x-x-x opposite A-10-x-x if you have no clue as to the location of the Q is to play A and K and hope the Q drops. However, after a pre-empt, it is a sound approach to place any significant high cards outside the pre-empt suit with the partner of the pre-emptor, not with the pre-emptor. On this basis, you would assume the ♠ Q is with South and play to finesse the ♠ J if you were drawing trumps. There is further confirmation of this in the play so far. North has shown up with the ♡ A and ♣ K-Q, 9 HCP, and so is unlikely to hold the ♠ Q which would make 11 HCP, usually too much for a pre-empt. Once you decide to play South for the ♠ Q, do not ruff low in dummy — South will overruff. Ruff the 3rd club with the ♠ A and lead the ♠ 10, letting it run if not covered. Repeat the spade finesse and draw trumps. Making 10 tricks.

Hand 64 : Action after a vulnerable pre-empt — Card reading to avoid a fatal ruff

Dealer West : East-West vulnerable

NORTH
- ♠ A 9 4 2
- ♡ 10 7 4
- ◇ K 10
- ♣ 10 6 5 2

WEST
- ♠ K Q J 10 7 6 5
- ♡ 3 2
- ◇ Q J 9
- ♣ 9

EAST
- ♠ - - -
- ♡ 6 5
- ◇ 8 7 6 5 4 2
- ♣ K Q J 7 3

SOUTH
- ♠ 8 3
- ♡ A K Q J 9 8
- ◇ A 3
- ♣ A 8 4

WEST	NORTH	EAST	SOUTH
3♠ (1)	Pass	Pass (2)	4♡ (3)
Pass	Pass	Pass	

Bidding : (1) 6 tricks in spades, 1 in diamonds = 7, the number needed for a vulnerable pre-empt.

(2) Do not panic with a weak hand just because you are void in partner's suit. Do not try to rescue partner with weakness. A new suit is forcing and you are in sufficient peril at the 3-level without going any higher.

(3) It is reasonable to play partner for about 6-8 points or about 2 tricks after they pre-empt. With 8 tricks in hand and hoping for 2 tricks from partner, 4♡ is clearcut.

Lead : ♠ K. Prefer the solid sequence in spades rather than the near sequence in diamonds.

Correct play : The instinctive play is to rise with dummy's ♠ A, and only after East ruffs this, does it dawn on declarer that it was almost certain that the ♠ A would be ruffed. West would have 7 spades for the 3♠ opening, dummy has 4 spades and South has 2 spades, leaving East with a marked void. It is vital to count the spades *before* playing from dummy. Once you realise the ♠ A will be ruffed, it is clear that you must not play the ace. Duck the 1st spade, duck the 2nd spade, win the next lead in hand and draw trumps. Later cross to dummy with a diamond to the K or a trump to the 10 and cash the valuable preserved ♠ A on which you discard one of your club losers. You lose 2 spades and 1 club. Making 10 tricks.

REVISION TEST ON PART 2

The answers to all these questions can be found in Chapters 9-16. Give yourself 1 mark for each correct answer. If you score less than 40, it will profit you to revise the relevant sections.

A. Your right-hand opponent has opened 1♢. What action do you take on each of these hands?

1. ♠ K Q 2	2. ♠ A J 3 2	3. ♠ - - -	4. ♠ A 9 7	5. ♠ A 8 7 2
♡ 7 2	♡ 3	♡ A K J 8 7 6 2	♡ A J 3	♡ A 2
♢ A Q 9 6 4	♢ A 9 7	♢ 7 6	♢ K 9 8	♢ 3
♣ Q J 7	♣ Q 9 7 4 2	♣ K J 10 4	♣ A K J 2	♣ A K Q 8 6 3

B. Right-hand opponent has opened 1♠. What action do you take on each of these hands?

1. ♠ 3	2. ♠ 7	3. ♠ A	4. ♠ 3	5. ♠ A 10 4
♡ A Q J 3 2	♡ 3	♡ 7 3	♡ A Q 7	♡ A K 9
♢ 8 6	♢ Q J 9 6 3 2	♢ A Q 10 6 2	♢ K Q 3 2	♢ J 6 4 3
♣ K Q 10 5 4	♣ K J 10 8 6	♣ A 10 8 5 2	♣ K 9 8 4 2	♣ K Q 2

C. The bidding has been (1♢) : 1♠ : (Pass) to you. What action do you take in reply to partner's overcall?

1. ♠ 8 7	2. ♠ J	3. ♠ A 8 5 3 2	4. ♠ J 8 2	5. ♠ J 8 7 5
♡ K 7 3	♡ A Q 8 5 4 3	♡ K Q 6 2	♡ A Q 10	♡ 6
♢ A Q 9 2	♢ 7 6 4	♢ A 7 6	♢ K Q 10 3	♢ J 9 4 3
♣ A 10 5 2	♣ K J 3	♣ 4	♣ A J 10	♣ A K Q J

D. The bidding has been (1♡) : Double : (Pass) to you. What action do you take on these hands?

1. ♠ K 9 4 2	2. ♠ A 7	3. ♠ A 5 3	4. ♠ 3 2	5. ♠ 2
♡ A Q 7 3	♡ A Q 3 2	♡ J 7 2	♡ 9 6 4 3 2	♡ K 8
♢ J 9	♢ 7 6 4	♢ 8 7 2	♢ 9 6 2	♢ 9 7 5 3 2
♣ 9 5 2	♣ J 7 3 2	♣ J 8 5 4	♣ Q 9 7	♣ J 8 6 3 2

E. The bidding has been (1♢) : Double : (1♠). What action do you take on these hands?

1. ♠ Q 7	2. ♠ A J 7 5 2	3. ♠ A Q J 2	4. ♠ Q 7	5. ♠ A 8 3 2
♡ Q 8 4	♡ 6 4	♡ 8 2	♡ A J 9	♡ K J 6 4
♢ 7 6	♢ 9 7	♢ 6 3 2	♢ K J 6 2	♢ 9 4 2
♣ 9 8 7 5 3 2	♣ A 8 3 2	♣ J 8 5 4	♣ 9 7 3 2	♣ 6 2

F. What would your answers be on the hands in E. if the bidding had started (1♡) : Double : (2♡) to you?

G. What would your answers be on the hands in E. if the bidding had started (1♢) : Double : (Redouble) to you?

H. The bidding has started (1♠) : Double : (Redouble) to you. What action do you take on these hands?

1. ♠ 9 7 4 2	2. ♠ K 7 5 2	3. ♠ A 9 7 2	4. ♠ A Q 2	5. ♠ 8 7 4
♡ 6 3 2	♡ 9 6 4 2	♡ K J 6 4 3	♡ J 3 2	♡ Q 10
♢ 6 4	♢ Q 9	♢ 8	♢ Q 7 2	♢ K 3
♣ J 8 3 2	♣ 7 3 2	♣ 9 5 4	♣ 8 7 5 3	♣ K Q 9 8 5 2

I. Right-hand opponent opened 2♠, weak. What action do you take on each of these hands?

1. ♠ 9 7	2. ♠ A J 8 7 3	3. ♠ A	4. ♠ A Q 2	5. ♠ 2
♡ K 3	♡ A Q	♡ A K J 2	♡ A 8	♡ 6
♢ A Q 9 6 4	♢ Q 9 7 6	♢ 8 7 6 4	♢ A K 8 6 2	♢ K J 9 4 3
♣ K 9 7 3	♣ J 7	♣ K 8 5 4	♣ K Q 7	♣ K Q J 8 6 2

J. The bidding has been (3♢) : Double : (Pass) to you. What action do you take on each of these hands?

1. ♠ K 7 5 2	2. ♠ A 7	3. ♠ 9 7 5 4 2	4. ♠ A 7 2	5. ♠ Q 8 5 2
♡ K 8 7 3	♡ 8 7 5 3 2	♡ 8 6 4 3 2	♡ 9 7	♡ 6
♢ A	♢ 6 4	♢ K 7	♢ A K 8	♢ 9 4 3
♣ 9 8 5 3	♣ A K 3 2	♣ 4	♣ 9 6 5 4 2	♣ K 9 8 6 4

PART 3

EXPAND YOUR
CONSTRUCTIVE BIDDING

If you ever become satisfied with your level of competence and your mastery of the game, you will have reached a plateau and will remain at that level or fall below it. The true enthusiast is constantly aiming to improve the skills already acquired and to add new dimensions to the existing store of knowledge. This part delves further into actions after your side has opened the bidding and deals with areas which are considered part and parcel of being a competent bidder. If you propose to "grow up" as a bridgeplayer, you will want to rise beyond the basics and learn how to solve the problems and challenges which each new deal thrusts upon you. You will want to master the vital techniques which enable you to get the most out of the cards when they are running your way. Both partners need to be conversant with the principles in this section. If you have any doubts about your partner's expertise in any of these areas, make sure that you and your partner go through the relevant sections together thoroughly. A little study by both of you will repay you tenfold when you can cope with trouble situations confidently and competently.

In many of the chapters, hands are discussed in terms of losers. If you are not yet familiar with counting losers, take another look at Chapter 12, page 73 on "How to count your playing tricks" and also have a preview run through the text of Chapter 23 on *The Losing Trick Count*. Assessing the playing strength of a hand in terms of losers is a very valuable valuation technique in many areas of bidding.

Chapter 17 deals with 4th-suit-forcing; when to use it; when it is unnecessary; how the bidding develops after 4th-suit-forcing has been used; the effect of 4th-suit-forcing on other auctions which become non-forcing.

Chapter 18 is concerned with reverses and jump-shifts; the requirements for opener to make a reverse; responder's weak and strong continuations; opener's rebids; the forcing status of opener's and responder's subsequent actions; types of hands on which opener and responder should jump-shift; rebids after a jump-shift.

Chapters 19 and 20 cover the approach to show specific hand patterns; how to reveal to partner that you hold a 5-5, a 6-5, a 6-6, a 5-4 or a 6-4 pattern; how to recognise partner's pattern and how to choose the correct contract after the pattern has been disclosed; how to play such hands to best advantage as declarer.

Chapter 21 explores stopper-showing and stopper-asking; how to discover whether the partnership holds the stoppers vital to make a success of 3NT; how to avoid 3NT and locate the best alternative contract when the stoppers necessary for no-trumps are not present.

Chapter 22 examines responder's problems with a weak hand; the use of Stayman on weak hands; when you can afford to Stayman with junk in order to rescue the partnership from a rotten 1NT and when you must subside in 1NT and suffer the consequences; how to recognise the weak actions by responder in order to bail out in a partscore superior to 1NT; further, the use of the 1NT response when holding a long suit in a hand too weak to respond at the 2-level is covered; how to handle the later bidding; when to show the long suit and when to stick with partner's suit.

Chapter 23 provides an outline of the Losing Trick Count, a valuation technique superior to the point count when a trump fit has come to light; when to use it and when to avoid it; how the LTC operates; its limitations and the number of losers expected in partner's hand calculated by the actions taken by partner so far.

Chapter 24 is on long suit trials; how to recognise a long suit trial; when it should be used; when to accept partner's invitation and when to reject it. To be able to use long suit trials will provide an invaluable aid for reaching major suit games (and occasionally slams as well) when the fit is just right, even though the point count is minimal.

CHAPTER 17

FOURTH-SUIT-FORCING

The concept of 4th-suit-forcing is common to all standard bidding systems, whether one uses 5-card majors or 4-card majors, weak no-trump or strong no-trump, and so on. 4th-suit-forcing is a valuable adjunct to natural bidding methods because it enables one to explore the nature and strength of partner's hand without fear of being dropped. Without 4th-suit-forcing, one would be forced to jump to game and gamble on the correct contract instead of consulting and co-operating with partner on this decision.

After the partnership has bid 3 suits (e.g. 1♢ : 1♠, 2♣), the following principles apply :

1. A 2NT bid or higher no-trump bid *promises* at least 1 stopper in the unbid suit. It is attractive for a 1NT rebid by responder also to have a stopper in the unbid suit (e.g. after 1♣ : 1♡, 1♠), but it is not vital.

2. A rebid of 2NT by responder suggests around 11-12 points and is invitational, not forcing. This applies whether 2NT is a simple rebid (e.g. 1♢ : 1♠, 2♣ : 2NT *or* 1♠ : 2♣, 2♡ : 2NT) or whether it is a jump-rebid (e.g. 1♣ : 1♢, 1♡ : 2NT). With more than 12 points, bid 3NT or use the 4th suit.

3. If there is a clearcut, natural bid, make that bid and do not use 4th-suit-forcing.

4. If responder raises opener's *second* suit, that *promises* 4-card support.

5. A jump-rebid in responder's suit (e.g. 1♢ : 1♠, 2♣ : 3♠) *promises* a 6-card suit.

6. Responder's jump to the 3-level either in opener's suit or in responder's suit shows 10-12 points and is not forcing if opener's rebid is consistent with a minimum opening. For example, 1♢ : 1♠, 2♣ : 3♢ is based on a 10-12 range. Likewise, 1♣ : 1♡, 1♠ : 3♠ is not forcing but highly invitational, and responder's 3♡ or 3♣ rebid after the same start would also be a strong invitation but not forcing. In order to create a forcing auction, responder must first use the 4th suit. However, if only 2 suits have been bid so far, responder's jump rebid is best played as forcing. For example, 1♣ : 1♠, 2♣ : 3♠ should be used as forcing because otherwise responder could be stuck for a rebid, as new suit rebids would be natural, not artificial.

7. A *jump*-rebid in the 4th suit is *natural* and shows a 5-5 or 6-5 pattern with at least game expectations. For example, after 1♣ : 1♡, 1♠ ... responder's 3♢ shows 5+ hearts and 5+ diamonds and enough for game. Similarly, 1♣ : 1♢, 1♠ : 3♡ would reveal responder to hold 5 hearts and 6 diamonds at least, with enough strength for game. The jump-rebid in the 4th suit is a rare creature but a valuable descriptive technique.

8. A bid of the 4th suit is *artificial* and shows :

(a) A strong hand, worth at least an invitation to game (normally 11 points or better), and

(b) Inability to make a clearcut, natural bid. Perhaps responder has no stopper in the 4th suit. Perhaps the responder is too strong to bid just to game and is worth a slam invitation. Perhaps responder's suit is 5 cards long and not 6 cards and thus responder cannot make a minimum rebid in that suit (which would show a weak hand) or a jump-rebid in that suit (which would promise a 6-card suit). Perhaps it is a combination of these problems. Whatever the reason, responder needs more information about opener's values.

Responder's bid of the 4th suit is forcing on opener who must keep on bidding. After 4th suit, opener must not only reply but must also bid again after responder's next bid if responder rebids below game. Responder, however, is entitled to pass a minimum rebid by opener in reply to the 4th suit and therefore opener must make more than a minimum bid with 15 points up or even with a very good 14.

OPENER'S USE OF 4TH-SUIT-FORCING

When opener rebids the suit opened and responder changes suit (e.g. 1♢ : 1♠, 2♢ : 2♡), opener may also utilise 4th-suit-forcing (by bidding 3♣ in the above sequence). In this situation, opener is not showing any extra strength (the 2♢ rebid already showed a minimum opening) but is indicating a hand which is unable to support either of responder's suits and has no stopper in the 4th suit (otherwise no-trumps would be a convenient bid). Opener's use of 4th-suit-forcing may also arise after a strong auction where responder's suit has been rebid. After 1♢ : 1♡, 3♣ : 3♡, a 3♠ rebid by opener here would not be genuine but would deny support for hearts and deny a stopper in spades for 3NT, such as ♠864 ♡K ♢AQJ84 ♣AKQJ.

AFTER RESPONDER'S 4TH-SUIT-FORCING

Opener will have a choice of actions. In order of preference, opener should :

1. Give delayed 3-card support for responder's suit. Where responder's suit is a major suit, this delayed 3-card support takes precedence over other actions. Frequently responder will hold a strong hand with a 5-card major and also the requirements for a rebid of 3NT. Responder is unable to jump rebid in the major, since that promises a 6-card suit, so that in order to check whether opener holds 3-card support for the major, responder will use 4th-suit-forcing, planning to rebid 3NT if delayed 3-card support is not forthcoming.

2. Bid no-trumps with at least 1 stopper in the 4th suit. Where responder's suit is a minor, bidding no-trumps takes priority over giving 3-card delayed support for responder's suit.

3. Raise the 4th suit (but never beyond 3NT). If opener could genuinely hold the 4th suit, raising the 4th suit shows a 4-card holding in the suit. If opener has previously denied holding the 4th suit, raising the 4th suit shows a strong hand, too good to make the weakest rebid of opener's first suit, *but with no stopper in the 4th suit.* For example, after 1◇ : 1♠, 2♣ : 2♡ (4th suit), 3♡ by opener would show 4 hearts and either a 1-4-4-4 or a 0-4-5-4 pattern, since the 2♣ rebid did not deny 4 hearts. However, after 1◇ : 1♡, 2♣ : 2♠ (4th suit), 3♠ by opener cannot show 4 spades — opener would have rebid 1♠ over 1♡, not 2♣. In this situation, 3♠ says, "I have a strong opening (normally 15 HCP or more) but no stopper in spades and no 3-card support for hearts." Again, this is not a common situation but very useful when a problem hand occurs.

4. Rebid opener's 2nd suit with at least 5 cards in that suit.

5. Rebid opener's 1st suit with 5 cards in that suit.

With a minimum, opener takes the above action at the cheapest level. With a strong hand, make a jump-rebid.

AFTER OPENER'S REPLY TO THE 4TH SUIT

Responder's next bid is forcing if it is below game and indicates that responder was too strong to take that action on the previous round. For example, 1◇ : 1♠, 2♣ : 3♠, a jump-rebid by responder after 3 suits have been bid, is best played as non-forcing . . . a strong invitation on around 10-12 points and a good 6-card suit. If responder has a game-force with a 6-card suit, the auction should go 1◇ : 1♠, 2♣ : 2♡ (4th suit), any rebid by opener : 3♠ by responder which is forcing because 4th suit was used. This applies whether the rebid by responder is in opener's suit, in responder's suit or in no-trumps. If responder bids game after using 4th suit, this is stronger than bidding game on the previous round. For example, 1◇ : 1♡, 2♣ : 4♡ is not as strong as 1◇ : 1♡, 2♣ : 2♠, any rebid by opener : 4♡ by responder. If opener's rebid over 4th suit has not shown significant extra values, then a game rebid by responder has a slam invitation suggestion. With values beyond those already shown, either in good shape, good fit or extra high card strength, opener is entitled to push on to slam.

AFTER OPENER'S USE OF 4TH-SUIT-FORCING

Responder will bid no-trumps with a stopper in the 4th suit. With no stopper, responder may give delayed support for opener or rebid one of responder's suits. Delayed support will depend on what has been shown or denied so far. For example, after 1♠ : 2◇, 3♣ : 3◇, 3♡ (4th suit) responder's 3♠ would be based on a doubleton only, because of the failure to support spades earlier, and would deny a stopper in hearts. However, delayed support with a jump-rebid shows genuine support and a hand too strong to support earlier. For example, in the above auction, if responder bid 4♠ over 3♡, that would promise 3-card support and suggest slam with a strong diamond suit. With lesser values and no slam interest, responder should have bid 4♠ over 3♣. Responder's 3◇ rebid was forcing since opener's 3♣ rebid created a game force, but choosing 3◇ when holding spade support indicates that more than just game is in responder's mind.

THE 1♣ : 1◇, 1♡ : 1♠ AUCTION vs THE 1♣ : 1◇, 1♡ : 2♠ AUCTION

In standard methods, the 1♠ rebid after 1♣ : 1◇, 1♡ is 4th-suit-forcing but a very sensible modern development is to use the 1♠ rebid as a *natural* rebid, promising 4 spades, and forcing for 1 round. The 1♠ rebid does not promise more than 6 points, although it could be a very strong hand, just like an immediate 1♠ response to 1♣ which shows 6 points or more. Subsequent bidding is natural. The jump to 2♠ after 1♣ : 1◇, 1♡ is artificial and is used as 4th-suit-forcing, promising 11 points or more and specifically denying 4 spades. Bidding over 2♠ continues as after any 4th-suit-forcing rebid. If responder has a game-forcing hand with 6+ diamonds and 5 spades, then after 1♣ : 1◇, 1♡ responder shows this hand with a 3♠ rebid.

EXERCISES

A. Partner opened 1 ◇ and rebid 2♣ over your 1♡ response. What action do you now take on these hands?

1. ♠ 8 4 3 2
   ♡ A K 9 8
   ◇ K 6
   ♣ J 4 3

2. ♠ K Q 8
   ♡ K 9 8 6 3
   ◇ Q 9
   ♣ J 4 3

3. ♠ 8 4 3
   ♡ A K 9 8
   ◇ K 6
   ♣ J 8 6 3

4. ♠ 8 4 3
   ♡ A K J 3
   ◇ K 6
   ♣ K 8 6 3

5. ♠ K 8 6
   ♡ K Q 7 6 2
   ◇ A Q
   ♣ 8 4 2

6. ♠ 7 3
   ♡ A J 7 2
   ◇ K Q 4 3
   ♣ J 8 5

7. ♠ 7 3
   ♡ A K 7 2
   ◇ K Q 4 3
   ♣ K 7 6

8. ♠ 8 6
   ♡ A Q J 6 5 2
   ◇ 9 7
   ♣ 8 4 3

9. ♠ J 6
   ♡ A Q J 6 5 2
   ◇ K 7
   ♣ 8 4 3

10. ♠ 8 6
    ♡ A Q 8 6 4 2
    ◇ A 3
    ♣ A 7 2

B. With silent opponents, the bidding has been 1 ◇ : 1♡, 2♣ : 2♠ (4th suit). What is opener's next action?

1. ♠ 2
   ♡ 8 5 4
   ◇ K Q J 3 2
   ♣ A Q J 3

2. ♠ K Q 8
   ♡ 3
   ◇ K J 8 6 4
   ♣ A K 3 2

3. ♠ 3
   ♡ K 9 8
   ◇ A K 6 5 2
   ♣ A Q 6 3

4. ♠ 8 4
   ♡ K
   ◇ K Q 6 5 2
   ♣ A J 7 4 3

5. ♠ 6
   ♡ 2
   ◇ A Q 9 7 3 2
   ♣ A K J 5 2

6. ♠ Q J 6
   ♡ 2
   ◇ K Q 5 3 2
   ♣ A J 5 4

7. ♠ 7 3
   ♡ 8 4
   ◇ K Q 9 3 2
   ♣ A K J 2

8. ♠ J 6
   ♡ 5 2
   ◇ A K 8 5 2
   ♣ A K Q 9

9. ♠ J 6
   ♡ 2
   ◇ A K 7 5 3 2
   ♣ A 8 4 3

10. ♠ 8 6 2
    ♡ Q
    ◇ A K J 9 6
    ♣ A Q J 7

PARTNERSHIP BIDDING : How should the following hands be bid? West is the dealer on all hands.

SET 35 — WEST	SET 35 — EAST	SET 36 — WEST	SET 36 — EAST
1. ♠ A Q 8 7 ♡ K 3 ◇ 7 6 ♣ K Q 9 8 5	1. ♠ K 9 3 ♡ 7 6 2 ◇ A Q 4 3 2 ♣ A 4	1. ♠ A Q 8 6 ♡ 7 3 ◇ 9 4 ♣ K Q J 7 3	1. ♠ J 5 ♡ 8 5 4 ◇ A Q 6 3 2 ♣ A 8 2
2. ♠ A J 8 4 ♡ A Q 2 ◇ 6 ♣ K Q 9 8 4	2. ♠ K 5 2 ♡ 7 6 ◇ A K 9 7 3 ♣ J 3 2	2. ♠ A Q 10 8 7 ♡ A K 9 3 ◇ 7 4 ♣ 6 3	2. ♠ K 2 ♡ 8 7 2 ◇ 9 8 6 ♣ A K Q 5 4
3. ♠ K Q 4 2 ♡ 3 2 ◇ A 9 ♣ K 8 7 3 2	3. ♠ A 3 ♡ K 9 8 6 4 ◇ 7 4 3 ♣ A 6 5	3. ♠ - - - ♡ 8 3 2 ◇ A K 7 3 2 ♣ A Q 9 8 3	3. ♠ K Q 8 7 4 ♡ A J 10 7 4 ◇ Q ♣ J 2
4. ♠ A K 8 7 ♡ 8 4 3 ◇ 9 8 ♣ A Q 9 4	4. ♠ 6 4 ♡ A Q J 7 5 ◇ J 3 2 ♣ K J 2	4. ♠ A K J 7 ♡ 6 4 ◇ A Q 7 5 4 ♣ 9 3	4. ♠ 8 3 2 ♡ A K 9 8 3 2 ◇ K 8 ♣ 7 4
5. ♠ K Q 9 8 ♡ A 6 4 ◇ 2 ♣ A K 8 6 3	5. ♠ A 6 2 ♡ K Q 7 3 2 ◇ 7 4 ♣ J 4 2	5. ♠ A K J 7 ♡ 7 3 2 ◇ 8 ♣ A Q 9 8 5	5. ♠ Q 8 3 ♡ J 5 ◇ A Q 7 4 3 2 ♣ K J
6. ♠ - - - ♡ A J 4 2 ◇ K Q 8 6 3 ♣ K J 5 2	6. ♠ A J 10 9 6 ♡ 10 5 ◇ A 5 2 ♣ A 9 3	6. ♠ A K 9 8 5 ♡ K Q 3 2 ◇ 3 ♣ Q 7 6	6. ♠ 6 4 ♡ A 9 8 ◇ 7 6 ♣ A K J 5 3 2

PLAY HANDS ON FOURTH-SUIT-FORCING

Hand 65 : 4th-suit-forcing — Avoidance technique (keeping the danger hand off lead)

Dealer North : Nil vulnerable

NORTH
♠ A Q 7 2
♡ K J 6
♢ 8 4
♣ K 7 3 2

WEST
♠ J 8 4
♡ 10 7 4
♢ Q J 6 5
♣ Q 9 8

EAST
♠ 10 9 6 3
♡ A Q 8 5 3
♢ 10 2
♣ 5 4

SOUTH
♠ K 5
♡ 9 2
♢ A K 9 7 3
♣ A J 10 6

WEST	NORTH	EAST	SOUTH
	1♣	Pass	1♢ (1)
Pass	1♠ (2)	Pass	2♡ (3)
Pass	2NT (4)	Pass	3NT (5)
Pass	Pass	Pass	

Bidding : (1) 3♣ as a forcing raise does not appeal if opener might have only 3 clubs. 2NT is out with those rotten hearts.
(2) Do not bypass a 4-card major. 1♠ is superior to 1NT.
(3) 4th-suit-forcing. (Using 4th-suit-forcing, a jump to 3♣ would suggest only 10-12 points.) South is keen to reach 3NT but cannot bid no-trumps without a stopper in the unbid suit.
(4) Shows a stopper in hearts but only a minimum opening.
(5) 3NT is a much better spot than 5♣ and it is best played by North who has the danger suit covered.

Lead : ♡5. Do not be put off by the fact that North is known to hold a stopper in hearts. Your job is to knock out that stopper and set up your long suit.

Correct play : West plays the ♡10 and North wins the ♡J. With 1 trick in and 7 more tricks in top cards, North needs to set up one more trick and the club suit will provide that. North must keep West off lead and it would be an error to cash the ♣K and finesse the ♣J. West would win the ♣Q and a heart from West would give the defense 4 more tricks. North's remaining K-6 in hearts provides a stopper if East is on lead, but not if West is on lead. West thus is the danger hand and North plans to keep West off lead. Play a club to the ace and lead the ♣J, playing low if West plays low. Even if this finesse lost to East, the hearts would not be at risk and declarer would have 9 tricks. As it is, finessing clubs the safe way nets 10 tricks.

Hand 66 : 4th-suit-forcing — Delayed support — Setting up dummy's long suit — Ruffing finesse

Dealer East : North-South vulnerable

NORTH
♠ 8 6 5
♡ J 10 5
♢ A K 9 8 2
♣ 10 5

WEST
♠ K 3 2
♡ A K 7 6 2
♢ Q J 4
♣ 4 3

EAST
♠ A J 9 4
♡ 9 8 4
♢ 7
♣ A K 7 6 2

SOUTH
♠ Q 10 7
♡ Q 3
♢ 10 6 5 3
♣ Q J 9 8

WEST	NORTH	EAST	SOUTH
		1♣	Pass
1♡ (1)	Pass	1♠	Pass
2♢ (2)	Pass	2♡ (3)	Pass
4♡ (4)	Pass	Pass	Pass

Bidding : (1) It would be dreadful to respond 2NT as some players do ("just to show my points, partner"). Choose the major suit response when available.
(2) 4th-suit-forcing. West has enough for 3NT but should check first whether opener has 3-card support for hearts. If West does not receive delayed support in reply to the 4th suit, time enough then to rebid 3NT.
(3) Shows delayed 3-card support for hearts but only a minimum opening. With more, the rebid would have been 3♡.
(4) Note how poor a contract 3NT is on the marked diamond lead.

Lead : ♢K. An A-K suit lead is highly attractive, but a trump lead here would also be sensible.

Correct play : North should not continue diamonds but should switch to a spade (or a trump). If the switch is to a spade, West should win with the K, cash A-K of hearts and then play ♣A, ♣K and ruff a club. North may overruff and continue spades, but declarer wins with dummy's ace and ruffs another club, setting up the last club in dummy as a winner. Next the ♢Q is led : if North plays low, run the Q, as the ace is marked with North on the original K-lead. If North covers, ruff in dummy and cash the last club on which the spade loser is discarded. West has a trump and the winning ♢J left. Making 11 tricks. Note declarer's timing of the play.

Hand 67 : Hunting for the best spot when one suit is unguarded — Keeping control of the trump suit

Dealer South : East-West vulnerable

NORTH
♠ A Q 5
♡ 9 3 2
◇ A J 10 6 3
♣ Q 8

WEST
♠ 4 2
♡ K Q J
◇ Q 9 8 5
♣ 10 9 4 3

EAST
♠ 9 8 7 3
♡ A 10 7 6 5
◇ K 4
♣ 7 2

SOUTH
♠ K J 10 6
♡ 8 4
◇ 7 2
♣ A K J 6 5

WEST	NORTH	EAST	SOUTH
			1♣
Pass	1◇ (1)	Pass	1♠
Pass	2♡ (2)	Pass	3♣ (3)
Pass	4♠ (4)	All pass	

Bidding : (1) A response in no-trumps is not appealing with the weakness in hearts. Note that a heart lead quickly puts paid to 3NT.
(2) North has enough for a game, but the best contract is by no means clear. No-trumps is appealing but there is no indication that partner has anything in hearts and if South has a stopper in hearts, South should be the declarer in no-trumps. To discover more, North uses the 4th suit.
(3) Denies a stopper in hearts, denies 3 diamonds, shows 5 clubs and a minimum opening.
(4) North should discount no-trumps now that the hearts are known to be unprotected. While a 4-3 trump fit is not particularly desirable, it is acceptable if no-trumps is out of the question.

Lead : ♡K. The unbid suit is the normal lead.

Correct play : Hearts are continued and South must resist the natural inclination to ruff the third round. If South does ruff the 3rd heart and then leads 3 rounds of trumps, East would be left with the last trump plus 2 heart winners for 2 down. With only 7 trumps, the missing trumps are more likely to break 4-2 than 3-3. To protect the trump position, South should discard a diamond on the 3rd heart. If a 4th heart came, dummy could ruff. It is fine to ruff with the short trump hand but risky to ruff with the long trump hand. On anything but a heart at trick 4, declarer wins, draws 4 rounds of trumps and cashes the ◇ A and the 5 club winners. Play the ♣Q first when starting the clubs (high-card-from-shortage when cashing winners). 10 tricks.

Hand 68 : Bidding when 1♠ is the 4th suit bid — Keeping control of the trump suit

Dealer West : Both vulnerable

NORTH
♠ 10
♡ J 10 9 6
◇ 9 8 4 3 2
♣ K 10 6

WEST
♠ A K 7 6
♡ K Q 5 3
◇ 6
♣ A 5 4 2

EAST
♠ 5 4 3 2
♡ A 8 7
◇ K Q J 10 7
♣ 8

SOUTH
♠ Q J 9 8
♡ 4 2
◇ A 5
♣ Q J 9 7 3

WEST	NORTH	EAST	SOUTH
1♣	Pass	1◇ (1)	Pass
1♡ (2)	Pass	1♠ (3)	Pass
3♠ (4)	Pass	4♠ (5)	All pass

Bidding : (1) Longest suit first is the normal response. It would be abnormal to respond 1♠.
(2) 4-card suits are shown up-the-line even on the rebid.
(3) This is superior to a rebid in diamonds. In modern style, this shows 4 spades even though it is the 4th suit, since 2♠ over 1♡ is used as the 4th suit rebid when not holding a genuine spade suit. Even if 1♠ as 4th suit did not guarantee a spade suit, opener would raise spades with 4-card support, just in case responder did have spades. If responder did not hold spades, responder could always revert to no-trumps over a spade raise.
(4) Shows 4 spades and better than a minimum opening. 2♠ would show a minimum.
(5) 4♠ is the best spot. 3NT is beaten on a club lead.

Lead : ♣Q. Top of near sequence is best when all suits have been bid.

Correct play : It is instinctive to win with the ♣A and tackle trumps next, but this is risky. The normal split with 5 trumps missing is 3-2, but a 4-1 break occurs about ¼ of the time. If East were to play off ♠A-K first, South would get in with the ◇ A, draw declarer's trumps and cash clubs. Declarer should play a diamond before starting trumps, knocking out the ◇ A and setting up diamond winners in hand. Any return can be won, followed by ♠ A, ruff a club, ♠ K, ruff a club and then play the diamond winners. 10 tricks in comfort.

CHAPTER 18
REVERSES & JUMP-SHIFTS

REVERSES

The concept of the reverse is common to all standard bidding systems, whether one uses 5-card majors or 4-card majors, weak no-trump or strong no-trump, and so on. The reverse allows the opener to reveal a strong hand without a jump-rebid, but there are significant restrictions on the hands with which one is permitted to reverse. It is not sufficient to hold a strong hand — only specific hand patterns are allowed for a reverse.

A reverse bid by opener is a new suit at the 2-level and higher-ranking than opener's first bid suit.

Opener's rebids in these sequences are examples of a reverse :

WEST	EAST	WEST	EAST	WEST	EAST	WEST	EAST	WEST	EAST
1♣	1♠	1♢	1NT	1♣	1♡	1♡	2♢	1♢	2♣
2♡ ...		2♠ ...		2♢ ...		2♠ ...		2♡ ...	

Examples of sequences which do not constitute a reverse include 1♣ : 1♡, 1♠ (opener's rebid is at the 1-level), 1♢ : 1♠, 2♣ (opener's 2nd suit is *lower*-ranking), 1♠ : 2♡, 3♢ (opener's rebid is at the 3-level), 1♣ : 1♡, 2♠ (opener's rebid is a jump), 1♡ : 2♡, 2♠ (a game try as hearts have been raised), and so on.

WHAT DOES A REVERSE SHOW?

A reverse = better than a minimum opening and that opener's 1st suit is longer than the 2nd suit.

A reverse is never made on suits of equal length . . . never with a 5-5 pattern. The usual minimum for a reverse is 17 points in total (16 HCP with 1 length point for a 5-4 pattern, or 15 HCP with 2 length points for a 6-4 pattern, or 13-14 HCP and a 6-5 pattern). A hand worth a reverse bid normally contains 5 losers, but a 4-loser hand even with only 12 or 13 HCP would be strong enough for a reverse.

Note in particular that even though you may be playing 5-card majors together with a short club or with a "better-minor" club or a prepared club or a convenient club, or whatever, the standard approach if you do make a reverse bid is that you must have at least 5 cards in your first bid suit. Thus, 1♣ : 1♠, 2♡ will guarantee *five* or more clubs. If you cannot meet those requirements, you should not make a reverse bid. You may rebid in no-trumps or in a lower-ranking suit, but you should not reverse.

SUBSEQUENT BIDDING AFTER A REVERSE

After a 1-level response, opener's reverse is forcing for 1 round. If the response was at the 2-level, opener's reverse is forcing to game.

It is logical that a reverse showing 16 or more points should be game-forcing after a 2-level response which showed 10 or more points. Subsequent bidding after a reverse over a 2-level response follows standard principles : a bid of no-trumps promises a stopper in the missing suit and a bid of the 4th suit asks for a stopper in that suit or for further description of opener's shape and values.

After a 1-level response followed by opener's reverse, responder has 4 weak actions, each of which indicates a hand of about 6-8 HCP and is not forcing :

1. Raise opener's 2nd suit (e.g. 1♣ : 1♠, 2♢ : 3♢) . . . not forcing.
2. Rebid 2NT with a stopper in the 4th suit (e.g. 1♣ : 1♠, 2♢ : 2NT) . . . not forcing.
3. Give preference to opener's 1st suit (e.g. 1♢ : 1NT, 2` : 3♢) . . . not forcing.
4. Rebid responder's suit (e.g. 1♢ : 1♠, 2♡ : 2♠) . . . not forcing.

All other actions by responder are strong, indicating 9 HCP or more and therefore are logically forcing to game, as opener should have the equivalent of 17 points or more. Responder's strong actions will be :

1. 4th-suit-forcing (shows 9+ points after a reverse, e.g. 1♢ : 1♠, 2♡ : 3♣) . . . forcing to game.
2. Any jump rebid (e.g. 1♣ : 1♡, 2♢ : 3♡ *or* 1♣ : 1♡, 2♢ : 4♣) . . . forcing to game.

Suppose the bidding has started 1◇ : 1♠, 2♡ . . . Responder's possible rebids are : 3♡ (6-8 points and support for hearts), 2NT (6-8 points, stopper in clubs, denies support for hearts), 3◇ (6-8 points, preference for diamonds, at least 3-card support), 2♠ (6-8 points, 6-card spade suit or, at the worst, a very good 5-card suit; the rebid of your own suit is used as a last resort with only a 5-card suit), 3♣ (4th-suit-forcing, game-force; opener will support spades with 3 trumps, bid 3NT with a stopper in clubs, or otherwise make some other descriptive bid; if nothing clearcut is available, opener can rebid 3◇), 3♠ or 3NT or 4◇ or 4♡ (all natural and game-going; a bid of game is not forcing; a jump-rebid below game after a reverse is a game-force).

After responder has shown a weak hand in the 6-8 zone, opener with a minimum reverse (16-18 HCP and a 5-4 pattern) should not bid on, especially when responder has given preference to opener's minor. With a hand of 19 or more points, however, opener may still bid again in an effort to reach game. For example, after 1◇ : 1♠, 2♡ : 3◇, a 3♠ rebid by opener now would show 3-card support and indicate a total value of around 19 points, because opener bid again despite responder's minimum rebid. Responder would be expected to bid again over 3♠, choosing 4♠ with 5 spades or even with a strong 4-card suit, or chancing 3NT with a club stopper (unlikely as responder failed to bid 2NT over 2♡) or reverting to diamonds.

EXAMPLES

♠ 2 ♡ A Q 9 6 ◇ A K J 8 6 ♣ K 4 3	You open 1◇. If partner responds 1♠, you should rebid 2♡ (a reverse). You have the right shape (1st suit longer) and enough points. If partner then rebids 3◇ or 2♠ or 2NT, a weak rebid showing 6-8 points, you should pass. Over responder's 3♣ or 3♠ rebid, you should rebid 3NT.
♠ 2 ♡ A Q 9 6 ◇ A K J 8 7 ♣ 7 4 3	You open 1◇. If partner responds 1♠ or 1NT or 2♣, you should rebid 2◇. You have the correct shape for a reverse (1st suit longer than the 2nd suit), but your hand is too weak to make a reverse. 2◇ shows a minimum opening, while 2♡ would show a strong hand since it goes beyond your 2◇ barrier (see page 16).
♠ 7 ♡ A Q 9 8 4 ◇ A K 8 7 5 2 ♣ Q	You open 1◇. If partner responds 1♠ or 1NT or 2♣, you should rebid 2♡. Although your HCP count is not high, you are strong enough to reverse with just a 4-loser hand. Over any weak rebid by responder, you should rebid 3♡ to show that you hold 5 hearts and hence at least 6 diamonds, as you bid diamonds first.

WHEN IS A REVERSE NOT A REVERSE?

If the bidding has gone beyond opener's barrier (see page 16) before opener has had a chance to rebid, opener is allowed to rebid in a new suit at the 2-level without the normal requirements for a reverse. There are 2 common situations when this can arise, after a jump-shift or after a competitive auction. For example, after 1♣ : 2♡, a rebid of 2♠ shows 4 spades but does not promise a strong hand or a long club suit. The sequence is analogous to 1♣ : 1♡, 1♠ but one level higher. As the jump-shift is forcing to game, it is not vital for opener to show extra strength at this stage. Similarly, if the bidding has been, say, 1♣ : (1♠) : 2◇, a rebid of 2♡ by opener need not have extra strength, since responder's 2◇ was already beyond opener's 2♣ barrier. Likewise, after 1◇ : (2♣) : 2♡, a 2♠ rebid by opener may be made on minimum values.

JUMP-SHIFT BY OPENER

Opener's jump-shift is based on a hand worth game opposite a 1-level response and hence should contain 19 or more points or the equivalent. A 4-loser hand with about 16-18 HCP will normally warrant a jump-shift. If the partnership sensibly plays that a 1-level change of suit is forcing, opener's jump-shift to the 2-level (such as 1♣ : 1♡, 2♠) can be used to guarantee at least a 5-4 pattern (5 or more clubs, 4 spades). It would not be a balanced hand (rebid with a jump in no-trumps) or a 4-4-4-1 since the forcing 1♠ rebid would be available for that pattern. To play auctions like 1♣ : 1♡, 1♠ as forcing is no hardship. If partner was able to respond to 1♣, partner will be able to respond to 1♠ also (pretend the 1♠ rebid was the opening).

After a 2-level response, a change of suit is forcing, so that there is less need for opener's jump-shift. Consequently, many partnerships sensibly play that a jump-shift after a 2-over-1 response (e.g. 1♠ : 2♣, 3◇) shows a strong 5-5 pattern. With a strong 5-4 or with a weak 5-5, opener can change suit without jumping (e.g. 1♠ : 2♣, 2◇) and rebid the 2nd suit with the 5-5 (thus a weak 5-5 because of the failure to jump-shift earlier) or rebid strongly with the 5-4.

After the jump-shift, responder will rebid naturally, supporting opener's 2nd suit with 4-card support *or* giving delayed support for opener's 1st suit *or* giving jump-support below game for opener's 1st suit with 4-card support and prospects for slam (e.g. 1♢ : 1♠, 3♣ : 4♢) *or* rebidding responder's suit with a 6-card suit or a very strong (3 honors) 5-card suit *or* bidding 3NT with the 4th suit stopped. With no clearcut action or needing more information from opener, responder can make use of 4th-suit-forcing (e.g. 1♡ : 1♠, 3♣ : 3♢ = 4th-suit-forcing). However, in this situation, 4th-suit-forcing does not promise any extra strength since opener's jump-shift created a game force already. Responder may have a weak 5-card suit, too weak to rebid (e.g. ♠ Q7642 ♡ 72 ♢ Q63 ♣ Q82), or perhaps responder has no stopper in the 4th suit (e.g. ♠ AJ32 ♡ 53 ♢ 6432 ♣ J86), to justify the 3♢ 4th-suit-forcing in the above auction.

RESPONDER'S JUMP-SHIFT

Because responder can create an initial force with a change of suit and can later force again either via 4th-suit-forcing or via a jump-rebid, there is less incentive for responder to make an initial jump-shift, since it is not required in order to locate the best game. In addition, if responder has a very powerful hand, it is better for responder to bid at the cheapest level in order to find out more about opener's hand. It is usually preferable for the stronger hand to find out about the weaker than the other way around. Therefore, many partnerships restrict the use of responder's strong jump-shift to 2 types of hands, the powerful single-suiter (at least a 5-card suit containing 3 honors) or a hand with superb support for opener's suit. The jump-shift will be based on 19 points or more (or the equivalent in shape, i.e. a 4-loser hand) and is forcing to game, with significant slam aspirations. With a 2-suiter hand or with a balanced hand, bid at the cheapest level, even with 19 points or more. The jump-shift shows 19 points up, but not all hands with 19+ hands warrant a jump-shift. The jump-shift is used to look for slam, not to reach just a game.

THE JUMP-SHIFT TO THE 3-LEVEL AFTER PASSING

After passing, a 2-level response shows 10-12 points and a 5-card suit (see page 34). What then should one make of a jump-shift to the 3-level after passing (e.g. Pass : 1♠, 3♣)? It cannot show more points . . . how much more can you have if you could not open? Most partnerships, especially at duplicate, utilise the jump-shift after passing to show a maximum pass + a strong 5-card suit + support for opener's suit. The support will depend on what length is promised by the opening bid, but if playing 5-card majors, responder's 3♣ in Pass : 1♠, 3♣ would promise 5 good clubs, 10-11 points and 3 spades or more. If the club suit were not strong, responder should choose Pass : 1♠, 3♠ and not bother to show a weak secondary suit.

Using this approach, it follows that auctions like Pass : 1♠, 2♣ deny support for opener's suit and so opener would be less inclined to repeat an ordinary suit or to bid at all with a minimum opening as well as tolerance for responder's suit.

It is also cannot be rational for responder to make a *natural* jump to 3NT after passing. For example, Pass : 1♡, 3NT is logically impossible. If you had enough to warrant 3NT, you would have had enough to open the bidding. Some partnerships use this sequence to promise very strong support for opener's suit and a hand too good to jump to 3-of-opener's-suit which could be dropped. The jump to 3NT after passing says, "I have exceptional support for your suit and an absolutely maximum passed hand. It is so good that I cannot risk being dropped below game. If you have extra values, there could even be a slam on." Consequently, after passing, responder's raises of opener's major in order of strength would be to the 2-level (6-10 points), to the 4-level (pre-emptive, 6-9 HCP, 7 losers), to the 3-level (10-12 points, 8 losers) and to 3NT (10-12 points, 7 losers or better).

FAKE REVERSES AND FAKE JUMP-SHIFTS

Opener may choose to reverse or to jump-shift into only a 3-card suit when holding support for responder's suit. Since the reverse or jump-shift is forcing, opener will have another chance to show the values held. This is revealed if opener bids game in responder's suit without responder having shown more than 4-card length. For example, 1♢ : 1♠, 3♣ : 3NT, 4♠ . . . opener certainly has 4 spades, but may have only 3 clubs. Indeed, opener's most likely pattern is 4-1-5-3 with a hand too good to jump to 4♠ over 1♠. Likewise, after 1♣ : 1♠, it would be safe for opener to reverse into 2♡ with a strong hand and a 3-3-1-6 pattern, even though there are only 3 hearts. If responder raises hearts to show 4-card support, responder must hold 5 spades to have bid 1♠ ahead of the 4-card heart suit and so opener will be able to revert to spades over any heart raise.

EXERCISES

A. You opened 1♣ and partner responded 1♠. What is your rebid on these hands?

1.	♠ A 4	2.	♠ 7 3	3.	♠ 3	4.	♠ J 4 3	5.	♠ 8 6
	♡ A K 9 8		♡ A Q J 6		♡ A K 9		♡ A K J 3		♡ Q J 6 2
	◊ Q 6		◊ 9 2		◊ K 7 4 2		◊ K 6		◊ A
	♣ J 8 6 4 3		♣ A Q 9 8 2		♣ A K J 6 4		♣ A K 9 3		♣ A K Q 8 6 3

B. With silent opponents, the bidding has been 1◊ : 1♠, 2♡. What is responder's next action?

1.	♠ K J 6 3	2.	♠ J 8 6 4 2	3.	♠ Q J 9 7 3 2	4.	♠ J 9 8 4	5.	♠ Q J 9 8
	♡ Q 5 4		♡ K 8 6 3		♡ A K		♡ 7 3 2		♡ 9 2
	◊ 7 6 2		◊ 8 6		◊ 6 5 2		◊ 6 5		◊ 7 5 3
	♣ 9 8 4		♣ Q 2		♣ J 6		♣ A J 7 4		♣ A K J 5

6.	♠ 9 8 7 6 4 2	7.	♠ A K 7 3	8.	♠ K Q 8 4 3	9.	♠ A 8 6 2	10.	♠ A K 8 6 2
	♡ 2		♡ K 4		♡ 5 2		♡ 2		♡ K Q 7 3 2
	◊ 3 2		◊ 9 3 2		◊ 8 3		◊ K Q 7 3		◊ 9 6
	♣ A Q 5 4		♣ 7 6 3 2		♣ A 9 6 2		♣ K 8 4 3		♣ 7

C. The bidding has started 1◊ : 1♠, 3♣. What action should responder now take on these hands?

1.	♠ K Q 7 4	2.	♠ A 9 8 6 3	3.	♠ J 8 6 4 3	4.	♠ Q 10 9 7 3 2	5.	♠ Q J 8 6 5 2
	♡ 9 7 3		♡ 8 5 4		♡ J 3		♡ 8 7 4		♡ K J 9 8 6 3
	◊ Q 10 6		◊ 6 4		◊ A K 6 4		◊ 6 2		◊ 3
	♣ 6 5 2		♣ Q 5 2		♣ Q 9		♣ A 2		♣ - - -

PARTNERSHIP BIDDING : How should the following hands be bid? West is the dealer on all hands.

SET 37 – WEST	SET 37 – EAST	SET 38 – WEST	SET 38 – EAST
1. ♠ K 8 7 3 2	1. ♠ 4	1. ♠ A 7 6 2	1. ♠ K 4
♡ K 4	♡ A Q 9 6	♡ J 3 2	♡ K Q 7 6
◊ 7 5 4	◊ A K J 8 6	◊ 5 4	◊ A K Q 3 2
♣ 6 5 2	♣ K 4 3	♣ A J 10 8	♣ 9 3
2. ♠ K 8 7 3 2	2. ♠ 4	2. ♠ J 6	2. ♠ K 9 7 4 2
♡ K 4	♡ A Q 9 6	♡ A K 3 2	♡ 6 5
◊ 9 5	◊ A K J 8 6	◊ 7 6	◊ A 9 8
♣ 9 8 5 2	♣ 7 4 3	♣ A K Q 4 3	♣ 7 6 5
3. ♠ 3 2	3. ♠ A 8 7 5 4	3. ♠ Q 7 6 2	3. ♠ K 8 3
♡ A 9 8 6	♡ K 4 3 2	♡ 6 5 3	♡ K Q J 2
◊ A K J 8 6 4	◊ 5	◊ A J 10	◊ 8
♣ 7	♣ A 9 4	♣ 7 5 3	♣ A K Q 4 2
4. ♠ A Q	4. ♠ J 8 6	4. ♠ 4 3	4. ♠ A K 7 2
♡ 7 3	♡ K Q 8 6 5 4	♡ A K Q 2	♡ 7 6 5
◊ K Q 7 2	◊ 9 3	◊ A Q 8 6 2	◊ K 4 3
♣ A J 10 4 3	♣ 7 5	♣ K 3	♣ 8 6 2
5. ♠ A 10	5. ♠ 7 3	5. ♠ Q 10 6 5 2	5. ♠ A 8 3
♡ 7 3	♡ A Q 8 6 5 4	♡ 6 5	♡ K Q J 2
◊ K Q J 3	◊ A 2	◊ A J 4	◊ 8
♣ A Q 8 7 4	♣ 5 3 2	♣ K 5 3	♣ A Q J 4 2
6. ♠ A J 9 6	6. ♠ K 7 4	6. ♠ 4 2	6. ♠ A 9 6 5 3
♡ A K Q 8 6	♡ 3 2	♡ A K Q 3	♡ 9 6
◊ K 5	◊ 8 7 4 3	◊ K Q J 5 3 2	◊ A 8 7 6
♣ 7 2	♣ A K J 9	♣ Q	♣ A 6

PLAY HANDS ON REVERSES

Hand 69 : Rebidding after a reverse — Discarding a loser and ruffing in dummy

Dealer North : North-South vulnerable

NORTH
♠ A 9 6
♡ 10 8 3 2
◇ Q 10 3
♣ Q J 10

WEST
♠ 4
♡ A Q 9 6
◇ A K J 8 6
♣ K 4 3

EAST
♠ K 8 7 3 2
♡ K 4
◇ 7 5 4
♣ 6 5 2

SOUTH
♠ Q J 10 5
♡ J 7 5
◇ 9 2
♣ A 9 8 7

WEST	NORTH	EAST	SOUTH
	Pass	Pass	Pass
1◇	Pass	1♠	Pass
2♡ (1)	Pass	3◇ (2)	Pass
Pass (3)	Pass		

Bidding : (1) West has the right shape for the reverse (2-suiter, with the first suit longer) and the right strength, 16 HCP or more, or 5 losers or better.

(2) With a minimum responding hand, East should choose a minimum rebid. 2♠ is possible but 3◇ is superior : play in the known trump fit (since 2♡ promised 4 hearts and 5+ diamonds).

(3) With a minimum reverse (only 17 HCP, no better than 5 losers) West should respect East's sign-off. Although 3NT has some chance, the odds for success in 3NT are poor. The club lead is marked and the defense can take 3 clubs, 1 spade and 1 diamond. 3NT requires diamonds to break with the Q onside, less than 50%.

Lead : ♣Q. The unbid suit and top of sequence.

Correct play : South wins the first trick with the ♣A and West should win the club return. Rather than tackle trumps at once, declarer can discard the club loser : heart to the K, heart to the A and on the ♡Q, dummy's 3rd club is discarded. You could ruff the club loser in dummy next, but a sound move before ruffing the club is to lead the singleton spade. If North plays low, you have stolen a spade trick; if North takes the spade and returns a spade, discard a heart, play a diamond to the A and ruff the club. North's best defense is to take the ♠A and lead a heart, allowing South to overruff dummy. From the bidding, North knows that declarer has 4 hearts and thus South must now be void. On best defense, declarer will make just 9 tricks.

Hand 70 : Ducking a side suit to retain control and prevent trumps being drawn

Dealer East : East-West vulnerable

NORTH
♠ A J 6 4
♡ 7 5 2
◇ J 9 2
♣ 10 8 3

WEST
♠ Q 8 7
♡ Q 10 8 6
◇ K 7 5
♣ Q J 9

EAST
♠ K 10 9 5 2
♡ J 9
◇ A 6 4 3
♣ 7 2

SOUTH
♠ 3
♡ A K 4 3
◇ Q 10 8
♣ A K 6 5 4

WEST	NORTH	EAST	SOUTH
		Pass	1♣
Pass	1♠ (1)	Pass	2♡ (2)
Pass	3♣ (3)	Pass	Pass (4)
Pass			

Bidding : (1) 1♠ is much better than a 1NT response.

(2) South's 2♡ shows 4 hearts and longer clubs (even though the 1♣ opening might not have been a genuine club). The 2♡ rebid not only indicates the 4-card heart length but also simultaneously clarifies that the club opening was genuine and at least a 5-card suit. One of the advantages of the reverse is that it shows 5+ cards in the suit opened without having to rebid that suit.

(3) With no stopper in the unbid suit, North should give preference to partner's longer suit.

(4) With no extra values, South should accept the sign-off.

Lead : ◇5. It is natural to lead the unbid suit, diamonds, and the correct card from K-x-x is the bottom card.

Correct play : The defense takes the first 2 diamonds, declarer winning the 3rd round. It is tempting to draw 2 rounds of trumps and then play A, K and a 3rd heart. This plan would work if hearts were 3-3 or the player who wins the 3rd heart does not hold the last trump. However, as the cards lie, West would win the 3rd heart, draw dummy's trump with the ♣Q and then cash the heart winner for one off. In situations like these, where a heart has to be lost anyway, concede a heart before touching trumps. Then you can win any return, cash A-K of trumps, A-K of hearts and ruff the heart loser in dummy. South loses 2 diamonds, 1 heart and 1 club.

Hand 71 : Discarding a loser before touching trumps − Double finesse.

Dealer South : Both vulnerable

WEST	NORTH	EAST	SOUTH
			Pass
1♣	Pass	1♡	Pass
2♢ (1)	Pass	3♡ (2)	Pass
4♡ (3)	Pass	Pass	Pass

NORTH
- ♠ K 10 8 4 2
- ♡ J 9
- ♢ 9 7 6 5
- ♣ 9 8

WEST
- ♠ A J
- ♡ 7 3
- ♢ K Q 8 2
- ♣ A Q 10 4 3

EAST
- ♠ 7 3
- ♡ A Q 8 6 5 4
- ♢ A 3
- ♣ 6 5 2

SOUTH
- ♠ Q 9 6 5
- ♡ K 10 2
- ♢ J 10 4
- ♣ K J 7

Bidding : (1) 2♢ shows 4 diamonds, 5+ clubs and 16+ HCP (or if less than 16 HCP, 5 losers or better).

(2) As 2♡ would be a weak rebid, showing just 6-8 points, East must take stronger action. With 9 HCP or more opposite a reverse, either make a jump-rebid or bid the 4th-suit to make a forcing bid. 3♡ shows 9 points or more with at least 6 hearts.

(3) West could rebid 3NT since West has a stopper in spades, but 4♡ is superior, as West has doubleton support for the 6-card suit shown by East's 3♡ rebid. 3NT can be made on the normal spade lead (win ♠ A; cross to ♢ A; finesse the ♣10; cross to ♡ A; finesse the ♣Q; making 5 clubs, 3 diamonds and 2 aces), but if either club finesse were to lose, you would go down.

Lead : ♠4. The natural lead is a spade, the unbid suit.

Correct play : Declarer can make 11 tricks because of the lucky club position : win the ♠ A, play a diamond to the A, diamond to the K and discard the spade loser on the ♢ Q. Then finesse the ♡ Q. This loses, but declarer ruffs the spade return, cashes the ♡ A and, leaving the top trump out, leads a club, finessing the 10. (With A-Q-10 opposite x-x-x, finesse the 10 first unless you need *only one* extra trick.) A diamond ruff back to hand allows declarer to finesse the ♣ Q. (As a heart trick must be lost in any event, the technically superior line is : win ♠ A; *cash* ♡ A; ♢ A; ♢ K; ♢ Q, discarding the spade loser; heart to the Q, and so on.)

Hand 72 : Strong action after a reverse − Ruffing a loser − Coping with a bad trump break

Dealer West : Nil vulnerable

WEST	NORTH	EAST	SOUTH
Pass	1♢	Pass	1♠ (1)
Pass	2♡	Pass	4♢ (2)
Pass	4NT	Pass	5♠
Pass	5NT (3)	Pass	6♢
Pass	7♢ (4)	All pass	

NORTH
- ♠ K 2
- ♡ A K Q 3
- ♢ K Q J 9 3
- ♣ 7 5

WEST
- ♠ Q J 10
- ♡ 8 7
- ♢ 10 5 4 2
- ♣ 9 8 3 2

EAST
- ♠ 9 8 7 4
- ♡ J 10 5 4 2
- ♢ - - -
- ♣ Q J 10 6

SOUTH
- ♠ A 6 5 3
- ♡ 9 6
- ♢ A 8 7 6
- ♣ A K 4

Bidding : (1) 1♠ is much better than 2NT. Firstly, prefer to show a major suit; secondly, the weakness in hearts is a drawback to 2NT.
(2) Better than 4NT, since if you are holding only aces and kings, it is better to answer Blackwood than to ask for aces yourself. If North were to bid 5♢ next, South is worth 6♢ simply on values.
(3) Confirms all the aces are held and shows grand slam ambitions. If South shows no king, North will settle in 6♢.
(4) North can count on 12 top tricks for no-trumps via 2 spades, 3 hearts, 5 diamonds and 2 clubs. If not bidding a grand slam, North would choose 6NT, but the chance of ruffing a heart for the extra trick makes the grand slam in diamonds attractive.

Lead : ♣Q. The unbid suit is normal unless there are strong reasons for a different choice.

Correct play : Win the lead and play a diamond to the K. With no possible trump losers, keep the trump suit "fluid" by keeping a top trump in each hand. If trumps were 2-2 or 3-1, the hand would be child's play, drawing trumps and ruffing the heart loser. With the bad break, North must ruff the heart loser before drawing trumps, so switch to ♡A, ♡K and then the ♡3, *ruffing with the ace of diamonds*, finesse the 9 of diamonds, draw trumps and claim. Traps to avoid include playing off the ace, king *and queen* of hearts *or* failing to ruff the 3 of hearts high *or* drawing 4 rounds of trumps at once *or* playing the ♢ A on the first round of trumps.

CHAPTER 19

SHAPE-SHOWING — 5-5, 6-6 AND 6-5 PATTERNS

Balanced hands are generally described with one or two bids, but for unbalanced hands, it frequently takes three bids to convey the hand pattern to partner. Consequently, one should be reluctant to jump to game, particularly 3NT, if partner has not yet had the chance to reveal the shape of the hand.

Certain hand patterns are described in a standard way, whether one plays 4-card majors or 5-card majors, and it is important to be aware of the technique to show specific hand patterns. Shape-showing bids continue, provided that the hands are strong enough to keep bidding, until either a trump fit has been located or one partner's shape has been fully revealed. The other partner should then be able to decide on the contract. Once a trump suit has been agreed, shape-showing is usually discontinued and the value of the hand is then bid (pass, invite game, bid game, explore slam, and so on).

THE 5-5 PATTERN

OPEN WITH THE HIGHER RANKING SUIT (regardless of suit quality)

NEXT BID THE LOWER-RANKING SUIT

THEN REBID THE LOWER SUIT

You can train your ear to listen for the sequence: first suit, second suit, second suit again (Code: ABB). These are typical auctions where the opener has revealed at least a 5-5 pattern:

WEST	EAST		WEST	EAST
1♢	1♠		1♠	2♢
2♣	2NT		2♡	3♣
3♣ . . .			3♡ . . .	

West has at least 5 diamonds and 5 clubs.   West has at least 5 spades and 5 hearts.

While this is the most common approach, it is also standard that a jump to game in a new suit shows at least a 5-card suit. Accordingly, West is showing at least a 5-5 pattern in the major suits in each of these auctions:

WEST	EAST		WEST	EAST
1♠	1NT			1♣
4♡ . . .			1♠	2NT
			4♡ . . .	

THE 6-6 PATTERN

The description of the freak 6-6 pattern commences the same way as the 5-5 (Higher Suit, Lower Suit, Repeat Lower Suit) but if suit agreement has not been reached after the first three shape-showing bids, the 6-6 hand rebids the lower suit once more. A jump to 5-of-a-minor is also often indicative of the 6-6 pattern, for example, 1♢ : 1♠, 5♣.

THE 6-5 PATTERN

OPEN WITH THE 6-CARD SUIT (regardless of suit quality)

NEXT BID THE 5-CARD SUIT

THEN REBID THE 5-CARD SUIT

The sequence to show a 6-5 pattern is also first suit, second suit, second suit again (Code: ABB). Where the 6-card suit is also higher-ranking than the 5-card suit, the sequence will follow the same path as for 5-5s. Each of the auctions in the 5-5 section is consistent with West holding a 6-5 pattern. Where the 6-card suit is lower-ranking, there will be no ambiguity and partner will be able to identify the pattern as 6-5.

WEST	EAST
1♦	1♠
2♡	2NT
3♡ ...	

WEST	EAST
1♣	1♡
1♠	2♦
2♠ ...	

West has at least 6 diamonds and 5 hearts.

West has at least 6 clubs and 5 spades.

West's rebid of the second suit confirms five cards in the second suit, but had the pattern been 5-5, the higher-ranking suit would have been opened. The logical explanation is that the lower suit must be longer.

Since a jump to game in a new suit promises five cards in that suit, West is also taken as showing at least a 6-5 pattern in each of these auctions :

WEST	EAST
1♣	1♠
4♡ ...	

WEST	EAST
	1♣
1♦	1NT
4♡ ...	

EXERCISE

Assuming you do not find a trump fit early and partner forces you to keep bidding, what three bids should you utilise to show the following hand patterns?

1. ♠ 7	2. ♠ A	3. ♠ A 8 6 4 3 2	4. ♠ 7	5. ♠ A J 6 5 2
♡ 7 3	♡ Q	♡ A	♡ A J 9 8 4 2	♡ 6
♦ A Q 9 6 4	♦ Q J 7 6 4	♦ K 8 7 6 4 3	♦ A K 8 6 2	♦ A K 9 5 3 2
♣ A K J 3 2	♣ A K 8 7 3 2	♣ - - -	♣ 7	♣ J

PARTNERSHIP BIDDING : How should these hands be bid? West is the dealer on all hands.

SET 39 — WEST	SET 39 — EAST	SET 40 — WEST	SET 40 — EAST
1. ♠ K Q 8 7 6	1. ♠ 3	1. ♠ K Q 9 4 3	1. ♠ A 5 2
♡ A K 9 4 3	♡ J 5 2	♡ 8	♡ K J 9 7 4
♦ J 3	♦ A K 9 7	♦ A Q J 6 4 2	♦ 7 3
♣ 2	♣ A J 6 4 3	♣ 3	♣ A J 6
2. ♠ A 2	2. ♠ K Q 8 6 4	2. ♠ 8 3 2	2. ♠ A K 7 5 4
♡ Q 9 2	♡ J 10 8 6 5	♡ A K J 8 5 3	♡ 4
♦ 7 6	♦ A J 3	♦ 8 7 2	♦ 5
♣ A K 9 8 7 3	♣ - - -	♣ A	♣ K Q 7 6 4 3
3. ♠ J 2	3. ♠ A 9 7 6 5	3. ♠ A Q J 6 2	3. ♠ 5
♡ 9 8	♡ A K 7 3 2	♡ K Q 9 8 4 3	♡ A 2
♦ A Q 8	♦ J	♦ - - -	♦ J 8 7 6
♣ A K 9 8 7 3	♣ 4 2	♣ J 2	♣ K Q 8 5 4 3
4. ♠ J 3 2	4. ♠ K Q 9 7 4	4. ♠ 6 4	4. ♠ A K 8 3 2
♡ K 6	♡ A 9 5 4 2	♡ 3 2	♡ K Q 7 6 5 4
♦ A Q 7 6 3 2	♦ 8	♦ A Q 2	♦ 5
♣ K 2	♣ A 3	♣ A K 8 7 4 2	♣ 3
5. ♠ 3 2	5. ♠ Q J 8 7 6 5	5. ♠ 4 3	5. ♠ A Q 9 6 5
♡ 2	♡ K Q 3	♡ J 2	♡ 7 3
♦ A K 8 4 3	♦ 5	♦ K 8 7	♦ A Q 9 5 4 2
♣ K Q 9 8 7	♣ 4 3 2	♣ A K Q 10 4 2	♣ - - -
6. ♠ - - -	6. ♠ Q 9 8 6 5 4	6. ♠ A Q 8 6 4	6. ♠ 7 3 2
♡ J 3 2	♡ A 8 7	♡ 3	♡ K Q 9 8
♦ A K 8 4 3	♦ 6	♦ 7	♦ Q 4 3 2
♣ K Q 9 6 2	♣ J 5 4	♣ A Q 9 6 5 2	♣ 4 3

PLAY HANDS ON SHAPE-SHOWING — 5-5 AND 6-5 PATTERNS

Hand 73: 5-5 pattern — Misfit — Ducking to set up a long suit

Dealer North : East-West vulnerable

NORTH
♠ 9 3
♡ Q 10 6 5
♢ K 7 6 4
♣ Q 6 3

WEST
♠ A 7 6 5 4
♡ A K 7 3 2
♢ J
♣ 4 2

EAST
♠ J 2
♡ 9 8
♢ A Q 8
♣ A K 9 8 7 5

SOUTH
♠ K Q 10 8
♡ J 4
♢ 10 9 5 3 2
♣ J 10

WEST	NORTH	EAST	SOUTH
	Pass	1♣	Pass
1♠	Pass	2♣	Pass
2♡	Pass	2NT	Pass
3♡ (1)	Pass	3NT (2)	All pass

Bidding : (1) Repeating the hearts to confirm the 5-5.
(2) With no fit for either major and the diamonds well stopped.

Lead : ♢ 3. As declarer and dummy have at least 5 cards in spades, hearts and clubs, it is normal to lead the unbid suit.

Correct play : North plays the ♢ K and declarer wins the ace. With 7 top tricks, declarer sees that the club suit offers the best chance for extra tricks. It may work to play ♣A, ♣K and give up a club if the opponents continue diamonds, but if the opponents do not cooperate and lead either major, declarer would have no entry to hand and 3 club winners and a diamond winner would be stranded.

It does not pay to rely on the opponents to help you, particularly when you can help yourself. Since a club trick has to be lost anyway, declarer should simply "duck a club" (play a low club from both hands) at trick 2. Now even if the opponents fail to continue diamonds, dummy has a club to reach declarer's hand. As long as the clubs divide 3-2, declarer has an easy path to 10 tricks (1 spade, 2 hearts, 2 diamonds and 5 clubs). Declarer could also have attempted to establish the hearts, but it is better to go for the clubs since you have more of them and so a favourable break in clubs is more likely than in hearts or spades.

Hand 74: How to handle a 2-suiter in the play — Setting up the 2nd suit early

Dealer East : Both vulnerable

NORTH
♠ 9 2
♡ K 7 6
♢ A 8 3
♣ A Q 7 4 3

WEST
♠ J 4
♡ Q J 5 2
♢ Q 10 6 4
♣ J 8 5

EAST
♠ A 10 8 5
♡ 10
♢ J 9 7 5
♣ K 10 9 6

SOUTH
♠ K Q 7 6 3
♡ A 9 8 4 3
♢ K 2
♣ 2

WEST	NORTH	EAST	SOUTH
		Pass	1♠
Pass	2♣	Pass	2♡
Pass	3♢ (1)	Pass	3♡ (2)
Pass	4♡ (3)	All pass	

Bidding: (1) 4th-suit-forcing, planning to rebid 3 NT over a 3♠ rebid by opener. 2NT instead of 3♢ would be fine if the partnership played 2NT in this auction as forcing.
(2) Confirms the 5-5 by rebidding the lower-ranking suit.
(3) The 5-3 heart fit is now known. 4♡ is far superior to 3NT, which is almost hopeless on a diamond lead. 4♡ can be made by skilful play despite the bad trump break and poor split in spades.

Lead : ♢ 4. The unbid suit is the natural lead.

Correct Play : The best way to play a pronounced 2-suiter is to set up the 2nd suit if it is not already high. Where losers in the 2nd suit need to be ruffed and dummy has only a few trumps, it is normal to set about the 2nd suit early, usually before drawing trumps. It also does not pay you to ruff in the long trump hand unless this is unavoidable. Declarer's trump length will be needed later as entries for the established 2nd suit.

Win the ♢ A and lead a spade to the king (East should duck). Play a heart to the king in order to lead dummy's last spade, taken by East who will return a diamond (or a trump). Win the diamond and play the ♡ A, followed by a low spade to ruff in dummy. It would be an error to lead the ♠ Q first, since West could ruff this high and lead the other top trump, eliminating dummy's last trump and leaving you with an extra spade loser. When you regain the lead, just keep on playing spades, forcing West to ruff.

Hand 75 : 6-5 pattern — Setting up the 2nd suit before drawing trumps

Dealer South : Nil vulnerable

NORTH
- ♠ A K 7 5 4
- ♡ A 8 6 5 3 2
- ◇ 6
- ♣ 5

WEST
- ♠ Q 10 9 2
- ♡ K J 9
- ◇ K 10 4 2
- ♣ 6 3

EAST
- ♠ J
- ♡ Q 10 4
- ◇ Q J 9 8 3
- ♣ Q 10 9 2

SOUTH
- ♠ 8 6 3
- ♡ 7
- ◇ A 7 5
- ♣ A K J 8 7 4

WEST	NORTH	EAST	SOUTH
			1♣
Pass	1♡	Pass	2♣
Pass	2♠ (1)	Pass	2NT (2)
Pass	3♠ (3)	Pass	4♠ (4)
Pass	Pass	Pass	

Bidding : (1) New suit by responder is forcing.
(2) Merely confirms a stopper in diamonds and no support yet for either of responder's suits.
(3) The spade rebid confirms 5 spades and therefore 6 hearts, as hearts were bid first. With a 5-5, spades would have been bid first.
(4) It is clearcut to support now that partner has shown 5 spades. It would have been premature to raise spades over 2♠, as it might then have been only a 4-card suit. With a doubleton in each major, responder would have supported hearts here. Note that 3NT is hopeless on the obvious diamond lead.

Lead : ◇ Q. The unbid suit is normal. Top of a near-sequence.

Correct play : Win the ◇ A and continue with the ♡ A and ruff a heart, spade to the ace and ruff another heart. When hearts divide 3-3, declarer's remaining hearts are high. Ruff a diamond to hand and cash the ♠ K. When spades do not break, keep on leading hearts. *Do not play a third trump.* If hearts had not been 3-3, you may hope that a defender who overruffs is using what would have been a trump winner anyway. It would also have been an error to play trumps early, as dummy's trumps are needed to ruff hearts. Another error would be to ruff clubs or diamonds in hand. It is normally wrong to shorten the long trump hand. Ruffing with the long trump hand is appropriate if you need an entry to hand, or you are playing on a cross-ruff, or you are in the process of setting up a long suit in dummy.

Hand 76 : 6-5 pattern — Setting up the 2nd suit early

Dealer West : North-South vulnerable

NORTH
- ♠ J 10 8 7
- ♡ A 9 2
- ◇ 10
- ♣ Q 9 8 7 4

WEST
- ♠ K Q 9 4 3
- ♡ 8
- ◇ A Q J 6 4 2
- ♣ 3

EAST
- ♠ A 5 2
- ♡ K J 10 7 4
- ◇ 7 3
- ♣ A J 6

SOUTH
- ♠ 6
- ♡ Q 6 5 3
- ◇ K 9 8 5
- ♣ K 10 5 2

WEST	NORTH	EAST	SOUTH
1◇	Pass	1♡	Pass
1♠	Pass	2♣ (1)	Pass
2♠ (2)	Pass	4♠ (3)	All pass

Bidding : (1) 4th-suit-forcing, planning to rebid 3NT unless opener shows a significant distributional feature. If the partnership plays all jump rebids by responder as forcing to game, a 2NT rebid by East would be all right and West would rebid 3♠ over 2NT. It is unnecessary to rebid the hearts. If opener holds 3 hearts, such secondary supprt will be shown in response to 4th-suit-forcing.
(2) Confirms the 6-5 shape with at least 6 diamonds.
(3) With support for both the major and the minor, prefer to support the major.

Lead : ♣7. The unbid suit is normal. The ◇ 10 would be a poor lead. With a natural trump trick, it is rarely desirable to lead a singleton, looking for a ruff. Furthermore, it is almost always poor strategy to lead declarer's 2nd suit.

Correct play : Win the ♣ A and finesse the ◇ Q. Cross to dummy's ♠ A and finesse the ◇ J. If North ruffs and returns a club, you ruff, cash the ♠ K, ♠ Q and continue with the ◇ A and another diamond, setting up your diamonds. You lose just 1 spade, 1 heart and 1 diamond. It would be an error to draw trumps early (you may need dummy's trumps to ruff diamonds) or to ruff a club in hand (do not shorten the long trump hand). Whenever West leads a heart, North should rise with the ace, as the ♡ 8 must be a singleton. As West's bidding has shown 6 diamonds, 5 spades and West followed to the 1st club, West cannot hold more than 1 heart.

CHAPTER 20
SHAPE-SHOWING — 6-4 AND 5-4 PATTERNS

Showing the 6-4 and 5-4 patterns is not as cut and dried as the 5-5 and 6-5 patterns, because the way to treat them will depend on which is the long suit and which the short and also the strength of the hand. One of the major obstacles to revealing the complete shape is the inability to "reverse" when the hand is minimum (see Chapter 18 on Reverses). *Bidding a new suit at the 2-level higher-ranking than your 1st suit shows a better-than-minimum hand.* Therefore, when opener's hand *is* minimum, opener should not bid the 2nd suit at the 2-level if the 2nd suit is higher-ranking. For example, 1♢ : 1♠, 2♡ is a reverse and shows extra values, while 1♢ : 1♠, 2♣ does not. Similarly, after a 2-level response, the opener is not permitted to proceed to the 3-level with minimum values : *opener's rebid at the 3-level after a 2-level response shows a better-than-minimum hand.* Therefore, when the hand *is* minimum, opener may bid a new suit at the 2-level lower than the suit opened or, if this is not possible, opener will have to rebid the original suit. For example, 1♠ : 2♢, 3♣ shows extra values, while 1♠ : 2♢, 2♡ does not promise more than a minimum, because the rebid is at the 2-level and lower than the suit opened. **The Barrier Principle :** The 2-level rebid of the suit opened creates a barrier and opener's rebids higher than the barrier show a strong opening (see Chapter 2, page 16).

THE 6-4 PATTERN : If the hand is not minimum, the standard approach is :

Start with the 6-card suit — Next bid the 4-card suit — Then rebid the 6-card suit

The order this time is : first suit, second suit, first suit again (Code : ABA). These are typical auctions where the opener has revealed at least a 6-4 pattern :

WEST	EAST		WEST	EAST
1♢	1♡		1♠	2♢
2♣	2NT		2♡	3♢
3♢ …			3♠ …	

West has at least 6 diamonds and 4 clubs.   West has at least 6 spades and 4 hearts.

Where the opener has a minimum hand, it will depend on which suits are held. With a 6-card minor and a 4-card major, open the 6-card minor and bid the 4-card major next at the 1-level if possible. If this is not possible (e.g. you hold 6 clubs and 4 hearts and the bidding has started 1♣ : 1♠), repeat the 6-card minor. Do not bid your 4-card major at the 2-level with only minimum values, because it is higher than your barrier.

With a 6-card major and a 4-card minor, open the major and bid the minor next if possible at the 2-level. If the 2-level is not possible (e.g. you have 6 spades and 4 clubs and the bidding has started 1♠ : 2♡), repeat your 6-card major. Do not bid to the 3-level with only minimum values. Also if your 6-card major is very strong and your 4-card minor is very weak, do not show the minor but rather repeat the major suit.

With 6 spades - 4 hearts, follow the normal order (spades, hearts, then spades again) unless a fit has been found earlier. With 4 spades and 6 hearts, you open 1♡ but with only minimum values, you are not strong enough to reverse with 2♠ over a 1NT or 2♣ or 2♢ response. Rebid just 2♡ to confirm the minimum opening.

THE 5-4-4-0 PATTERN : Open with the 5-card suit and if the hand is not minimum, show the cheaper 4-card suit next and, if still no trump fit has been found, bid the 3rd suit (e.g. 1♡ : 1♠, 2♣ : 2NT, 3♢ …). The same applies if the hand is minimum except that you must not make a reverse bid, or bid a new suit at the 3-level over a 2-level response. For example, if you held 4 hearts, 4 diamonds and 5 clubs and opened 1♣, if partner responded 1♠, you could rebid 2♢ (a reverse) if better than minimum, but should rebid only 2♣ if the hand is minimum. Likewise, if you held 5 spades, 4 diamonds and 4 clubs and opened 1♠, if partner responded 2♡, you could rebid 3♣ if better than minimum but should rebid 2♠ with a minimum.

THE 5-4-2-2 PATTERN : It is normal to open the 5-card suit and then bid the 4-card suit. However, if the hand is minimum, the rebid in the 2nd suit must not be a reverse bid or a bid at the 3-level. Where the hand is minimum and most of the high card points are in the doubletons, prefer to rebid in no-trumps. However, if your 2nd suit is a major, show the major if it can be done without bidding beyond your barrier.

THE 5-4-3-1 PATTERN: Open with the 5-card suit and then bid the 4-card suit (with the usual restriction that you must not reverse or venture to the 3-level with only a minimum). If your hand is too weak to bid your 4-card suit beyond your barrier, you may repeat your 5-card suit *or* raise partner with just 3-card support *or* rebid 1NT if the singleton is in partner's suit and your 5-card suit is very weak.

If no fit has been found after you have shown both your suits and you are obliged to bid again, then if your 3-card holding is in partner's original suit, support that suit ("delayed support") but if your 3-card holding is in the unbid suit, accept your partner's suggestion for no-trumps or bid no-trumps yourself if the 3-card holding amounts to a stopper (Q-x-x or better = a stopper). If your 3-card suit is J-x-x or worse and partner has not bid no-trumps, rebid your 5-card suit as a last resort.

EXERCISES

A. You opened 1 ◊ and partner responded 1♠. What is your rebid on each of these hands?

1. ♠ 8 2	2. ♠ A 2	3. ♠ A 2	4. ♠ A 2	5. ♠ A 8 7 2
♡ 3	♡ 3	♡ K J 6 4	♡ K J 6 4	♡ 6
◊ A Q J 8 6 4	◊ A K J 9 7 2	◊ A J 6 4 3 2	◊ A J 6 4 3 2	◊ A K J 4 3 2
♣ K Q 9 3	♣ 8 7 3 2	♣ 7	♣ A	♣ A 3

B. You opened 1 ◊ and partner responded 1♠. What is your rebid on each of these hands?

1. ♠ K 7	2. ♠ Q	3. ♠ A 6 3	4. ♠ - - -	5. ♠ - - -
♡ K J 7 3	♡ A K Q	♡ K Q 7 2	♡ A J 7 2	♡ A Q 7 2
◊ A Q 9 6 4	◊ Q 9 7 6 4	◊ K 8 6 4 3	◊ A K 8 6 2	◊ A K 9 4 3
♣ 4 2	♣ J 7 3 2	♣ 4	♣ Q 8 6 2	♣ K J 7 2

PARTNERSHIP BIDDING: How should the following hands be bid? West is the dealer on all hands.

SET 41 − WEST	SET 41 − EAST	SET 42 − WEST	SET 42 − EAST
1. ♠ K Q 8 7 4 3	1. ♠ J 6	1. ♠ Q 6 5	1. ♠ K J 9 3 2
♡ A K 9 2	♡ Q 4	♡ 6	♡ A J 4 3
◊ J 3	◊ K Q 5 4 2	◊ A K J 4 3	◊ Q 7
♣ 7	♣ A 8 6 3	♣ K Q J 6	♣ 3 2
2. ♠ 8 4	2. ♠ K Q J 2	2. ♠ K 5 3	2. ♠ 9 6 2
♡ K 8 6 4	♡ 7 3	♡ A 8 6 3	♡ 7
◊ 5 4 2	◊ A Q 9 8 7 3	◊ 7 4 3	◊ A K Q 6 2
♣ A J 8 7	♣ 2	♣ A 9 8	♣ K Q J 5
3. ♠ A 2	3. ♠ K 8 7 6 4 3	3. ♠ K 9	3. ♠ A Q 7 2
♡ 7 6	♡ A Q J 2	♡ J 6 3	♡ A 10 8 4
◊ A 9 3	◊ K 8	◊ A 7 4 3 2	◊ - - -
♣ K Q 8 5 4 2	♣ 3	♣ 7 6 2	♣ K Q 9 8 4
4. ♠ 8 6	4. ♠ K 7 3 2	4. ♠ J 6 2	4. ♠ A Q 8 7 4
♡ A 9 5 3	♡ 6	♡ A K 8 7 2	♡ - - -
◊ K 7 6 2	◊ A Q	◊ K J 9 3	◊ Q 5 4 2
♣ Q 9 2	♣ A K 8 7 4 3	♣ 9	♣ A J 9 2
5. ♠ K Q	5. ♠ J 8	5. ♠ Q 7 4 3	5. ♠ K 10
♡ K 7 3 2	♡ Q J 6 4	♡ J 7 5 2	♡ A Q
◊ A 9 8 6 5 3	◊ 7	◊ Q 3	◊ 8 7 6 4 2
♣ 7	♣ A K 8 6 5 2	♣ A 5 4	♣ K 10 3 2
6. ♠ A Q 9 8 6 4	6. ♠ 2	6. ♠ 8 3	6. ♠ A Q 9 6 5
♡ 4 2	♡ K Q J 7 5 3	♡ 4 2	♡ A 10 8 7
◊ K Q 7 3	◊ A J 9 8	◊ A Q 8 7 4	◊ K 3
♣ Q	♣ K 3	♣ A Q J 6	♣ 4 3

PLAY HANDS ON SHAPE-SHOWING — 6-4 AND 5-4 PATTERNS

Hand 77 : 6-4 pattern — Establishing an extra winner in dummy for a discard

Dealer North : Both vulnerable

NORTH
- ♠ J 6
- ♡ K 6 2
- ◇ K Q 8 6 5
- ♣ Q 4 3

WEST
- ♠ A 10 5 2
- ♡ 8 5
- ◇ A 10 3 2
- ♣ 10 9 2

EAST
- ♠ 9
- ♡ J 10 9 7
- ◇ J 9
- ♣ K J 8 7 6 5

SOUTH
- ♠ K Q 8 7 4 3
- ♡ A Q 4 3
- ◇ 7 4
- ♣ A

WEST	NORTH	EAST	SOUTH
	Pass	Pass	1♠
Pass	2◇ (1)	Pass	2♡ (2)
Pass	2NT (3)	Pass	3♠ (4)
Pass	4♠	All pass	

Bidding : (1) A 2-over-1 by a passed hand shows 10-12 points and a 5-card suit (see Chapter 4, page 34) but change of suit by a passed hand is not forcing.
(2) Change of suit by opener after a 2-over-1 response is forcing, even where responder is a passed hand.
(3) Confirms a stopper in clubs, the unbid suit, and denies support for either major, i.e. not 3 spades and not 4 hearts.
(4) The ABA Pattern showing 6 spades and 4 hearts. 3NT would be defeated easily on a club lead, followed by a club return when West wins the lead with either ace.

Lead : ♣10. Lead the top card from a 3-card suit, if the top cards are touching *and* include an honour.

Correct play : Win the ♣A and lead a spade to dummy's jack, followed by a spade to your king. Had trumps divided 3-2, you would not lose more than 1 spade, 1 heart and 1 diamond. Ruff the club return and play the ♠Q. Do not play a 4th spade and do not start on the hearts yet. Lead a diamond to dummy's king, cross back to your ♡A, and lead another diamond, playing low if West takes the ace, or playing the queen if West plays low again. Either you lose no diamond or the ◇Q is high for a heart discard. The ♡K in dummy is your entry to the established queen of diamonds if West takes the ◇A on the 2nd round of diamonds.

Hand 78 : How to handle the 5-4-3-1 — Setting up the stronger suit

Dealer East : Nil vulnerable

NORTH
- ♠ 7 3
- ♡ Q 8 7
- ◇ K Q J 10 8
- ♣ A 10 8

WEST
- ♠ A J 10 5
- ♡ 9 5 3
- ◇ 9 5 3 2
- ♣ 7 6

EAST
- ♠ 4 2
- ♡ J 10 6
- ◇ A 6 4
- ♣ K J 9 5 2

SOUTH
- ♠ K Q 9 8 6
- ♡ A K 4 2
- ◇ 7
- ♣ Q 4 3

WEST	NORTH	EAST	SOUTH
		Pass	1♠
Pass	2◇ (1)	Pass	2♡ (2)
Pass	2NT (3)	Pass	3NT (4)
Pass	Pass	Pass	

Bidding : (1) Bid a good 5-card suit rather than 2NT which implies no powerful suit and diminishes your chances of reaching a possible diamond slam.
(2) Change of suit after a 2-over-1 response is forcing.
(3) Showing a club stopper and giving the opener a chance to show 5 hearts (3♡) or 6 spades (3♠).
(4) Holding a 5-4-2-2 pattern, opener would choose 3NT. Similarly, with a 5-4-3-1 and a singleton in responder's suit, opener should opt for 3NT. Note that 3NT makes easily while 4♠ fails easily.

Lead : ♣5. With nothing startling elsewhere, the unbid suit is the natural lead, even though the opponents have a stopper in the suit.

Correct Play : Play low from dummy, not the honor, when you have honor-10 in hand. As it happens the 10 wins and you should set up the diamond winners, making at least 10 tricks. Even though you have more spades and hearts than diamonds, it would be an error not to start the diamonds at once. The diamond suit is more solid, has greater depth and can provide more tricks. As the hearts do divide 3-3, declarer should make 10 tricks (4 hearts, 4 diamonds and 2 clubs). If declarer played a spade before the diamonds (error), West could win and return a club, setting up East's clubs which East could cash upon winning the ◇A.

Hand 79 : 5-4-3-1 pattern — Tend to be highly suspicious when dummy's long suit is led

Dealer South : North-South vulnerable

NORTH
- ♠ 9 2
- ♡ K J 10 3 2
- ◊ 9 6
- ♣ A 6 5 4

WEST
- ♠ Q 4 3
- ♡ A Q 9 8 4
- ◊ K Q J 2
- ♣ K

EAST
- ♠ A J 10 6 5
- ♡ 7 6
- ◊ A 4 3
- ♣ Q 9 7

SOUTH
- ♠ K 8 7
- ♡ 5
- ◊ 10 8 7 5
- ♣ J 10 8 3 2

WEST	NORTH	EAST	SOUTH
			Pass
1♡	Pass	1♠	Pass
2◊ (1)	Pass	2NT (2)	Pass
3♠ (3)	Pass	4♠	All pass

Bidding: (1) As 1♠ may be only a 4-card suit, prefer not to give a 3-card raise. 2◊ is the natural bid.

(2) 2NT is better than repeating the spades. 2♠ would show the five spades but only a weak hand (6-10) while 3♠ would show a strong hand but promises *six* spades. 2NT is forward-going and allows opener to reveal any further shape.

(3) This now shows *three*-card support (delayed support = 3 trumps, not 4).

Lead: ♡5. The jack of clubs, the unbid suit, would be reasonable, but a singleton is very attractive when you have a weak hand (as partner then will have an entry) and you have trump control (A-x, A-x-x or K-x-x prevents declarer drawing trumps quickly).

Correct play: Win the ♡ A and lead the ♠ Q . . . If South wins and leads a club to the ace and North plays king and another heart, East ruffs high. East then draws trumps and discards a club on the 4th diamond. *Trap: Do not take the heart finesse at trick 1.* If declarer succumbs to the lure of the heart finesse, North wins ♡ K, gives South a heart ruff and declarer still has to lose the ♠ K and ♣ A. Be very suspicious when an opponent leads dummy's long suit. The lead is usually a singleton.

Hand 80 : 6-4 pattern — Jump-shift — Utilising the ruffing finesse

Dealer West : East-West vulnerable

NORTH
- ♠ K 9 8 4 3
- ♡ 9 7 5
- ◊ Q 10 5 2
- ♣ 7

WEST
- ♠ 2
- ♡ A K J 8 6 4
- ◊ A K
- ♣ K 8 6 3

EAST
- ♠ A Q J 6
- ♡ Q 3
- ◊ 6 4 3
- ♣ 9 5 4 2

SOUTH
- ♠ 10 7 5
- ♡ 10 2
- ◊ J 9 8 7
- ♣ A Q J 10

WEST	NORTH	EAST	SOUTH
1♡	Pass	1♠	Pass
3♣ (1)	Pass	4♣ (2)	Pass
4♡ (3)	Pass	Pass (4)	Pass

Bidding: (1) The jump-shift is normally based on at least a 5-4 pattern, 19 points or more and is forcing to game. 3♣ is superior to 3♡ (the hand is too strong for 3♡) or 4♡, since partner could have a singleton or void in hearts and have 4 or 5 good clubs, making a club slam possible.

(2) Delayed heart support with 3♡ or a 4th-suit 3◊ rebid would also be reasonable.

(3) Showing 6-4 and allowing partner to revert to 5♣ if 4♡ is out of the question.

(4) Very happy to pass 4♡. 3NT is best but not easy to reach.

Lead: ♣7. Although it is usually not attractive to lead declarer's suit and the ◊ 2, the unbid suit, is normal, the singleton club is a reasonable gamble with a weak hand.

Correct play: South wins the ♣ A and continues with the ♣ Q, North ruffing declarer's king. North exits with a trump or a diamond. How can declarer make 4♡ with two losing clubs in each hand?

Win the red suit exit in hand and do not draw trumps yet. Play a spade to the ace and lead the ♠ Q. If South were to produce the king, you would ruff and cross to the ♡ Q to discard a club loser on the ♠ J. When South plays low on the ♠ Q, do not ruff — discard a club instead. Even though North wins, North has no club to cash and the ♠ J is now established as a winner to allow you to discard the other club loser, with the ♡ Q as the required entry. This play in the spade suit is known as a "ruffing finesse" and the manoeuvre of discarding a loser while setting up an extra trick goes by the name of "loser-on-loser play".

CHAPTER 21

FINDING THE STOPPERS FOR 3NT

There are many situations where you feel no-trumps is the right spot but you are worried about a particular suit. The suit might be completely unguarded or partner might have it stopped. If partner has already bid no-trumps indicating a balanced hand, it is reasonable to take your chances in raising no-trumps, but in a suit auction, partner might not only have no cover in the danger suit but might be very short in that suit. The real risk in 3NT is not an unguarded suit, but shortages. You are more likely than not to make 3NT if your only danger is a suit where you hold x-x-x opposite x-x-x, since the opponents may not lead that suit and if they do, it is about 60% likely that the suit will divide 4-3 and the defence can take only 4 tricks. When you have an unguarded suit with x-x opposite x-x, or x-x-x opposite a singleton, then you have real problems. Even one stopper, such as A-x-x opposite a singleton, may prove to be insufficient unless you can run 9 tricks.

The technique of searching for a stopper will differ according to what has taken place in the auction so far.

1. The opponents have bid a suit — you want to bid no-trumps, but you have no stopper in their suit.

Solution: Bid their suit. Bidding the enemy suit is covered in detail in Chapter 25, but one of its functions is to *ask partner for a stopper in their suit.* See Chapter 25 for further information.

2. The partnership has bid 3 suits — you want to bid no-trumps, but you have no stopper in the 4th suit.

Solution: Use 4th-suit-forcing. 4th-suit-forcing was the subject matter of Chapter 17 but one of its functions is to *ask partner for a stopper in the 4th suit.* Partner has a specific set of priorities in replying to 4th-suit-forcing. See Chapter 17 for further information.

3. The partnership has a minor suit fit and has the values for a game — you want to be in 3NT rather than 5-of-a-minor, but do not hold a stopper in every outside suit. An outside suit might be wide open.

Solution: After minor suit agreement, bidding a new suit below 3NT is forcing and shows a stopper.

For example, after 1♡ : 2♣, 3♣ a rebid of 3◇ by responder would *show* a stopper in diamonds and thus indicate that the worry for 3NT is spades. Likewise, after 1♡ : 2♣, 3♣ a rebid of 3♠ by responder would *show* a stopper in spades and indicate that diamonds is the worry. If partner has the danger suit held, partner will bid 3NT, but with no stopper in the danger suit, partner will take some other descriptive action.

After 1♣ : 2♣, a rebid of 2◇ is forcing and *shows* a diamond stopper. Responder should now show a stopper in a major if possible (the 2♣ response already denied a 4-card major), *or* bid 2NT (minimum) or 3NT (maximum) with a stopper in both majors, *or* 3♣ (minimum) or 4♣ (maximum) with no major stopper.

After 1♣ : 3♣, a rebid of 3◇ is forcing and *shows* a diamond stopper. Responder should now bid 3♡ or 3♠ with a stopper in the suit bid, or bid 3NT with stoppers in both majors. After 1♣ : 3♣, a rebid of 3♡ is forcing, *shows* a stopper in hearts and *denies* a stopper in diamonds. Stoppers are shown up-the-line and bypassing a suit denies a stopper in the suit passed. Over 3♡, responder must not bid 3NT without a stopper in the danger suit, diamonds. After 1♣ : 3♣, a rebid of 3♠ is forcing, *shows* a stopper in spades and *denies* a stopper in hearts and in diamonds (both suits bypassed). With stoppers in hearts and diamonds, responder will bid 3NT, while with no stopper in one of the danger suits, responder will revert to clubs.

After minor suit agreement and a stopper bid by partner at the 3-level (e.g. 1♡ : 2♣, 3♣ : 3◇), if you have no stopper in the danger suit, the options are :

● Repeat your major suit with a powerful holding in that suit (at least 3 honors) which partner may then raise to the major suit game with just a doubleton, *or*

● Revert to 4-of-the-agreed-minor with a 2 or 3 cards (no stopper) in the danger suit. Partner may pass or push on to 5-of-the-minor, *or*

● Jump to 5-of-the-agreed-minor with a singleton in the danger suit. Partner may pass or push on to slam. This jump to 5-minor to show a singleton applies only if there is just one danger suit. Where there are two danger suits (e.g. 1♣ : 3♣, 3♠), a jump to 5-minor simply shows maximum values, not a specific singleton.

After major suit agreement, stopper showing is not used, since the assumption is that the partnership will finish in the major suit at some level. After 1-Major : 2-Major, a change of suit is forcing and is a trial bid (see Chapter 24 on Long Suit Trials), while after 1-Major : 3-Major, a new suit is a cue bid, looking for slam.

Because *stopper-asking* is the approach when bidding the enemy suit or when using 4th-suit-forcing, some partnerships sensibly use *stopper-asking* after minor suit agreement. Clearly you must agree with your partner if you switch to stopper-asking here. If so, a new suit at the 3-level after a minor suit has been raised (e.g. 1♠ : 2♣, 3♣ : 3♡) *asks for a stopper in the suit bid.* With a stopper in that suit, partner bids 3 NT. With no stopper, partner may rebid a powerful 5-card major, bid 4-of-the-agreed-minor with 2 or 3 cards (but no stopper) in the asked suit, bid 5-of-the-agreed-minor with a singleton in the asked suit, and raise the asked suit with a void in that suit. Asking-for-stoppers has definite advantages over the standard stopper-showing methods and is recommended at duplicate for serious and regular partnerships.

EXERCISES

A. The bidding has started 1♡ : 2♣, 3♣ . . . How should responder continue with these hands?

1. ♠ K 7	2. ♠ 9 7	3. ♠ A 8 2	4. ♠ 7 2	5. ♠ A 2
♡ 7 3	♡ 5 2	♡ J	♡ Q J 3	♡ 6
◇ A Q 9 6	◇ A K 3	◇ 6 4 3	◇ A K 8	◇ A K 9 4
♣ K J 7 3 2	♣ A J 8 7 3 2	♣ A K J 8 5 4	♣ K 9 7 4 3	♣ K Q 9 7 5 2

B. The bidding has begun 1♠ : 2♣, 3♣ : 3♡ . . . How should opener continue with these hands?

1. ♠ Q J 8 5 2	2. ♠ Q J 8 5 2	3. ♠ A Q J 10 2	4. ♠ A Q 7 5 2	5. ♠ A 8 7 4 2
♡ 7	♡ A 2	♡ J 3	♡ A 7 2	♡ 9 6
◇ A Q 9	◇ 6 4	◇ 8 7	◇ 2	◇ K 2
♣ K J 7 3	♣ A J 3 2	♣ A J 5 4	♣ A 8 6 3	♣ K Q J 4

PARTNERSHIP BIDDING : West is the dealer on all hands. How should the bidding go :—
(a) Using stopper-showing methods, and **(b)** Using stopper-asking methods?

SET 43 – WEST	SET 43 – EAST	SET 44 – WEST	SET 44 – EAST
1. ♠ A Q J 8 6	1. ♠ 7 4	1. ♠ J 6	1. ♠ 8 4 2
♡ K 3	♡ 9 6 2	♡ A 9 8 4 3	♡ K
◇ 9 5	◇ A K J	◇ 9 2	◇ A K Q 3
♣ K 8 4 3	♣ A Q 9 7 5	♣ A K 8 6	♣ Q J 9 5 4
2. ♠ J 4 3	2. ♠ A Q 7	2. ♠ A K J 10 3	2. ♠ Q 5
♡ J 5	♡ A K 6 4 2	♡ 7 6	♡ 8 3
◇ A K	◇ 7 5 4	◇ 8 4	◇ K Q 7 2
♣ A K J 8 6 2	♣ 9 3	♣ K J 9 7	♣ A Q 8 6 5
3. ♠ 7 2	3. ♠ A 4 3	3. ♠ K J 8 6 2	3. ♠ A
♡ K 5	♡ A 8 7 2	♡ K Q 3	♡ A J 2
◇ K Q J	◇ 6 2	◇ 7	◇ 8 6 3 2
♣ A J 8 7 5 3	♣ K 9 4 2	♣ A J 9 2	♣ K Q 10 8 7
4. ♠ K Q 9 8 5	4. ♠ J 4 2	4. ♠ A Q J	4. ♠ K 9
♡ Q 4	♡ A K	♡ 7 6	♡ 5 2
◇ A J 8 3	◇ K Q 9 7 5 2	◇ 9 4	◇ A K 3 2
♣ 7 5	♣ 8 2	♣ A Q 9 8 3 2	♣ K J 7 6 5
5. ♠ 7 3	5. ♠ Q J 4	5. ♠ K Q	5. ♠ 7 6
♡ A Q 9 8 2	♡ 6 5	♡ A J 10 3 2	♡ 9 6 4
◇ A J	◇ K Q 6	◇ 8 7	◇ K Q J
♣ K 8 6 3	♣ A Q 10 7 5	♣ K 9 3 2	♣ A Q J 7 5
6. ♠ K Q 2	6. ♠ 7 6	6. ♠ '	6. ♠ 7 6
♡ 8	♡ K Q 3	♡ A J	♡ K Q
◇ A J 6 4	◇ K Q 8 7 3	◇ A J 6 4	◇ K Q 9 7 3 2
♣ K Q 6 4 3	♣ A 8 2	♣ K Q J 6 '	♣ A 8 7

PLAY HANDS ON STOPPER-SHOWING

Hand 81 : Stopper-showing for no-trumps — Catering for a bad split

Dealer North : Nil vulnerable

NORTH
- ♠ A J 10 8 6
- ♡ K 10
- ◇ 9 6
- ♣ A 8 4 3

WEST
- ♠ Q 9 5 2
- ♡ Q 8 5
- ◇ Q 10 7 5 4 3
- ♣ - - -

EAST
- ♠ K 3
- ♡ A J 7 4 3
- ◇ 8 2
- ♣ J 10 6 2

SOUTH
- ♠ 7 4
- ♡ 9 6 2
- ◇ A K J
- ♣ K Q 9 7 5

WEST	NORTH	EAST	SOUTH
	1♠	Pass	2♣ (1)
Pass	3♣ (2)	Pass	3◇ (3)
Pass	3NT (4)	All pass	

Bidding : (1) Not 2NT with nothing in hearts.
(2) Minimum with club support. Far better than rebidding 2♠.
(3) Shows a stopper in diamonds and pinpoints hearts as the problem suit. (Using stopper-asks, South would bid 3♡ here to ask for a stopper in hearts. North would reply 3NT.)
(4) Shows at least 1 stopper in hearts. K-x is quite adequate as a stopper. The expectation is that there will be 9 tricks to run as long as the opponents cannot run 5 first.

Lead : ♡4. The long suit is the normal lead. As East seems to have the clubs stopped, East can afford to give up a trick to North's stopper in hearts. With no club values, East might try a diamond, hoping for West to gain the lead and lead hearts through North. This could work when West has ♡Q-10-x and North ♡K-x.

Correct play : When 3NT looks easy, ask yourself what could go wrong. Here a 4-0 club break, though unlikely, could make life difficult. Just in case, you should cash the ♣A first, not the K or Q. With 2 honors missing, you need 2 honors to capture them, so keep dummy's 2 club honors intact on the first club lead. If clubs broke 2-2 or 3-1, the rest would be easy. When the bad break appears, lead a 2nd club. East will play the 10 (else you finesse the 9) and the Q wins. Back to hand via the ♠A and another club allows you to finesse against East's J-x. On an initial diamond lead, win ◇A, club to A, club to East's 10 won by the Q, finesse ♠J, win the diamond exit with the K, finesse the ♠10, cash the ♠A and then lead a club to finesse dummy's 9.

Hand 82 : Finding the right spot after a stopper auction — Catering for a bad break

Dealer East : North-South vulnerable

NORTH
- ♠ 10
- ♡ Q J 10 5 4
- ◇ 10 9 6 3
- ♣ 10 8 5

WEST
- ♠ K 9 8 5 4
- ♡ 7 6 3
- ◇ A J 4 2
- ♣ K

EAST
- ♠ A 3 2
- ♡ 9 2
- ◇ K Q
- ♣ A Q J 6 4 3

SOUTH
- ♠ Q J 7 6
- ♡ A K 8
- ◇ 8 7 5
- ♣ 9 7 2

WEST	NORTH	EAST	SOUTH
		1♣	Pass
1♠	Pass	3♣ (1)	Pass
3◇ (2)	Pass	3♠ (3)	Pass
4♠ (4)	Pass	Pass	Pass

Bidding : (1) Shows 6+ clubs and about 16-18 points, denies support for responder and denies a 2nd suit.
(2) Shows a stopper in diamonds and focusses attention on the heart suit as the problem for no-trumps. Even though clubs have not been raised here, a new suit is still treated as a stopper, since 3♣ denied any 2nd suit. (Using stopper-asks, West would bid 3♡ here to ask for a stopper in hearts, but the rest of the bidding would be identical.)
(3) Delayed 3-card support for spades.
(4) If West held only 4 spades and did not wish to play in a 4-3 spade fit, West could choose 5♣ if 3NT was not available.

Lead : ♡Q. Top of sequence.

Correct play : After 2 heart tricks, declarer wins any switch. The ♠A is cashed and when North drops the 10, West can guard against a 4-1 break. On the next spade, South should play low (to insert an honor makes it easier for declarer) and West should play the 9. If this lost to the J or Q with North, the ♠K would draw the last trump later. As it is, the ♠9 wins. Cash the ♠K and the club and diamond winners. If the defense takes 2 hearts and West plays ♠A and ♠K, 4♠ would fail if South scores 2 trump tricks. If North did not lead a heart, declarer should cash ♠A, ♠K, ♣K, diamond to dummy and discard heart losers on the club winners.

Hand 83 : Stopper location for 3NT — Catering for a bad break

Dealer South : East-West vulnerable

```
              NORTH
              ♠ 5 3
              ♡ 8 4 3
              ◊ A K 5 2
              ♣ A K 8 4
WEST                        EAST
♠ Q 10                      ♠ K 9 8 6
♡ J 10 6 5 2                ♡ Q 9 7
◊ J 6                       ◊ 10 9 8 7 4
♣ J 10 7 2                  ♣ Q
              SOUTH
              ♠ A J 7 4 2
              ♡ A K
              ◊ Q 3
              ♣ 9 6 5 3
```

WEST	NORTH·	EAST	SOUTH
			1♠
Pass	2♣ (1)	Pass	3♣ (2)
Pass	3◊ (3)	Pass	3NT (4)
Pass	Pass	Pass	

Bidding : (1) 4-card suits are shown up-the-line. Not 2NT with nothing in hearts.

(2) 3♣ is much better than 2♠. Too weak in diamonds for 2NT.

(3) Showing a stopper and emphasising the need for hearts to be covered before trying 3NT. (Using stopper-asks, North would bid 3♡, asking for a stopper in hearts and South would reply 3NT.)

(4) Delighted to bid 3NT with hearts well held.

Lead : ♡5. The natural lead.

Correct play: Declarer can count on 8 top tricks. The best chance for a 9th trick is from the club suit, where any 3-2 split will allow an extra trick to be set up. So, win the ♡A and a lead a club to the A. As a trick has to be lost in clubs no matter what, a low club at trick 3 cannot harm your chances and when any honor drops from East, it is vital to continue with a low club to your 9. If the suit does break 3-2, the ♣K will later capture the missing club and the 4th round of clubs will be high. If clubs break 4-1 with East holding the 10, J or Q, the low club to your 9 forces an honor from West and when you regain the lead, you can lead a club and finesse dummy's 8. East's ♣Q dropping should tip you off to the bad break but any honor dropping would be the same. Note that if you play off the ♣A and ♣K, 3NT should be defeated. Similar strategy applies if you hold A-K-8-x opposite 10-x-x-x : cash the A and if the 9, J or Q drops over the A-K-8-x, low to your 10 next guarantees 3 tricks for you, although it does give up the chance of 4 club tricks and an overtrick when there is ♣Q-J doubleton.

Hand 84 : Bidding after a stopper auction — Ruffing losers in dummy before drawing trumps

Dealer West : Both vulnerable

```
              NORTH
              ♠ 8 7 4
              ♡ 7 5 3
              ◊ K Q 8 7 5 4
              ♣ 4
WEST                        EAST
♠ K Q 3                     ♠ A J 2
♡ K 10 8 6 2                ♡ A
◊ 10                        ◊ 9 6 3 2
♣ A J 9 2                   ♣ K Q 10 8 7
              SOUTH
              ♠ 10 9 6 5
              ♡ Q J 9 4
              ◊ A J
              ♣ 6 5 3
```

WEST	NORTH	EAST	SOUTH
1♡	Pass	2♣	Pass
3♣ (1)	Pass	3♠ (2)	Pass
5♣ (3)	Pass	6♣ (4)	All pass

Bidding : (1) Not quite strong enough for 4♣.

(2) Showing the spade stopper and indicating concern about diamonds. It is tempting to bid 3NT and the length in diamonds will usually protect you. Here 3NT would succeed but it is a risk since partner could be singleton or void in diamonds. On different diamond layouts, 3NT could fail and if 3NT is the right spot, partner will usually be able to bid it over 3♠. (If using stopper-asks, East bids 3◊ over 3♣ — the rest of the auction is the same.)

(3) The jump to 5-minor indicates a singleton in the danger suit.

(4) Although 6♣ might not be a certainty, it figures to be a very good chance with only 1 diamond loser. Rag cards opposite a shortage mean all the high cards figure to be in the right place.

Lead: ♠5 or a trump. If ruffs in dummy are vital, lead a trump.

Correct play: Whether a trump or a spade is led, the best plan is to ruff 2 diamonds in dummy and discard a diamond on the ♡K. Therefore, win the lead in dummy and lead a diamond at trick 2. Win any return in hand and ruff a diamond. Cross to hand, ruff another diamond and then proceed to draw their remaining trumps. It would be an error to draw trumps early because if you draw 3 rounds of trumps, you cannot ruff 2 diamonds in dummy. A different line of play would work on this hand : ♡A, play a trump to dummy, ruff a heart and eventually set up the heart suit by ruffing. This plan is inferior and could fail if the heart split is unfriendly.

CHAPTER 22

PART A : USING STAYMAN WITH WEAK HANDS

The primary function of Stayman is to reach the best game or slam contract by locating a 4-4 major fit (see Chapter 6). When Stayman is used for this purpose, responder will hold 8 points or more if facing a 16-18 or 15-18 1NT. However, simple Stayman may also be used on very weak hands when there is no chance for game at all and the object is to find a safer partscore than 1NT. There are 3 hand types where Stayman can be safely used for rescue purposes even though responder has a hand in the 0-7 range :

1. Responder has 6 or more clubs and judges 3♣ to be a better spot than 1NT: With this type, respond 2♣ and rebid 3♣ over opener's reply to Stayman. Your 3♣ rebid is an absolute sign-off— opener *must* pass 3♣.

2. Responder has at least 5-4 in the majors : With this type, respond 2♣ and then if opener bids a major, you pass while if opener bids 2◇, you rebid 2-of-your-5-card-major. Your 2-major rebid is not encouraging and opener should pass. With game values and a 5-card major, you would rebid 3-major over the 2◇ reply.

3. Responder has a 3-suiter (5-4-4-0 or 4-4-4-1) with clubs as the short suit: With this type, respond 2♣ and pass opener's reply, whatever it is. You have judged that this figures to be a better spot than 1NT.

♠ 8 ♡ 9 4 ◇ 8 6 2 ♣ Q J 8 6 5 3 2	What action do you take if partner opens 1NT? Unless partner has A-K-x in clubs, your hand is likely to be useless in no-trumps. Clubs is a far safer partscore. You cannot stop in 2♣ (that is the price for using the Stayman Convention), but you can stop in 3♣. Respond 2♣ and rebid 3♣ over any reply to 2♣. Opener *must* pass 3♣.
♠ 9 7 5 3 2 ♡ J 9 6 4 ◇ 8 ♣ Q 4 2	What action do you take if partner opens 1NT? Your hand looks better in a suit contract and you could reply 2♠, a weakness takeout. However, that risks playing in 2♠ when partner has 2 spades and 4 hearts when 2♡ would be better. Respond 2♣ and pass a 2♠ or 2♡ reply. Over 2◇, rebid 2♠ which opener is expected to pass.
♠ 9 6 4 2 ♡ 8 7 5 3 ◇ 9 7 6 4 3 ♣ - - -	What action do you take if partner opens 1NT? You could bid 2◇, a weakness takeout, but 2♣ is superior, planning to pass any reply by opener. If opener bids 2♡ or 2♠, you are in a better spot than 1NT and perhaps a better spot than 2◇, while if opener bids 2◇, you are better off since opener is playing the 2◇ contract.

After Stayman, responder's 2NT (8-9) is encouraging and 3-major rebids are forcing, but responder's 3♣ or 2-major rebids are sign-offs, which opener is expected to pass. This allows responder to use a 2♣ rescue. However, shapes other than the above are unsuitable for a rescue Stayman. For example, with a 1-4-4-4, singleton spade, and rubbish, pass 1NT. Do not Stayman. You cannot handle a 2♠ reply.

PART B : THE 1NT RESPONSE WITH A LONG SUIT

♠ 6 ♡ K 8 6 5 3 2 ◇ Q J 4 ♣ 8 7 2	If partner opens 1♣ or 1◇, you have an easy 1♡ response, and after 1♡ or 1NT, you are worth 4♡, but what action do you take after a 1♠ opening? You are not strong enough for 2♡ which shows 10 points or more. You might fudge by 1 point, but not by 4 points. The solution is to respond 1NT and hope for another bid later.

Hands with 5-8 HCP and a 6-card or longer suit respond 1NT when the suit cannot be shown at the 1-level. It is better to respond 1NT and show the weak strength even if the hand is not suitable for no-trumps than to respond at the 2-level and promise 10 points up when you are nowhere near that. With 9 HCP and a 6-card suit, you have enough to respond at the 2-level and below 5 HCP, it is better to pass.

If partner passes 1NT, do the best you can and console yourself that you never could have stopped in 2-of-your-suit since your new suit response would have been forcing. If partner bids again over 1NT, you may be able to show your suit then, depending on opener's rebid, or you may be happy to pass opener's rebid.

The 1NT response followed by a new suit rebid shows 5-8 HCP and a 6-card or longer suit.

In addition, responder will not have a fit for opener's suit(s), since responder would be happy to play in opener's suit if a fit existed. If opener bids a 2nd suit, opener will be at least 5-4 in the 2 suits, while if opener rebids the suit opened, that will be at least a 6-card suit, which responder will often be happy to pass. After opener rebids the suit opened, you have to decide whether to pass or whether to show your own suit. With a void in partner's suit and 6 in your own *or* with a singleton in partner's suit and 7 in your own, bid your own suit (i.e. bid your own suit if the difference in lengths is 6 or more). With doubleton support for opener or with a difference in lengths of 5 or less, pass opener's rebid. Even if opener's rebid was a reverse, responder's 1NT-then-new-suit is still weak and indicates no fit for opener's suits. If opener's rebid was 2NT, about 17-18 points, responder can show the long suit at the 3-level, as a degree of tolerance will exist.

If responder bids 1NT and later a new suit, *opener should almost always pass.* The hand is a misfit and will usually play better in responder's suit. With a significant fit for responder, opener may raise the suit if game chances still exist despite responder's announced weakness (via 1NT). Opener should not rebid a suit previously bid by opener unless opener has both greater length in that suit than already promised *and* absolutely no tolerance for responder's suit (such as a void). Opener should not rebid 2NT as a rescue or 3NT over responder's 3-level bid without significantly extra strength. 3NT on a misfit needs lots of HCP.

EXERCISE

A. The bidding has been 1♠ : 1NT, 2◇. What action should responder now take with each of these hands?

1. ♠ 82	2. ♠ 82	3. ♠ - - -	4. ♠ 7	5. ♠ - - -
♡ Q J 8 6 4 2	♡ Q J 8 6 4	♡ K 9 6 4 3	♡ K Q 6	♡ J 8 4
◇ 4	◇ 5 4	◇ J 6 4	◇ 3 2	◇ 9 8 4 3
♣ K 9 7 3	♣ K 9 7 3	♣ Q J 7 3 2	♣ J 9 7 5 4 3 2	♣ K Q 9 6 4 3

B. What would your answer be on the hands above if the bidding had started 1♠ : 1NT, 2♠?

PARTNERSHIP BIDDING : How should the following hands be bid? West is the dealer on all hands.

SET 45 – WEST	SET 45 – EAST	SET 46 – WEST	SET 46 – EAST
1. ♠ A Q 9 8 4	1. ♠ 6	1. ♠ 9 4 3	1. ♠ 6 2
♡ 3 2	♡ Q J 8 7 6 4	♡ 5	♡ A K J 8 7 6
◇ 6 4	◇ A 9 3 2	◇ K 8 7 6 4 2	◇ A 3
♣ K Q J 9	♣ 6 2	♣ A 8 3	♣ 7 6 4
2. ♠ 3	2. ♠ A Q 7 5 4	2. ♠ K 5 4	2. ♠ A 3 2
♡ 9 7 4 3	♡ K 6 2	♡ A K 8 5 4 3	♡ 2
◇ A Q 10 8 6 5	◇ 3	◇ A 8 4	◇ J 2
♣ 9 5	♣ K Q 8 3	♣ 6	♣ Q 9 8 7 5 4 2
3. ♠ A Q 9 6 5	3. ♠ 4 2	3. ♠ 8 5	3. ♠ K Q 9 3 2
♡ 5 3	♡ A 8 7 6 4 2	♡ K J 7 4	♡ A 3 2
◇ A 8 6 5 2	◇ K	◇ Q J 9 8 7	◇ 4
♣ K	♣ 8 7 5 3	♣ 9 5	♣ A Q 6 2
4. ♠ - - -	4. ♠ A Q J 10 8 5	4. ♠ A K 8 7 4	4. ♠ 3
♡ A 6 3 2	♡ 9 5 4	♡ A 4 3	♡ K Q 9 8 6 2
◇ 9 7 4 2	◇ A J	◇ A Q 9 2	◇ 7 5
♣ K J 8 6 2	♣ 7 4	♣ 6	♣ J 7 4 3
5. ♠ J 3 2	5. ♠ A K 6	5. ♠ A K 9 8 2	5. ♠ 5
♡ J	♡ A K 6 4 2	♡ K Q J 4	♡ A 2
◇ 7 5 3	◇ Q 6 4	◇ 7 3	◇ 8 4 2
♣ A 8 7 6 4 3	♣ Q 2	♣ A Q	♣ K 9 8 7 6 4 3
6. ♠ J 6 2	6. ♠ Q 7	6. ♠ J 10 5 4	6. ♠ A 9 8
♡ A 9 6 4	♡ 7	♡ Q 9 5 3	♡ K 7 6 4
◇ A K 9 7	◇ 6 5 2	◇ 8 7 5 2	◇ A Q 3
♣ A 7	♣ J 9 8 6 5 3 2	♣ 3	♣ A 7 2

PLAY HANDS ON RESCUE STAYMAN

Hand 85 : Removing 1NT into a club partscore — Leading towards honors

Dealer North : North-South vulnerable

NORTH
- ♠ A K 3
- ♡ Q 6 5 3
- ◇ A Q J
- ♣ 8 7 2

WEST
- ♠ 10 7 2
- ♡ K 10 7
- ◇ K 8 7 4
- ♣ A Q 6

EAST
- ♠ Q 9 8 5
- ♡ A J 9 4 2
- ◇ 9 6 2
- ♣ J

SOUTH
- ♠ J 6 4
- ♡ 8
- ◇ 10 5 3
- ♣ K 10 9 5 4 3

WEST	NORTH	EAST	SOUTH
	1NT	Pass (1)	2♣ (2)
Pass	2♡ (3)	Pass	3♣ (4)
Pass	Pass (5)	Pass	

Bidding : (1) Too weak to overcall, even at this vulnerability.
(2) It would be an error to pass 1NT which would be easily beaten, starting with the ♡4 lead to the K and the ♡10 return. With a weak hand and a long suit, responder should rescue 1NT.
(3) 4 hearts. Opener gives the normal reply to Stayman.
(4) Sign-off in clubs. Shows 6+ clubs and no prospects for game.
(5) Opener *must* pass this 3♣ sign-off.

Lead : ♠2, lowest from 3 to an honor. There is no attractive lead.

Correct play : You might duck the spade lead in dummy, hoping that West has led from the Q. Although this loses to East, you can hold the losers to 1 spade, 1 heart and 2 clubs. You will have to take the diamond finesse twice and by leading a club from dummy and covering East's J with the K, there are only 2 club losers.

Hand 86 : Using Stayman on a weak hand with both majors — Ruffing losers in dummy

Dealer East : East-West vulnerable

NORTH
- ♠ A J 10 8
- ♡ Q 7
- ◇ 7 5
- ♣ K J 9 5 2

WEST
- ♠ K 9
- ♡ A K 3 2
- ◇ K Q J 10
- ♣ 7 6 4

EAST
- ♠ Q 7 6 5 2
- ♡ 9 6 5 4
- ◇ 4 3 2
- ♣ 8

SOUTH
- ♠ 4 3
- ♡ J 10 8
- ◇ A 9 8 6
- ♣ A Q 10 3

WEST	NORTH	EAST	SOUTH
		Pass	Pass
1NT	Pass	2♣ (1)	Pass (2)
2♡	Pass	Pass (3)	Pass (4)

Bidding : (1) It would be an error to pass 1NT which would fail by 1 or 2 tricks on straightforward defense. 2♠ over 1NT is better than passing, but not best, as it puts all your eggs in one basket. 2♣ allows you to play in hearts *or* spades. Against 2♠, the ♡J would be led and as the cards lie, declarer figures to lose 3 spades, 1 heart, 1 diamond and 1 club, one off.
(2) If South were to double 2♣, a lead-directing double, North would later bid 3♣ which makes.
(3) Had West bid 2◇, East would now sign off in 2♠.
(4) A delayed 2NT takeout for the minors, by no means a clearcut action with a balanced hand but reasonable as the opponents have stopped in 2♡, would put North-South into the making 3♣.

Lead : ◇7 or ♣5. Neither major is attractive.

Correct play : While trumps are likely to divide 3-2, it is risky to play off the ♡ A-K early. If hearts are 4-1, an opponent may draw the rest of your trumps when you give up the lead later. It is better to set up the club ruff and the diamond and spade winners before cashing up the ♡ A-K. Against a diamond lead and return, West should immediately lead a club. Even though the defense can take a diamond ruff, West can arrange to ruff 2 clubs in dummy and lose just 1 spade, 1 heart, 1 diamond, a diamond ruff and 1 club. On a club lead and trump switch, win the ♡ A, ruff a club and lead a diamond. Ruff your other club at your first opportunity and then lead another diamond if they are not yet set up, or lead a spade if the diamonds are high.

EXERCISE : Partner has opened 1NT. What is your response on each of these hands?

1.	2.	3.	4.	5.
♠ 7	♠ - - -	♠ A 6 4 2	♠ 7	♠ Q 9 7 5 4
♡ J 9 7 3	♡ Q 6 4 2	♡ Q 9 5 3	♡ J 9 6 2	♡ J 10 5 3 2
◇ 9 6 4 3	◇ 8 7 6 4	◇ 8 7	◇ 6 2	◇ 4 3
♣ 8 6 5 2	♣ 9 7 5 3 2	♣ 8 5 4	♣ Q 9 7 5 4 2	♣ 6

PLAY HANDS ON 1NT RESPONSE WITH A LONG SUIT

Hand 87 : Removing opener's rebid to a safer partscore — Ruffing finesse — Compulsory duck

Dealer South : Both vulnerable

```
            NORTH
            ♠ - - -
            ♡ 8 6 4
            ◇ A J 9 5 3 2
            ♣ Q 7 4 3
WEST                    EAST
♠ A J 10 8             ♠ 9 5 3
♡ J 7 5               ♡ K Q 10 9
◇ K 7                 ◇ Q 10 8
♣ J 8 6 5             ♣ K 10 9
            SOUTH
            ♠ K Q 7 6 4 2
            ♡ A 3 2
            ◇ 6 4
            ♣ A 2
```

WEST	NORTH	EAST	SOUTH
			1♠
Pass	1NT (1)	Pass	2♠ (2)
Pass	3◇ (3)	Pass	Pass (4)
Pass			

Bidding: (1) Too weak for 2◇ which would show 10 points up.
(2) Repeating spades over 1NT promises a 6-card suit.
(3) To pass 2♠ is possible but not recommended. In 2♠ South might manage 6 tricks at most (and no-trumps is even worse). 3◇ denies any tolerance for spades and shows 6+ diamonds.
(4) It would be very poor for South to bid again.

Lead : ♡K. K from K-Q suits is normal in a trump contract.

Correct play : Win the ♡A and lead the ♠K (ruffing finesse), planning to discard a heart if West plays low, thus setting up the ♠Q as a winner. When West plays the ♠A, you ruff, cross to the ♣A and discard a heart loser on the ♠Q. It is still too soon to lead trumps as you need to ruff clubs. Lead the ♣2 from dummy.

When West plays low on this club, you should assume East has the ♣K (West would rise with the K when the last club from dummy is played), so there is no point playing the ♣Q which would be taken by the K. Duck the club, won by East who would cash a heart and may play a 3rd heart. You ruff this, lead a low club and ruff in dummy, noting with satisfaction the fall of the ♣K, which makes your ♣Q high. Now lead a diamond to your ace and a diamond back, clearing 2 rounds of trumps. You later lose another diamond, but make your contract, losing just 1 heart, 2 diamonds and 1 club.

Hand 88 : Responding 1NT with a long suit — Compulsory duck — Card combination

Dealer West : Nil vulnerable

```
            NORTH
            ♠ 10 9 8 2
            ♡ K 4 2
            ◇ A 9 6 4
            ♣ A 5
WEST                    EAST
♠ A Q 7 5 4           ♠ 3
♡ 3                  ♡ A Q 10 8 6 5
◇ K Q 8 3            ◇ J 5
♣ K 6 2              ♣ 9 7 4 3
            SOUTH
            ♠ K J 6
            ♡ J 9 7
            ◇ 10 7 2
            ♣ Q J 10 8
```

WEST	NORTH	EAST	SOUTH
1♠	Pass	1NT (1)	Pass
2◇	Pass	2♡ (2)	Pass
Pass (3)	Pass		

Bidding : (1) Much too weak to respond 2♡.
(2) No tolerance for West's suits; shows 6+ hearts and 5-8 HCP.
(3) It would be poor for West to bid again. West has already shown 5 spades and 4 diamonds and a 2NT rebid would suggest about 17-18 HCP, still looking for game. 2NT is not a rescue move and is not an attractive spot if the hands are weak and misfits.

Lead : ♣Q. Top of sequence in the unbid suit is natural.

Correct play : Do *not* play the ♣K at trick 1. The lead marks North with the ♣A and you just lose dummy's K if you play it. If the ♣K is played, 2♡ is beaten easily : ♣A wins; a club is returned to South who continues the clubs. Dummy ruffs the 4th club and whether North overruffs or not, declarer will fail, losing another 2 hearts and the ◇A.

Play low in dummy on the ♣Q lead (North's ace might be singleton). If South continues clubs, play low in dummy again. When North's ace falls, the ♣K is high. With a tough lead to make, North might switch to a heart or cash the ◇A and lead a second diamond. On a heart switch, East should play the Q from hand, not the 10. When you have only one finesse available with an A-Q-10 combination, choose the Q finesse. When the ♡Q wins, cash the ♡A and then lead the ◇J or a 3rd heart. If North had switched to ace and another diamond, win the ◇J, cross to the ♠A, cash ◇K to discard 1 club, and then lead a heart to your Q, cash the ♡A and play a 3rd heart. Careful play can restrict the losers to 1 heart, 1 diamond and 2 clubs.

CHAPTER 23
THE LOSING TRICK COUNT

The Losing Trick Count is a more accurate guide than point count in assessing the playing potential of the partnership hands when a good trump fit exists. Players who count their points at the outset and do not change that total as the bidding progresses fail to get an accurate picture of their assets. Counting HCP is best for balanced hands and misfit hands. The Losing Trick Count is not used for opening the bidding, for no-trump hands or for misfit hands. It becomes useful only after a trump fit has been established, but once the trump fit exists, it can be used by opener, responder or the overcalling side. You are able to use the LTC even though partner may never have heard of it. The LTC is not a convention but a technique for valuation. Using the LTC replaces the use of the 5-3-1 shortage point count because the trick-taking capacity revealed by the LTC is more accurate more often than that indicated by point count. The following is a brief summary of how the LTC works and how you can use it to value your trump fit hands, but for a complete treatment, you should acquire a copy of *The Modern Losing Trick Count* by Ron Klinger.

THE LTC FORMULA

Count Your Losers — Add Partner's Losers — Deduct This Total From 24

The answer is the number of tricks the partnership will win most of the time when playing in the known trump fit. The answer is correct almost all of the time when suits break normally and half of your finesses work. If trumps split 4-0 or every finesse is wrong, clearly you will not make the number of tricks expected.

COUNTING YOUR OWN LOSERS

3-card or longer suit: Count losers only in the top 3 cards of the suit; everything beyond the 3rd card counts as a winner. *No suit ever counts more than 3 losers.* In the top 3 cards, count the ace and king as winners, and everything lower than the queen as a loser. Count the queen as a winner if there is a second honor card in the suit; if the queen is the only honor card in the suit, count the queen as a ½-winner, ½-loser. For example, A-6-4-2 is 2 losers, A-K-5-4-2 is 1 loser, 8-6-3-2 is 3 losers, Q-J-5-4 is 2 losers, but Q-9-6-3 is 2½ losers.

Short suit holdings: A void counts as no losers (since you are playing in your trump fit), a singleton counts as 1 loser, except for ace-singleton which is no losers, and a doubleton is 2 losers, except for A-x (1 loser), K-x (1 loser) and A-K (no loser). K-Q-doubleton, A-Q-doubleton, and K-singleton are all 1 loser holdings.

ASSESSING PARTNER'S LOSERS

Just as an average minimum opening is around the 13-point mark, so the average minimum opening in terms of the LTC is 7 losers. This applies to a normal balanced opening. The more freakish the shape, the fewer losers the hand will have. Note that when opening with a 1-bid, use the point count, not losers.

♠ A 7　　　　This is minimum 1-opening in almost any standard system, but you will note that it
♡ K Q 7 4　　contains just 7 losers. There is 1 loser in spades, 1 loser in hearts (the 4th card counts
♢ K 9 5　　　as a winner), 2 losers in diamonds and 3 losers in clubs (in the LTC, no suit counts
♣ 8 6 4 2　　more than 3 losers). Thus, 7 losers is a good estimate for a minimum opening hand.

Just as a minimum opening may be 14-15 points or occasionally 10-11 points, so a minimum opening may be 6½ losers or 7½ or 8 losers. An extra loser is common when the hand pattern is 4-3-3-3.

If partner's bidding promises minimum opening strength, play partner to hold a 7-loser hand.

For example, if the bidding has started 1♣ : 1♡, 2♡ opener has shown a minimum opening and you should play opener for 7 losers. Likewise, 1♡ : 1♠, 1NT indicates a minimum opening and so 7 losers. 1♠ : 2NT indicating a 13-15 balanced response should be taken as 7 losers, 1♡ : 3♡ as a game-forcing raise would be 7 losers or better, a minimum takeout double would be 7 losers, and so on. Where opener rebids the suit opened, e.g. 1♣ : 1♢, 2♣, normally a 6-card suit, opener will commonly hold 7 losers, but may have only 6 losers because of the significant extra length.

If partner shows more than a minimum opening, play partner to have fewer than 7 losers.

The number of losers depends on how strongly partner has bid, but if you can work out partner's points, you have a good basis for assessing partner's losers, (work on 16-18 points 6 losers, 19-21 points 5 losers and 22-24 points 4 losers). Thus, for a strong 1NT opening (c. 16-18 points), opener usually has 6 losers, a reverse has 5-6 losers, a jump-shift has 4 losers, a jump-rebid of opener's suit (1♣ : 1◊, 3♣) has 5-6 losers, a game-force opening has 3 losers, and so on. When raising partner, a single raise (1◊ : 1♠, 2♠) would show 7 losers, a jump raise to the 3-level would show 6 losers and a jump raise to game would be a 5-loser hand.

If partner's bidding shows less than opening strength, play partner to hold more than 7 losers.

Play a hand of 10-12 points to hold 8 losers, a hand of 7-9 points to hold 9 losers, and worse hands to have 10 losers or more. If partner is a passed hand, assume partner to hold 8 losers at best. A jump raise after passing (Pass : 1♡, 3♡) shows 10-12 points and 8 losers. A single raise (1♠ : 2♠) has about 6-10 points, and thus 8-9 losers. A 2-level response (1♡ : 2♣) has at least 10 points and so will hold 8 losers or better, while a 1-level response should be played for 9 losers or better. Whenever partner has a long suit, there are fewer losers. Expect a weak 2-opening to have 8 losers if minimum, 7 losers if maximum. A 3-level pre-empt has 7 losers not vulnerable, 6 losers vulnerable, while a 4-level pre-empt should have 6 losers not vulnerable, 5 losers vulnerable (see Chapter 12). A 1-level overcall is 8 losers or better, and an overcall at the 2-level is normally 7 losers or better. Playing weak jump overcalls, your methods would be :

Weak jump overcall, e.g. (1◊) : 2♠, = Good 6-card suit, 6-10 HCP, 7-8 losers.

Simple overcall at the 1-level = 8 losers up to 6 losers; simple overcall at the 2-level = 7 losers up to 6 losers.

Overcall-type hand with 5 losers : Double, then bid your suit next.

Overcall-type hand with 4 losers : Double, then jump bid your suit.

Overcall-type hand with 3 losers : Force to game.

When responding to a takeout double with a suit bid, with 9-10 losers, bid your suit at the cheapest level, while with 8 losers you can jump bid your suit, and with 7 losers you can bid game if a trump fit is certain.

WHY 24?

Why is the total of your losers and partner's losers deducted from 24? As there are at most 3 losers per suit, there are at most 12 losers in a hand. The maximum possible number of losers in your hand and partner's hand is therefore 24, and by deducting the actual losers from the maximum possible, the difference is the number of tricks the partnership figures to win.

KEY FIGURES TO REMEMBER

1. If partner opens and you have a 7-loser hand : Game in a major should be bid if a good fit is found.

2. If partner opens and you have a 5-loser hand : There is slam potential if a good fit is found, but you still must check whether the partnership has sufficient controls (Blackwood for aces, etc.).

3. Partner opens and shows better than a minimum opening. If you have a 7-loser hand or better, there is slam potential if a good trump fit can be found.

COVER CARDS

The concept of cover cards devised by George Rosenkranz works very well in conjunction with the LTC. Where you have a trump fit and have ruffing potential, use the LTC as above, but where a trump fit exists and either you have no ruffing value for partner or you hold the long trump suit and know you are facing a balanced hand (e.g. partner has opened 1NT), it is better to estimate the partnership potential through cover cards. The method is quite simple. If you have the balanced hand :

Estimate partner's losers − Count your cover cards − Deduct the cover cards from the losers

If you have the long suit or the freakish shape and partner has the balanced hand :

Count your losers − Estimate partner's cover cards − Deduct the cover cards from the losers

Deduct this answer from 13 to arrive at the number of tricks the hand with the long suit figures to win. For example, partner is expected to hold 6 losers, you have 3 cover cards. 6 − 3 = 3, so the partnership has 3 losers and hence 13 − 3 = 10 winners.

The cover card approach works well when partner is known to have a long, strong suit (as after a weak 2 or after a pre-empt) or when partner's shape is clearly revealed (as after a reverse, 5-4 at least, or when the shape has been shown to be 5-5, 6-5, 6-4 etc. as in Chapters 19 and 20).

A cover card is any card that eliminates or is likely to eliminate a loser in partner's hand. In partner's known long suit or suits, each ace, king or queen counts as a cover card. Outside partner's known long suits, the lower the honor the less valuable it is as a cover card. An outside ace is almost always a cover card (it may not be, if partner is void in that suit), a king might cover a loser, but an outside suit headed by the queen or jack is of limited value for partner. For example, opposite a pre-empt you would not count Q-J-x-x-x as removing any of partner's losers. A-K probably covers 2 losers and K-Q will cover 1 loser unless partner has a singleton in that suit. The more you know about partner's hand pattern, the more accurate will be your assessment of the cards that will count as cover cards.

An opening hand of 13-15 points will usually contain 3-4 cover cards, and you can expect 4-5 cover cards from a 16-18 point hand, 5-6 cover cards from a 19-21 point hand, and so on, while 2-3 cover cards will be normal for a 10-12 point hand and 1-2 cover cards for a 7-9 point hand, and 0-1 cover cards for less than 7.

EXERCISES

A. How many losers do each of these card combinations contain?

1. J 7 3 2	4. K Q 7 5 4 3	7. 8 3	10. A 8 4	13. A K 6 3 2	16. Q J 8 6 4 2
2. A Q 9 5 4 2	5. K Q 7 3	8. Q 3	11. A K 3	14. Void	17. Q 8 7 5 4 2
3. A Q 6	6. Q 10 6	9. K 3	12. K Q	15. A K Q 8 5 3	18. 10 9 7 4 3

B. For these hands, state : **(a)** The number of losers   **(b)** The number of cover cards for a spade contract.

1. ♠ K 4	2. ♠ 9 7 5 4 2	3. ♠ A	4. ♠ Q 7 2	5. ♠ 2
♡ A 3 2	♡ A K	♡ A K	♡ A J	♡ A 9 6
◇ A 9 6 2	◇ Q 9 7 6	◇ 8 7 6 4 3 2	◇ A K 8 6 2	◇ A K 9 4 3
♣ A 9 7 3	♣ J 7	♣ K Q 5 4	♣ 10 9 7	♣ A K 5 2

PARTNERSHIP BIDDING : How should these hands be bid? West is the dealer unless stated otherwise.

SET 47 — WEST	SET 47 — EAST	SET 48 — WEST	SET 48 — EAST
1. ♠ K Q 6 5 4	1. ♠ A 8 3 2	1. ♠ A 7 6 3	1. ♠ K 9 8 5 4 2
♡ K 8	♡ 6 3	♡ 9 8	♡ 6 4
◇ 7 6 4	◇ 9	◇ K Q	◇ A 7 5 4
♣ A 8 3	♣ K 9 7 6 5 4	♣ K 8 6 5 4	♣ 7
2. ♠ 7 5 4 2	2. ♠ 8	2. ♠ K 8 4 2	2. ♠ A J 6 3
♡ A 7 6 2	♡ K Q 9 4 3	♡ Q 10	♡ J 9 8
◇ K 5 4	◇ A Q 8 7 6	◇ J 2	◇ K 7 4
♣ 3 2	♣ Q 10	♣ A K 7 4 2	♣ Q 6 3
3. ♠ K 8 6 4	3. ♠ A Q 9 7 5 3	3. ♠ A 10 7 4 2	3. ♠ K Q 6 3
♡ K 4	♡ A 6	♡ A 6 4 2	♡ 10
◇ A 10 8 3	◇ 2	◇ A 9	◇ K 8 3 2
♣ 7 5 4	♣ A K 6 2	♣ 7 4	♣ A K Q J
4. ♠ 9 6 3	4. ♠ A K 8 7 5 4 2	4. ♠ A 6 3 2	4. ♠ K Q 9 8 5
♡ Q 8 4 3	♡ 7 5 2	♡ 7	♡ A K Q 8 6 2
◇ A K	◇ 9 8	◇ A J 9 3 2	◇ 4
♣ A 9 8 3	♣ 5	♣ A 4 2	♣ 3
5. South opens 1♣.	5. South opens 1♣.	5. South opens 1♡.	5. South opens 1♡.
♠ A Q 8 3 2	♠ K 9 7 5 4	♠ A 9 7 4	♠ K 8 5 3
♡ 7 5	♡ A K 8 3 2	♡ Q 9	♡ J 4
◇ K 9 4	◇ 8 2	◇ A K 9	◇ Q J 7 3
♣ 8 6 2	♣ 7	♣ J 7 5 3	♣ A 8 6

PLAY HANDS ON THE LOSING TRICK COUNT

Hand 89 : Hand valuation after a 2-over-1 response — Card combination — Setting up a long suit

Dealer North : East-West vulnerable

NORTH
♠ A K Q 8 6 4
♡ K 8 6 5 2
♢ 7
♣ 2

WEST
♠ J 10 5
♡ - - -
♢ Q 6 5 4 3 2
♣ K Q 10 7

EAST
♠ 9 7
♡ Q 10 9
♢ K J 10 9
♣ A 6 5 3

SOUTH
♠ 3 2
♡ A J 7 4 3
♢ A 8
♣ J 9 8 4

WEST	NORTH	EAST	SOUTH
	1♠	Pass	2♡ (1)
Pass	4NT (2)	Pass	5♡
Pass	6♡ (3)	All pass	

(1) Shows 10+ points and 5+ hearts (see page 33).

(2) With an excellent fit for hearts, North heads for slam, counting 4 losers in hand and assessing responder as 8 losers or better for the 2♡ response on 10+ points (10-12 points = about 8 losers). 4 + 8 = 12; 24 − 12 = 12 tricks potential. With 2 singletons, asking for aces is the best approach. It would be an error to jump straight to 6♡, as 2 aces could be missing, and it would be a serious underbid to jump to 4♡. This would miss a slam as responder would surely pass 4♡.

(3) When 1 ace is missing, bid the small slam if the LTC potential indicates 12 tricks. You can afford to lose 1 trick.

Lead : ♣K. K from a K-Q-10 suit is an attractive start.

Correct play : The defense wins the 1st trick, but South wins the next trick and should draw trumps. With only 3 trumps missing, the split will usually be 2-1, but the correct play is to cash the ♡K first to guard against 3 hearts with East. (If West has the 3 hearts, a trick will have to be lost, no matter what.) When the ♡K reveals the bad break, South finesses next against East's Q. The 3rd round draws the trumps and then declarer runs the spade suit. If West had not led a club, declarer would draw trumps as above and then discard all the clubs on the spade suit and ruff the diamond loser in dummy.

Hand 90 : Hand valuation for a grand slam — Rufffing losers, discarding losers

Dealer East : Both vulnerable

NORTH
♠ J 9 8
♡ Q J 8
♢ 7 6 5 2
♣ 10 6 3

WEST
♠ K Q 6 2
♡ 10
♢ K 8 4 3
♣ A K Q J

EAST
♠ A 10 7 4 3
♡ A 6 4 2
♢ A 9
♣ 7 4

SOUTH
♠ 5
♡ K 9 7 5 3
♢ Q J 10
♣ 9 8 5 2

WEST	NORTH	EAST	SOUTH
		1♠	Pass
4NT (1)	Pass	5♠	Pass
5NT (2)	Pass	6♣	Pass
7♠	Pass	Pass	Pass

Bidding : (1) As soon as East opens 1♠, West should recognise the grand slam potential. West knows there is a strong spade fit and West has 4 losers. Crediting East with a 7-loser hand for the opening bid, West calculates 4 + 7 = 11; 24 − 11 = 13 tricks potential. West could bid 2♣ first for more information and rebid 4NT over East's 2♡ rebid, but with solid clubs and 2nd round control in each outside suit, asking for aces straight away is sensible.

(2) Once East shows the 3 missing aces, West can count 13 tricks in spades if using 5-card majors (5 spades, 4 clubs, 2 diamonds, 1 heart and 1 heart ruff) and could bid 7♠ over 5♠. If the LTC potential is 13 tricks and you have all the aces and the K-Q of trumps, bid your grand slam. West asks for kings with 5NT, so that if East had the ♡K, West could bid 7NT. When the ♡K is missing, West is content with 7♠. Note that there are only 12 tricks in no-trumps.

Lead : ♢Q. Top of sequence is normal.

Correct play : Cash the ♠K first, not the ♠A first, just in case North has J-9-8-5 in trumps. When all follow to the 1st round of trumps, draw the remaining trumps, cash ♡A and ruff a heart and discard the other heart losers on the clubs. Had South been void in spades, then after winning ♠K, East would play ♡A and ruff a heart before drawing all the trumps. Then ♠Q and a finesse of the ♠10 allows the trumps to be drawn.

Hand 91 : Hand valuation for slams — Setting up a long suit — Managing your entries

Dealer South : Nil vulnerable

NORTH
- ♠ K 8 7 6 5 3
- ♡ 4
- ◇ 6 3
- ♣ A 5 4 2

WEST
- ♠ J 10 4
- ♡ Q 9 6 5 3 2
- ◇ 9 8
- ♣ Q 3

EAST
- ♠ - - -
- ♡ A K 8 7
- ◇ Q 10 5 2
- ♣ J 10 8 7 6

SOUTH
- ♠ A Q 9 2
- ♡ J 10
- ◇ A K J 7 4
- ♣ K 9

WEST	NORTH	EAST	SOUTH
			1◇
Pass	1♠	Pass (1)	4♠ (2)
Pass	4NT (3)	Pass	5♡
Pass	6♠	All pass	

Bidding: (1) Despite the low count, a takeout double would not be unreasonable because of the excellent shape.
(2) South has 5 losers, 2 tricks better than a minimum opening of 7 losers, and so bids 2 tricks more than a minimum 2♠. Another way of reasoning: South has 5 losers, a 1-level response is usually 9 losers or better. $5 + 9 = 14$; $24 - 14 = 10$ tricks.
(3) North counts 7 losers in hand and assesses South for a 5-loser hand (as South should have 19 points or more to jump to game opposite a possible 6-count). $7 + 5 = 12$; $24 - 12 = 12$ tricks potential. With a singleton in hearts, Blackwood is best (but if North had a rag doubleton in hearts, a cue bid of 5♣ would be a better approach.). With 1 ace missing, North bids the small slam.

Lead : ♡K. It is natural to try to cash 2 tricks against a slam.

Correct play: North ruffs the 2nd heart and should draw trumps. If trumps were 2-1, the hand would be over very quickly, drawing trumps and ruffing the 2 club losers in dummy. When trumps break 3-0, North should still draw all the trumps and avoid the trap of trying to ruff a club in dummy before trumps have been drawn (West would overruff). After trumps have been drawn, set up the diamond suit via ◇ A, ◇ K, ruff a diamond, club to the king, ruff a diamond (which sets up the 5th diamond as a winner). Cash the ♣ A and ruff a club to reach dummy to discard the other club loser on the 5th diamond. Note that diamonds must be started before playing ♣ K, ♣ A and ruffing a club. The ♣ K and the club ruff are vital entries to dummy to utilise the diamonds.

Hand 92 : Grand slam valuation — Suit combination — Setting up a long suit — Timing

Dealer West: North-South vulnerable

NORTH
- ♠ J 10 7
- ♡ J 9
- ◇ K Q 7
- ♣ J 10 8 6 5

WEST
- ♠ A 6 3 2
- ♡ 7
- ◇ A J 9 3 2
- ♣ A 4 2

EAST
- ♠ K Q 9 8 5
- ♡ A K Q 8 6 2
- ◇ 4
- ♣ 3

SOUTH
- ♠ 4
- ♡ 10 5 4 3
- ◇ 10 8 6 5
- ♣ K Q 9 7

WEST	NORTH	EAST	SOUTH
1◇	Pass	1♡ (1)	Pass
1♠ (2)	Pass	4NT (3)	Pass
5♠	Pass	7♠ (4)	All pass

Bidding: (1) A jump-shift to 2♡ is reasonable but with a strong 2-suiter, it is superior simply to change suit (see page 107).
(2) Always show the major. 1♠ is far superior to 1NT or 2◇.
(3) Once West introduces spades, East applies the LTC since it was not until then that a good trump fit had come to light. East counts 3 losers, West's opening indicates 7 or better, so that there is potential for a grand slam ($3 + 7 = 10$; $24 - 10 = 14$ tricks potential!!). With 2nd round control in all suits, asking for aces is best. 4♠ would be a gross underbid. (Had East responded 2♡ initially, West would rebid 2♠ and East again would jump to 4NT.)
(4) Because it may be necessary to ruff 1 or 2 hearts, 7♠ is much better than looking for 7NT.

Lead : ♣J. The ◇ K is more dangerous as West bid diamonds.

Correct play: Win the ♣ A and draw trumps, starting with the A, just in case North holds J-10-7-4. When all follow, draw the trumps in 3 rounds and then play ♡ A, ♡ K, ♡ Q and ruff a heart, setting up the remaining hearts as winners. If North had held J-10-7-4 in spades, then after ♠ A, a 2nd spade would see North play the 10, taken by the K. Then cash the ♡ A and ruff a heart to set the hearts up before all of West's trumps have gone. This would be followed by a spade to finesse against North's remaining J-x, and trumps would be drawn, after which the rest is easy.

CHAPTER 24

LONG SUIT TRIAL BIDS

WEST A	EAST A	WEST B	EAST B	WEST C	EAST C
♠ AQ854	♠ KJ92	♠ AQ854	♠ KJ92	♠ AQ854	♠ KJ92
♡ A863	♡ K5	♡ A863	♡ 954	♡ A863	♡ 954
◊ A7	◊ 954	◊ A7	◊ K5	◊ A7	◊ 8653
♣ Q2	♣ 8653	♣ Q2	♣ 8653	♣ Q2	♣ K5

It is worth studying the above hands. On Hand A, 4♠ is a very good contract. Declarer would plan to ruff 2 hearts in the East hand before drawing trumps and could afford to ruff the 4th round of hearts with a top trump. Hands B and C, however, offer no prospects of game. Yet the West hand is identical in all 3 cases and the East hand in each case has the same number of points and the same number of losers. How can we account for this difference and how can we reach the good game while avoiding the hopeless ones? The *location* of key high cards and short suits are also vital for accurate assessments. Long Suit Trial Bids are a method of discovering whether partner's high cards or short suits are "in the right place", whether the fit is excellent.

WHAT IS A LONG SUIT TRIAL BID?

A long suit trial bid is a *change of suit after a major suit has been raised to the 2-level,* whether it is opener or responder who makes the change of suit. The final bid in each of these auctions is a long suit trial bid:

Long suit trial bids by opener :

Opener	Responder	Opener	Responder
1♡	2♡	1♡	2♡
3♣ . . .		2♠ . . .	

Long suit trial bids by responder :

Opener	Responder	Opener	Responder
1♣	1♡	1◊	1♠
2♡	3◊ . . .	2♠	3♡ . . .

WHAT DOES THE TRIAL BID MEAN?

The long suit trial bid is an invitation to game *in the agreed major suit.* The suit in which the trial bid is made is known as "the trial suit". A long suit trial bid promises 3 or more cards in the *trial suit* and asks for help in the trial suit. For example, 1♠ : 2♠, 3♣ means "I am interested in 4♠ and need help in clubs."

STRENGTH OF THE TRIAL SUIT

A long suit trial bid is always made in a weak suit, typically a suit with 2 or 3 losers. The trial suit should not be headed by A-K, A-Q, K-Q or A-J-10 (these holdings make the trial suit too strong, as there could be no losers or just 1 loser in that suit even if partner has no helpful cards in the trial suit). The typical trial suit contains 3 or 4 cards either with no top honor at all or with at most 1 top honor of the A, K or Q. If there are 2 trial suits available, choose the weaker suit. If the suits are about equal, make the trial bid in the cheaper suit.

WHEN TO MAKE A TRIAL BID

After 1♡ : 2♡ or 1♠ : 2♠, opener makes a trial bid on an invitational hand, normally with about 16-18 points (including the 5-3-1 shortage count) or a hand with 6 losers. With a 7-loser hand in the 12-15 point range, opener should pass, while with a sound 5-loser hand, opener has enough to bid game without inviting. Responder's raise to the 2-level can be expected to be around the 8 to 9 loser mark.

After responder has been raised to the 2-level (e.g. 1♣ : 1♡, 2♡ . . .), responder may trial with around 10-12 points, about 7½ to 8 losers. With a 7-loser hand or 13 points or more, responder has enough to bid straight to game without inviting. Even with 8 losers and 10-12 points, responder should try for game. Although opener will usually have 7 losers, opener may have a bit extra, such as 6½ losers, or 6 losers but in a hand of only 12-13 HCP, and even if opener has 7 losers, opener's values may be just in the right spot for responder. That is exactly what the long suit trial bid is trying to discover: *whether partner's values cover your losers.*

Occasionally, responder may have slam interest after a raise to the 2-level and can use a trial bid to find out whether opener has help in a 2nd suit held by responder. Responder would intend to bid on to slam if opener can show help in the required suit or to bid on just to game if opener's reply indicates no help in the trial suit.

REPLYING TO THE LONG SUIT TRIAL BID

No losers in the trial suit :	Bid game in the agreed major suit.
1 loser in the trial suit :	Bid game in the agreed major suit.
2 losers in the trial suit :	Bid game if maximum, but sign off in 3-of-your-major if minimum.
3 losers in the trial suit :	Sign off in 3-of-your-major.

NO LOSERS IN THE TRIAL SUIT

Holdings which are "no losers" are a void, ace-singleton, A-K-doubleton or A-K-Q in the trial suit.

1 LOSER IN THE TRIAL SUIT

Holdings which count as only 1 loser are a singleton, A-x or K-x, or 3-card or longer suits including 2 of the top 3 honors, i.e. A-K-x, A-Q-x or K-Q-x. If holding just 1 loser in the trial suit, bid the major suit game.

2 LOSERS IN THE TRIAL SUIT

Holdings which count as 2 losers are any doubleton headed by the Q or worse, or any 3-card or longer suit which contains 1 of the top 3 honors, such as A-x-x, K-x-x or Q-J-x. Tend to upgrade holdings like A-J-x or K-J-x in the trial suit (give a huge upgrade to A-J-10), but tend to downgrade Q-x-x without either the jack or ten as well. With 2 losers in the trial suit, bid 3-of-your-major if your hand is minimum for the raise, but if you have maximum values for the raise, accept the invitation and bid 4-of-your-major.

3 LOSERS IN THE TRIAL SUIT

Holdings which count as 3 losers are any 3-card or longer suit headed by the jack or weaker. With 3 losers in the trial suit, normally sign off in 3-of-your-major suit, which partner is expected to pass (unless, of course, responder made the trial bid with slam in mind, which is revealed when responder bids on to game despite the intended sign-off in 3-of-the-major).

PARTNERSHIP BIDDING : How should the following hands be bid? West is the dealer on all hands.

SET 49 – WEST	SET 49 – EAST	SET 50 – WEST	SET 50 – EAST
1. ♠ 8 7 3 2	1. ♠ 9 6	1. ♠ 7	1. ♠ K Q
♡ K 7 6 2	♡ A Q J 5 4	♡ A K Q 6 2	♡ J 10 8 4
◇ 7 5 4	◇ A 2	◇ 7 6 5	◇ 9 8 4
♣ K 5	♣ A 6 3 2	♣ A J 8 2	♣ K 7 6 4
2. ♠ 8 7 3 2	2. ♠ 9 6	2. ♠ 9 8 4 3	2. ♠ Q J 10 6 5 2
♡ K 7 6 2	♡ A Q J 5 4	♡ 7 6 5	♡ A 8
◇ K 5	◇ A 2	◇ 4	◇ A 7 3
♣ 7 5 4	♣ A 6 3 2	♣ K Q 9 8 2	♣ A 4
3. ♠ 8 7 3 2	3. ♠ 9 6	3. ♠ A J 7 2	3. ♠ K 9 8 4 3
♡ K 7 6 2	♡ A Q J 5 4	♡ Q	♡ A J 9
◇ 7 5	◇ A 2	◇ A Q 2	◇ 10 5 4 3
♣ K 5 4	♣ A 6 3 2	♣ J 8 6 4 2	♣ 7
4. ♠ A K 9 7 3	4. ♠ Q 10 4 2	4. ♠ 8 3	4. ♠ A 2
♡ K 6	♡ A 4	♡ A J 4 2	♡ K 10 9 8 6
◇ K Q	◇ 10 6 5 3	◇ A J 8 3 2	◇ 7
♣ 9 8 3 2	♣ Q J 10	♣ K 4	♣ A Q 7 3 2
5. ♠ A K 9 7 3	5. ♠ Q 10 4 2	5. ♠ A Q J 8 6	5. ♠ K 7 5 2
♡ K 6	♡ Q 4	♡ 7	♡ 9 5 3
◇ K Q	◇ 10 6 5 3	◇ A 8 6 4 2	◇ K 3
♣ 9 8 3 2	♣ Q J 10	♣ Q 5	♣ 8 6 4 2
6. ♠ A K 9 7 3	6. ♠ Q 10 4 2	6. ♠ A Q J 8 6	6. ♠ K 7 5 2
♡ K 6	♡ Q J 10 6	♡ 7	♡ 8 6 4 2
◇ K Q	◇ 10 6 5 3	◇ A 8 6 4 2	◇ 9 5 3
♣ 9 8 3 2	♣ J	♣ Q 5	♣ K 3

PLAY HANDS ON LONG SUIT TRIAL BIDS

Hand 93 : Bidding after a trial bid — Ruffing losers in dummy — Delaying trumps

Dealer North : Both vulnerable

NORTH
♠ 9 6
♡ A Q J 5 4
♢ A 2
♣ A 9 3 2

WEST
♠ Q J 10 4
♡ 9
♢ K Q 10
♣ J 10 7 6 4

EAST
♠ A K 5
♡ 10 8 6
♢ J 9 8 6 3
♣ Q 8

SOUTH
♠ 8 7 3 2
♡ K 7 3 2
♢ 7 5 4
♣ K 5

WEST	NORTH	EAST	SOUTH
	1♡	Pass	2♡
Pass	3♣ (1)	Pass	4♡ (2)
Pass	Pass	Pass	

Bidding : (1) Long suit trial bid. North is worth 17 points and has 6 losers. On either basis, North is worth an invitation to game and the 3♣ trial is more precise and more co-operative than a simple raise to 3♡ (which South would pass).

(2) South has only 1 loser in the trial suit and should therefore accept the invitation by bidding 4♡ even though the South hand is minimum for the 2♡ raise. With 1 loser, the strength of the hand is not relevant.

Lead : ♠ K. It is natural for East to start with 3 rounds of spades. On the ♠ K, West should signal with the ♠ Q. The Q-signal on a K-lead is either a singleton or promises the J and lets partner know that it is safe to lead low next. Here East has no reason to want West on lead urgently and so continues with ♠ A and a 3rd spade.

Correct play : After ruffing the 3rd spade, North should not yet draw trumps, since North needs to ruff 2 clubs in dummy. North could draw 2 rounds of trumps, using the A and Q, but this also has some risk (East's ♡ 10 might get promoted). Either draw no trumps at all or draw just 1 round of trumps with the A before starting on the clubs : club to the K, club to the ace, and a 3rd club. If East discards, ruff low; come to the ♢ A and ruff the 4th club, followed by trumps. If East ruffs in on the 3rd club, overruff with the ♡ K, draw the trump still out with a heart to hand, and then ruff the last club. North should lose only 2 spades and 1 diamond.

Hand 94 : Rejecting a trial bid — Leading towards honors to set up winners rather than finessing

Dealer East : Nil vulnerable

NORTH
♠ A 9 5 4
♡ 9 7 3
♢ K Q 4
♣ Q 10 8

WEST
♠ 7
♡ A K Q 6 2
♢ 7 6 3
♣ A J 4 2

EAST
♠ K Q 8
♡ J 10 8 4
♢ 9 8 5
♣ K 7 6

SOUTH
♠ J 10 6 3 2
♡ 5
♢ A J 10 2
♣ 9 5 3

WEST	NORTH	EAST	SOUTH
		Pass	Pass
1♡	Pass	2♡	Pass
3♢ (1)	Pass	3♡ (2)	All pass

Bidding : (1) Trial bid. West is worth 17 points (counting 3 for the singleton) and has 6 losers. Either way, the hand warrants an invitation to game. West could make a trial bid in clubs or in diamonds, but should choose the suit where help is needed most.

(2) With 3 losers in the trial suit, East should reject the invitation by reverting to 3♡, even though East has a maximum raise to the 2-level.

Lead : ♢ K. The K-Q combination is the most attractive holding in North's hand, but the trial suit is often the most attractive lead anyway if the trial bid invitation is rejected. The trial bid is made in a weakish suit and if the response indicates no help in the trial suit, it follows that the defense figures to have strength in that suit. South encourages and the defense takes 3 rounds of diamonds.

Correct play : South is likely to win the 3rd diamond and might switch to clubs, dummy's weaker suit outside trumps, or might lead a trump, which is safer than either black suit. In either case, West should win and draw trumps, ending in hand. Before tackling the clubs (club to the K, club back and finesse the J), declarer should lead the singleton spade from hand. If North has the ace and ducks, dummy wins and there is no spade loser, and now the club finesse can be taken. If North takes the ♠ A, dummy's K-Q are high and will provide discards for West's clubs without needing to resort to the club finesse. If it turns out that South has the ♠ A, so that the ♠ K loses to South and dummy has only 1 spade winner, then the club finesse is needed.

Hand 95 : Playing safe — Playing for an overtrick at duplicate — Setting up a long suit

Dealer South : North-South vulnerable

NORTH
- ♠ 9 8 4 3
- ♡ 7 6 5
- ♢ J
- ♣ K Q 9 7 6

WEST
- ♠ A
- ♡ Q J 10 4
- ♢ Q 9 8 6
- ♣ 10 8 5 4

EAST
- ♠ K 7
- ♡ K 9 3 2
- ♢ K 10 5 4 2
- ♣ J 3

SOUTH
- ♠ Q J 10 6 5 2
- ♡ A 8
- ♢ A 7 3
- ♣ A 2

WEST	NORTH	EAST	SOUTH
			1♠
Pass	2♠	Pass	3♢ (1)
Pass	4♠ (2)	All pass	

Bidding: (1) Long suit trial bid. South is worth 17 points and has 6 losers. 3♢ is the best invitation.

(2) North has only 1 loser in the trial suit and should therefore accept the game invitation even though North's raise is minimum in high cards.

Lead : ♡Q. Top of sequence is most attractive.

Correct play: South can make 4♠ safely by winning the ♡A and leading a trump, thus losing only 1 heart and 2 spades. South can later ruff a diamond in dummy and discard the other diamond loser on the 3rd round of clubs. This would be the correct play at rubber bridge where the emphasis is on making your contract. It would be risky to play clubs first, in case an opponent ruffs the 2nd round of clubs with the ♠7 and 4♠ might then go down.

At duplicate pairs, however, you are rewarded for outscoring other pairs and it is worthwhile to try for an overtrick in order to obtain a higher score. Win the ♡A and play ♣A, club to the king and lead the ♣Q. If East were to follow suit or discard, South would discard the heart loser. If East ruffs with a top spade, South again discards the heart loser and concedes only 2 trump tricks. If East ruffs with the ♠7, South can either discard the heart loser and hope the trumps are now 1-1 (which they are) so that both trumps fall when South later leads a trump, or South can overruff, play ♢A and ruff a diamond and lead another club. If East ruffs high, discard the heart loser; if East discards, ruff the club, ruff a diamond and then discard the heart loser on the 5th club. No matter who ruffs, South loses only 2 trump tricks.

Hand 96 : Slam exploration via a long suit trial — Using a long suit for a discard

Dealer West : East-West vulnerable

NORTH
- ♠ 10 9 7 6 5 4
- ♡ 10
- ♢ K 9
- ♣ J 9 8 5

WEST
- ♠ 8 3
- ♡ A J 4 2
- ♢ A J 8 3 2
- ♣ K 4

EAST
- ♠ A 2
- ♡ K 9 8 6 5
- ♢ 7
- ♣ A Q 7 3 2

SOUTH
- ♠ K Q J
- ♡ Q 7 3
- ♢ Q 10 6 5 4
- ♣ 10 6

WEST	NORTH	EAST	SOUTH
1♢	Pass	1♡	Pass
2♡ (2)	Pass	3♣(1)	Pass
4♡ (2)	Pass	4NT (3)	Pass
5♡	Pass	6♡	All pass

Bidding : (1) With 5 losers, East is worth a move towards slam and could simply ask for aces but the 3♣ trial bid is preferable. If West rejects the game try (thus indicating that the ♣K is probably missing) and it turns out that an ace is also missing, East should avoid the slam.

(2) With only 1 loser in the trial suit, bid the major suit game.

(3) Checking on aces and bidding the excellent small slam. With 5 losers opposite a likely 7 losers, a grand slam is unlikely and to attempt a grand slam, East would need to find West with the ♡Q as well. Do not bid a grand slam with 9 trumps missing the Q or the K. There is too great a chance of losing a trump trick.

Lead : ♠K. Top of sequence is best.

Correct play: Win the ♠A and draw trumps, playing the ♡K and a heart to the A. Even though the trump finesse does in fact work here, it is not the best play. If the trump finesse were to lose to North's queen, the defense could cash a spade and defeat the slam. After the ♡A does not drop the ♡Q, leave the trump queen out and start on the clubs: ♣K; a club to the A and then the ♣Q, pitching the losing spade from dummy. South can ruff this with the ♡Q, but that is the only trick for the defense. It was far more important to eliminate the spade loser from dummy on the club suit than to concern yourself about a possible trump loser.

REVISION TEST ON PART 3

The answers to all these questions can be found in Chapters 17-24. Give yourself 1 mark for each correct answer. If you score less than 40, it will profit you to revise the relevant sections.

A. The bidding has been 1♠ : 2♣, 2♡ : 3♢. What action should opener take next on each of these hands?

1.	♠ A9743	2.	♠ AJ832	3.	♠ KQ863	4.	♠ AJ972	5.	♠ AK872
	♡ KJ72		♡ KQ964		♡ AKJ8		♡ A972		♡ AJ97
	♢ AQ		♢ 9		♢ 76		♢ 8		♢ K3
	♣ 97		♣ K3		♣ J4		♣ AQ2		♣ 52

B. The bidding has started 1♢ : 1NT, 2♠. What action should responder now take on each of these hands?

1.	♠ K53	2.	♠ 752	3.	♠ J2	4.	♠ 932	5.	♠ AJ
	♡ QJ3		♡ KJ9		♡ 732		♡ KQ10		♡ 862
	♢ 863		♢ 632		♢ 94		♢ 832		♢ A94
	♣ 10542		♣ QJ108		♣ KQ9863		♣ KJ104		♣ 87532

C. The bidding has started 1♢ : 1♡, 1♠ : 2NT. What action should opener take next on these hands?

1.	♠ AJ87	2.	♠ Q10762	3.	♠ A853	4.	♠ QJ82	5.	♠ A875
	♡ K73		♡ 3		♡ Q6		♡ Q2		♡ ---
	♢ AQ1092		♢ AK9832		♢ AQ962		♢ AKQ863		♢ AQJ43
	♣ 2		♣ A		♣ K5		♣ 5		♣ KJ73

D. The bidding has started 1♢ : 1♠, 3♢. What action should responder now take on these hands?

1.	♠ K942	2.	♠ AJ742	3.	♠ AQ972	4.	♠ KJ9732	5.	♠ AJ82
	♡ 873		♡ KQ32		♡ A72		♡ 32		♡ K83
	♢ J9		♢ 76		♢ 872		♢ 962		♢ 97
	♣ K952		♣ 84		♣ 54		♣ AJ		♣ QJ32

E. The bidding has been 1♣ : 2♣, 2♢. What action should responder now take on these hands?

1.	♠ J7	2.	♠ AQ7	3.	♠ K72	4.	♠ 652	5.	♠ 32
	♡ J64		♡ K96		♡ QJ4		♡ AK9		♡ 64
	♢ K6		♢ 97		♢ 63		♢ 62		♢ A42
	♣ J87532		♣ 98532		♣ J8542		♣ Q9732		♣ A98632

F. The bidding has started 1♠ : 1NT, 2♣. What action should responder now take on these hands?

1.	♠ 97	2.	♠ 42	3.	♠ ---	4.	♠ 92	5.	♠ 7
	♡ A63		♡ 4		♡ Q4		♡ J3		♡ A9863
	♢ KJ9742		♢ K97632		♢ 9865432		♢ QJ7642		♢ A3
	♣ 32		♣ QJ32		♣ A954		♣ K32		♣ 98652

G. What would your answers be on the hands in F. if the bidding had started 1♠ : 1NT, 2♡?

H. What would your answers be on the hands in F. if the bidding had started 1♠ : 1NT, 2♠?

I. The bidding has started 1♠ : 2♠. What action should opener now take on each of these hands?

1.	♠ J76532	2.	♠ AJ873	3.	♠ AQ7632	4.	♠ A9852	5.	♠ AQJ84
	♡ AK2		♡ AQ		♡ AKJ9		♡ AK		♡ 6
	♢ KQ		♢ 76		♢ 4		♢ 9762		♢ AQJ43
	♣ K2		♣ J752		♣ 96		♣ KJ		♣ 62

J. The bidding has been 1♠ : 2♠, 3♡. What action should responder now take on each of these hands?

1.	♠ Q752	2.	♠ A74	3.	♠ 9754	4.	♠ A72	5.	♠ Q852
	♡ K87		♡ K76532		♡ 643		♡ K7		♡ 6
	♢ A3		♢ 64		♢ Q7		♢ 863		♢ 943
	♣ 9853		♣ 32		♣ KJ42		♣ 96542		♣ K9864

PART 4

EXPAND YOUR
COMPETITIVE AND DEFENSIVE BIDDING

This part covers more advanced situations where the opponents have opened the bidding or where your side has opened the bidding and the opponents intervene, situations which you and your partner must get right to score what is rightfully yours or to avoid a horrible debacle. Here also, both partners need to be conversant with the relevant principles and rather than wait until a calamity occurs at the table, make sure that you and your partner go through the relevant areas together thoroughly. The groundwork by both of you will be well rewarded by success when the difficult situations do arise.

Chapter 25 deals with bidding the enemy suit: what it means if you bid the enemy suit directly over an opponent's opening bid and what it means later in the auction or in response to partner's action, and how the bidding proceeds after a bid of the enemy suit has been used.

Chapter 26 is concerned with responder's strong hands after a takeout double, how responder conveys enough strength for game and how the bidding then develops, and also how opener can use the takeout double to show various types of strong hands, particularly the strong balanced types.

Chapter 27 covers actions by the third player after an opponent makes a takeout double, including the redouble and subsequent bidding after the redouble, as well as the 2NT Convention (Truscott) over an opponent's takeout double which has become an integral part of most standard systems.

Chapter 28 comprises overcalling their 1NT opening (what conventions are commonly used and what you need to implement them) and coping with opposition interference over your partner's 1NT (which bids are merely competitive, which are invitational and which are forcing).

Chapter 29 deals with bidding in 4th seat after a 1-level or 2-level bid by an opponent is passed back to you: when to pass, when to reopen the bidding and how such actions differ from bidding in the direct seat.

Chapters 30 and 31 illustrate the use of negative doubles: how to recognise them, when to use them and how the bidding continues after a negative double has been made. Chapter 30 covers responder's hands in the 6-9 and 10-12 zone, while Chapter 31 deals with responder's game-going hands of 13 or more points and opener's rebids when holding game-invitational or game-forcing values after responder has made a negative double.

Chapter 32 concludes by treating penalty doubles: what you need to make a penalty double of 1NT, of a suit overcall, of opponents' games and slams and how to collect penalties even though your partnership is playing negative doubles.

CHAPTER 25
BIDDING THE ENEMY SUIT

Bidding the enemy suit is also sometimes called "cue bid of the enemy suit". A cue bid implies control of a suit, such as a void in the suit or holding the ace in the suit. Cue bids are often used in slam going auctions *after suit agreement has been reached.* For example, after 1♠ : (2◇) : 3♠ : Pass, a bid of 4◇ by opener would in standard methods indicate the ◇ A or a void in diamonds, as well as interest in slam. Bidding the enemy suit before your side has agreed on a suit, however, does not promise the ace or a void in their suit. The expression "cue bid of the enemy suit" still appears because it used to be a requirement 40 or 50 years ago that a bid of the enemy suit did imply such control even before your side had agreed on a suit.

Today, bidding the enemy suit *before suit agreement* is played in standard methods as an artificial, strong action, normally forcing to game. The meaning will vary depending on how the auction has started. The principles are not difficult as long as you realise that bidding the enemy suit is a strong artificial action. The concept of bidding the enemy suit by responder later in the auction is very similar to 4th-suit-forcing (see Chapter 17) and if the 4th-suit-forcing area has been absorbed, this chapter will pose no difficulties.

BIDDING THE ENEMY SUIT DIRECTLY OVER THEIR OPENING BID e.g. (1♡) : 2♡ ...

(A) STANDARD APPROACH : Whether their suit is a major or a minor, bidding their suit directly over the opening is artificial, forcing to game and shows values equivalent to a demand opening bid (23 HCP or more, or a hand with 3 losers or fewer). All bidding is natural after this start and a no-trump bid by either partner promises a stopper in the enemy suit. Bidding must continue until game is reached or, if the opponents bid again, a penalty double is made. All doubles by either player after bidding the enemy suit are for penalties.

(B) MICHAELS CUE BID : Popular at duplicate pairs, this convention shows a weakish 2-suiter, similar in strength and shape to the unusual 2NT overcall, about 8-12 HCP and at least a 5-5 pattern (see Chapter 11). The suits shown, however, are not the minors. (1♣) : 2♣ or (1◇) : 2◇ shows both majors, while (1♡) : 2♡ or (1♠) : 2♠ promises 5 cards or more in the other major plus a 5-card or longer minor. The minor suit is not disclosed. If you cannot fit the major and need to know which minor suit is held, bid 2NT which asks partner to bid the minor. Any double by you or partner after using Michaels is for penalties.

(C) MICHAELS OVER MAJORS, NATURAL OVER MINORS : In this method, the Michaels Cue Bid is used only if the opponents open with a major suit, while (1♣) : 2♣ and (1◇) : 2◇ are played as natural overcalls, just as though the bidding had started (1♡) : 2♣ or (1♠) : 2◇ and later bidding is exactly the same as after a natural overcall. This approach is very sensible. If they open with a major suit bid, it almost never makes sense to play in their major. Bidding their suit with an artificial meaning is therefore quite logical. However, when they open with a minor suit, they frequently do not have significant length or strength in the minor suit bid. Convenient clubs, prepared clubs, short clubs, better minor diamonds and Precision diamonds all may hold 3 cards or even fewer in the suit bid. Thus you may well hold length and strength in that suit and it makes sense to be able to bid that suit with a natural meaning. If they open with a minor suit and you have 5-5 in the majors, the Michaels' hand, you can cope via an overcall or a double.

Obviously the partnership must agree which of the above approaches is to be used. If you and partner adopt either (B) or (C), then the game-forcing demand after they open is shown by doubling first and bidding their suit after partner's reply to the double. The sequence double first, bid their suit next, is forcing to game.

BIDDING THE ENEMY SUIT LATER IN THE AUCTION

(A) AFTER YOUR SIDE OPENED 1NT : This is covered in Chapter 28 (Interference Over 1NT). Basically, bidding the enemy suit here, e.g. 1NT : (2♡) : 3♡, is used to replace Stayman.

(B) AFTER PARTNER MADE A TAKEOUT DOUBLE : See Chapter 26 (Takeout Doubles : Strong Replies & Strong Rebids). Basically, bidding the enemy suit in response to a takeout double, e.g. (1◇) : Double : (Pass) : 2◇, merely confirms a strong hand, usually 13 points or more, and asks the doubler to keep bidding till game (or, in some partnerships, until suit agreement has been reached).

(C) AFTER A MAJOR SUIT HAS BEEN RAISED TO THE 2-LEVEL : Bidding the enemy suit in this situation, e.g. 1♠ : (2♢) : 2♠ : (Pass), 3♢, is a long suit trial bid (see Chapter 24). It is forcing for one round, like any normal long suit trial bid, and is not necessarily forcing to game.

(D) OTHER SITUATIONS : Bidding the enemy suit in other cases is primarily a strong action, normally leading to a game somewhere, Bidding the enemy suit denies an available clearcut action. If you have an obvious, natural bid, make the natural bid and do not bid the enemy suit. Bidding the enemy suit is almost always used when you have enough points for a game but you cannot tell yet which is the correct contract. Perhaps your natural bid would go beyond 3NT and yet 3NT could be the correct spot. Perhaps you would like to play in 3NT but you do not have a stopper in the enemy suit, yet partner could have a stopper.

After partner has bid the enemy suit, your priorities are :

● Give delayed support for partner's suit if it is a major and an 8-card fit is possible.

● Bid no-trumps with a stopper in the enemy suit.

● Without a stopper, give delayed support for partner's suit if it is a minor.

● Without a stopper and without delayed support, make the most descriptive bid possible. You must not pass, so cope as best you can.

PARTNERSHIP BIDDING : How should the following hands be bid? West is always the dealer unless otherwise stated and there is no opposition bidding other than that given.

SET 51 − WEST	SET 51 − EAST	SET 52 − WEST	SET 52 − EAST
1. South opens 1♢.	**1. South opens 1♢.**	**1. N. overcalls 2♢.**	**1. N. overcalls 2♢.**
♠ 6 5	♠ K 10 9	♠ 7 6	♠ A K 5 3 2
♡ K 3	♡ A Q 5	♡ 4 2	♡ A J 10
♢ A 4 3	♢ 6 5 2	♢ K Q 3	♢ 4 2
♣ K Q 10 9 8 4	♣ A J 7 2	♣ A K J 8 7 4	♣ Q 5 3
2. South opens 1♡.	**2. South opens 1♡.**	**2. S. overcalls 2♠.**	**2. S. overcalls 2♠.**
♠ K Q J 3	♠ A 9 8	♠ 7 4 3	♠ Q J 2
♡ K J	♡ 4 3	♡ A Q 7	♡ 9 5
♢ A Q J 10 7 5	♢ K 9 3	♢ K Q 2	♢ A 9 7 5 4 3
♣ 9	♣ Q J 5 3 2	♣ A K J 10	♣ 7 5
3. South opens 3♣.	**3. South opens 3♣.**	**3. S. overcalls 1♠.**	**3. S. overcalls 1♠.**
♠ K 9 6 5 4	♠ A 7 3 2	♠ 7 4 3	♠ 6 2
♡ A J 7 3	♡ K 6 4 2	♡ K 7 2	♡ A 9 6 4 3
♢ K Q J	♢ A 5	♢ A K Q 3	♢ 6 4 2
♣ 6	♣ J 4 2	♣ A K 2	♣ Q 5 4
4. N. overcalls 2♢.	**4. N. overcalls 2♢.**	**4. S. overcalls 2♠.**	**4. S. overcalls 2♠.**
♠ A Q 9 5 4	♠ 7	♠ K Q	♠ 4
♡ K 2	♡ A Q 8 6 4 3	♡ Q J 4 2	♡ K 9 6 5
♢ 5 2	♢ 9 8 4	♢ A J 8 3 2	♢ K 6 5
♣ Q J 8 4	♣ A K 3	♣ 7 2	♣ A K 6 4 3
5. N. overcalls 2♡.	**5. N. overcalls 2♡.**	**5. South opens 1♡.**	**5. South opens 1♡.**
♠ A Q 7 6 3	♠ 2	♠ A Q 9 8 6 2	♠ - - -
♡ K 2	♡ 7 4 3	♡ - - -	♡ J 10 9 3
♢ A J 9 4 2	♢ Q 5 3	♢ A K Q J 2	♢ 10 7 4 3
♣ 9	♣ A K Q J 7 2	♣ A J	♣ 10 7 6 4 2
6. S. overcalls 2♡.	**6. S. overcalls 2♡.**	**6. South opens 1♠.**	**6. South opens 1♠.**
♠ A 9 7 4 3	♠ K	♠ 7 6 3	♠ 4
♡ 7 6	♡ 8 4 3	♡ - - -	♡ A K Q 7 3 2
♢ A Q 5	♢ K J 2	♢ A 9 6 4 2	♢ 7
♣ K 4 2	♣ A Q J 9 5 3	♣ J 7 6 5 4	♣ A K Q 9 3

PLAY HANDS ON BIDDING THE ENEMY SUIT

Hand 97 : Bidding the enemy suit — Leading a high card for a finesse

Dealer North : Nil vulnerable

NORTH
- ♠ 10 7
- ♡ A Q 10 9 6 5
- ◇ K 8 4
- ♣ A 10

WEST
- ♠ A 9
- ♡ 8 3 2
- ◇ 10 3 2
- ♣ K Q 7 4 3

EAST
- ♠ K Q J 3
- ♡ K J
- ◇ A Q J 7 6 5
- ♣ 9

SOUTH
- ♠ 8 6 5 4 2
- ♡ 7 4
- ◇ 9
- ♣ J 8 6 5 2

WEST	NORTH	EAST	SOUTH
	1♡	Dble (1)	Pass
3♣ (2)	Pass	3◇ (3)	Pass
3♡ (4)	Pass	3NT (5)	All pass

(1) Unsuitable for a strong jump overcall because of the spades.
(2) Shows 10-12 points, 4+ clubs and denies 4 spades.
(3) East could bid 3NT here but this might be too hasty. 3◇ is forcing and does not preclude 3NT. 5◇ could be the correct spot.
(4) With a balanced hand, West prefers to look for 3NT. 3♡ *asks* East for a stopper in hearts.
(5) With a stopper, East bids 3NT. If East did not have a stopper, East would bid 3♠ or 4◇. As the cards lie, 5◇ is on, but 3NT is safer. You also score more for 11 tricks in 3NT than in 5◇.

Lead : ♡7. Partner's suit and top of a doubleton.

Correct play: North wins the ♡A and knocks out declarer's ♡K. Declarer needs to tackle the diamond suit and it is standard to finesse for the king. In addition, East-West hold 26 HCP and North-South therefore have 14 HCP. The ◇K is thus almost certainly with North who opened the bidding. Without the ◇K, North would have opened with 11 HCP, possible but not likely. Win the ♡K, cross to the ♠A and lead the ◇10, playing low from hand when North plays low. Repeat the diamond finesse and claim 6 diamonds, 4 spades and 1 heart. It would have been an error to lead a low diamond from dummy instead of the 10. The finesse would win but you would be stuck in hand without another entry to dummy to repeat the finesse. If you then continue with the ◇A, North would get in with the ◇K and cash the hearts.

Hand 98 : Searching for a stopper in the enemy suit — High cards from shortage — Marked finesse

Dealer East : North-South vulnerable

NORTH
- ♠ Q J 2
- ♡ 9 5 3
- ◇ A 9 7 4 3
- ♣ 5 4

WEST
- ♠ 8 5
- ♡ J 8 4 2
- ◇ J 8 6 5
- ♣ Q 9 2

EAST
- ♠ A K 10 9 7
- ♡ K 10 6
- ◇ 10
- ♣ 8 7 6 3

SOUTH
- ♠ 6 4 3
- ♡ A Q 7
- ◇ K Q 2
- ♣ A K J 10

WEST	NORTH	EAST	SOUTH
		Pass	1♣ (1)
Pass	1◇ (2)	1♠ (3)	2♠ (4)
Pass	2NT (5)	Pass	3NT (6)
Pass	Pass	Pass	

Bidding: (1) South's standard approach with strength is to open and rebid with a jump in no-trumps. If East had not intervened, the bidding would have been 1♣ : 1◇, 2NT : 3NT.
(2) It is normal to respond 1◇ rather than 1NT. If no-trumps is the contract, allow the stronger hand to bid no-trumps first.
(3) Although just short of an opening, the hand is ideal for an overcall with length and strength in the spades.
(4) No-trumps by South is out of the question with no spade cover. With the values for game but unsure of the best spot, bid their suit.
(5) Confirms at least 1 stopper in spades.
(6) Exactly what South wanted to hear. 5◇ can be defeated via ♠K, ♠A and a spade ruff.

Lead: ♠10. Prepared to give North a trick and hoping East or West can get in before North can win 9 tricks.

Correct play: North wins the first spade trick and should tackle the diamonds. The correct order is to play off the ◇K and ◇Q first (high cards from shortage). East drops the 10 on the 1st round and when East shows out on the 2nd round, continue with a low diamond and finesse the 9 if West plays low. Play off the remaining diamonds. If North would have cashed the ◇A on the 1st or 2nd round of diamonds, West's J-8-6-5 could not have been captured and 3NT should then be defeated.

Hand 99 : Bidding the enemy suit to ask for a stopper in their suit — Card combination

Dealer South : East-West vulnerable

NORTH
♠ 10 6 4 3 2
♡ 9 5 2
◇ 10 7 5 3
♣ J

WEST
♠ A Q
♡ 7 4
◇ 9 4 2
♣ A Q 10 9 6 2

EAST
♠ K J 8 7
♡ J 6
◇ A K Q 8
♣ 8 7 5

SOUTH
♠ 9 5
♡ A K Q 10 8 3
◇ J 6
♣ K 4 3

WEST	NORTH	EAST	SOUTH
			1♡
2♣	Pass	2♡ (1)	Dble (2)
3♣ (3)	Pass	4♣ (4)	Pass
5♣ (5)	Pass	Pass	Pass

Bidding : (1) A sound opening hand opposite a 2-level overcall is usually enough for game in no-trumps or a major. 2♡ is the best action, since 2◇ or 2♠ would indicate a 5-card or longer suit. Opposite a minor suit overcall, bidding the enemy suit primarily asks for a stopper in their suit. If West were able to bid 2NT, East would raise to 3NT.

(2) Confirms very strong hearts and asks partner to be sure to lead a heart if West becomes declarer.

(3) Denies a stopper in hearts and denies 4 spades.

(4) This is no longer forcing. While East has enough for 3NT, East's values may not be enough for 5-in-a-minor. 4♣ allows West to pass if minimum for the 2♣ overcall.

(5) Just worth a shot at 5♣. West figures that if either black king is missing, the finesse is almost sure to work, since South opened the bidding.

Lead : ♡5. Partner's suit and M.U.D. to deny a doubleton.

Correct play : After cashing 2 hearts, South might switch to a spade or continue with a third heart. Declarer's only problem is the trump suit. With A-Q-10-x-x-x opposite x-x-x, it is normal to finesse the Q, not the 10. This wins against (K-x) and (J-x) as well as against (K-x-x) and (J). The ♣K is marked with South for the opening bid but with 14 points missing, the ♣J could be in either hand. With no overwhelming reason to go against the normal line, cross to dummy and lead a club to the Q. When North's J drops, return to dummy and lead another club, finessing the 10 and then cash the ♣A, picking up South's K.

Hand 100 : Locating the best trump fit — Loser count — Slam exploration — Setting up a long suit

Dealer West : Both vulnerable

NORTH
♠ 10
♡ A K Q 8 6 4
◇ 9
♣ A K Q 7 6

WEST
♠ A K Q 9 5 3
♡ J 5 3
◇ Q J 7
♣ 9

EAST
♠ 7 6 4
♡ 10 9 7 2
◇ K 10 4 3
♣ 10 3

SOUTH
♠ J 8 2
♡ - - -
◇ A 8 6 5 2
♣ J 8 5 4 2

WEST	NORTH	EAST	SOUTH
1♠	2♠ (1)	Pass	3◇ (2)
Pass	3♡ (3)	Pass	4♣ (4)
Pass	4NT (5)	Pass	5◇
Pass	6♣	All pass	

Bidding : (1) The North hand has only 2 losers and must insist on game. To jump to 4♡, as some would do, is very lazy. Firstly, the correct contract may be in clubs, not hearts. Secondly, more than just game might be available. The challenge in the bidding is to locate the best trump fit and to get the most out of your cards. 2♠ insists on game, but if the partnership uses the bid of the enemy suit here for other purposes (e.g. Michaels Cue Bid), North would double first and rebid 2♠ over South's 2 ⁚ reply. The 2♠ rebid would then create a game force and when South rebid 3♣, North would then Blackwood with 4NT and bid 6♣.

(2) With 5-5, show the higher suit first.

(3) Longer suit first. 3♡ is forcing here because of the 2♠ bid.

(4) It is natural to show the 2nd suit. 3NT is out with no spade stopper. If desperate, 3♠ could be used.

(5) With the club fit known and only 2 losers, North asks for aces, planning to pass 5♣ if South has none.

Lead : ♠K. A 2nd spade hoping partner might overruff if dummy ruffs low is about the only hope to beat 6♣.

Correct play : Draw trumps in 2 rounds, ending in dummy. Continue with the top hearts, ruffing the 4th round of hearts. Dummy's remaining hearts are winners. 6♣ made.

CHAPTER 26

TAKEOUT DOUBLES: STRONG REPLIES & STRONG REBIDS

Responding to a takeout double with 0-5, 6-9 or 10-12 points was covered in Chapters 13, 14 and 15.

PARTNER DOUBLES FOR TAKEOUT : REPLYING WITH 13 POINTS OR MORE

With 13 points up, you have enough for game opposite the double. Therefore :

BID GAME   **or**   **BID THE ENEMY SUIT**

With a long, strong major, bid 4♡ or 4♠. With a balanced hand, no major and their suit well stopped, bid 3NT. With a weak major *or* with a choice of contracts *or* with no obvious game contract at this stage, bid the enemy suit. This is forcing until suit agreement (i.e. until a suit has been bid and raised). For example, (1♠): Double : (Pass): 2♠, (Pass): 3♢ : (Pass): 4♢ is encouraging but not forcing. 13 points opposite a double does not mean that game in a minor is a good bet.

Unless your game bid is clearcut, choose the bid of the enemy suit. If the opponents have bid 2 suits, such as (1♢): Double: (1♠) or (1♢): Pass: (1♠): Double, a bid of their 1st suit (2♢) is natural, but a bid of their 2nd suit (2♠) is artificial and game-going. If 3rd player raises opener's suit, you may still bid their suit to ask the doubler to choose a suitable contract, e.g. (1♢): Double: (3♢): 4♢ asks partner to bid a major.

AFTER PARTNER BIDS THEIR SUIT IN REPLY TO YOUR DOUBLE

The bidding continues until a game is reached or a suit is bid and raised. Suits are shown in the normal order: longest first; the higher first with a 5-5 pattern, and the cheapest first with 4-card suits. Higher suit followed by lower suit shows at least a 5-4 pattern, as usual. 2NT after the enemy suit has been bid is still forcing, shows a stopper in their suit and suggests a contract of 3NT. If stuck later for a natural bid below 3NT, you can fall back on a bid of the enemy suit again. This asks partner to bid 3NT with a stopper in their suit or to make some other descriptive bid with no stopper in their suit.

OPENER'S POWERFUL DOUBLING HANDS

After partner's suit reply showing 0-9 points : Pass below 16 points. Otherwise :

Doubler's holding	*Doubler's rebid*	*Doubler's holding*	*Doubler's rebid*
Long suit, 5-loser hand	Bid suit (not forcing).	19-21, balanced	1NT if possible, else 2NT.
Long suit, 4-loser hand	Jump suit (not forcing).	22-23, balanced	Jump rebid no-trumps.
3-loser hand or better	Bid game or enemy suit.	24 up, balanced	Rebid 3NT.

The doubler's no-trump rebids assume a stopper is held in the enemy suit. With 19 HCP or more and no long suit, no support for partner's suit and no stopper in their suit, the doubler has a serious problem. Best is to bid their suit and play it by ear from there. You may then elect to pass partner's rebid below game.

THE DOUBLE AND SUBSEQUENT 1NT REBID

WEST	NORTH	EAST	SOUTH
1♢	**Double**	Pass	**1♠**
Pass	**1NT ...**		

North's rebid does not *sound* strong, but it shows 19-20-21 points, balanced, with a stopper in their suit. With 12-15 points, North would pass South's 1♠ reply. Double and bid again opposite a weak reply always shows more than a minimum double. With 16-18 points balanced and a diamond stopper, North would have bid 1NT at once rather than double. Therefore, to double and rebid 1NT, North must be stronger than 18 points.

After partner's reply showing 6-9 points (1NT or a suit bid over interference) : A new suit by the doubler shows a 5-card suit and is encouraging but not forcing. Jump in a new suit is a game force and a bid of the enemy suit is a game-force, asking partner for a stopper in their suit. Where partner has bid 1NT, already suggesting a stopper in their suit, bidding the enemy suit shows a powerful hand with a void or singleton in their suit. This warns partner against no-trumps unless the enemy suit is well covered, at least a double stopper.

After partner's reply showing 10-12 points (a jump response to the double): A new suit by the doubler shows a 5-card suit and is forcing. A rebid of 2NT by the doubler is also forcing and promises a stopper in their suit. If the doubler bids the enemy suit, this is forcing to game and asks for a stopper in their suit. If partner's reply was a jump to 2NT, a bid of the enemy suit by the doubler shows a void or singleton in the enemy suit. It warns partner against no-trumps unless partner has the enemy suit well stopped.

A. Partner has doubled their 1♡ opening, pass on your right. What is your reply on each of these hands?

1.	♠ Q J 7	2.	♠ A J 9 8 6 3	3.	♠ 7 2	4.	♠ 8 7 6 4 2	5.	♠ A Q 7
	♡ 8 6		♡ 7 6		♡ A Q J		♡ A J		♡ 8 6 4 3
	◇ A Q 8 6		◇ K 9 2		◇ K Q 7 2		◇ K Q		◇ A K
	♣ K J 9 3		♣ A 2		♣ J 9 8 4		♣ K 9 4 3		♣ J 7 6 2

B. You doubled their 1◇ opening and partner replied 2◇. What is your rebid on each of these hands?

1.	♠ K 8 7 4	2.	♠ A 9 7 4 2	3.	♠ K 7 6 4 2	4.	♠ Q 7 3 2	5.	♠ A Q 3
	♡ 8 6 4 3		♡ K Q 9 3		♡ Q 9 4 3 2		♡ A 8 3		♡ K Q 6
	◇ A 7		◇ 7		◇ A K		◇ 9 6		◇ 8 7 3 2
	♣ A Q 3		♣ K J 2		♣ 7		♣ A K 5 4		♣ A Q 4

PARTNERSHIP BIDDING: How should these hands be bid? There is no bidding other than that given.

SET 53 — WEST	SET 53 — EAST	SET 54 — WEST	SET 54 — EAST
1. South opens 1♡.	**1. South opens 1♡.**	**1. South opens 1♣.**	**1. South opens 1♣.**
♠ A 8 7 2	♠ Q J 10 9 4 3	♠ K Q 8 5	♠ 9 3
♡ 8 2	♡ A K 7	♡ A J	♡ 8 7 6 5 4 2
◇ K 5 4	◇ 6	◇ A 8 2	◇ 6 4
♣ K Q 7 3	♣ 9 4 2	♣ A Q 9 2	♣ 8 6 3
2. (a) S. opens 1♠.	**2. (a) S. opens 1♠.**	**2. (a) S. opens 1♣.**	**2. (a) S. opens 1♣.**
♠ A	♠ 8 6	♠ K 9	♠ A 3 2
♡ K Q 9 3	♡ J 7 5 4 2	♡ A K 3 2	♡ 6 5 4
◇ A 7 6 5 2	◇ K 8 3	◇ K Q 9	◇ J 10 4 3 2
♣ J 7 3	♣ A K Q	♣ A J 5 4	♣ Q 2
(b) South opens 1♣.	**(b) South opens 1♣.**	**(b) South opens 1◇.**	**(b) South opens 1◇.**
3. South opens 1◇.	**3. South opens 1◇.**	**3. South opens 1◇.**	**3. South opens 1◇.**
♠ K Q 4 3	♠ A 2	♠ A Q 9 7 2	♠ J 4 3
♡ A 9 3 2	♡ 8 7	♡ A K 4 3	♡ 8 2
◇ A 8	◇ 7 6 4 2	◇ 8	◇ A Q 9 7
♣ 7 5 4	♣ A K Q 8 6	♣ K Q 10	♣ 9 7 6 4
4. South opens 1♣.	**4. South opens 1♣.**	**4. South opens 1♣.**	**4. South opens 1♣.**
♠ A Q 4 3	♠ K 9 7 6	♠ 6 5	♠ J 8 2
♡ A 8 2	♡ K 9 7 6	♡ A Q 8 7 6 4	♡ K 9 5
◇ A 9 8 3	◇ K Q J	◇ A K	◇ 8 7 4 3 2
♣ 7 4	♣ J 3	♣ K Q J	♣ 8 6
5. South opens 1◇.	**5. South opens 1◇.**	**5. South opens 1♡.**	**5. South opens 1♡.**
♠ A Q 6 5	♠ K 7	♠ A 7	♠ J 8 4 2
♡ K 9 7 4	♡ A 8 3	♡ 6 4	♡ 7 3
◇ 8 2	◇ Q J 4 3	◇ A K 3	◇ 8 5 4 2
♣ A J 10	♣ K 4 3 2	♣ A K Q 8 6 2	♣ 7 5 3
6. South opens 1♣.	**6. South opens 1♣.**	**6. South opens 1♡.**	**6. South opens 1♡.**
♠ Q J 5 4 2	♠ K 7 3	♠ A 2	♠ J 7 6 5
♡ A Q J 3	♡ K 6 5	♡ 7 6	♡ A 3
◇ K 4 3	◇ A 7 2	◇ A K Q 8 6 2	◇ 7 5 3
♣ 9	♣ A 8 4 2	♣ A K 3	♣ 8 5 4 2

PLAY HANDS ON STRONG DOUBLES & STRONG REPLIES TO DOUBLES

Hand 101 : Bidding the enemy suit — Counting your tricks — Card combination

Dealer North : North-South vulnerable

NORTH
- ♠ Q 9
- ♡ Q J
- ◊ A Q J 10 7
- ♣ Q 9 8 5

WEST
- ♠ A 4
- ♡ K 6 3
- ◊ K 6 4 3
- ♣ K 7 3 2

EAST
- ♠ K 8 6 5
- ♡ A 7 4 2
- ◊ 9 5
- ♣ A J 10

SOUTH
- ♠ J 10 7 3 2
- ♡ 10 9 8 5
- ◊ 8 2
- ♣ 6 4

WEST	NORTH	EAST	SOUTH
	1◊	Dble	Pass
2◊ (1)	Dble (2)	2♡ (3)	Pass
2NT (4)	Pass	3NT (5)	All pass

(1) Artficial, showing enough values for game.
(2) Shows a strong suit and asks partner to lead diamonds. Double of an artificial bid is usually lead-directing.
(3) 4-card suits are bid up-the-line.
(4) Promises a diamond stopper and denies 4 spades.
(5) No point showing the spades, as partner's 2NT rebid denied 4 spades. East would rebid 3♡ with a 5-card suit.

Lead : ◊ Q. Prepared to concede a trick to the ◊ K in order to set up the rest of the diamonds.

Correct play : West should win with the ◊ K. If not, North may switch and then even with 4 club tricks, West does not have enough winners. West needs the ◊ K in order to score 9 tricks. Continue with a low club and finesse the 10. Cross back to hand with a heart to the K and lead another low club, finessing the J. Cash the ♣ A, come to hand with the ♠ A and cash the ♣ K. Making 2 spades, 2 hearts, 1 diamond and 4 clubs. It would be an error to cash the ♣ K before taking the club finesse. ♣ K first would limit you to 3 club tricks whenever North has Q-singleton, Q-x, Q-x-x-x or Q-x-x-x-x in clubs. Taking the first round finesse scores 4 club tricks whenever North has the ♣ Q, regardless of length. ♣ A first and then lead ♣ J is not as good. This scores 4 tricks only if South has the ♣ Q *and* clubs are 3-3, and the ♣ Q is far more likely to be with North, the opening bidder.

Hand 102 : Exploring for the best game — Card reading and counting — Endplay

Dealer East : East-West vulnerable

NORTH
- ♠ K 10 4
- ♡ A 5 4
- ◊ A 4 3
- ♣ Q 7 4 3

WEST
- ♠ 6 5
- ♡ J 10 8 2
- ◊ Q 10 8 7 2
- ♣ 10 5

EAST
- ♠ A 8 2
- ♡ 9 7
- ◊ 9 5
- ♣ A K J 8 6 2

SOUTH
- ♠ Q J 9 7 3
- ♡ K Q 6 3
- ◊ K J 6
- ♣ 9

WEST	NORTH	EAST	SOUTH
		1♣	Dble (1)
Pass	2♣ (2)	Dble (3)	2♠
Pass	2NT (4)	Pass	3♡
Pass	4♠ (5)	All pass	

Bidding : (1) With 5-4 in the majors, double rather than overcall.
(2) Artificial and showing values for game.
(3) Shows strong clubs. Lead-directing.
(4) Shows a stopper in clubs and seeks further information.
(5) South's 2♠, then 3♡ shows at least 5 spades and 4 hearts. Therefore, North elects to play in the spade game.

Lead : ♣10. Partner's suit. Top from a doubleton.

Correct play : South should play low from dummy and East encourages with the ♣8. The next club is ducked in dummy and East's ♣J is ruffed. A spade to the 10 loses to East's ace, and East's ♣K is ruffed high by South, West discarding a diamond. West's ♣10, then ♣5 indicates a doubleton, so that South must ruff high to avoid the risk of an overruff. Trumps are drawn, West discarding another diamond. West must hang on to all 4 hearts, as South bid hearts : *keep length with declarer*. If West discards a heart. South has 4 heart tricks instead of just 3. Having lost 2 tricks, it seems that South needs hearts 3-3 or the ◊ Q onside. However, South can manage even though neither hearts nor diamonds are favourable. Play off the top hearts. When they do not break 3-3 and West has the last heart, play the 4th heart and put West on lead. West is known to be out of clubs and out of spades. With only diamonds left, West has to lead into South's ◊ K-J-6. Thus, the losing diamond finesse is avoided by *endplaying* West.

Hand 103 : Doubling with a strong balanced hand — Ducking in defense — Setting up the right suit

Dealer South : Both vulnerable

NORTH
♠ Q 9 7 4
♡ A 6
♢ K 9 8 3
♣ A 8 3

WEST
♠ 8 3
♡ 10 9 8 3
♢ A 7
♣ Q J 10 5 2

EAST
♠ A K 6 2
♡ K Q J
♢ Q J 4
♣ K 7 4

SOUTH
♠ J 10 5
♡ 7 5 4 2
♢ 10 6 5 2
♣ 9 6

WEST	NORTH	EAST	SOUTH
			Pass
Pass	1♢	Dble (1)	Pass
1♡ (2)	Pass	1NT (3)	Pass
3NT (4)	Pass	Pass	Pass

Bidding : (1) Too strong for a 1NT overcall.
(2) Show the major first in reply to a double.
(3) The 1NT rebid after doubling shows 19-21 balanced.
(4) 3NT is much better than a 3♣ rebid.

Lead : ♢ 2. 4th highest is the standard card from your own long suit or when leading partner's suit. Reject partner's suit only when you have a good long suit and outside entries.

Correct play : Win the ♢ A at once — do not duck. Lead *hearts* next, not clubs. Knock out the ♡ A and on regaining the lead, cash your hearts. Continue by leading the ♣ K (North should duck this) and a second club to dummy. When you reach dummy, now or later, cash the heart winner and, if North had switched to spades after winning the ♡ A, lead a diamond. You win 2 spades, 3 hearts, 2 diamonds and 2 clubs. Traps to avoid : (1) If you duck the first diamond, North could win the ♢ K and switch to spades. On winning ♣ A or ♡ A, North could lead another spade. The defense would then score 2 spades, the ♢ K and 2 aces before declarer could make 9 tricks. (2) Ducking the first diamond, winning North's diamond return (it is not easy for North to find the spade switch) and tackling clubs next. If North ducks the first two club leads, declarer cannot reach the extra heart winner in dummy and makes only 8 tricks. When declarer is trying to set up dummy's long suit and dummy has no outside entry, it pays you to hold off with the ace in dummy's suit.

Hand 104 : Doubling with a powerful hand — Bidding the enemy suit — Creating an entry to dummy

Dealer West : Nil vulnerable

NORTH
♠ A 5 3
♡ A K Q J 10 8
♢ A Q 3 2
♣ - - -

WEST
♠ K Q 10 9 8
♡ 7 2
♢ K 10 7
♣ K Q 9

EAST
♠ J
♡ 9 6 5 3
♢ 9 8 5 4
♣ 10 8 5 4

SOUTH
♠ 7 6 4 2
♡ 4
♢ J 6
♣ A J 7 6 3 2

WEST	NORTH	EAST	SOUTH
1♠	Dble (1)	Pass	2♣
Pass	3♡ (2)	Pass	3♠ (3)
Pass	4♡ (4)	All pass	

Bidding : (1) Much too good for an overcall, even a strong jump overcall, or a pre-emptive jump to 4♡.
(2) North has 8 obvious tricks and the ♢ Q could be a 9th trick. For 4♡ to be a worthwhile risk, South needs to produce at least 1 trick. Double then jump rebid is the way to show a hand which is just 1 trick short of game.
(3) South has the trick needed for game but has no clear idea which game is best. Bidding the enemy suit solves the problem. It shows the values for game but doubt as to the best contract.
(4) 4♡ is safer than 3NT because of the club void. If South has the values to allow 3NT to make (such as the ♢ K or ♠ K), 4♡ should make as well. However, 4♡ may be on where 3NT cannot be managed, because of only 1 stopper in spades.

Lead : ♠ J. Partner's suit. The ♠ J would be considered clearcut and automatic by almost everyone and yet it is a trump lead that can defeat 4♡. Bridge is a tough game!

Correct play : West should overtake the ♠ J with the ♠ Q and North wins the ♠ A (else East ruffs the ♠ A). North must not lead trumps next. Instead, North leads the ♢ Q to create an entry to dummy (via the ♢ J) to reach the ♣ A. If West ducks the ♢ Q, cash ♢ A and ruff a diamond. Then discard a loser on the ♣ A and make 11 tricks. If West takes the ♢ Q with ♢ K, North will ruff high on the 4th round of spades. Trumps are drawn in 4 rounds and a diamond to dummy's jack allows declarer to play ♣ A to discard a diamond loser.

CHAPTER 27

BIDDING OVER AN OPPOSITION TAKEOUT DOUBLE

After partner has opened with a suit bid and 2nd player has doubled, e.g. 1 ◊ : (Double) : to you, different approaches are possible. It is recommended that your partnership adopts the Modern Style (see below).

STANDARD TREATMENT

1. All hands with 10 HCP or more will REDOUBLE (the "omnibus redouble").
2. Change of suit is 6-9 points and non-forcing, whether the new suit is at the 1-level or at the 2-level.
3. Jump-shift = 6-9 points and an excellent suit. Not forcing.
4. With 0-5 points, to pass is normal, but with decent support and 4-5 points, a raise to the 2-level is acceptable.
5. A jump raise, e.g. 1♡ : (Double) : 3♡, is pre-emptive with less than 10 HCP.

BARON OVER THE DOUBLE : In this method, which is not recommended, you REDOUBLE with 10 HCP up, PASS with 6-9 HCP and BID with 0-5 HCP. Bidding with 0-5 points and passing with 6-9 points may occasionally trap the unwary, but it is unsound against competent opposition. It is especially risky to bid with 0-5 points and a misfit after partner has opened with a major. The penalties can be severe.

MODERN STYLE

1. Change of suit retains its normal meaning and is forcing. The same applies to a jump-shift.
2. 1NT is 6-9 or 6-10 points, as usual.
3. 2NT is not used in its normal, powerful balanced sense. With a hand suitable for a natural 2NT reply, REDOUBLE first and bid no-trumps later if a penalty double is not appropriate.
4. The structure for raising opener is :
  ● Raise to the 2-level = 4-9 HCP and 9 losers.
  ● Raise to the 3-level = 6-9 HCP and 8 losers.
  ● Raise to the 4-level = 6-9 HCP and 7 losers.
  ● With support and 10 HCP or more bid 2NT over the double, e.g. 1♠ : (Double) : 2NT. This artificial strong raise over their double is known as the TRUSCOTT 2NT Convention.
5. Without support for opener and 10 HCP or more, REDOUBLE if you wish to penalty double a bid by an opponent. If your hand is not suited for a penalty double, make your normal response (except for 2NT). Hands suitable for a penalty double are covered in Chapter 32.

Bidding after a new suit response, a jump shift, a raise or a 1NT response follows normal lines.

BIDDING AFTER THE TRUSCOTT 2NT RESPONSE

The Truscott 2NT Response over a double is very sensible. It allows responder to distinguish between weak, shapely hands (raise according to the number of losers) and raises backed by high card strength. It also usually shuts out the 4th player. If the bidding starts 1♡ : (Double) and you have to *redouble* to show a strong hand with support, you allow 4th player an easy entry to the auction. Over your redouble, 4th player can make a cheap lead-directing bid or suggest a sacrifice. By contrast, if you bid 2NT over the double to show support plus strength, 4th player is rarely strong enough to come in at the 3-level.

The Truscott 2NT is forcing and promises support for opener's suit. Support depends on what length was promised by the opening bid.

If opener has a dead minimum opening, opener signs off in 3-Major. Responder may still bid game with more than just 10-11 HCP, or even with 10 HCP if holding 7 losers. With game possibilities, opener can bid a new suit as a trial bid (see Chapter 24), e.g. 1♡ : (Double) : 2NT : (Pass), 3♣ . . . The trial bid must be below 3-of-the-agreed-major. With enough for game but no slam interest, opener bids 4-Major over 2NT. With slam values after 2NT, opener may cue bid by bidding a new suit higher than 3-of-the-agreed-major, e.g. 1♡ : (Double) : 2NT : (Pass), 3♠ or 4♣ or 4◊ by opener. A new suit below 3-Major is a trial bid and a new suit above 3-Major is a cue bid. It is even sensible to use 3NT over Truscott 2NT as Blackwood.

Where opener's suit is a minor, Truscott 2NT denies a major. For example, 1♣ : (Double) : 2NT shows club support, 10 HCP or more and no 4-card major. With support and a major suit as well, bid the major.

If your opponent has bid 2NT over partner's takeout double, you are worth a bid with a 4-card major or a 5-card minor and about an 8-loser hand. With fewer losers, you may jump bid pre-emptively.

BIDDING AFTER THE REDOUBLE

1. *The doubler's partner should bid.* Say the bidding has started (1♠): Double: (Redouble)... Do not pass the redouble even with a very weak hand. The bidding so far has shown that 4th player can have very little. However, it is correct for 4th player to bid for psychological reasons. A pass reveals weakness and will encourage the opponents to double later actions for penalties. A bid *sounds* stronger even though a bid does not promise any strength at all. 4th player should also bid to take pressure off partner. The doubler usually has no clear idea of the best trump suit — after all, that is why the double was chosen originally. 4th player should therefore indicate the desired suit. The best principle is: *After partner's takeout double, bid over a redouble as you would bid over a pass.* The bidding over a redouble is no higher, so that there is no greater difficulty. If you would have bid over a pass, what is so tough about bidding over a redouble? Unlike a bid, the redouble has not cancelled the double, so that 4th player should take out the double. If 4th player is worth a jump reply to the double, make the jump reply. The redoubler could be bluffing or the opening might have been a "psyche".

2. *The opener should pass unless able to make a penalty double.* After a redouble, all doubles are for penalties. A strong 4-card or better holding in a suit they bid is adequate for a penalty double. If opener is unable to make a penalty double, opener should pass on all normal hands. The redouble promises another bid, so that partner will not let the bidding die out. The redoubler may want to double for penalties and if opener bids first, the opponents are let off the hook. A bid by opener ahead of the redoubler would show a weak, distributional hand.

Suppose the bidding has started 1♠ : (Double) : Redouble : (2♣) to the opener. With 4 or more strong clubs, double for penalties. With other normal opening hands, pass. A new suit bid such as 2♡ or 2♢ would suggest a weak 5-5 or 6-5 with only 10 or 11 HCP, unsuitable to defend for penalties. Rebidding the suit opened, 2♠, ahead of the redoubler would suggest 6-7 spades, 10 or 11 HCP and unsuited for defense.

Opener may pass 4th player's bid and later bid a new suit to remove a penalty double by the redoubler. This shows a shapely hand, usually 5-5, but not a weak, sub-minimum opening. Opener is suggesting that game chances offer a better reward than defense.

3. *The doubler takes normal action.* Suppose the bidding has been (1♡): Double: (Redouble): 1♠, (Pass) to you. You would bid now only if you would normally have bid over a weak reply to your double. Any further action by the doubler shows a strong doubling hand.

4. *The redoubler must take action if 4th player's bid is passed around.* Suppose partner opened 1♡ and you redoubled RHO's takeout double. LHO bids 2♣ passed back to you. You may double 2♣ for penalties with 4 or more good clubs. A misfit with opener makes penalties attractive. A new suit by the redoubler is natural and forcing, and subsequent bidding is natural. Reverting to opener's suit (2♡ in the given auction) suggests only delayed, secondary support because of the failure to use 2NT over the double. A 2NT rebid by the redoubler is not forcing and shows 10-12 points and at least 1 stopper in their suit. Bidding the enemy suit (3♣ above) would be forcing to game and ask for a stopper for 3NT.

OPENER'S REDOUBLE WHERE THE 4TH PLAYER MAKES A TAKEOUT DOUBLE

If partner changes suit over your opening and 4th player doubles, e.g. 1♢ : (Pass) : 1♠ : (Double), opener's rebids have their normal meaning. Redouble by the opener indicates 16 HCP or better, denies support for responder and suggests a desire for penalties. All doubles following the redouble are for penalties.

The function of the redouble by responder or by opener is to indicate that your side holds the balance of power (12 + 10 or 16 + 6). If the hand is also a misfit and you have a strong 4-card or longer holding in their suit, you will usually score more via a penalty double than by bidding on. Redoubles suggest penalties.

AFTER THE DOUBLE OF PARTNER'S 1NT RESPONSE

The double of a 1NT *response* is commonly played as a takeout double (see page 78). For example, 1♡ : (Pass) : 1NT : (Double) is used as a takeout double of 1♡. Opener takes normal action here just as if 4th player had passed 1NT. Redouble by opener indicates 16 HCP or more, asks the responder to pass 1NT redoubled with any normal 1NT response and suggests penalties if either opponent bids again.

A. Partner opened 1♡, next player doubled. What action do you take, in the modern style, on these hands?

1. ♠ K 7 4 3	2. ♠ 7	3. ♠ A J 9 8 4	4. ♠ - - -	5. ♠ A Q 6 3
♡ A 2	♡ K 7 4 3	♡ 2	♡ K 8 4 3 2	♡ K 8 6 4
◇ A 9 8 4	◇ A 9 4 3	◇ A Q 10 2	◇ 8 6 4 3 2	◇ Q 7
♣ Q 6 3	♣ J 5 3 2	♣ 8 6 4	♣ K 7 5	♣ 9 8 3

B. Partner doubled their 1♡ opening and next player redoubled. What should you do now with these hands?

1. ♠ Q 9 5 2	2. ♠ 9 7	3. ♠ A Q 9 5 4	4. ♠ 8 6 3	5. ♠ A Q 6
♡ 7 6	♡ 6 5 3 2	♡ 6 4 3	♡ 7 4 3 2	♡ Q 7
◇ 8 5 3 2	◇ 6 4	◇ Q J 7	◇ Q 7 6	◇ Q 9 4 3
♣ 8 7 3	♣ 9 6 5 3 2	♣ 5 3	♣ 8 4 2	♣ K J 7 6

C. The bidding has been 1♡ : (Double) : Redouble : (1♠) back to opener. What should the opener do now?

1. ♠ A 7	2. ♠ A K 10 9	3. ♠ K 5 4	4. ♠ 7	5. ♠ 9
♡ A 9 7 4 3	♡ K Q 8 7 3	♡ A J 7 4 3	♡ K 9 8 6 4 2	♡ A K Q 8 6 3
◇ K Q 6 2	◇ 4	◇ K Q 3	◇ A Q J 6 3	◇ J 8 4
♣ 8 3	♣ J 10 2	♣ 9 2	♣ 4	♣ J 5 2

D. The bidding starts 1♠ : (Double) : Redouble : (2♡), Pass : (Pass) back to you, the redoubler. What now?

1. ♠ 7	2. ♠ 8 6	3. ♠ 5 2	4. ♠ 7 2	5. ♠ 6
♡ A J 9 3	♡ Q J 4	♡ K 8 4	♡ 8 6 3	♡ 7 2
◇ K Q 7	◇ A 9 8 2	◇ A J 8 6	◇ A K 4 3	◇ A Q 8 3
♣ J 10 7 4 2	♣ K Q J 2	♣ Q J 7 4	♣ K Q J 4	♣ K Q 9 7 4 2

PARTNERSHIP BIDDING: How should these hands be bid? There is no bidding other than that given.

SET 55 — WEST	SET 55 — EAST	SET 56 — WEST	SET 56 — EAST
1. N doubles W's 1♡.	1. N doubles W's 1♡.	1. N doubles W's 1♣.	1. N doubles W's 1♣.
♠ 7 2	♠ 8 5	♠ K Q 7 4	♠ A 2
♡ A Q 7 6 2	♡ K 9 4 3	♡ 8 3	♡ K Q 9 6 5 2
◇ K 3	◇ A Q J 5	◇ A 2	◇ J 3
♣ K Q 8 4	♣ J 9 2	♣ A Q 9 3 2	♣ 8 6 4
2. S doubles E's 1♠.	2. S doubles E's 1♠.	2. N doubles W's 1◇.	2. N doubles W's 1◇.
♠ 9 7 6 4	♠ A K 8 5 2	♠ A Q 7 5	♠ 6 4
♡ 7	♡ A K 9 4	♡ 7	♡ A 9 6
◇ A K 4 3	◇ 7 6	◇ A K 8 6 4	◇ Q J 7 3 2
♣ 8 6 4 2	♣ 5 3	♣ K Q 3	♣ A 8 5
3. N doubles W's 1♣.	3. N doubles W's 1♣.	3. S doubles E's 1♣.	3. S doubles E's 1♣.
♠ 8 3 2	♠ K Q J	♠ A 9 7 4 2	♠ K 8
♡ A Q 4	♡ 7 3	♡ 7 6 4	♡ K J 2
◇ 7 2	◇ Q 4 3	◇ Q 9 5	◇ 7 2
♣ A Q 9 6 4	♣ K 8 5 3 2	♣ J 5	♣ A Q 7 6 3 2
4. N doubles W's 1♡.	4. N doubles W's 1♡.	4. N doubles W's 1♠.	4. N doubles W's 1♠.
South bids 2♣.	South bids 2♣.	South bids 2♡.	South bids 2♡.
♠ K J 8	♠ Q 9 5 2	♠ A Q J 6 4 3	♠ 8 7
♡ A Q 7 5 4	♡ 2	♡ 7 4	♡ J 3
◇ K 9 3 2	◇ A 6 4	◇ A J 4	◇ K 10 8 3
♣ 7	♣ A J 8 6 2	♣ 8 2	♣ A K Q 6 4
5. N doubles W's 1♠.	5. N doubles W's 1♠.	5. N doubles W's 1♠.	5. N doubles W's 1♠.
South bids 2◇.	South bids 2◇.	South bids 2♣.	South bids 2♣.
♠ A K 9 7 2	♠ 6 3	♠ K Q 8 7 3 2	♠ 5
♡ 7	♡ A Q 8 5 3	♡ A J 9 5 4	♡ K 10 8 2
◇ K Q 10 6	◇ 7 2	◇ J 2	◇ A 9 7 4
♣ J 6 2	♣ K Q 9 3	♣ - - -	♣ A 7 4 3

PLAY HANDS ON BIDDING OVER AN OPPOSITION TAKEOUT DOUBLE

Hand 105 : Truscott 2NT − Defensive technique − Signalling with a queen − Cashing out

Dealer North : East-West vulnerable

NORTH
- ♠ 4 3 2
- ♡ 4 2
- ◇ Q J 10 7 4
- ♣ 9 5 4

WEST
- ♠ K 10 7 6
- ♡ A Q J 6 5
- ◇ 9 3
- ♣ 7 2

EAST
- ♠ A Q J 9 5
- ♡ K 8
- ◇ 6 5
- ♣ K J 10 6

SOUTH
- ♠ 8
- ♡ 10 9 7 3
- ◇ A K 8 2
- ♣ A Q 8 3

WEST	NORTH	EAST	SOUTH
	Pass	1♠	Dble
2NT (1)	Pass (2)	4♠ (3)	All pass

Bidding : (1) 10 or more HCP plus support for opener's suit.
(2) Not strong enough for 3◇, but had West redoubled, North would have bid 2◇.
(3) East with 16 points or 6 losers is better than minimum and on either basis is worth game opposite the values shown by 2NT.

Lead : ◇ K. An A-K suit is almost always the most attractive. It allows you to see dummy and partner's signal. You can then decide whether to continue or whether to switch. On a spade or a heart lead, East wins, draws trumps and discards 2 diamond losers and a club on the hearts to make 11 tricks. A club lead is awful.

Correct play : If South continues with the ◇ A at trick 2, declarer makes 4♠. Declarer will discard 3 club losers on the hearts after trumps are drawn and lose only 2 diamonds and 1 club. It does not help South to switch to ♣ A at trick 3. To defeat 4♠, the defence must take 2 diamonds and 2 clubs before declarer gets in. This can be achieved only if North can play a club through East. To help South find the defense, North signals with the *queen* of diamonds on the ◇ K lead. The Q-signal on the king promises the J or the Q is a singleton. In either case, it tells partner you will win if partner leads low, away from the ace, on the next trick. Either your J wins or you ruff. You never signal with the Q on the K from Q-doubleton (except Q-J doubleton). The defense goes : ◇ K lead, North plays ◇ Q; ◇ 2 from South, North wins ◇ 10; North switches to ♣ 5 − J − Q; ♣ A cashed; one off. It is true that if North signalled with the ◇ 10 on the ◇ K, South might lead a low diamond at trick 2, but the ◇ Q signal makes it easier.

Hand 106 : Q signal on K lead − Recognising the danger of a ruff − The scissors coup

Dealer East : Both vulnerable

NORTH
- ♠ Q 10 5 2
- ♡ A 7 6
- ◇ 3
- ♣ A K 8 4 2

WEST
- ♠ 8 3
- ♡ K Q 10 8 3
- ◇ 10 7 5 4
- ♣ 10 5

EAST
- ♠ A K J
- ♡ J 9 5 2
- ◇ A K Q J
- ♣ 6 3

SOUTH
- ♠ 9 7 6 4
- ♡ 4
- ◇ 9 8 6 2
- ♣ Q J 9 7

WEST	NORTH	EAST	SOUTH
		1◇ (1)	Pass
1♡ (2)	Dble (3)	4♡ (4)	All pass

Bidding : (1) Too strong to open 1NT.
(2) Too good to pass. Bid 1♡ rather than support diamonds.
(3) Better to double with both unbid suits than to overcall 2♣.
(4) With 20 points and support for hearts, East is worth game. With support, choose the raise rather than the redouble.

Lead : ♣ K. An A-K suit is highly attractive.

Correct play : South should signal with the *queen* of clubs under the ♣ K. Recognising that South surely has the ♣ J (rather than a singleton). North should switch to the singleton ◇ 3 at trick 2. If declarer wins and leads a trump, North takes the ♡ A, leads a low club to South's jack and South returns a diamond for North to ruff, one down. (If the ♣ Q were singleton, this defense would still work as long as South started with 2 hearts : South would ruff when North led a low club and give North a diamond ruff.)

Declarer should recognise what is happening after the ♣ Q signal and the switch to the obviously singleton diamond. Declarer can do nothing if South has the ♡ A entry, but may be able to to remove the club entry via a loser-on-loser play. Win the ◇ A at trick 2 and play ♠ A, ♠ K and lead the ♠ J. When South follows low on the ♠ J, do not ruff − discard your club (loser-on-loser). North wins ♠ Q, but South can no longer gain the lead. Declarer later forces out the ♡ A and draws trumps, losing 1 spade, 1 heart and 1 club. This technique is called the "scissors coup" because it *cuts* the communications (entries) between the defenders.

Hand 107 : Truscott 2NT — Using a strip-and-throw-in to avoid tackling Q-x-x opposite J-x-x

Dealer South : Nil vulnerable

WEST	NORTH	EAST	SOUTH
			1♠
Dble (1)	2NT (2)	Pass	4♠ (3)
Pass	Pass	Pass	

NORTH
♠ K Q 6 5
♡ 8 6 4
◇ Q 6 2
♣ A 9 3

WEST
♠ 10 9
♡ Q 10 7 5
◇ A 10 9
♣ K Q J 7

EAST
♠ 8
♡ J 9 2
◇ K 8 7 3
♣ 10 8 6 4 2

SOUTH
♠ A J 7 4 3 2
♡ A K 3
◇ J 5 4
♣ 5

Bidding : (1) Just enough for a double.
(2) Truscott 2NT, showing 10+ HCP and support for opener.
(3) Only 7 losers which would suggest a 3♠ rebid, but because of the extra trump length and the singleton, South is worth 4♠.

Lead : ♣K. Clearcut.

Correct play : There is a danger of losing 3 diamonds and 1 heart. Correct technique can limit the opposition to 2 diamond tricks by forcing an opponent to start the diamond suit or concede a ruff and discard. Win ♣A and ruff a club high. Cash a top spade and lead a spade to dummy, which draws trumps. Ruff dummy's last club, creating a void opposite a void. Then play ♡A, ♡K and exit with a heart. You have now "stripped" the hearts also (void opposite void) and the 3rd heart forces an opponent on lead ("throw in").

No matter who wins the 3rd heart, declarer is safe. A heart or a club gives declarer a ruff and discard, while a diamond guarantees 1 diamond trick as long as declarer plays 2nd hand low. If declarer starts diamonds, the defense can come to 3 diamonds (also by playing 2nd hand low), plus a heart. If the defense can be forced to start diamonds, declarer loses only 2 diamonds and 1 heart. Note the above technique : Q-x-x opposite J-x-x and other holdings where it is better to let the defenders start the suit occur frequently.

Hand 108 : Sign off after Truscott 2NT — Card combination — Throw-in to avoid guessing a finesse

Dealer West : East-West vulnerable

WEST	NORTH	EAST	SOUTH
Pass	1♠	Dble (1)	2NT (2)
Pass	3♠ (3)	Pass	4♠ (4)
Pass	Pass	Pass	

NORTH
♠ K J 6 4 3
♡ 8 6 3
◇ A 10 4
♣ A 8

WEST
♠ Q 10 8
♡ 10 9 7
◇ Q 8 6
♣ 10 7 5 4

EAST
♠ - - -
♡ K Q J 2
◇ 9 7 5 2
♣ K Q J 6 3

SOUTH
♠ A 9 7 5 2
♡ A 5 4
◇ K J 3
♣ 9 2

Bidding : (1) Much better to double than to overcall 2♣.
(2) Truscott 2NT, 10 or more points, plus support for opener.
(3) Sign off with a minimum opening, and no extra length and no singleton or void as compensation.
(4) Has enough to bid game despite opener's sign-off. Opening + opening = game. If South had a stronger hand and slam ambitions, South could continue with a cue bid, as 2NT already agreed spades as trumps, or with 4NT for aces.

Lead : ♡K. With 2 sequences, lead the stronger, but with equal sequences, lead the shorter suit. On the actual hand, it is immaterial whether ♡K or ♣K is led. However, declarer or dummy figures to be shorter in clubs than in hearts. Therefore you are likely to take more tricks in hearts than in clubs.

Correct play : Win the ♡A. There is no benefit here in ducking. Cash the ♠A and when East shows out, finesse the ♠J and cash the ♠K to draw trumps. It would be an error to cash the ♠K first as a trump loser can be avoided only if trumps are 2-1 or West has Q-10-8. If Q-10-8 is with East, a trump loser is inevitable. If South held ♠A-10-7-5-2, so that there is a 2-way finesse in spades, cashing the ♠A first would still be correct. East is more likely to be short in spades because of the takeout double.

After drawing trumps, cash the ♣A and exit with a heart or a club. After 2 hearts and 1 club, the defense must lead a diamond (thus eliminating a diamond loser if you play 2nd hand low) or give you a ruff and discard. Either way you lose only 3 tricks. Avoid the temptation of finessing against East for the ◇ Q. The ◇ Q is *likely* to be with East because of the double, but the throw-in play makes a game a *certainty*.

CHAPTER 28

INTERFERENCE OVER 1NT

THEY OPEN 1NT – YOUR ACTIONS

1. DOUBLE

It is standard to play a double of their 1NT opening for penalties. Over a weakish 1NT opening (12-14 or 12-15 or 13-15 points), the strength for a double should be 15 HCP or more. With a long, strong suit and 7 or more potential winners, you may double with fewer than 15 HCP. A suitable holding for such a double might be ♠ A93 ♡ K2 ◇ KQJ10842 ♣ 6. With a solid suit, such as A-K-Q-J-x or better, but below 7 winners, pass. Do not double and certainly do not bid your suit in 2nd seat. You have ideal defense and you are on lead against no-trumps. If 3rd player bids and a no-trumps contract no longer seems likely, you should be prepared to bid your solid suit later, if you can do so at a convenient level. For example, with ♠ AKQJ72 ♡ 86 ◇ 743 ♣ 62, you would pass RHO's 1NT opening. If the bidding continues (1NT) : Pass : (2♡) : Pass, (Pass) to you, you should bid 2♠. Likewise, if responder had bid 2♣ Stayman and the 1NT opener rebid 2♡, it would be opportune for you to bid 2♠ now. It is clear that 3rd player was certainly not looking for a spade fit and if you do not bid 2♠, 2♡ might end the bidding. Again, if responder had bid 2◇ as a transfer to 2♡ and opener duly bid 2♡, you should bid 2♠. While the bidding might continue to a higher level, there is too great a risk that if you pass, 2♡ could become the contract.

In 4th seat, after (1NT) : Pass : (Pass), double is still for penalties but it should be based on the 15 HCP or stronger hand. Since you are not on lead, it is too risky to double with just a long, strong suit and one or two entries if your suit needs to be set up. Partner is unlikely to lead your long suit and declarer may make 7 tricks before your long suit is established or your entries may be knocked out and you are unable to regain the lead later when your suit is established. Holding ♠ A93 ♡ K2 ◇ KQJ10842 ♣ 6 in 4th seat, bid 2◇ or 3◇, according to vulnerability. Similarly, with a solid suit such as A-K-Q-J-x or better in 4th seat, bid the suit. You are not on lead and partner is bound to make a worse lead unless you indicate your suit.

After partner doubles 1NT, you normally pass with 6 HCP or more, regardless of shape. However, with 9 HCP or more and a 6-card or longer major, you may score more in a major suit game. Jump to 3♡ or 3♠ with a 6-card major and 9 HCP up, and 4♡ or 4♠ with a 7-card suit (or a 6-card suit with 4 honours).

If you have 0-5 HCP, pass the double if your hand is balanced, but bid a 5-card or longer suit if unbalanced. A suit bid at the 2-level after partner's penalty double is a very weak action. If 3rd player redoubles, remove the redouble on any hand with 0-5 points. If they make 1NT redoubled (quite probable if your hand is so weak), they score a game. It is usually better to concede a penalty at the 2-level than to let them make 1NT redoubled. In addition, redoubled overtricks score very heavily. See Chapter 32 on the S.O.S. Redouble for further information on this and related areas.

2. BIDDING A MAJOR AT THE 2-LEVEL : This shows a powerful 5-card suit or a strong 6-card suit. The suit needs to conform to the Suit Quality Test (see Chapter 9, page 58). The strength is about 9-14 HCP and good playing strength : 5½-6 tricks if not vulnerable (7-7½ losers) *or* 6-6½ playing tricks vulnerable (6½-7 losers) *or* 7-7½ playing tricks when vulnerable against not vulnerable (6 losers or better). A raise is invitational. A new suit is strong (not a rescue) and is forcing (except if 3rd player doubled the 2-Major bid for penalties). 2NT is strong and encouraging but shows only doubleton support.

3. BIDDING A SUIT AT THE 3-LEVEL : The suit will be a powerful 6-card or a strong 7-card suit, satisfying the Suit Quality Test. The hand will have about 9-14 HCP and should contain 6½-7 playing tricks not vulnerable, 7-7½ playing tricks vulnerable and 8-8½ tricks at adverse vulnerability.

4. JUMPS TO 4♡ OR 4♠ : These are based on playing strength and at least a strong 7-card suit. The basic minimums are 7½+ tricks not vulnerable, 8+ tricks vulnerable and 8½+ tricks at adverse vulnerability.

5. 2NT OVER THEIR 1NT : This shows a freak 2-suiter, at least a 5-5 pattern and no more than 3 losers. It may contain any 2 suits, not just the minors. Bidding continues until at least game.

6. 2♣ OR 2♢ OVER 1NT: There are many possible uses for 2♣ and 2♢. You and partner need to agree on which method the partnership should adopt. Possibilities include:

(a) Natural overcalls: In this case, the hand type is the same as bidding a major at the 2-level. See 2. above.

(b) 2♣ for the majors — The Landy Convention: In this method, (1NT): 2♣ normally shows at least 5-4 in the majors. The strength is about 8-14 HCP, but at the lower end, the pattern should be at least 5-5. Partner chooses the major where longer support is held, or bids hearts with equal support. With a total misfit, you may pass 2♣ with 6+ clubs or bid 2♢ with 6+ diamonds. With game chances, jump to 3♡ or 3♠ as an invitation to game with 4-card or better support. A 2NT response to 2♣ is strong and asks for further information. A sensible structure of replies to 2NT could be: 3♣ = any minimum; 2♢ = maximum with 5-5 in the majors; 3♡ or 3♠ = maximum with 5+ cards in the suit bid.

(c) 2♣ for the minors, 2♢ for the majors: The strength and shapes will be as those for Landy 2♣, with 8-14 HCP and at least a 5-4 pattern. Over 2♣, partner may pass or bid 2♢ with preference for diamonds. A major suit bid is encouraging and doubleton support would be adequate. Over 2♢, the bidding would proceed in the same manner as over Landy 2♣ and 2NT would again operate as a strong enquiry.

(d) The Ripstra Convention: In this method, 2♣ shows both majors and 3 or more clubs. 2♢ shows both majors and 3 or more diamonds. The typical patterns are 4-4-4-1s, 5-4-3-1s, 6-4-3-0s and 5-4-4-0s.

Other methods exist over 1NT and no method is wholly satisfactory. You and partner need to settle in advance the methods you will adopt. Either (b) or (c) above are reasonable for casual partnerships.

7. AFTER 3RD PLAYER RESPONDS TO 1NT

(a) Stayman: After (1NT): Pass: (2♣), 4th player should double to show a strong 5-card or longer club holding. It asks partner to lead a club. The club suit should contain 3 honors if a 5-card suit, e.g. K-Q-J-x-x, or 2 top honors if a 6-card or longer suit, e.g. A-Q-x-x-x-x. After 1NT: (Pass): 2♣: (Double), opener should make the normal reply to Stayman if also holding a stopper in clubs and should pass with no stopper in clubs. If opener passes, a redouble by the 2♣ bidder asks opener to make the normal reply. This allows the partnership to avoid a silly 3NT when the club suit is wide open.

(b) Other artificial bids: Double of any artificial response by 3rd player shows a strong holding in the suit bid. For example, (1NT): Pass: (2♡-Transfer): Double shows strong hearts. Partner should lead the suit doubled.

(c) Natural bids: Double of a natural bid is for takeout in the direct seat or the pass-out seat. For example, (1NT): Pass: (2♡): Double or (1NT): Pass: (2♡): Pass, (Pass): Double. Both doubles are for takeout.

YOUR SIDE OPENS 1NT — THEY INTERVENE

1. They double your 1NT: Over the double, your first concern is self-preservation and all suit bids at the 2-level are natural. They show a weak hand and at least a 5-card suit. In particular, 1NT: (Double): 2♣ shows 5+ clubs and is *not* Stayman. Playing 1NT as 16-18 or 15-18, you should redouble with 6 HCP or more, since your side will have greater strength than theirs. You will thus make 1NT redoubled more often than not, and if they flee to a suit at the 2-level, you and partner should be alert for penalty doubles. Jumps to the 3-level over a penalty double are based on 5-7 HCP and a 6-card or longer suit. With a fit *and* a maximum, opener may bid on. With a freak 2-suiter and game chances more profitable than penalties, bid 2NT over the double. Subsequent bidding is natural, showing the suits held, until the best fit is found.

2. They intervene with a natural suit bid, e.g. 1NT : (2♢)

(a) *Suit bids at the 2-level are competitive and non-forcing.* The strength is about 4-7 points. Opener may raise responder's suit with a fit *and* maximum values.

(b) *A suit bid at the 3-level lower-ranking than their suit is not forcing.* For example, 1NT: (2♢): 3♣.

(c) *Jumps to the 3-level are forcing.* For example, 1NT: (2♡): 3♠ is forcing and shows a 5-card suit.

(d) *Jumps to game are normal.* The jump to 3NT does *not* promise a stopper in their suit. No stopper is needed since their suit will not be solid (they would pass and defend with a solid suit). Therefore, opener figures to hold the missing honors and thus has a stopper in their suit. While a stopper in opener's hand is not guaranteed, this is a sound and reasonable working assumption. Do not fear bidding 3NT with no stopper.

(e) *Double is for penalties.* With 6 HCP or more *and* a strong 4-card holding in their suit, be quick to double.

(f) *2NT is invitational, as usual.* As with 3NT, the 2NT response need not contain a stopper in their suit.

(g) *Bidding the enemy suit is Stayman and forces to game.* For example, 1NT : (2♡) : 3♡ promises 4 spades, 1NT : (2♠) : 3♠ promises 4 hearts, 1NT : (2♣) : 3♣ or 1NT : (2♢) : 3♢ promises at least one 4-card major. 1NT : (2♣) : Double is for penalties, not Stayman. If their suit is a minor, e.g. 1NT : (2♢) : 3♢ : (Pass), opener bids a 4-card major, bids 3NT with no major and bids 3♡ with both majors. Over this 3♡, responder will raise to 4♡ with support or bid 3NT with 4 spades. Over this 3NT, opener bids 4♠ with 4 spades or passes with fewer spades. Responder promised a major by bidding the enemy suit and 3NT must deny hearts.

3. They intervene with an artificial suit bid

(a) *Double is for penalties.* The double suggests a desire to play for penalties in the suit(s) *actually shown.*

(b) *Bidding the artificial suit is natural and non-forcing.* For example, 1NT : (2♢ -Transfer) : 3♢ shows real diamonds and is *not* Stayman. A 5-card or longer suit is promised and about 5-7 HCP. *If their overcall is natural, bidding that suit is artificial. If their overcall is artificial, bidding that suit is natural.*

(c) *Bidding the suit actually shown is artificial, game-forcing and replaces Stayman.* For example, after 1NT : (2♣), if 2♣ shows hearts and a minor suit, 2♡ by you is artificial and takes the place of Stayman. Similarly, after 1NT : 2♢, if 2♢ is a transfer showing 5 or more spades, 2♠ by you replaces Stayman.

(d) *Other actions have the same meaning as over a natural overcall.*

A. Partner opened 1NT and next player overcalled a natural 2♡. What action do you take on these hands?

1. ♠ A	2. ♠ A Q 7 2	3. ♠ K J 8 6 4 3	4. ♠ A J 6	5. ♠ A 9 7 4 3
♡ K 10 8 3	♡ 7 4	♡ 7 2	♡ 6 4 2	♡ 6
♢ 9 7 4 2	♢ K 9 3	♢ 8 6	♢ K Q 3	♢ A 8 5
♣ 7 6 4 3	♣ J 8 5 4	♣ 7 3 2	♣ J 8 4 2	♣ Q 9 5 2

B. Partner opened 1NT and next player bid 2♡, an artificial transfer, showing 5 or more spades. Your action?

1. ♠ 8 7	2. ♠ 9 3	3. ♠ A J 8 7	4. ♠ 9 7 2	5. ♠ 6
♡ K 4	♡ A Q 6 2	♡ J 8 7 2	♡ 6 4 3	♡ A Q J 7 4 3
♢ 8 3 2	♢ K 8	♢ 7	♢ A K 8 6	♢ Q 9 4 2
♣ Q J 8 7 4 2	♣ J 6 4 3 2	♣ Q 9 4 2	♣ K 9 4	♣ 6 2

PARTNERSHIP BIDDING : West is the dealer on all hands. Bid the hands with the interference given. All bids by North or South are natural.

SET 57 − WEST	SET 57 − EAST	SET 58 − WEST	SET 58 − EAST
1. South bids 2♡.	**1. South bids 2♡.**	**1. North bids 2♡.**	**1. North bids 2♡.**
♠ K J 9 8 4	♠ 10 7 3	♠ K 8 6 4	♠ Q J 5 2
♡ 7 5	♡ A 8	♡ A J	♡ 8 7 2
♢ 9 6 5 3	♢ K Q 7	♢ Q J 7	♢ K 9
♣ 6 4	♣ A K 10 3 2	♣ A Q 3 2	♣ K J 6 4
2. North bids 2♢.	**2. North bids 2♢.**	**2. South bids 2♢.**	**2. South bids 2♢.**
♠ A K J 4	♠ 8 7 2	♠ 6 3	♠ A 9 7 4
♡ Q 8 7 5	♡ K 3 2	♡ Q J 8 7	♡ A K 2
♢ K 5 3	♢ 7	♢ A 5	♢ 9 7 2
♣ K 9	♣ Q J 10 7 4 3	♣ K 10 6 4 2	♣ A J 5
3. South bids 2♠.	**3. South bids 2♠.**	**3. North bids 2♢.**	**3. North bids 2♢.**
♠ 8 2	♠ A 9 7	♠ A J	♠ Q 9 7 3
♡ K J	♡ A Q 3	♡ K 10 7 4	♡ A 8
♢ A 9 6 4 3 2	♢ K Q 7	♢ A K 6	♢ 8 3 2
♣ J 5 2	♣ Q 8 6 3	♣ Q 7 4 2	♣ A J 9 6
4. North bids 2♡.	**4. North bids 2♡.**	**4. South bids 2♢.**	**4. South bids 2♢.**
♠ A J 7	♠ Q 9 2	♠ A J 7 4	♠ Q 9 6 2
♡ 9 3 2	♡ A J 8 7	♡ 8 6	♡ A K 5 3
♢ A K 5 4	♢ 3	♢ 9 3 2	♢ K 7 6
♣ K Q 7	♣ 8 6 5 3 2	♣ K Q 9 5	♣ A J

PLAY HANDS ON INTERFERENCE OVER 1NT

Hand 109 : Coping with interference over 1NT — Throw-in to increase chances of a vital finesse

Dealer North : Both vulnerable

NORTH
♠ A J 3
♡ K 9 8 6
♢ A 7
♣ K Q 4 3

WEST
♠ 10 8 5 4
♡ 5 3
♢ Q 8 5
♣ J 10 9 7

EAST
♠ Q 7 6
♡ A 4 2
♢ K J 10 9 6 4
♣ 8

SOUTH
♠ K 9 2
♡ Q J 10 7
♢ 3 2
♣ A 6 5 2

WEST	NORTH	EAST	SOUTH
	1NT	2♢ (1)	3♢ (2)
Dble (3)	3♡ (4)	Pass	4♡ (5)
Pass	Pass	Pass	

(1) Just enough for 2♢ vulnerable because of the good suit quality.
(2) Bid the enemy suit when you would have used Stayman.
(3) Double of an artificial bid asks partner to lead the suit doubled. With a top diamond, West does not want East to try any other lead.
(4) Answering Stayman. In an expert partnership, North's 3♡ promises 4 hearts *and* a diamond stopper. With no diamond cover, North would pass the double and South then has to redouble to obtain the Stayman answer.
(5) 3NT could be defeated on a diamond lead even if clubs were 3-2 and the spade finesse worked. 4♡ can be made even though clubs are 4-1 and the ♠Q is offside.

Lead : ♣8 or ♢J. The singleton club is best, looking for a ruff if West holds the ♢A, distinctly possible after the double of 3♢.

Correct play : North wins with the ♣K and leads a low heart. East wins the 1st or 2nd heart and switches to the ♢J, taken by North. Trumps are drawn and the top clubs are cashed. When clubs split 4-1, declarer has a loser in clubs, diamonds and hearts. Declarer cannot afford a spade loser as well. The simple line is to finesse the ♠J, a 50% line. A superior move is to exit with a diamond. If East wins this, the hand is over : East leads a spade into North's A-J-3 or concedes a ruff and discard. If West wins the diamond exit, West cashes a club and then leads a low spade (a diamond gives a ruff and discard). North plays low from hand and East must insert the Q to beat dummy's 9. If the ♠Q and ♠10 were reversed, East's ♠10 would be taken by the K and then the ♠J finessed. Forcing West to lead a spade increases the chances of no spade loser from 50% to 75%. Only if East began with ♠Q *and* ♠10 would there be a spade loser. If West exits with ♠10, North plays the ♠J to ensure no loser.

Hand 110 : Interference over 1NT — Elimination and throw-in to force a ruff and discard

Dealer East : Nil vulnerable

NORTH
♠ Q 10 8
♡ A K 9 6 5 3
♢ 9
♣ J 10 2

WEST
♠ A J 5 2
♡ Q 8
♢ A 7 4 3
♣ A Q 4

EAST
♠ K 9 6 4 3
♡ 7 2
♢ K 8 6 2
♣ K 7

SOUTH
♠ 7
♡ J 10 4
♢ Q J 10 5
♣ 9 8 6 5 3

WEST	NORTH	EAST	SOUTH
		Pass	Pass
1NT	2♡ (1)	3♠ (2)	Pass
4♠ (3)	Pass	Pass	Pass

Bidding : (1) Certainly worth 2♡ not vulnerable.
(2) Game force with 5 spades, just as 1NT: 3♠ with no interference.
(3) 3NT fails even if the ♡Q wins on a low heart lead by North.

Lead : ♡J. Partner's suit and top when holding J-10-x.

Correct play : After 2 heart tricks, North should switch to the ♢9. Declarer wins and plays ♠K and a 2nd spade. When South shows out, win the ♠A. Leave North with the ♠Q for the time being — do not duck the 2nd spade to North and do not play a 3rd spade yet. Next cash the ♣K, lead a club to the A and discard a diamond on the ♣Q. Hearts and clubs have now been stripped — you hold a void in each suit in both hands. Then play your other top diamond. If North ruffs, North must give you a ruff and discard. If North discards on the top diamond, do not play another diamond.

You have lost 2 hearts and you are bound to lose a spade — you cannot afford to lose a diamond as well. The solution is to throw North in with a spade. Out of diamonds, North has to give you a ruff and discard. You ruff in dummy and discard the last diamond from hand. Make sure you do not ruff in hand, for that still leaves you with a diamond loser. The recommended line also works if North began with a doubleton diamond.

Hand 111 : Bidding the enemy suit — Setting up a long suit and keeping the danger hand off lead

Dealer South : North-South vulnerable

NORTH
♠ J 9 4 2
♡ 10
♢ Q 6 4
♣ A K 8 6 3

WEST
♠ A 7
♡ K 9 8 6 5 3 2
♢ 8 2
♣ Q 9

EAST
♠ Q 10 8 6
♡ Q 7
♢ 10 9 7 5
♣ J 10 5

SOUTH
♠ K 5 3
♡ A J 4
♢ A K J 3
♣ 7 4 2

WEST	NORTH	EAST	SOUTH
			1NT
2♡ (1)	3♡ (2)	Dble (3)	3NT (4)
Pass	Pass	Pass	

Bidding : (1) With 7 losers, this is worth only 2♡ despite the 7-card suit and the favourable vulnerability.
(2) Game force and Stayman enquiry.
(3) Lead-directing. Shows a top honour in hearts.
(4) Denies 4 spades and confirms hearts are stopped. With no heart stopper, South would pass the double and leave it to North.

Lead : ♡6. Especially after partner's lead-directing double.

Correct play : South must capture East's ♡Q with the ace. If South ducked, East would continue hearts and West's hearts would be set up, with the ♠A as entry. South could then be held to 7 tricks at best. After winning ♡A, South must prevent East from gaining the lead. It would be disastrous, for example, to play ♣A, ♣K and a 3rd club. East would be in and a heart lead by East through South's J-4 gives West 6 heart tricks. However, South's ♡J-4 does operate as a stopper against West. After winning ♡A, lead a low club. If West plays ♣9, win the ace. Do *not* cash the ♣K. Return to hand with a diamond to the ace and lead another club. When West plays the ♣Q, play low in dummy and leave West on lead. You would also have ducked on the 1st round of clubs if West had played the ♣Q. With West on lead, you are safe and you now make at least 1 heart, 4 diamonds and 4 clubs. An overtrick is yours if West cashes ♡A or ♠A.

Hand 112 : Coping with interference over 1NT — Keeping the dangerous hand off lead

Dealer West : East-West vulnerable

NORTH
♠ A Q 9 6 5 3
♡ 8 7
♢ K Q 2
♣ J 7

WEST
♠ K J 10
♡ A K J 3
♢ 8 7 5
♣ A 9 2

EAST
♠ 4 2
♡ Q 5 4
♢ A 6 3
♣ K 10 6 4 3

SOUTH
♠ 8 7
♡ 10 9 6 2
♢ J 10 9 4
♣ Q 8 5

WEST	NORTH	EAST	SOUTH
1NT	2♠ (1)	3NT (2)	All pass

Bidding : (1) The spades are not strong enough to justify 3♠, despite the favourable vulnerability.
(2) 9 HCP plus a 5-card suit is enough for game and 3NT is the only attractive game. 3♣ is out, as that is not forcing. 3♠ is unsuitable, since that would be Stayman and you are not looking for a 4-4 major fit. 3NT is not 100% safe but it is a sound practical bid. With solid spades, North would pass and defend 1NT. Here, North's spades are not solid and the 1NT opening is highly likely to include a spade stopper.

Lead : ♠6. This is the best shot, hoping that partner can get in and lead a spade back. ♢K is a reasonable second choice.

Correct play : Win the spade lead with ♠J. It is clear that North has led from a long suit headed by the A-Q. You must develop club tricks but cannot afford to let South in. ♣A, club to the king and a 3rd club would be a disaster. South wins and a spade through your K-10 is curtains. It is not good enough to play ♣A and then a low club, planning to duck if North plays ♣Q. If North held ♣Q-x, North should pitch the ♣Q under the ace to avoid being stuck on lead. The best chance is to play the ♣2 to the ♣K and a low club back, finessing the 9. This works whenever the ♣Q and ♣J are split, whenever North has Q-J-x and whenever either opponent holds a singleton honor. It fails if South has ♣Q-J-x, but then nothing would work. On this line North wins the second club with the J, but a spade lead *by North* gives you an extra trick. If North exits with ♢K, win ♢A, unblock ♣A, cross to the ♡Q and cash 2 more clubs, making 10 tricks. Note that if North started with ♣Q-x, it would not help North to rise with ♣Q when you lead ♣2. You win ♣K, finesse ♣9 and lose no club tricks. (If North leads ♢K originally, duck the first 2 diamonds and later play the clubs as above, cashing the ♣K first.)

CHAPTER 29

RE-OPENING THE BIDDING

When the bidding is at a low level and it goes Pass : (Pass) to you, there are many situations where it is unsound to pass, even with the most modest values. Finding an action in the pass-out seat is known as "balancing", "protecting" or "re-opening the bidding", for if you pass, the auction is over.

1. (1NT) : Pass : (Pass) to you : Bid in this auction only if you would have bid in the direct seat. There is no urgency to compete against 1NT and it is not advisable to balance with light values or weak suits. Any action taken over 1NT in 4th seat has the same meaning as that action in the direct seat.

2. (1-suit) : Pass : (1NT) : Pass, (Pass) to you : Again it is not worthwhile finding heroic bids here on light values and weak suits. The balancing double of a 1NT response indicates about 13-15 points and some strength in opener's suit. It suggests penalties but partner may remove the double with a long suit. It does not demand the lead of opener's suit, but such a lead is acceptable if there is no good, long suit available.

If the bidding has started (1◇) : Pass : (1NT) : Pass, (Pass) to you, it is reasonable to bid a 6-card major, one which is too weak for an immediate overcall, such as J-x-x-x-x-x or x-x-x-x-x-x. Do not back in with 2♣ in this auction, however. The 1NT responder is marked with length in clubs because of the failure to bid a major or raise diamonds. Consequently, a re-opening 2♣ risks a hefty penalty.

3. (1-suit) : Pass : (Pass) to you : With length and strength in the suit opened, you may pass for penalties, but otherwise you should be reluctant to pass. Find some action or other, even on slender values.

(a) *Overcall a suit at the 1-level :* The suit need not conform to the Suit Quality Test (see page 58) and a strong 4-card suit will do. The strength may be as little as 7 HCP.

(b) *Overcall a suit at the 2-level :* The Suit Quality Test does not apply, but a 5-card or longer suit is expected. The hand should contain at least 9 HCP, a fraction less than the normal 2-level overcall.

(c) *Jump overcalls :* Even if you use weak jump overcalls in the direct seat, they are not appropriate in the pass-out seat. A hand with 12-15 HCP and a powerful 5-card suit is suitable for a 4th seat jump overcall. If the suit qualifies via the Suit Quality Test, it is strong enough for a 4th seat jump overcall.

(d) *1NT and 2NT in 4th seat :* There are several different structures and the partnership should choose the method preferred. For maximum action with reasonable safety, method (i) is recommended.

(i) 1NT is 9-12 points balanced, with a stopper in their suit. 2NT is 17-18 points balanced, with a stopper in their suit. The unusual 2NT does not apply in 4th seat. With 13-16 points balanced, double, and with 19-up balanced, double and jump bid in no-trumps later. One advantage of this method is that a 4th seat double will have good shape if it contains less than 13 HCP.

(ii) 1NT is 11-14 points, balanced, with a stopper in their suit. With no stopper, double. Below 11 points, pass or double. Bid 2NT with 19-20 points balanced. With 15-18 points balanced, double first and rebid 1NT if no fit is found. If partner bids at the 2-level, pass with 15-16 and rebid 2NT with 17-18. With 21-up balanced, double first and jump rebid in no-trumps.

(iii) 1NT is 13-16 points, balanced, with a stopper in their suit. With no stopper, double. 2NT is 17-18 points balanced. Below 13 and above 19, double first.

(iv) 1NT is 15-18 points balanced, much the same as a 1NT opening or a 1NT overcall in the direct seat. One advantage of this approach is that you do not need to learn a new set of point ranges, but it also means that you are likely to sell out at the 1-level with 9-10 point hands where both sides can make a low contract. However, until you are confident in other areas of your system, it is not a bad idea to have the same range in 2nd seat and 4th seat. If so, bid 2NT with 19-20 balanced. Below 15 or above 20, double first.

Each of the above methods can present problems and gaps. None is perfect, but whichever 1NT range you select for re-opening, a 2♣ reply should be Stayman, 2-level suit replies are weak and jumps force to game.

(e) *Double in 4th seat:* The double includes all the hands usually covered by a takeout double in 2nd seat, plus the hands not covered by the 1NT and 2NT re-openings in (d). Since you are anxious not to sell out at the 1-level, your 4th seat doubles can easily drop to 10 HCP or even 9 HCP with good shape. Partner should be conservative in making a jump reply to a 4th seat double when holdi﹏ only a weakish 4-card suit.

The desire to compete creates a loss of accuracy and definition after a 4th seat takeout double. It is quite normal to take action in 4th seat on hands with 2-3 HCP less than required in the direct seat. If in doubt, *bid.*

(f) *Bidding their suit in 4th seat:* This is used as a game-force takeout, even though it might be used as a weakish 2-suiter in the direct seat (Michaels Convention). If the bidding has stopped at the 1-level, you have no need for pre-empts or unusual weak 2-suiter re-openings. The hand probably belongs to you.

4. You open, LHO bids a suit, passed back to you: For example, 1 ◇ : (1 ♠) : Pass : (Pass) to you. If LHO's overcall was at the 1-level or 2-level, you should be reluctant to pass. With length and strength in the suit overcalled, you should pass. If LHO made a strong jump overcall, you may pass. You may also pass any jump overcall to the 3-level — bid again only with extra values. If LHO made an *intermediate* jump overcall and you hold K-x-x or Q-x-x or better in that suit, pass unless you have better than a minimum opening. On all other hand types, be quick to compete — do not sell out.

With any ordinary competing hand, re-open with a double. It is the most efficient and most flexible competitive move. A new suit, lower-ranking, normally implies a 5-5 pattern, e.g. 1 ◇ : (1 ♠) : Pass : (Pass), 2 ♣. Re-opening with 1NT indicates 19-20 points, too strong for a 1NT opening, e.g. 1 ◇ : (1 ♠) : Pass : (Pass), 1NT.

5. They open, you overcall, LHO raises opener's suit and this is passed back to you: For example, (1 ♡) : 1 ♠ : (2 ♡) : Pass, (Pass) to you. With most hands worth another action, compete via a takeout double. If you repeat your suit, you should have at least a 6-card suit. A new suit, lower ranking, usually indicates a 5-5 pattern. Be wary of doubling if you hold strength in their suit and cannot stand a particular new suit by partner. A double would be misguided in the above auction if you could not handle a 3 ◇ reply. Double would be all right if you were short in clubs but could bid 3 ◇ over an unwelcome 3 ♣ response from partner.

6. They bid and raise a suit to the 2-level, passed back to you: For example, (1 ♠) : Pass : (2 ♠) : Pass, (Pass) to you. Be reluctant to sell out when they find a fit and stop at the 2-level. In these situations, it is almost always correct to compete to the 3-level even on very light values and even when vulnerable. Your options are:

Delayed overcall: This promises a 5-card or longer suit but not good enough for an immediate overcall.

Delayed double: Promises any unbid major and tolerance for other unbid suits. Usually will be less than 12 HCP as you did not double on the previous round.

Delayed 2NT: This cannot be a strong balanced hand, as you would have bid earlier. It promises 4-4 or more in the minor suits. It could be 5-5 in the minors, but this is not likely, as you did not use the unusual 2NT on the first round. It will not contain 4 cards in an unbid major, since you would prefer to double with that.

Whichever delayed action you choose, partner will be conscious of the limited nature of your values because of your failure to bid on the first round. Accordingly, partner will not compete beyond the 3-level.

7. Other competitive situations: Whenever the auction reveals that the opponents have a primary trump fit and the bidding is dying out at the 2-level, you should be reluctant to sell out. Under these conditions, your partnership should use takeout doubles and the unusual 2NT even on minimal values.

WEST	NORTH	EAST	SOUTH	
1 ♡	Double	Pass	2 ♠	What action should East take with J-x-x-x-x in each
Pass	Pass	?		minor and nothing more? Rather than sell out, bid 2NT,
				which must be for the minors. You would have bid 1NT
				earlier with 6-9 balanced or redoubled with 10 or more points.

WEST	NORTH	EAST	SOUTH	
1 ♡	1 ♠	2 ♡	2 ♠	Almost regardless of values, East should compete to 3 ♡.
Pass	Pass	?		It is tactically unsound to pass. Bid a new suit with 5-6 cards
				and only 3-card support for hearts, but do not pass. The
				meek may inherit the earth but they do not win at bridge!

Once the bidding has reached the 3-level, be prepared to compete at the 3-level if you have a 9-card trump fit, but prefer to defend at the 3-level on most hands where you have only an 8-card trump fit. If the values indicate that there is no more than a partscore available, do not compete to the 4-level.

A. You opened 1◇, LHO overcalled 1♡, passed back to you. What action do you take in the pass-out seat?

1. ♠ K 7 6 3	2. ♠ K 9 8 6	3. ♠ 7 6	4. ♠ A 7 2	5. ♠ 2
♡ 7	♡ 6 2	♡ A K 9 2	♡ A Q J	♡ 6
◇ A Q 8 5	◇ A Q 7 5	◇ 8 7 6 4 3	◇ A K 8 6	◇ K Q 9 4 3 2
♣ A K 4 3	♣ K 8 2	♣ A Q	♣ Q 9 7	♣ A Q J 6 4

B. You opened 1♡, LHO overcalled 2♣, passed back to you. What action do you take in the pass-out seat?

1. ♠ K 7 3	2. ♠ A 7 2	3. ♠ A	4. ♠ A Q 7 2	5. ♠ 7 2
♡ A Q 8 6 2	♡ A Q 8 5 4 2	♡ A K J 8 7	♡ A J 9 8 6 2	♡ A J 9 7 2
◇ Q J 6 4	◇ Q 9 7	◇ 9 3 2	◇ A 2	◇ A
♣ 3	♣ 2	♣ Q 8 5 4	♣ 7	♣ K Q 8 6 2

C. Partner opened 1♡, your RHO overcalled 2◇, passed back to opener who re-opened with a double, passed to you. What action do you take now on each of these hands?

1. ♠ Q 7 4	2. ♠ A 7 5 3 2	3. ♠ K 8	4. ♠ 8 7 2	5. ♠ 8 7 2
♡ 7 3 2	♡ 7	♡ J	♡ A J	♡ 6
◇ J 9 6 4	◇ 9 7 6 4	◇ 8 7 6 4	◇ K 8 6 2	◇ Q J 9 4 3
♣ J 7 3	♣ 7 3 2	♣ J 9 8 5 4 2	♣ 9 7 5 2	♣ K 9 3 2

D. The bidding has been (1♠) : Pass : (2♠) : Pass, (Pass) to you. What action do you take on these hands?

1. ♠ 7	2. ♠ A 7 3 2	3. ♠ 2	4. ♠ 7 2	5. ♠ 7 2
♡ 7 6 4 3	♡ 8	♡ A J 5	♡ A J 9 2	♡ 6 2
◇ A Q 9 6	◇ Q 9 7 6	◇ Q 8 7 6 4 3	◇ Q 9 8 6 4 2	◇ Q J 9 4 3
♣ K J 7 3	♣ K 6 5 2	♣ J 8 5	♣ 7	♣ K Q 8 5

PARTNERSHIP BIDDING : How should these hands be bid? West is the dealer on each hand. All bids by North or South are natural, jump overcalls are weak and there is no North-South bidding other than given.

SET 59 – WEST	SET 59 – EAST	SET 60 – WEST	SET 60 – EAST
1. North bids 2♣.	**1. North bids 2♣.**	**1. South bids 1♠.**	**1. South bids 1♠.**
♠ K 9 2	♠ Q 7 5 4 3	♠ 8 6	♠ A K 10 2
♡ A Q 8 7 4	♡ 2	♡ 9 8 6 4 3 2	♡ A 5
◇ K 8 6 3	◇ J 4 2	◇ J 8	◇ K 7 5
♣ 7	♣ Q 9 6 4	♣ 9 3 2	♣ K Q 8 6
2. South bids 2♡.	**2. South bids 2♡.**	**2. North bids 1♠.**	**2. North bids 1♠.**
♠ 5 2	♠ K Q 4 3	♠ A Q J	♠ 8 3 2
♡ A 6 3 2	♡ 8	♡ K Q 9	♡ 7 5
◇ 3	◇ A Q 8 7 5	◇ A K 4	◇ Q J 9 3 2
♣ J 10 7 5 3 2	♣ K 6 4	♣ J 7 3 2	♣ A 6 5
3. North bids 2◇.	**3. North bids 2◇.**	**3. South bids 2♡.**	**3. South bids 2♡.**
♠ A Q 7 6 3	♠ 9	♠ 9 5	♠ A K 8 2
♡ K 5	♡ 9 8 4 2	♡ 8 7 4	♡ A 9
◇ K 9 8 4 2	◇ J 3	◇ Q 7	◇ A J 8 6 3 2
♣ 4	♣ Q 8 7 5 3 2	♣ Q 8 6 5 3 2	♣ 7
4. North opens 1♡.	**4. North opens 1♡.**	**4. North opens 1♠.**	**4. North opens 1♠.**
South raises to 2♡.	**South raises to 2♡.**	**South raises to 2♠.**	**South raises to 2♠.**
♠ A 4 2	♠ 8 6 5	♠ 9 4 3 2	♠ 6
♡ 9 7 4 3	♡ 2	♡ J 9 7 4 2	♡ Q 8 6 5
◇ A 8 7 2	◇ K 9 4 3	◇ K Q 3	◇ A 7 6 2
♣ Q 9	♣ K J 5 4 2	♣ Q	♣ K 10 3 2
5. North opens 1♠.	**5. North bids 1♠.**	**5. North opens 1◇.**	**5. North opens 1◇.**
South raises to 2♠.	**South raises to 2♠.**	**South raises to 2◇.**	**South raises to 2◇.**
♠ 8 7 5 2	♠ 4	♠ J 8 4	♠ A 6 3
♡ 6 4 2	♡ A J 9 3	♡ 3	♡ A J 10 7 4
◇ 3	◇ K Q 8 7 4	◇ A 7 5 2	◇ 8
♣ K 8 5 4 2	♣ A Q 6	♣ Q J 8 4 3	♣ K 6 5 2

PLAY HANDS ON RE-OPENING THE BIDDING

Hand 113 : Coping with a bad trump break — Trump reduction — Management of entries

Dealer North : Nil vulnerable

WEST	NORTH	EAST	SOUTH
	1♡	Pass (1)	Pass (2)
2♠ (3)	Pass	2NT (4)	Pass
4♠ (5)	Pass	Pass	Pass

NORTH
- ♠ 4
- ♡ K Q 9 7 5
- ◇ 7 4 3 2
- ♣ A K Q

WEST
- ♠ A Q J 8 6 3
- ♡ 6
- ◇ K J 8
- ♣ J 6 2

EAST
- ♠ 10 9
- ♡ A J 4 3
- ◇ A Q 10
- ♣ 10 7 4 3

SOUTH
- ♠ K 7 5 2
- ♡ 10 8 2
- ◇ 9 6 5
- ♣ 9 8 5

Bidding : (1) Certainly not worth any action at this stage.
(2) Much too weak to respond.
(3) The jump overcall in 4th seat shows a strong suit with a minimum opening hand.
(4) Shows the hearts stopped and about 10-12 points, normally without 3 or more spades.
(5) Worth a shot at game. Excellent spades and the singleton make 4♠ more attractive than 3NT. Had West doubled initially, East would respond 2NT and again West would rebid 4♠.

Lead : ♣K. North naturally cashes the 3 club winners.

Correct play : After taking 3 clubs, North's natural continuation is the ♡K. The ace wins and the ♠10 is run. There is no strong evidence to reject the normal spade finesse. When the ♠10 holds, the ♠9 is continued, also winning. When North shows out, it seems that South must win a trick with the ♠K. However, West can capture South's ♠K by *trump reduction technique.* Declarer's trumps must be reduced to the same length as South's and the lead must be in dummy at trick 11. So, ruff a heart, play a diamond to the 10, ruff another heart and lead a diamond to the Q. Lead dummy's 13th club (just in case South is now out of diamonds). If South ruffs, overruff and draw the last trump. If South discards, pitch your ◇ K. There are only 2 cards left in each hand : lead either red card from dummy. South holds ♠ K-7 and West has ♠ A-Q and thus South's ♠ K is trapped in this ending. (If North switches to a diamond at trick 4 or declines to cash 3 clubs and switches to a heart or a diamond, the same reduction technique is used after running the ♠ 10 and ♠ 9.)

Hand 114 : 4th seat bidding — Avoiding an overruff — Coping with a bad break — Trump reduction

Dealer East : North-South vulnerable

WEST	NORTH	EAST	SOUTH
		1◇	Pass
Pass (1)	Dble (2)	Pass	1♡
Pass	2NT (3)	Pass	4♡ (4)
Pass	Pass	Pass	

NORTH
- ♠ A K 6 2
- ♡ A K
- ◇ J 8 5 2
- ♣ A K 8

WEST
- ♠ 8 7 5 4 3
- ♡ 8
- ◇ 9 7
- ♣ Q 7 6 3 2

EAST
- ♠ Q J 10
- ♡ J 6 5 2
- ◇ A K Q 10
- ♣ 10 5

SOUTH
- ♠ 9
- ♡ Q 10 9 7 4 3
- ◇ 6 4 3
- ♣ J 9 4

Bidding : (1) It is unsound to bid when hopelessly weak, even though you are not keen on diamonds.
(2) Not quite strong enough to insist on game. Double is the best start. If partner bids spades, 4♠ would be a fair gamble.
(3) Opposite 1♡, it is best to jump to 2NT to show around 21-22 points balanced, equivalent to a 2NT opening.
(4) Exactly what you would bid over a 2NT opening and the double followed by a jump in no-trumps shows a 2NT opening.

Lead : ◇9. Partner's suit and top from a doubleton.

Correct play : East wins and cashes 2 more diamonds. East continues with the 4th diamond winner, which would ensure defeat of 4♡ if West held the ♡10. South should ruff the 4th diamond with the ♡10 or ♡9. To ruff with the ♡Q and hope for the ♡J to fall has far less chance of success. When the heart ruff holds, South cashes the ♡A and ♡K. When West shows out, South must plan to trap East's ♡J-6 via trump reduction : ♠A, ♠K (discard a club), ruff a spade, ♣A, ♣K and lead either black card from dummy at trick 12 when East has ♡J-6 and South has ♡Q-9 left. If East fails to lead the 4th diamond or a diamond is not led, declarer cashes ♡A and ♡K and then uses the same trump reduction technique.

Hand 115 : 4th seat bidding — Card combination — Card reading

Dealer South : East-West vulnerable

NORTH
- ♠ 10 8 4
- ♡ A 5
- ♢ 9 7 5 4
- ♣ 9 4 3 2

WEST
- ♠ 9 6 5
- ♡ 9 7 2
- ♢ A Q 10 3
- ♣ 8 6 5

EAST
- ♠ A Q J 7 3 2
- ♡ 8 6 3
- ♢ 6
- ♣ A K Q

SOUTH
- ♠ K
- ♡ K Q J 10 4
- ♢ K J 8 2
- ♣ J 10 7

WEST	NORTH	EAST	SOUTH
			1♡
Pass	Pass (1)	Dble (2)	Pass
2♢	Pass	2♠ (3)	Pass
3♠ (4)	Pass	4♠ (5)	All pass

Bidding : (1) There is no shame in passing with a weak hand.
(2) Too strong for a jump to 2♠ which would be based on 6-7 losers.
(3) Double then new suit is still a strong action in the re-opening position. 2♠ here implies 5+ spades, 16+ points and 5-5½ losers.
(4) West has 1½ quick tricks and is thus worth an invitation.
(5) With an extra spade and a shortage, East accepts the invitation, hoping West might hold shorter hearts.

Lead : ♡K. Obvious.

Correct play: North should overtake the ♡K with the A and return a heart. South wins and cashes the ♡Q. (Had South wanted a club switch, South leads the ♡4 for North to ruff instead of cashing the ♡Q.) South should switch to a diamond, taken by the A.

The normal play with this trump combination is to finesse the Q but here declarer should lead a spade and play the A! When the ♠K falls singleton, declarer's card reading is rewarded. Once North turned up with the ♡A, North could not hold the ♠K as well. That would give North 7 points and then North would not have passed 1♡. Once the ♠K is placed with South, the spade finesse becomes futile. Play the ace and pray for the king to be singleton. (If North lets the first heart go and wins ♡A at trick 2, declarer again has the information needed to forego the spade finesse. The best chance for declarer to go wrong is for South to lead ♡K and switch to a low diamond. If declarer takes the ♢A, declarer may misguess the spade position. However, declarer might finesse the ♢Q and discard a heart on the ♢A. Further, a canny declarer should ask why the defenders with hearts to cash, have been so eager to put declarer into dummy. A justifiably suspicious declarer would know the answer and cash the ♠A anyway.)

Hand 116 : 4th seat bidding — Strip and throw-in to avoid a finesse

Dealer West : Both vulnerable

NORTH
- ♠ J 9 2
- ♡ 10 9 4 3 2
- ♢ 8 7 3
- ♣ 7 2

WEST
- ♠ Q 10 8 6 5
- ♡ A K
- ♢ K J 10
- ♣ J 10 4

EAST
- ♠ 7 4 3
- ♡ 7
- ♢ 6 5 4 2
- ♣ Q 9 8 6 3

SOUTH
- ♠ A K
- ♡ Q J 8 6 5
- ♢ A Q 9
- ♣ A K 5

WEST	NORTH	EAST	SOUTH
1♠	Pass	Pass (1)	Dble (2)
Pass	2♡ (3)	Pass	4♡ (4)
Pass	Pass	Pass	

Bidding : (1) Too weak to raise to 2♠. If East did bid 2♠, South would still double and raise North's 3♡ to 4♡.
(2) Best to start with a double and see what develops.
(3) You do not have to enjoy bidding — you just have to do it.
(4) With 5 hearts and 24 points, a mere 3♡ would not do this justice.

Lead : ♠4. Partner's suit. Middle-up-down from 3 rags.

Correct play: Win ♠A and lead a trump. West wins ♡K. If West cashes ♡A and exits with a black suit, declarer cashes the top spades and clubs, ruffs a club in hand and ruffs a spade in dummy. Spades and clubs have now been eliminated (void opposite void). Now a low heart to North's 10 is followed by a diamond, playing dummy's 9 when East plays low. West must return a diamond or concede a ruff and discard. The trap to avoid is to play a diamond to the Q. West wins and a diamond return leaves declarer with a diamond loser. (If West wins ♡K and does not cash ♡A, eliminate the spades and clubs before leading the 2nd heart. West is again endplayed. If East should hit on a diamond lead, declarer can still succeed: win ♢A; eliminate the black suits: ♠A, ♠K, ♣A, ♣K, club ruff, spade ruff; then lead a heart. West wins and must set up the ♢Q or give a ruff and discard.

CHAPTER 30
NEGATIVE DOUBLES (1)

In standard methods, when partner opens and the next player intervenes, responder's double is for penalties, unless the partnership is using negative doubles. A negative double is simply a takeout double *by responder.* The normal takeout double arises *after an opponent has opened.* The negative double is for takeout *after partner has opened.* If the partnership has decided to use negative doubles, then a double is for takeout if:

● Partner opened with a suit bid *and*

● Second player overcalled in a suit at the 1-level or 2-level.

For example :

WEST	NORTH	EAST	SOUTH
1♡	2♣	Double . . .	

If not using negative doubles, East's double is for penalties, asking West to *pass.*

If using negative doubles, East's double is for takeout, asking West to *bid.*

If West opened 1NT, East's double is for penalties. Negative doubles apply only after a suit opening.

If North overcalled 1NT or 2NT, East's double is for penalties. Negative doubles apply only after a suit overcall, not after a no-trump overcall.

If North overcalled 3♣, East's double is for penalties. Negative doubles apply only after intervention at the 1-level or 2-level unless the partnership has specifically agreed to extend negative doubles to higher levels.

Without the negative double many hands become difficult and even impossible to bid sensibly after opposition interference. This is particularly so because of the very strict requirements for a 2-level response (10 points or more). Suppose you picked up ♠ A765 ♡ K642 ◇ 763 ♣ 87 and partner opened 1◇. You intend to respond 1♡, allowing the partnership to find any available major suit fit. However, when 2nd player intervenes with 2♣, you have a problem. You are too weak to respond at the 2-level and in standard methods you would have to pass. Obviously a good fit in either major could be lost.

Similarly, if you held ♠ 76 ♡ K874 ◇ A732 ♣ 852 and the bidding began 1♣ from partner, 1♠ on your right, you would be lost and the hearts might likewise be lost in standard methods, since there is no satisfactory response (too weak for 2♡ or 2◇, support too poor for 2♣ and the absence of a stopper in spades makes 1NT unattractive).

Negative doubles are popular, especially at duplicate, because :

● They cater for more hand types than penalty doubles do.

● They occur far more frequently than penalty double types.

● One can play negative doubles and still catch the opponents for penalties — see Chapter 32.

● They are a very effective competitive device.

● They solve the problems in 5-card major systems when the opponents intervene. Pairs playing 5-card majors should feel obliged to incorporate negative doubles in order to obtain the best results from the system they play. Pairs using 4-card majors will also do better if they use negative doubles, but for 5-card majorites, negative doubles are really essential.

WHAT DOES THE NEGATIVE DOUBLE PROMISE?

(1) 6 points or more. The negative double promises enough strength to have made a 1-level response. There is no top limit. Just like a 1-level suit response, responder might have enough for game and if so, this will be revealed by a strong rebid later (see Chapter 31).

(2) Specific suit holdings. *The negative double denies support for a major suit opening.* There could be support if opener began with a minor. Responder guarantees certain suit holdings, depending on what has been bid so far. The negative double caters for unbid major suits and will promise 4 cards in any *unbid* major. The negative double promises both minors only when both majors have already been bid.

(a) *Minor — Minor:* Partner opens with a minor and they overcall in a minor, e.g. 1♢ : (2♣) or 1♣ : (1♢). **The double promises both majors, at least 4–4, but could be 5–4 or 6–4.** A major suit response at the 1-level, e.g. 1♣ : (1♢) : 1♡ or 1♠, need not be more than a 4-card suit, but a response in a major suit at the 2-level, e.g. 1♢ : (2♣) : 2♡ or 2♠, would show at least a 5-card suit. A new suit response at the 2-level would show 10 points or more and would be forcing (except by a passed hand).

(b) *Major — Minor or Minor — Major:* **The double promises the other major.** At least 4 cards are promised in the unbid major. However, if the overcall was 1♡, the double shows precisely 4 spades, 6+ points, while 1♠ over the 1♡ overcall would promise 5 or more spades and 6+ points. Where their overcall was 1♠, a 2♡ response shows 5 or more hearts and 10+ points. The double over the 1♠ overcall will contain either 4 hearts exactly and 6+ points (no upper limit) *or* 5+ hearts and 6-9 points. With 5+ hearts and 10+ points, bid 2♡ — do not use a negative double. It follows that if responder doubles the 1♠ overcall and later bids hearts to show 5+ hearts, responder's range must be just 6-9 points because of the failure to bid 2♡ at once.

(c) *Major — Major:* **Double shows both minors.** Responder will hold at least 4 cards in each minor and 6 or more points. If, instead of doubling, responder bids a new suit at the 2-level, this promises 10 points up.

OPENER'S REPLY TO THE NEGATIVE DOUBLE

1. Where 4th player passes partner's double: Opener is required to bid unless prepared to make a penalty pass (having trump length and trump winners in the suit overcalled). Where the negative double promised a specific major, opener replies as if responder had bid that major at the 1-level. For example, if the bidding has started 1♣ : (1♠) : Double : (Pass), a 2♡ rebid by opener would be equivalent to 1♣ : 1♡, 2♡ without interference. Likewise, opener's 3♡ or 4♡ reply to the double would be equivalent to 1♣ : 1♡, 3♡ or 1♣ : 1♡, 4♡ without interference. A no-trumps rebid by opener would deny support for any major shown by responder and would promise at least one stopper in the enemy suit. A jump-rebid by opener is encouraging, around 17-18 points and 6 losers, but is not forcing. With 12-16 points, the opener can afford to make a minimum rebid because responder will bid again if holding 10 points or more and so game will not be missed. Rebids by the negative doubler with 10 points or more are covered in Chapter 31. If opener has 19 points or more, that should be enough for game opposite the 6+ points promised by the negative double. Opener can bid the game at once or, if not sure of the best game, bid the enemy suit as a force to game.

2. Where 4th player bids over partner's double: Opener is not obliged to bid, but may do so. If able to make a convenient bid at the 1-level or 2-level, opener should do so and this does not promise any extra strength. If 4th player changes suit, a double by either the opener or by the negative doubler is best played for penalties. If 4th player's action means opener would have to bid at the 3-level, opener should bid only with extra values. This situation usually arises when 4th player raises the overcalled suit. With 16 or more points or a 6-loser hand, opener should feel free to bid at the 3-level. With a minimum opening, opener should pass. Responder will have another opportunity to compete and responder knows not to sell out at the 2-level when they have a fit.

REBIDS BY THE NEGATIVE DOUBLER

Responder holds 6-9 HCP : Responder will normally pass any minimum action by opener, unless dissatisfied with opener's rebid as the final contract. Where opener rebids with a jump, responder should pass with 6-7 points and accept the invitation to game with 8-9 points. Opener's jump will be 17-18 points. Where the negative doubler rebids with a change of suit, this promises a 5-card or longer suit and therefore only 6-9 points. With 10 points up *and* a long suit, responder should have bid the suit initially.

Where 4th player has bid over the double and this is passed back to the negative doubler, a double of a new suit or 1NT by 4th player is for penalties. The negative doubler is also permitted to pass 4th player's new suit or 1NT but may bid with something worthwhile to show. However, *if 4th player raised the overcalled suit to the 2-level, the negative doubler should take some action.* It is unsound strategy to pass out their 2-level contract if they have found a trump fit. The negative doubler may support opener's suit at the 3-level, bid a 5-card or longer suit or double again. *The second double is still for takeout if 4th player raised the overcalled suit.* Any of these rebids may be made with just 6-9 points since the situation demands action.

WEST	NORTH	EAST	SOUTH
1♢	1♠	Dble	2♠
Pass	Pass	?	

Even with 6-9 points, East should take action. The choices are 3♢ with support, 3♣ or 3♡ with a 5-card or longer suit, or double, again for takeout, if nothing better is available.

Responder holds 10-12 points or 13 points or more : These ranges are covered in Chapter 31.

A. Partner opened 1♣ and RHO overcalled 1◇. What is your response on each of these hands?

1. ♠ K752	**2.** ♠ K752	**3.** ♠ A853	**4.** ♠ K72	**5.** ♠ 872
♡ A873	♡ 73	♡ 86532	♡ AJ42	♡ 6
◇ 964	◇ 964	◇ A7	◇ 9862	◇ AK9432
♣ 73	♣ A873	♣ 54	♣ 63	♣ K85

B. Partner opened 1◇ and RHO overcalled 1♠. What action do you take each of these hands?

1. ♠ 97	**2.** ♠ A7	**3.** ♠ A72	**4.** ♠ 962	**5.** ♠ A72
♡ Q873	♡ QJ9642	♡ 953	♡ AJ	♡ AJ974
◇ A964	◇ 64	◇ 87	◇ 86	◇ K94
♣ 632	♣ 762	♣ KJ854	♣ Q97542	♣ Q2

C. You opened 1◇ and partner doubled LHO's 1♠ overcall. What is your rebid on each of these hands?

1. ♠ K7	**2.** ♠ 97	**3.** ♠ A2	**4.** ♠ 72	**5.** ♠ 2
♡ 732	♡ 852	♡ 42	♡ AJ32	♡ AK92
◇ AQ964	◇ AQ964	◇ AJ643	◇ AJ862	◇ AK943
♣ KJ7	♣ AK2	♣ KJ75	♣ K7	♣ KJ5

D. Partner opened 1♣, RHO overcalled 1♠ and you doubled. LHO raised to 2♠, back to you. Your action?

1. ♠ 97	**2.** ♠ 74	**3.** ♠ 542	**4.** ♠ 64	**5.** ♠ 4
♡ Q873	♡ AQ8642	♡ KQ52	♡ AJ72	♡ 76432
◇ AQ96	◇ J102	◇ QJ943	◇ 862	◇ AQ43
♣ 862	♣ 32	♣ 8	♣ K974	♣ QJ2

PARTNERSHIP BIDDING : How should the following hands be bid? West is the dealer on all hands. The North-South bidding is natural, jump overcalls are weak and there is no other North-South bidding.

SET 61 – WEST	**SET 61 – EAST**	**SET 62 – WEST**	**SET 62 – EAST**
1. South bids 1♠.	**1. South bids 1♠.**	**1. North bids 1♠.**	**1. North bids 1♠.**
North raises to 2♠.	**North raises to 2♠.**	**South raises to 2♠.**	**South raises to 2♠.**
♠ 92	♠ A8	♠ A8	♠ 97
♡ AJ73	♡ K862	♡ K843	♡ QJ62
◇ J1093	◇ Q4	◇ KQ	◇ A542
♣ J65	♣ AQ743	♣ J8652	♣ Q73
2. North bids 1♠.	**2. North bids 1♠.**	**2. North bids 2♣.**	**2. North bids 2♣.**
♠ A8	♠ 32	♠ AK83	♠ J765
♡ 64	♡ QJ10853	♡ K62	♡ A943
◇ KQ762	◇ 84	◇ AK432	◇ Q7
♣ KJ32	♣ A64	♣ 9	♣ 742
3. South bids 2♡.	**3. South bids 2♡.**	**3. North bids 2♡.**	**3. North bids 2♡.**
♠ A632	♠ K874	♠ K73	♠ AQ854
♡ 65	♡ AJ	♡ 95	♡ 32
◇ J1032	◇ 76	◇ KQ7532	◇ A4
♣ K87	♣ AJ432	♣ KJ	♣ Q986
4. North bids 2♡.	**4. North bids 2♡.**	**4. North bids 1♠.**	**4. North bids 1♠.**
♠ A8642	♠ 9	♠ A764	♠ 3
♡ 863	♡ 105	♡ AJ72	♡ K965
◇ AQ	◇ K8654	◇ 6	◇ 98532
♣ K72	♣ A9843	♣ KQ93	♣ AJ6
5. North bids 1♡.	**5. North bids 1♡.**	**5. North bids 1♠.**	**5. North bids 1♠.**
South raises to 2♡.	**South raises to 2♡.**	**South raises to 2♠.**	**South raises to 2♠.**
♠ J7	♠ A962	♠ A7	♠ 94
♡ 843	♡ 62	♡ 86	♡ QJ10743
◇ AK2	◇ Q853	◇ AJ943	◇ K8
♣ AJ984	♣ Q72	♣ K652	♣ Q105

PLAY HANDS ON NEGATIVE DOUBLES (1)

Hand 117 : Negative double — Coping with interference — Setting up a secondary suit

Dealer North : North-South vulnerable

NORTH
♠ 9 3
♡ A K 8 3
♢ 7 2
♣ A K 10 5 2

WEST
♠ K 6 4 2
♡ J 10 4
♢ K J 10 5
♣ J 6

EAST
♠ A Q J 8 7
♡ 9 7
♢ Q 6 4
♣ Q 8 3

SOUTH
♠ 10 5
♡ Q 6 5 2
♢ A 9 8 3
♣ 9 7 4

WEST	NORTH	EAST	SOUTH
	1♣	1♠	Dble (1)
2♠	3♡ (2)	Pass (3)	Pass (4)
Pass (5)			

Bidding: (1) Negative double on minimum values. Do not reject normal competitive moves because of the vulnerability.
(2) With only 6 losers, North is entitled to compete with 3♡ over 2♠. With a minimum, opener should pass at this stage and allow responder to push the bidding to the 3-level. With this arrangement, the partnership can distinguish between minimum openings and those openings worth an invitation to game.
(3) With a minimum overcall, do not bid again in the direct seat.
(4) With a minimum negative double, do not bid again if partner does not make a forcing bid.
(5) West should not pass, but should compete to 3♠. In a partscore competitive auction, you should bid on if your side holds 9 trumps as long as you do not push to the 4-level. On some days 3♠ will

make. On others 3♠ will be a good sacrifice, one off when 3♡ is making. That is the case here. 3♡ is on and 3♠ has just 5 losers.

Lead: ♡7. A spade is unappealing from an A-Q suit, even though partner supported, and Q-x-x is not attractive either. A trump lead is safe and when leading a trump it is standard to lead low-high from a doubleton.

Correct play: On a trump lead, draw trumps and then play ♣A and give up a club. Later you cash the clubs and lose 2 spades, 1 diamond and 1 club. The play is equivalent if the opponents cash 2 spades first.

Hand 118 : Negative double to show the minors — Competitive bidding — Crossruff

Dealer East : East-West vulnerable

NORTH
♠ Q J 10 8 6
♡ 10 5
♢ K 9 7 4
♣ 10 2

WEST
♠ 7
♡ 8 4 3
♢ A 10 6 5 3
♣ K 9 7 3

EAST
♠ A K 5 3 2
♡ J 6 2
♢ 8
♣ A Q J 5

SOUTH
♠ 9 4
♡ A K Q 9 7
♢ Q J 2
♣ 8 6 4

WEST	NORTH	EAST	SOUTH
		1♠	2♡ (1)
Dble (2)	Pass	3♣ (3)	Pass (4)
Pass (5)	Pass		

Bidding: (1) With a strong 5-card holding in the other major, it is much better to overcall in the major suit than to double. The overcall promises at least a good 5-card suit (and does not deny opening strength), while a double does not suggest any more than 4 cards in the other major.
(2) With both majors bid, the negative double shows at least 4-4 in the minors and 6+ points. It would be timid of West to pass 2♡.
(3) East would need partner to hold about 12 points (or 4 cover cards) to make 5♣, so there is no need to jump to 4♣. If West has the values to allow 5♣ to make, West will raise to 4♣ at least.
(4) Once the bidding has reached the 3-level, there is no urgency to compete unless you have significant extra values or a strong trump fit. There is no evidence of either here, so South should

pass 3♣. If South were to bid 3♡, this could be defeated by 3 tricks : ♠7 lead, ♠K wins; ♢8 to the ♢A; ♢3 returned for a ruff; ♣A; club to the K; diamond ruff; ♠A; 3 off.
(5) With a minimum double, do not bid again if opener makes a minimum rebid.

Lead: ♡K. It is natural for South to cash 3 hearts. The best switch then is to a trump as dummy is short in spades, and declarer must be short in diamonds. The best attack against a cross ruff is repeated trump leads.

Correct play: Do not draw trumps. When dummy is short of your long suit and you are short in dummy's long suit, choose a cross ruff. Cash ♠A, ♠K, ♢A and ruff a diamond, ruff a spade, ruff a diamond, ruff a spade, etc. etc.

Hand 119 : Replying to a negative double with a strong hand — Drawing trumps with care

Dealer South : Both vulnerable

NORTH
♠ 8 6 4 3
♡ A J 9 3
♢ J 7 6
♣ 9 2

WEST
♠ A K Q 10 5 2
♡ 5
♢ 5 4 3
♣ J 6 5

EAST
♠ J 9
♡ 10 8 7 4
♢ A K 10 8 2
♣ 10 4

SOUTH
♠ 7
♡ K Q 6 2
♢ Q 9
♣ A K Q 8 7 3

WEST	NORTH	EAST	SOUTH
			1♣
1♠ (1)	Dble (2)	Pass (3)	4♡ (4)
Pass	Pass	Pass	

Bidding : (1) This would be worth 2♠ if playing weak jump overcalls (6-10 HCP and a good 6-card or longer suit).
(2) Promises 4+ hearts and 6+ points.
(3) Opposite a 1♠ overcall, East is not worth any action. The hand is not strong enough for 2♢. Opposite a weak jump to 2♠, East could increase the pressure with a raise to 3♠. An advance sacrifice to 4♠ is not recommended, even though 4♠ goes 2 off only on good defense. However, North-South have not yet bid 4♡ and with East holding 4 hearts, there is nothing to say that they will bid it or make it. Do not sacrifice against a game that might fail.
(4) Worth around 20 points and therefore good enough for 4♡. South has only 4 losers and it is reasonable to expect partner to be able to cover one of those losers at least.

Lead : ♠K. East should signal with the ♠J. It is natural for West to try to cash another spade.

Correct play : South ruffs the 2nd spade and must take care with the trump suit. With a strong outside suit, it is imperative to draw trumps and all the trumps must be drawn. They are likely to break 3-2, but a 4-1 break is not that improbable (a 28% chance). When cashing a suit or when drawing trumps, it is usually best to play the high cards first from the shorter holding. Therefore continue with ♡K and ♡Q (noting the 4-1 break), a heart to dummy and play dummy's last heart to draw the outstanding trump, discarding a diamond. Then run the clubs. The contract will fail if a low heart is led to dummy first or if the trumps are not all drawn.

Hand 120 : Strong reply to the negative double — Do not put all your eggs in one basket — Timing

Dealer West : Nil vulnerable

NORTH
♠ J 3
♡ A Q J 9 8 3
♢ 7
♣ A 10 6 4

WEST
♠ A K 10
♡ K 7 2
♢ A 5
♣ K Q 8 3 2

EAST
♠ Q 7 6 2
♡ 6 5
♢ K Q J 4 3
♣ 7 5

SOUTH
♠ 9 8 5 4
♡ 10 4
♢ 10 9 8 6 2
♣ J 9

WEST	NORTH	EAST	SOUTH
1♣ (1)	1♡ (2)	Dble (3)	Pass
3NT (4)	Pass	Pass	Pass

Bidding : (1) The standard way to show a balanced 19-20 points is to open with a suit and rebid with a jump in no-trumps.
(2) Too strong for a weak jump overcall. If using intermediate jumps, this would be suitable for 2♡. If North did bid 2♡, East would still double and West would still jump to 3NT.
(3) Too weak for 2♢. The double promises precisely 4 spades and 6 or more points. With 5 spades, East would respond 1♠.
(4) West knows that there is no 8-card spade fit and with enough for game, the practical shot is 3NT.

Lead : ♡Q. Prepared to concede a trick to the ♡K and set up the rest of the hearts. North hopes to get in with the ♣A before West can score 9 tricks. It is usually best to set up your long suit even though it gives declarer a trick in the process. Holding the ♣A, North could also lead the ♡A and continue with the ♡Q at trick 2.

Correct play : West wins the ♡K and must resist the instinctive play of ♢A and a diamond to dummy, planning to take 5 diamond tricks, 3 or 4 spades and the ♡K. When everything looks rosy, cater for the worst. If diamonds are 5-1, you have only 4 diamond tricks and you then need 4 spade tricks. Spades could be 3-3, but you can also take 4 spade tricks if the ♠J is singleton or doubleton. In that case, however, you need an entry to dummy to reach the ♠Q after cashing A, K and 10 of spades. If the diamonds behave, they will do so later also. There is no rush for the diamonds. Correct is to cash the ♠A and ♠K first, then the ♠10 after the ♠J has dropped, then ♢A, diamond to dummy, cash the ♠Q and 2 more diamonds for your 9 tricks.

CHAPTER 31

NEGATIVE DOUBLES (2)

RESPONDER'S APPROACH WITH 10-12 POINTS

With 10-12 points, responder would be strong enough to change suit at the 2-level and thus could forego the use of a negative double. However, the negative double still has many benefits with strong hands. In general, if you hold 10 or more points and a 5-card or longer suit, bid the long suit first — do not double. With a 2-suiter you will be able to bid your other suit on the next round if you wish. If you hold 10 points up and no 5-card suit, it is better to use the negative double as long as your hand has the correct suit content. On the next round, you will bid again to reveal the extra strength held.

Double and later raise opener to the 3-level shows 10-12 points and support for opener's suit.

Double and later rebid 2NT shows 10-12 points, a balanced hand and a stopper in their suit.

Where responder with 10-12 points has a choice whether to rebid 2NT or support opener to the 3-level, responder should raise opener's suit if it is a major and should prefer 2NT if opener's suit is a minor. Responder cannot show 10-12 points by doubling and then changing suit. That would show only 6-9 points since the suit change shows at least a 5-card suit and if responder had a 5-card suit and 10+ points, the proper course of action would have been to bid the long suit initially, not double.

After responder has shown 10-12 points and support by raising opener to the 3-level, opener passes with a bare minimum opening and bids on to game with better than a minimum. If responder raised opener's major, opener passes or bids 4-Major. If responder raised opener's minor, opener may be interested in 3NT rather than 5-Minor and a new suit at the 3-level is stopper-showing (see Chapter 21), while a bid of the enemy suit asks for a stopper in that suit. If responder rebid 2NT, opener may pass or rebid a suit at the 3-level to sign off, or bid 3NT or some other game or a new suit at the 3-level as a forward-going move. If stuck for a bid, opener can always bid the enemy suit to force responder to bid again. Bidding the enemy suit would *ask* for a stopper.

RESPONDER'S APPROACH WITH 13 POINTS OR MORE

Responder should have enough for game with 13 points or more but may still use a negative double. With 13 points or more and a 5-card or longer suit, responder would bid the long suit initially and would not use a negative double. However, with 13 points or more, balanced shape and 4 cards in an unbid major, the negative double is the best initial response. With support for opener's minor and a 4-card unbid major as well, responder should use the negative double initially. After opener's reply to the negative double, responder may have sufficient information to bid to the best game. If not, responder should bid the enemy suit as a force to game. Note the difference between these auctions :

A. WEST	NORTH	EAST	SOUTH		B. WEST	NORTH	EAST	SOUTH
1◇	1♠	2♠			1◇	1♠	Dble	Pass
					2◇	Pass	2♠	

In A, East is showing the values for game with 2♠ but has denied 4 hearts because of the failure to double. In B, East's double of 1♠ promised 4 hearts, the unbid major. The subsequent 2♠ bid was a game force. In other words, East B has a game force with 4 hearts while East A has a game force without 4 hearts. In each case, East figures to have a balanced hand and is asking opener for a stopper in spades. For example :

♠ A 8 3 2 Suppose partner opened 1◇. You already know you have enough for game. If RHO bids
♡ 9 7 4 2 1♠, you double to show 4 hearts. If opener then bids 2♡, you would raise to 4♡, while if
◇ A K opener rebids 1NT, 2♣ or 2◇, your sensible rebid is 3NT. Now suppose RHO bid 1♡.
♣ Q J 6 Again you double, showing 4 spades. If partner bids spades, raise to 4♠ and over 1NT,
bid 3NT. However, over 2♣ or 2◇, your best continuation is 2♡, forcing to game and asking for a stopper in hearts. Opener will bid no-trumps with a stopper or make some other descriptive rebid without a stopper. If opener has no stopper, clearly it is vital for you to avoid 3NT.

If the values for game are present but you cannot tell which game is best, bid the enemy suit as a game force.

A. Partner opened 1♦ and RHO overcalled 1♠. What is your response on each of these hands?

1. ♠ 6 2	2. ♠ 6 2	3. ♠ 8 5 3	4. ♠ K 7 2	5. ♠ 8 6 3 2
♡ A 8 7 3	♡ A 8 7 3	♡ A Q 5 3 2	♡ A J 4 2	♡ A K J
◇ J 9	◇ A K J 7 3	◇ A 7	◇ Q 8	◇ A 3 2
♣ A K J 7 3	♣ J 9	♣ J 5 4	♣ K 9 6 2	♣ Q 8 5

B. You opened 1♡, LHO overcalled 2♣, doubled by partner (negatively), passed to you. What action do you take on each of these hands?

1. ♠ A 7	2. ♠ A 7	3. ♠ A Q	4. ♠ A Q 6 2	5. ♠ A 7
♡ Q 8 7 3 2	♡ A J 9 6 4	♡ A K 9 6 4	♡ A J 9 5 4	♡ A J 10 8 7 4
◇ A 9 6 4	◇ A Q J 3	◇ K Q J 2	◇ A 8 6	◇ K Q J
♣ K 2	♣ 6 2	♣ 5 4	♣ 2	♣ Q 2

C. Partner opened 1◇, RHO bid 1♠ and you doubled. Partner replied 2♣ to your double, passed to you. What is your rebid on each of these hands?

1. ♠ K 7 5	2. ♠ 10 7	3. ♠ 9 6 2	4. ♠ A J 2	5. ♠ 8 6 2
♡ J 7 3 2	♡ A 8 5 2	♡ K J 4 2	♡ A J 3 2	♡ A Q 9 2
◇ A 6 4	◇ J 4 3	◇ A J 6 3	◇ 9 8 6 2	◇ K J
♣ K 8 7	♣ A Q 8 2	♣ Q 9	♣ K 7	♣ A 8 5 3

D. What would your answers be on the hands in C. if partner's reply to your double had been—
(i) 1NT?   (ii) 2◇?   (iii) 2♡?

PARTNERSHIP BIDDING : How should the following hands be bid? West is the dealer on all hands. The North-South bidding is natural and there is no North-South bidding other than that given.

SET 63 – WEST	SET 63 – EAST	SET 64 – WEST	SET 64 – EAST
1. North bids 1♠.	**1. North bids 1♠.**	**1. North bids 1♠.**	**1. North bids 1♠.**
♠ A 7	♠ K 9 2	♠ 7 3	♠ A 10
♡ 7 2	♡ A 10 9 5	♡ A 8 6 5	♡ K J 7 3
◇ K Q 8 6 3	◇ J 5 2	◇ A J 7 3 2	◇ K Q 4
♣ A Q 9 2	♣ K 6 4	♣ A 5	♣ 7 4 3 2
2. South bids 1♠.	**2. South bids 1♠.**	**2. North bids 1♠.**	**2. North bids 1♠.**
♠ K 5 3	♠ 8 2	♠ 7 3	♠ A 10
♡ K Q 9 6	♡ A 3	♡ A 5	♡ K J 7 3
◇ K 8 4	◇ Q 7 2	◇ A 9 7 3 2	◇ K Q 4
♣ 7 4 2	♣ K Q J 9 6 5	♣ A J 6 5	♣ 7 4 3 2
3. North bids 1♠.	**3. North bids 1♠.**	**3. South bids 1♠.**	**3. South bids 1♠.**
♠ 8 4 2	♠ A 9	♠ Q J 4	♠ 7 6 5
♡ A J 9 4 3	♡ K 5	♡ Q J 6 3	♡ A K 8
◇ K Q	◇ A 7 6 4 3	◇ K 6 4 2	◇ A Q 3
♣ K 6 2	♣ 10 9 8 3	♣ 3 2	♣ A Q J 6
4. South bids 1♠.	**4. South bids 1♠.**	**4. South bids 1♠.**	**4. South bids 1♠.**
♠ 8 6 3	♠ A 2	♠ 8 4	♠ 7 6 5
♡ A K 9 2	♡ 8 7 4 3	♡ Q J 6 3 2	♡ A K 8
◇ J 8 7 3	◇ K Q	◇ K 6 4	◇ A Q 3
♣ K 9	♣ A J 7 6 2	♣ 9 3 2	♣ A Q J 6
5. North bids 2♡.	**5. North bids 2♡.**	**5. North bids 2◇.**	**5. North bids 2◇.**
♠ A K J 9 7 3	♠ 8 6	♠ 7	♠ A K Q 2
♡ A 8 3	♡ 4 2	♡ A J 9 7 2	♡ 6 5
◇ K 10	◇ A Q J 5	◇ Q J 4	◇ 6 3 2
♣ J 10	♣ K 9 8 6 5	♣ K Q 8 3	♣ A J 9 6

PLAY HANDS ON NEGATIVE DOUBLES (2)

Hand 121 : Setting up extra winners via ruffing finesse — Keeping danger hand off play

Dealer North : East-West vulnerable

WEST	NORTH	EAST	SOUTH
	1♠ (1)	2◇ (2)	Dble (3)
Pass	3♠ (4)	Pass	4♠ (5)
Pass	Pass	Pass	

NORTH
- ♠ K Q 10 8 4 3 2
- ♡ K 6 5
- ◇ 4 2
- ♣ A

WEST
- ♠ 9 7 5
- ♡ J 10 9
- ◇ K 8
- ♣ 7 6 4 3 2

EAST
- ♠ 6
- ♡ A Q 7
- ◇ Q J 10 9 7 5
- ♣ K 9 5

SOUTH
- ♠ A J
- ♡ 8 4 3 2
- ◇ A 6 3
- ♣ Q J 10 8

Bidding : (1) Too strong to pre-empt. To open 3♠ or 4♠ in 1st or 2nd seat with such strength may result in missing a slam. (2) With 12-15 HCP and a 1-suiter, prefer the overcall to the double. (3) Better to show the hearts first via the double than to reply 2NT. (4) Despite holding only 12 HCP, this is worth a jump to 3♠ with just 5 losers. You may add 3 points when holding a good 7-card suit. (5) South is worth only 4♠, but if South had a stronger hand and slam ambitions, a 4◇ cue bid or 4NT could be used.

Lead : ◇ Q. Avoid abnormal leads.

Correct play : North has 9 obvious winners. The 10th could come from the heart finesse. However, the ♡ A is almost certainly with East. The ◇ Q lead denies the ◇ K and East-West are known to hold 16 HCP. If West has the ♡ A as well as the ◇ K, East would have overcalled on an aceless 9 count, possible but very unlikely. Do not duck the first diamond : West could overtake with the ◇ K and switch to a heart — disaster. The best chance is to use dummy's clubs. Win the ◇ A; cross to the ♣ A; back to dummy with a spade to the J; lead the ♣ Q. If West were to cover, you would ruff and lead a spade back to dummy to cash as many clubs as possible. When West plays low, do not ruff: discard your diamond loser (loser-on-loser and scissors coup), not a heart. (If you discard a heart, East can lead a diamond to West's K and a heart through defeats the contract.) East wins the ♣ K but now there is no entry to the West hand. Ruff the diamond return, cross to the ♠ A and discard 2 hearts on the club winners. 11 tricks.

Hand 122 : Discarding a loser before touching trumps — Insuring against a bad break

Dealer East : Both vulnerable

WEST	NORTH	EAST	SOUTH
		1♣	1♠ (1)
Dble (2)	Pass (3)	2♡ (4)	Pass
4♡ (5)	Pass	Pass	

NORTH
- ♠ 9 8 3
- ♡ J 10 7 5
- ◇ 10 8 7 6
- ♣ A 9

WEST
- ♠ A 5
- ♡ A K 9 4
- ◇ Q 5 4
- ♣ 8 7 5 4

EAST
- ♠ 7 6
- ♡ 8 6 3 2
- ◇ A K
- ♣ K Q J 6 2

SOUTH
- ♠ K Q J 10 4 2
- ♡ Q
- ◇ J 8 3 2
- ♣ 10 3

Bidding : (1) Worth 2♠ if playing weak jump overcalls. (2) Show the other major first via the double rather than reply in no-trumps first. West has enough for game and plans to play in 4♡ if a fit is found and in 3NT if no heart fit exists. (3) Too weak to support to 2♠ and a raise on 3 rags may encourage partner to lead a broken suit with dire results. North should pass now but plan to compete with 2♠ if East-West stop at the 2-level. (4) No need to do more. With 10+ points, responder will bid again. (5) Clearcut. 3NT is easily defeated on a spade lead.

Lead : ♠ K. How come you have such easy leads?

Correct play : Win the ♠ A. Do not cash the ♡ A and ♡ K yet. If you do, there is no easy entry back to dummy to reach the ◇ Q after cashing ◇ A-K. You have to lose 1 club and 1 heart. If hearts are not 3-2, you will lose 2 hearts and cannot also afford to lose a spade. Therefore, play off the ◇ A-K first, cross to the ♡ A and discard the spade loser on the ◇ Q. Still do not cash the other top heart. If you do and trumps *are* 4-1, you could find an opponent, when in with the ♣ A, drawing *your* trumps for down 3 or 4. You have lost no tricks so far and can afford to lose 1 club and 2 hearts, so that a club ruff would not defeat you. When a bad trump break is a risk, set up the side suit first. Here you should lead clubs before playing off the other top heart. North wins ♣ A, but you win the return, cash the ♡ K and then lead clubs at each opportunity.

Hand 123 : Play from dummy at trick 1 — Keeping the danger hand off lead

Dealer South : Nil vulnerable

NORTH
- ♠ Q 5
- ♡ K Q 6 3
- ◇ 10 9 5 2
- ♣ A 6 2

WEST
- ♠ A J 9 7 4 3
- ♡ 9 2
- ◇ K 6
- ♣ K 8 3

EAST
- ♠ 10 8
- ♡ J 10 8 7 4
- ◇ 8 3
- ♣ Q J 9 5

SOUTH
- ♠ K 6 2
- ♡ A 5
- ◇ A Q J 7 4
- ♣ 10 7 4

WEST	NORTH	EAST	SOUTH
			1◇
1♠ (1)	Dble (2)	Pass	1NT (3)
Pass	2NT (4)	Pass	3NT (5)
Pass	Pass	Pass	

Bidding : (1) This would be worth 2♠ if playing intermediate jump overcalls (11-15 HCP and a good 6-card or longer suit).
(2) Promises 4+ hearts and 6+ points.
(3) With a stopper in their suit and a 5-3-3-2 pattern, it is better to rebid 1NT than to repeat the 5-card suit.
(4) With 11-12 points and balanced shape, North is worth a raise to 2NT. Where opener rebids 1NT, responder can pass with a balanced 10 count, since opener's maximum for a 1NT rebid should be 15 points.
(5) Worth 15 points, allowing 1 for the length in diamonds. With a maximum, accept the invitation.

Lead : ♠7. 4th-highest of your long suit is normal.

Correct play : Play the *queen* from dummy, do not play low. With K-x-x opposite Q-x, or Q-x-x opposite K-x, play the honor from dummy's doubleton. If the honor wins, you then try to keep RHO, the danger hand, out of the lead. Here the ♠Q wins and you lead the ◇10, finessing. West wins but your ♠K-6 is a stopper when West is on lead. If West switches to a club, play the A and take your 9 tricks. If you duck the club switch, East wins and a spade from East takes you 3 off. If you fail to play the ♠Q from dummy at trick 1, you will go down. East plays the ♠10 and if you take the K, West cashes 5 spades when in with the ◇K. If you duck East's ♠10, East leads another spade to West's A and West clears out your ♠K. Either way you are at least 2 off. (If West leads a club initially, duck the first 2 clubs, win the 3rd club and finesse diamonds. If East wins the 1st club and switches to a spade, duck it to dummy's Q and again finesse diamonds.)

Hand 124 : Holdup play — Card combination — Keeping the danger hand off lead

Dealer West : North-South vulnerable

NORTH
- ♠ Q 7 5
- ♡ A 10 8 7 5
- ◇ J 8 3
- ♣ K 8

WEST
- ♠ A 9 3
- ♡ K J 4
- ◇ A K 6 2
- ♣ 5 4 3

EAST
- ♠ K 6 4 2
- ♡ 9 3 2
- ◇ Q 5
- ♣ A Q 10 9

SOUTH
- ♠ J 10 8
- ♡ Q 6
- ◇ 10 9 7 4
- ♣ J 9 6 2

WEST	NORTH	EAST	SOUTH
1◇	1♡ (2)	Dble (3)	Pass
1NT (3)	Pass	2NT (4)	Pass
3NT (5)	Pass	Pass	Pass

Bidding : (1) Only just worth an overcall. The strength is fine but the suit quality is minimal.
(2) Over 1♡, the negative double shows *four* spades precisely.
(3) Denies 4 spades. Shows 12-15 points and a heart stopper.
(4) Shows 11-12 points and invites 3NT.
(5) West is maximum with 15 points and accepts the invitation.

Lead : ♡7. No reason to avoid the normal long suit lead.

Correct play : Let South's ♡Q win. It would be all right to win the ♡K if you could keep South off lead, since your ♡J-4 is a stopper against North. If you take the ♡Q with the K, and South gains the lead, a heart through your J-4 gives North 4 heart tricks for one off. To score 9 tricks, you need to tackle clubs which involves two finesses. Unless North holds both the ♣K and ♣J, South will gain the lead. As you are unlikely to keep South off lead, it is better to duck the first heart. You still score a heart trick but if North has the 5 hearts expected for the overcall, South will be out of hearts after the next heart lead. South returns a heart, North wins and plays a 3rd round. Now North with 2 heart winners is the danger hand, but you can keep North off lead. Finesse the ♣9 (not the Q), win the return and another club sees you home when the ♣K appears. If the ♣K did not pop up, you would keep finessing in clubs.

CHAPTER 32

PENALTY DOUBLES & PENALTY PASSES

The principles for successful penalty doubles vary according to the level of the bidding. The most rewarding doubles are usually those of low-level contracts when an opponent overcalls and you sit over them with a strong trump holding. An overcall is a risky venture (although the risk must be taken), because there may be a worthless hand opposite or even if there are some values, there may be little or no support for the suit overcalled. On the other hand, by the time the opponents have exchanged plenty of information and have reached a game or a slam, it is unlikely that you will be able to collect a huge penalty.

PARTNER OPENS WITH A SUIT BID, RHO MAKES A SUIT OVERCALL

In order to look for penalties, you should have :

● *A strong trump holding* − see the Rule of 6 and the Rule of 4 below.

● *8 HCP or more* so that your side has at least 20 HCP and figures to take at least half the tricks.

● *A misfit with the suit opened.* A singleton holding is ideal, and a void is excellent also. A doubleton is acceptable but with 3 cards or more in partner's suit, you should be reluctant to go for penalties at the 1-level or the 2-level. This misfit feature is important. If you are short in partner's suit, partner's winners in that suit will take tricks and you can ruff quickly if necessary. However, if you have length in partner's suit, partner's winners there are unlikely to survive as declarer or dummy is likely to ruff and you will be unable to overruff.

How much length and strength is needed in their trump suit to go for penalties at the 1-level, 2-level or 3-level? If your hand conforms to both the Rule of 6 and the Rule of 4, your trump quality is adequate for penalties :

The Rule of 6 : Add the number of trumps you hold to the level at which the opponent has overcalled. If the answer is 6 or more, you have enough trumps for penalties. If the answer is below 6, you have insufficient trumps. For example, if the overcall was at the 1-level, you need at least 5 trumps $(1 + 5 = 6)$. At the 2-level, you need at least 4 trumps $(2 + 4 = 6)$, while at the 3-level you need at least 3 trumps $(3 + 3 = 6)$.

The Rule of 4 : Add the number of expected winners you hold *in their suit* to the level at which the opponent has overcalled. If the answer is 4 or more, you have enough trump winners to go for penalties. If the answer is below 4, you do not have sufficient trump winners and should not play for penalties (yet). For example, if the overcall was at the 1-level, you need at least 3 trump winners $(1 + 3 = 4)$. At the 2-level you need 2 trump winners $(2 + 2 = 4)$, while at the 3 level you need at least 1 trump winner $(3 + 1 = 4)$.

The Rule of 6 measures the trump *length* and the Rule of 4 measures the trump *strength* needed for penalties. On the above basis, if partner opens say 1♡ and RHO overcalls 2♣, you need 4 clubs including 2 club winners plus the HCP and misfit requirements in order to try successfully for penalties.

HOW DO YOU COLLECT YOUR PENALTIES?

If you hand fits the above requirements, how can you collect the penalties bonanza? If you are not playing negative doubles, you have no difficulty : simply double. In standard methods, a double is for penalties if partner has already bid.

However, if you are playing negative doubles (see Chapters 30 and 31) − and it is very sensible to use negative doubles − you can still collect penalties. The principle is : *Pass For Penalties.* If partner opens with a suit bid and next player overcalls in a suit at the 1-level or 2-level and your hand fits the above requirements for penalties, you *pass*. If the bidding then goes Pass : (Pass) to opener, partner will keep the bidding alive. Partner's No. 1 choice when re-opening the bidding is a takeout double on all normal hands (see Chapter 29). If partner makes this re-opening takeout double, you *pass for penalties*. In other words, you convert partner's takeout double into penalties by passing. You are said to be making a "penalty pass". If opener does not re-open with a double, do not fret that you have missed out on penalties. This just means that if you would have made a penalty double, opener would have removed it anyway. The typical sequences for these penalty passes look like this :

WEST	NORTH	EAST	SOUTH
1♣	1♠	Pass	Pass
Dble	Pass	Pass ...	

WEST	NORTH	EAST	SOUTH
1♠	2◇	Pass	Pass
Dble	Pass	Pass ...	

In each auction, East's second pass is a penalty pass and East is stacked in North's suit. If East has a poor hand and passed on the first round simply because of weakness, East would now reply to West's double, just as one normally replies to a takeout double. You pass the takeout double when you are strong in their suit and you take out the double on all other hand types when you are not looking for penalties.

WHEN CAN THE OPENER DECLINE TO RE-OPEN WITH A DOUBLE?

When the bidding has been 1-suit: (Suit overcall): Pass: (Pass) back to the opener, the opener should usually re-open the bidding with a double. However, the opener should re-open with some other action on a freak hand (such as a 6-5) or with exceptional length in the suit opened (see Chapter 29). The opener should pass when holding length and strength in the overcalled suit since responder then cannot have a penalty pass type. In this case, responder's pass indicates a weak hand without support for opener and unsuitable for a negative double. Opener is therefore better off defending with length and strength in their suit, so again, *pass for penalties*. Opener is not obliged to re-open when LHO's action was a strong jump overcall *or* when LHO's overcall was at the 3-level *or* when LHO's action was an intermediate jump overcall and opener has Q-x-x or better in their suit. In addition, if 4th player makes a bid, e.g. 1◇: (1♡): Pass: (2♡) *or* 1◇: (1♡): Pass: (1♠), there is no obligation on opener to bid. Indeed, if opener does bid over 4th player's bid, opener would be showing better than a minimum opening.

PASSING OUT OTHER TAKEOUT DOUBLES

1. Partner makes a takeout double of their 1-level suit opening: To pass this, your hand must satisfy the Rule of 6 and the Rule of 4. You need at least 5 trumps and at least 3 trump winners, and about 8 points up. You do not pass a takeout double out of weakness, but out of a deliberate desire to penalise their contract. To defeat their contract you need to win at least 7 tricks. Thus you have to make 1-in-their-suit and to do this, naturally you need excellent trumps as there is known to be a bad break against you. Where a 1-level takeout double has been passed out, if the doubler is on lead, the doubler should lead a trump. As partner's trumps should be better than declarer's, partner will want to draw declarer's trumps. A trump lead will assist partner.

2. Partner makes a negative double at the 1-level or 2-level: Opener may pass partner's negative double with a strong holding the suit overcalled (use the Rule of 6 and Rule of 4) and no fit for responder's suit(s). The bidding might go like this: 1♡: (2♣): Double: (Pass) ... With strong clubs and no spade fit, opener should pass. Opener also knows that responder has no fit with hearts, since the negative double denies support for opener's major. This kind of penalty can only be obtained by pairs using negative doubles.

SUBSEQUENT DOUBLES

After a penalty pass has been made, all subsequent doubles are for penalties. Thus, if they try to rescue themselves from one penalty, you should continue to double with a strong 4-card or better holding in any suit they try. Note that East's double in this auction is for penalties:

WEST	NORTH	EAST	SOUTH
1◇	1♠	Pass	Pass
Dble	2♠	Dble	

West's re-opening double was for takeout. East's double cannot be negative. If East has a negative double of 2♠, East would have made a negative double of 1♠. It is clear that East had a penalty pass of 1♠ doubled and North is about to regret bidding 2♠.

DOUBLES AFTER A 1NT OPENING

1. They open 1NT: The double of a 1NT opening is for penalties, not for takeout. See Chapter 28. You should double a weak 1NT with 15 HCP or more and a strong 1NT when you hold the equivalent of the top of their range. You may double a 15-17 1NT with 17 HCP or more, a 16-18 1NT with 18 HCP or more, or slightly less if you have an excellent suit to lead. After a penalty double of 1NT, all subsequent doubles are also for penalties and you need only a strong 4-card holding in their suit and at least 20 HCP together with partner.

2. Your side opens 1NT, they overcall: All doubles after a 1NT opening are for penalties in standard methods. You need a strong 4-card holding or better in their suit and at least 20 HCP together with partner. After one penalty double has been made, all subsequent doubles are also for penalties and a strong 4-card holding or better in their suit is sufficient.

DOUBLING THEIR 1NT OVERCALL

When partner has opened and RHO overcalls 1NT, you should double if your side has more points than they do. If they are trying to win more than half the tricks with less than half the points, they will generally fail. Accordingly, as partner's opening is usually based on 12 HCP or more, double their 1NT overcall whenever you hold 9 HCP or better. If unable to double, raise partner to the 2-level (5-8 points), bid your own suit at the 2-level (5-8 HCP and a 6-card suit), bid 2NT (a freak 2-suiter with game values) or jump to the 3-level (forcing, with a 6-card suit). After their 1NT has been doubled, if either opponent tries to escape by bidding a suit, you or partner should double this rescue attempt with a strong 4-card holding in the suit they have bid. If unable to double their suit in 2nd seat, pass it to partner who may be able to double. If their suit has been passed to you in 4th seat and you do not have a strong 4-card holding, you may support partner, bid a new suit or rebid 2NT. A new suit or a jump would be forcing, but supporting partner or 2NT could be passed.

PENALTY DOUBLES AFTER A STRENGTH-SHOWING REDOUBLE

Where the bidding has started 1-Suit : (Double) : Redouble, responder is looking for penalties. All doubles following this redouble are for penalties. A strong 4-card or better holding in their suit is enough to double. Where the bidding has started 1NT : (Double) : Redouble, responder has indicated enough strength to guarantee that the opening side holds more HCP than the doubling side. If either opponent now runs to a suit (as they probably will), all doubles are for penalties. Again, a strong 4-card holding in the suit bid is enough.

THE S.O.S. REDOUBLE – REDOUBLING FOR RESCUE

Where your side has been doubled for penalties or where a takeout double of a suit bid by your side has been passed for penalties (a penalty pass has been made), redouble is used for takeout as a means of rescue. *The redouble of a takeout double shows strength, the redouble of a penalty double is S.O.S. for rescue.* In each of the following auctions, the final Redouble . . . is for rescue (and PP indicates a penalty pass) :

WEST	NORTH	EAST	SOUTH		WEST	NORTH	EAST	SOUTH
1♣	Dble	Pass	Pass (PP)		1♡	Pass	Pass	Dble
Rdble . . .					Pass	Pass (PP)	Rdble . . .	

WEST	NORTH	EAST	SOUTH		WEST	NORTH	EAST	SOUTH
1♡	1♠	Pass	Pass		1♠	Dble	Rdble	2♣
Dble	Pass	Pass (PP)	Rdble . . .		Dble	Rdble . . .		

WEST	NORTH	EAST	SOUTH		WEST	NORTH	EAST	SOUTH
1NT	Dble	2♣	Dble		1NT	Dble	Rdble	2♢
Pass	Pass	Rdble . . .			Dble	Rdble . . .		

The above illustrates that you may make an S.O.S. redouble of your own suit as well as of partner's suit. One of the most useful positions for an S.O.S. redouble is after they have doubled partner's 1NT opening and you have started rescue operations. Suppose the bidding has started 1NT : (Double) : and you hold ♠ 9 7 4 3 ♡ 8 5 4 2 ◇ J 5 3 2 ♣ 8. You would be better off in a suit, but which suit? Bid 2♣ and if this is doubled for penalties (as it almost certainly will be), redouble for rescue. Whichever other suit is chosen by partner will be better than 1NT doubled. If they do pass you out in 2♣, at least you are not doubled. Similarly, after 1NT : (Double), what should you do with ♠ 9 7 5 3 2 ♡ 8 6 4 3 2 ◇ 9 ♣ 7 4 ? You belong in a major but which one? Since 2♣ over a double is clubs and not Stayman, you might feel that you have to take a guess. Not at all. Bid 2♣ anyway, pretending you have clubs. If this is doubled, redouble for rescue. If partner bids a major, you are in your best spot. If partner bids something useless such as 2◇ and this is doubled, redouble for rescue again, forcing partner to choose a major. The S.O.S. redouble is fun!

In other situations where partner's suit has been doubled for penalties (or a penalty pass has been made), you should not make an S.O.S. redouble with tolerance for partner's suit. You may be in a worse trump suit and at a higher level if you start rescue operations. However, with a void in partner's suit and the other 3 suits, or a singleton plus a 5-5 or freakier pattern, redouble for rescue. A better trump suit is likely to exist.

Note that the redouble of a takeout double or a negative double (which is a form of takeout double) is showing strength and is not S.O.S. If partner's 1NT has been doubled, the redouble is strength-showing and to play in 1NT redoubled. It is not S.O.S. in standard methods, even though the double of 1NT was for penalties.

PENALTY DOUBLES AT THE 3-LEVEL

As doubles above 2◊ give them a game if they succeed, you need to be confident you will defeat them. At a lower level, you may occasionally try a speculative double. If it fails to come off, you have not lost much. If the double gives them a game, however, you should have a safety margin and the best approach is not to make a penalty double above 2◊ unless you expect to defeat the contract by at least 2 tricks. In that way, if one of your tricks fails to materialise because of an unexpected singleton or void with the opposition, you will at least still defeat the contract. If you follow the advice on page 170 of what you need for a penalty double or a penalty pass of a suit overcall (a trump stack, high card strength and a misfit), you should be able to defeat the opponents' contract normally by about 3 tricks. The safety margin is built into the requirements.

For a penalty double at the 3-level, you should expect to take 6 or more tricks between you and partner, including at least 1 trump trick. It is risky to double at the 3-level without any trump winners. You can expect partner to hold 1-2 tricks with 6-10 HCP and 2-3 tricks with 11-15 HCP. Add your winners to this expectancy.

If you are highly likely to make a game, do not settle for a small penalty. Prefer to bid on to your best game. If you can make a game, you need at least 500 points from the double as compensation for the game missed. On the other hand, if game chances are doubtful, take the penalty. Better to be a small plus from a penalty than to be minus because your game was not on.

PENALTY DOUBLES OF GAME CONTRACTS

The odds are stacked heavily against doubles of game contracts or higher, unless the opponents are taking a sacrifice or have been forced to guess at the contract because of a pre-emptive opening or pre-emptive overcall. By the time the opponents have reached a game or higher, they have usually been able to exchange enough information to have a good idea of their combined assets. In such circumstances, it is not common to collect a large penalty because they rarely go more than one off. If, without any pre-emptive bid by your side, the opponents have bid a game, expecting it to make, and you feel that they are too high, take your profit and pass . . . do *not* double. If they make their doubled contract they score an extra 150 or 170. If you defeat them by 1 trick, you score an extra 50 or an extra 100. Depending on vulnerability, you have to be right more than 2 times out of 3 or 3 times out of 4 to start showing any profit. In addition, any doubled overtricks are hideously expensive (100 or 200 each, according to vulnerability) and if they redouble and make it, you have a real disaster. *Never double a freely bid game for just one off.* You need an expectancy of at least 2 down to make the double worthwhile. Do not expect to defeat them just because you have a lot of points. If they have bid to the 4-level or 5-level and you hold 18 HCP or more, what allows them to bid so high? Excellent distribution . . . voids and singletons . . . and some of your hoped for tricks are likely to be ruffed.

Worst of all, an ill-judged double of a game contract can alert declarer to bad breaks and may indicate how the contract should be handled. Without warning, declarer might have gone down. What a calamity if your double tips declarer off and allows the contract to be made! If the opponents are in a contract you are happy to defend since they are almost sure to fail, do not become greedy and double if they might run to some other contract which might not be defeated. So do not double them unless you can double them if they run to some other contract. However, if declarer has offered a choice of suits and dummy has chosen one, do not be afraid to double if you have the values for a penalty double in the suit chosen even though you do not have such values in the other suit. The fact that they have already made a choice means it is unlikely that they will run to the other suit (possibly at a higher level). Also, if you have their first choice sewn up, partner is bound to be stacked in their other possible trump suit if you are not, since their 2nd choice figures to be a worse spot for them than their 1st choice. If their 1st choice is terrible for them, because *you* have a trump stack, their 2nd choice will be just as terrible since *partner* figures to have the trump stack there.

If the opponents have had a strong auction to reach game, e.g. 1♠ : 2NT, 4♠ *or* 1♡ : 3♡, 4♡, it is not a good idea to double them just because you know they are in for a bad trump break. They may have plenty of points to spare and you may make just your trump tricks. The best time to double their suit game is when they have struggled to reach the game *and* they are in for a bad break. Auctions like 1♠ : 2♠, 3♠ : 4♠ and 1♠ : 1NT, 2♡ : 2♠, 3♠ : 4♠ are ripe for a penalty double if their suits split badly. The auction shows that they have barely enough high card strength for game and if they are running into bad breaks as well, they are likely to go 3 or 4 down when the hand blows up. Double their limping auctions when the breaks are bad for them and you will collect big.

If you have more high card strength than the opponents and they bid above your game contract, make sure that you double them. Do not let them play in any sacrifice undoubled. You do not need trump tricks to double a sacrifice and you do not need to be sure where your tricks are coming from. The fact that you know that you have more strength than they do is sufficient. When they take a sacrifice and you have to decide whether to double or whether to bid on, the more balanced your hand, the more inclined you should be to defend. The more distributional your hand, the more inclined you are to bid on. The more strength you hold in their suit(s), especially kings and queens, the more you should double. Occasionally in such competitive situations, you double their sacrifice to warn partner not to bid on. When you are in 2nd seat and you are short in their suit, pass the decision to partner if you are not sure what to do. As you are short in their suit, partner will have length in their suit and partner will be in a better position to know whether to double or whether to bid on. The best lead after doubling a sacrifice is often a trump. If the enemy have less strength, they must be hoping to make tricks by ruffing. The more trump leads you can manage, the fewer ruffs they will obtain.

DOUBLING THEIR 3NT CONTRACT

When the opponents have bid to 3NT, double by the player not on lead calls for a specific lead :

● If the player on lead has bid a suit, the double asks for that suit.

● If the player doubling has bid a suit, the double asks for that suit.

● If both defenders have bid a suit, the double asks for the suit bid by the player on lead.

● If neither defender has bid a suit, the double asks for the first suit bid by dummy.

● If no suit has been bid at all, e.g. (1NT) : (3NT), the double asks for a spade lead. Other methods exist but they leave room for error in deciding which suit is requested. It is better to be certain of the suit partner will lead so the demand for a spade if no suit has been bid is sensible, practical and handy when it arises.

DOUBLING SLAMS FOR PENALTIES

The worst reason for doubling a slam is that you know you can defeat it! Suppose their bidding has been (1♡) : (3♣), (3♡) : (4NT), (5♢) : (6♡) and there you are, holding Q-J-10-9 of hearts! Do you double? There is no way that they can make 6♡ but it would dreadful to double! You are sure that you will defeat 6♡ but you cannot be sure that you will also defeat 6NT. If you double 6♡, they may suspect a bad trump break and run from the contract you can defeat to one which is unbeatable. Thus, for a measly extra 50 or 100 points, your greedy double has cost you over 1000 points. Be content to take their slams down undoubled and you will gradually acquire a reputation for being a kindly and sporting player, even though your motivation for not doubling is purely self-interest.

Similarly, if they have an auction like (1♠) : (3♠), (6♠) *or* (1♡) : (2♢), (4♢) : (6♢), and you hold 2 aces, it is extremely naive to double. The opponents know about aces also and even the rawest novice has heard of Blackwood and how to ask for aces. When you hold 2 aces and they did not ask for aces, you can be confident that the slam bidder has a void where you have an ace. Otherwise they *would* have asked for aces. If, in fact, you are able to cash both your aces and defeat their slam, what more do you want? With opponents like that, you do not want to double and *stop* them bidding such slams, do you? And again, by not doubling, you will prove to the world what a nice and magnanimous player you are. Little do they know . . .

DOUBLING THEIR SLAM FOR A PARTICULAR LEAD

Since we saw above that it is unsound to double their slam just because you feel you can defeat it (unless they are sacrificing), the double of their slam by the player not on lead demands a specific lead. This idea was devised by the late Theodore Lightner and is known as the Lightner Double. When partner doubles their slam and you are on lead, the double asks you to make an unusual lead. Do not lead a suit your side has bid (that is usual), do not lead an unbid suit (that is usual), do not lead a trump (that is not unusual). **Lead the first suit bid by dummy** — *that is unusual.* The doubler has either a void or a powerful holding in dummy's first bid suit and fears that you would never make that lead under normal circumstances. If dummy has not bid a suit, study the bidding and your cards and deduce the suit in which partner is likely to be void. The double alerts you to the fact that partner has a void and you should normally lead your longest suit. That is where partner's void figures to be. The double of an artificial bid while they are en route to slam, such as the double of the answer to an ask for aces or the double of a cue bid, asks partner to lead the suit doubled. Use such doubles sparingly since they also tip off the opposition and it may help them more than your side.

A. Partner opened 1♡ and RHO overcalled 2♣. Which of these hands are suitable for penalties?

1. ♠ 6 2	2. ♠ 9 8 6 2	3. ♠ 8 6 5 3 2	4. ♠ 9 7 5 2	5. ♠ K 6 3
♡ A 8 7 3	♡ 3	♡ 2	♡ 2	♡ 8 7
◇ J 9 3	◇ A K J 7 3	◇ A 7	◇ 9 3	◇ K 6 3 2
♣ A K 7 6	♣ J 9 3	♣ A J 8 5 4	♣ Q J 7 6 4 3	♣ K J 10 5

B. You opened and LHO overcalled 2♡, passed back to you. What action do you take on each of these hands?

1. ♠ A Q 9 7 2	2. ♠ A J 8 3 2	3. ♠ A Q 5	4. ♠ A Q 8 6 2	5. ♠ 9 7
♡ 2	♡ K Q 9	♡ 4	♡ A J 9 5 4	♡ A J 10 4
◇ A 9 6 4	◇ A J 3	◇ K Q J 2	◇ J 8	◇ K Q J 7 5
♣ K 9 2	♣ 6 2	♣ K Q 9 3 2	♣ 2	♣ Q 2

C. Partner opened 1♡, RHO bid 2♣, passed back to opener who doubled. This is passed to you. Your action?

1. ♠ K 7 5	2. ♠ 10 8 7 6 4 2	3. ♠ 9 6 2	4. ♠ 9 6 2	5. ♠ 8 6 2
♡ J 7 3	♡ - - -	♡ 4 2	♡ 2	♡ 9 2
◇ 7 6 4	◇ J 4 3	◇ A J 6 3	◇ A 8 6 2	◇ Q 6 3
♣ 9 7 3 2	♣ J 6 5 2	♣ Q 7 6 2	♣ K J 5 4 2	♣ 9 8 5 3 2

PARTNERSHIP BIDDING : How should the following hands be bid? West is the dealer on all hands. The North-South bidding is natural and there is no North-South bidding other than that given.

SET 65 − WEST	SET 65 − EAST	SET 66 − WEST	SET 66 − EAST
1. North bids 2◇.	**1. North bids 2◇.**	**1. North bids 1NT.**	**1. North bids 1NT.**
♠ A Q 8 7 4	♠ 3	♠ A K 3	♠ 8 5
♡ K Q 9 3	♡ J 7 6	♡ K J 9 5 2	♡ Q 7 3
◇ 7 2	◇ A J 9 8 5	◇ J 10 3	◇ A K 8 2
♣ Q 4	♣ K 9 8 2	♣ 9 7	♣ J 8 6 5
2. North bids 1♡.	**2. North bids 1♡.**	**2. South bids 2♠.**	**2. South bids 2♠.**
♠ K Q 9 4	♠ 7 3	♠ Q 10 8 3	♠ K 5
♡ 3	♡ A Q 10 8 6 5	♡ A 7	♡ K J 9 4
◇ A Q 6	◇ K 7 4 2	◇ 7 6 4	◇ A K 5
♣ Q 9 8 3 2	♣ 6	♣ 8 6 5 2	♣ K 9 4 3
3. North bids 1♡.	**3. North bids 1♡.**	**3. North bids 4♠.**	**3. North bids 4♠.**
♠ A 6 5 3	♠ 10 8 4 2	♠ 7 6 4	♠ 2
♡ 8 2	♡ 7 6 4 3	♡ 10 9 5 4 2	♡ K Q J 8 3
◇ A Q 6	◇ K 4 3	◇ A K	◇ J 6 4
♣ A K Q 8	♣ 6 5	♣ K Q J	♣ A 8 5 2
4. South bids 2♣.	**4. South bids 2♣.**	**4. South bids 2♣.**	**4. South bids 2♣.**
♠ Q 9 8	♠ A 7	♠ 7 2	♠ A Q 9 8 3
♡ 7 5 3	♡ K Q 9 8 6	♡ J 9 8 4	♡ 7 2
◇ 8 3 2	◇ K J 7 4	◇ 7 6 5 3 2	◇ K J
♣ J 7 4 3	♣ A 2	♣ 9 4	♣ K J 7 2
5. North doubles 1♠.	**5. North doubles 1♠.**	**5. North bids 1♡.**	**5. North bids 1♡.**
South bids 2♡.	**South bids 2♡.**	**South bids 2♡.**	**South bids 2♡.**
♠ A K 8 6 4 2	♠ 3	♠ A Q 3 2	♠ J 8 4
♡ 7	♡ A Q 10 4	♡ 7	♡ K J 10 6
◇ A J 3	◇ 10 9 5 2	◇ A K 8 4 3	◇ 7
♣ 9 4 2	♣ K Q 6 5	♣ A 9 6	♣ 8 7 5 4 3
6. South bids 2♣.	**6. South bids 2♣.**	**6. North bids 2♠.**	**6. North bids 2♠.**
♠ K 8 4 2	♠ J 10	♠ K Q 10 7	♠ 8 3
♡ 3 2	♡ A K 7 6 4	♡ A K 7 4 3	♡ 6 2
◇ A 9 8 6 4 2	◇ 7	◇ K 8 2	◇ A 9 7 5
♣ 3	♣ A J 10 8 5	♣ 9	♣ K Q 6 3 2

PLAY HANDS ON PENALTY DOUBLES & PENALTY PASSES

Hand 125 : Penalty double of 1NT overcall — Leading partner's suit — Suit preference signals

Dealer North : Both vulnerable

NORTH
♠ 7 6 3 2
♡ 10 2
♢ 9 8 4
♣ 8 5 4 3

WEST
♠ J 10 8
♡ Q 6 3
♢ K 10 7 2
♣ A 10 8

EAST
♠ K Q 9
♡ A 9 8 5 4
♢ 6 5
♣ Q J 7

SOUTH
♠ A 5 4
♡ K J 7
♢ A Q J 3
♣ K 9 2

WEST	NORTH	EAST	SOUTH
	Pass	1♡	1NT (1)
Dble (2)	Pass (3)	Pass (4)	Pass (5)

Bidding : (1) 16-18 balanced with a heart stopper.
(2) Double the 1NT overcall when your side has more HCP.
(3) Do not start rescue operations if balanced with no 5-card suit.
(4) You should remove a penalty double only on freak shapes.
(5) South could be excused for feeling mildly confident.

Lead : ♡3. Unless you have a very strong suit, prefer to lead partner's suit. Lead bottom from Honor-x-x.

Correct play : East should win the ♡A and return the ♡5. When returning a suit, lead top from a remaining doubleton. With more than 2 cards left, lead top from a remaining sequence but lead the original 4th highest card when there is no sequence. South should finesse the ♡J and West wins ♡Q. On the 3rd heart, East knows this will knock out the ♡K and should play the *nine*. When knocking out a stopper in declarer's hand, if your cards are immaterial, play low if your entry is in the lower outside suit and play high if your entry is in the higher suit. At trick 3, East's hearts are 9-8-4 and it does not matter to East which one is played. East therefore chooses the 9, the highest, to tell partner to lead the highest suit, spades, later to find North's entry. Note that if West later switched to ♣A, that would give South a trick with the ♣K. After winning ♡K, South plays ♢A and ♢Q: West wins and switches to ♠J. When East gains the lead, East cashes the 2 heart winners and switches to the ♣Q. This defense holds declarer to 4 tricks (1 spade, 1 heart, 2 diamonds) for +800. Note that if West incorrectly led the ♡Q, this would give South an extra trick in hearts. Lead lowest from Q-x-x.

Hand 126 : The penalty pass — Suit preference signal — Defensive technique

Dealer East : Nil vulnerable

NORTH
♠ 3
♡ A 6 4
♢ A Q 9 6 3
♣ J 7 6 5

WEST
♠ J 8 2
♡ 8 7
♢ K J 10 8 5 4
♣ A K

EAST
♠ K 10 5 4
♡ J 10 5 2
♢ 2
♣ 10 9 8 2

SOUTH
♠ A Q 9 7 6
♡ K Q 9 3
♢ 7
♣ Q 4 3

WEST	NORTH	EAST	SOUTH
		Pass	1♠
2♢ (1)	Pass (2)	Pass (3)	Dble (4)
Pass (5)	Pass (6)	Pass (7)	

Bidding : (1) A *very* sound overcall and yet it comes to grief. Imagine the possible damage if you overcall on a weakish suit.
(2) The North hand is ideal for penalties : misfit with opener, strong trumps and plenty of HCP. If playing penalty doubles, North would double and South would pass. Using negative doubles, you pass for penalties and hope partner re-opens with a double.
(3) Do not bid opposite an overcall with a weak hand. No heroics.
(4) Double is far superior to 2♡. If 2♡ is the right contract, North can bid it in reply to the double. However, North is unlikely to have hearts (no negative double) or spade support (no 2♠ raise).
(5) This would be a bad moment to bid 3♢ to push the bidding up.
(6) The penalty pass closes the trap.
(7) The outside suits are not good enough for an S.O.S. redouble.

Lead : ♠3. Partner should expect a spade shortage because you have made a low-level penalty pass.

Correct play : South wins and cashes the other top spade, North discarding ♡6. South now leads the *nine* of spades for North to ruff, a high card asking for the high suit back. North ruffs and cashes ♡A and leads a heart to South. The defense has already taken 5 tricks and North still has A-Q-9-6 left, sure to be 3 tricks, for +500. North exits each time with clubs and simply waits for the diamond tricks to come. On the spade lead, West should play low in dummy and drop the J from hand, trying to fool South that it is a singleton. South should not be misled, for if the ♠J were singleton, North would have 3 spades, inconsistent with a penalty pass.

Hand 127 : Penalty pass — Suit preference signal — Defensive technique

Dealer South : North-South vulnerable

```
              NORTH
              ♠ Q 10
              ♡ K Q 9 5 3
              ◇ J 8 7 6
              ♣ A K
WEST                        EAST
♠ A K J 8                  ♠ 9 6
♡ 7                        ♡ A J 10 8 6 2
◇ A Q 9 5 3                ◇ 4
♣ 6 3 2                    ♣ Q J 9 8
              SOUTH
              ♠ 7 5 4 3 2
              ♡ 4
              ◇ K 10 2
              ♣ 10 7 5 4
```

WEST	NORTH	EAST	SOUTH
			Pass
1◇	1♡ (1)	Pass (2)	Pass
Dble (3)	Pass	Pass (4)	Pass (5)

Bidding : (1) Worth 1♡ even at adverse vulnerability. Double is inferior without tolerance for the black suits.

(2) Perfect for penalties : strong trumps, misfit with opener and enough HCP. If using penalty doubles, East would double and West would pass. If sensibly using negative doubles, East passes for penalties and awaits a re-opening double.

(3) Double is superior to 1♠. If spades is the best contract, East will bid spades in reply to the double. East's failure to double or bid spades suggests East does not have spades. The double allows partner to bid or to pass, whichever is desired.

(4) Things have gone exactly as East hoped.

(5) South might think of running but if South bids 1♠, West will double. After a penalty double or a penalty pass, all later doubles are for penalties. Both 1♠ doubled and 1NT doubled can be defeated by 3 tricks.

Lead : ◇ 4. Partner's suit is the normal lead.

Correct play : West wins and cashes a 2nd diamond, East discarding a spade. West continues with the ◇ 9 (high card when giving a ruff — "Play back the higher suit.") and East ruffs. A spade allows West to cash a 2nd spade before giving East another diamond ruff. The defense have 6 tricks so far and East still has A-J-10-8 over North's K-Q-9-5-3. As long as East does not lead trumps but exits patiently with clubs, East will take 4 more tricks for 3 off, +800. (If South runs to 1♠, West doubles and leads a heart to East. East returns a diamond and after 2 diamond winners, a defensive cross-ruff ensues : diamond ruff, heart ruff, etc. for 3 off.)

Hand 128 : Negative double — Penalty pass — Suit preference signal — Defensive technique

Dealer West : East-West vulnerable

```
              NORTH
              ♠ J 10
              ♡ A K 7 6 5
              ◇ 7
              ♣ A J 10 8 5
WEST                        EAST
♠ Q 7 5 4 3                ♠ A
♡ Q J 9                    ♡ 10 4 3
◇ Q 4 3 2                  ◇ K J 5
♣ 2                        ♣ K Q 9 7 6 4
              SOUTH
              ♠ K 9 8 6 2
              ♡ 8 2
              ◇ A 10 9 8 6
              ♣ 3
```

WEST	NORTH	EAST	SOUTH
Pass	1♡	2♣ (1)	Dble (2)
Pass (3)	Pass (4)	Pass (5)	

Bidding : (1) An impeccable overcall, despite what happens.

(2) Negative double, promising 4+ spades and 6+ points. South is too weak to bid 2♠ or 2◇.

(3) There is no reason for West to panic. West is too weak to bid (since South's double showed spades, 2♠ would not be a bright move) and South's negative double is for takeout.

(4) What a delightful development! Only the negative doublers can score these penalties. If South bid 2◇ or 2♠, East would be off the hook and if South passed, North would pass out 2♣ (and collect undoubled penalties) since a double by North would be for takeout.

(5) East may have a fleeting thought that the opponents have muffed it and that 2♣ doubled might actually be making.

Lead : ♡8. Partner's suit and top from a doubleton.

Correct play : North wins ♡ K and, knowing South will not have heart support because of the negative double, cashes ♡ A. North continues with ♡5 when giving South a heart ruff, lowest card for the low suit back (excluding trumps, of course). South ruffs and switches to ace and another diamond, giving North a ruff. With 5 tricks in, North's remaining A-J-10-6 will be good for another 3 tricks at least. After winning ♡ K, North might consider switching to the singleton diamond at once. That is not best (although it works here). If East had the ◇ A, East would win and draw South's trump. The defense would then miss the heart ruff.

REVISION TEST ON PART 4

The answers to all these questions can be found in Chapters 25-32. Give yourself 1 mark for each correct answer. If you score less than 40, it will profit you to revise the relevant sections.

A. Partner opened 1♠, RHO bid 2♦. Using negative doubles, what action should you take on these hands?

1. ♠ A9	2. ♠ 83	3. ♠ 63	4. ♠ K8	5. ♠ 2
♡ KJ72	♡ KQ9	♡ AKJ8	♡ AK7	♡ AJ
◇ K32	◇ K832	◇ 76	◇ 8432	◇ KJ952
♣ 9742	♣ K762	♣ AQ972	♣ A942	♣ 98532

B. RHO opened 1◇ and partner replied 1♠ to your double. What action do you now take on these hands?

1. ♠ K53	2. ♠ Q52	3. ♠ A2	4. ♠ AQ9	5. ♠ A3
♡ AQJ932	♡ KQ9	♡ A2	♡ AKQ	♡ AK2
◇ 8	◇ AK2	◇ 94	◇ 832	◇ A94
♣ AKQ	♣ AJ108	♣ AKQ8632	♣ AKQ4	♣ AKQ32

C. Partner opened 1♡ and RHO doubled. What action should responder take on these hands?

1. ♠ 9852	2. ♠ A107	3. ♠ AJ53	4. ♠ QJ82	5. ♠ AQ75
♡ K732	♡ 842	♡ 6	♡ Q963	♡ - - -
◇ A1092	◇ AK9	◇ AQ962	◇ AQ8	◇ A9743
♣ 2	♣ QJ82	♣ 853	♣ 52	♣ KJ73

D. Partner opened 1NT, RHO bid 2♠. What action should responder take on these hands?

1. ♠ K942	2. ♠ 42	3. ♠ 72	4. ♠ 32	5. ♠ - - -
♡ 873	♡ KQ32	♡ QJ8632	♡ A2	♡ QJ32
◇ K952	◇ 762	◇ K72	◇ K962	◇ J976
♣ J6	♣ AJ64	♣ 54	♣ KJ643	♣ AJ1053

E. What would your answers be for D. if RHO bid an artificial 2◇ over 1NT to show a 2-suiter including spades?

F. You opened 1◇, LHO overcalled 2♣, passed back to you. What action do you take on these hands?

1. ♠ K7	2. ♠ KQJ	3. ♠ A3	4. ♠ K	5. ♠ AJ72
♡ 73	♡ AQJ	♡ AKJ4	♡ AJ	♡ 6
◇ AQ964	◇ KQ764	◇ QJ8742	◇ KQJ8542	◇ AKJ43
♣ KJ73	♣ 32	♣ 4	♣ 972	♣ 962

G. What would your answers be for F. if LHO's overcall had been 1♡, passed back to you?

H. You opened 1◇, LHO bid 2♡ (weak), negative double by partner, passed to you. Your rebid?

1. ♠ AK62	2. ♠ Q6	3. ♠ 83	4. ♠ 52	5. ♠ A872
♡ 3	♡ 973	♡ 72	♡ KQ109	♡ 6
◇ AQ65	◇ AKQ84	◇ AKQJ32	◇ A9862	◇ AK1093
♣ Q983	♣ AKJ	♣ AK5	♣ AK	♣ KQJ

I. Partner opened 1♠, RHO bid 2◇, you doubled (negative) and partner rebid 3♣, to you. Your action?

1. ♠ K7	2. ♠ A7	3. ♠ A	4. ♠ K72	5. ♠ 2
♡ Q973	♡ AQ63	♡ AKJ2	♡ AJ1093	♡ K963
◇ 964	◇ 764	◇ Q764	◇ 98632	◇ 943
♣ KJ73	♣ K732	♣ J854	♣ - - -	♣ KQJ92

J. Partner opened 1♡ and RHO overcalled 1NT. What action do you take on these hands?

1. ♠ K7	2. ♠ A7	3. ♠ 87542	4. ♠ AJ72	5. ♠ 92
♡ 73	♡ K764	♡ K954	♡ 7	♡ 6
◇ AQ96	◇ QJ86	◇ Q76	◇ Q973	◇ KQJ1083
♣ J10762	♣ 732	♣ 4	♣ 10975	♣ 9754

ANSWERS TO EXERCISES AND QUIZZES

(Note : In answers, No = No bid. In the Partnership Bidding Sets, dealer's action is given first)

Page	Answers and Comments

11   **Set 1 :** 1. 1NT : 3NT, No   2. No : 1NT, 3NT : No   3. No : 1NT, 2NT : 3NT, No   4. 1NT : 3NT, No
5. No : 1NT, 3NT : No   6. 1♣ : 1♠, 2NT : 3NT, No   **Set 2 :** 1. 2NT : No   2. No : 2NT, 3NT : No
3. 2NT : 3NT, No   4. No : 2NT, 3NT : No   5. 2NT : 6NT, No   6. 2NT : 7NT, No.

12   1. 2♣   2. 1NT   3. 1NT — all the strength is in the short suits   4. 2NT   5. 4♠ — Worth 20 points counting the singleton

13   1. 3NT   2. 2NT   3. 3NT — worth 10 points   4. 3NT — worth 10 points   5. 2NT — worth 8 points via the 6-card suit

15   **A.** 1. 1♠   2. 1♥   3. 1♦   4. 1♦ — with a weak hand and 4 diamonds and a 4-card major, bid the diamonds first   5. 1♠
B. 1. 1♠ — show the major before supporting a minor   2. 1♥   3. 1♥   4. 1♦   5. 1♠ — 2♣ would show 10 points up.
C. 1. 1♠   2. 2♥   3. 4♥   4. 2♥   5. 1♠   **D.** 1. 1♠   2. 2♠   3. 1NT — too weak for 2♦   4. 1NT   5. 2♠

18   **A.** 1. 1♠   2. 1♦   3. 1♦   4. 1♦   5. 1♥   **B.** 1. 2♥   2. 2♥   3. 1♠   4. 1♠ — just too weak for 2♦   5. 4♥
C. 1. 1♥   2. 1♥   3. 1NT   4. 1♠   5. 3♣   **D.** 1. 2♥   2. 4♥ — 5 points for the void   3. 1NT   4. 1♠   5. 3♣
E. 1. 1♠   2. 1♠ — bid the major rather than 1NT   3. 2♣   4. 3♣   5. 1NT   **F.** 1. 2♦   2. No   3. 2♣   4. 2♦   5. No
Set 3 : 1. 1♣ : 2♣, No   2. No : 1♦, 2♦ : 3NT   3. 1♦ : 2♦, No   4. No : 1♠, 2♠, 4♠ : No   5. 1♠ : 4♠, No
6. No : 1♠, 2♠ : 3♠, No.   **Set 4 :** 1. 1♦ : 1NT, No   2. No : 1♥, 1NT : 3NT, No   3. 1♠ : 1NT, 2♥ : No
4. No : 1♥, 1NT : 3♥, 4♥ : No   5. 1♠ : 1NT, 3♠ : No   6. No : 1♠, 1NT : 3♥, 4♥ : No.

19   **G.** 1. No   2. 4♠   3. 4♠   4. No   5. No   **H.** 1. No   2. 3NT   3. 3♠   4. 2♠   5. 2♠   **I.** 1. 2♠   2. 1NT
3. 2♣   4. 2♥   5. 1NT — prefer not to rebid a 5-card suit   **J.** 1. No   2. No   3. No   4. No   5. No — all too weak
K. 1. No   2. 2♠   3. 2♥ — too weak for 2♦ or 2NT   4. No   5. 2♠   **L.** 1. No   2. 4♠   3. 4♠   4. 4♠   5. 4♠.
Set 5 : 1. 1♣ : 1♥, 1NT : 2♥, No   2. No : 1♣, 1♥ : 1♠, 1NT : No   3. 1♣ : 1♥, 2♣ : No
4. No : 1♦, 1♥ : 1♠, 2♠, No   5. 1♦ : 1♠, 2♦ : 2♠, No   6. No : 1♦, 1♥ : 2♣, 2♦ : No
Set 6 : 1. 1♣ : 1♠, 4♠ : No   2. No : 1♦, 1♥ : 2NT, 3NT : No   3. 1♥ : 1♠, 3♦ : 3♠, 4♠ : No
4. No : 1♣, 1♦ : 1♥, 2♦ : 4♥, No   5. 1♣ : 1♥, 1♠ : 2♥, 4♥ : No   6. No : 1♥, 1♠ : 4♥ : No.

26   **A.** 1. 1♠   2. 1♥   3. 1♦ (or 1♠, intending to rebid 3NT if no spade fit is found)   4. 1♠   5. 1♦ —Longest first.
B. 1. 2♦   2. 2♣ — Longest first   3. 2♣   4. 1♠   5. 2♣ — Too strong for just 2♥ and not good enough for 3♥.
C. 1. 2♥   2. 2♥   3. 2NT — Partner can bid 3♥ with 4 hearts   4. 2♣ — Avoid the jump to 3♠ with only 3 trumps
as far as possible   5. 2♣ — Too strong for 2♥, not enough for 3♥, so mark time with a 2♣ response, even on 3 cards.
D. 1. 1♥ — Show 4-card suits up-the-line   2. 1♥ — it would be a serious error to rebid 1NT   3. 3♦   4. 2♣   5. 3♣.
Set 7 : 1. 1♣ : 1♥, 1♠ : 4♠, No   2. 1♣ : 1♥, 1NT : 3NT, No   3. 1♣ : 1♥, 2♥ : 4♥, No   4. 1♣ : 1♥, 1♠ : 4♠, No
5. 1♣ : 1♥, 2♣ : 3NT, No   6. 1♣ : 1♥, 3♣ : 3NT, No
Set 8 : 1. 1♦ : 1♠, 2♣ : 3♣, 4♠ : No   2. 1♦ : 1♥, 2♣ : 3♥, 3NT : No   3. 1♦ : 1♠, 2♦ : 2♥, 2♠ : 4♠, No
4. No : 1♦, 1♥ : 2♣, 3♣ : 3NT, No   5. 1♦ : 1♥, 3♣ : 3NT, No   6. 1♦ : 3♦, 3NT : No.

27   **E.** 1. 2♦   2. 2♥ — Too weak to bid 2♠, beyond the 2♥ barrier   3. 3♣   4. 4♣   5. 3♥ — Too good for just 2♥.
F. 1. 2♥   2. 2♠ — Too weak for 3♣, beyond your 2♠ barrier   3. 3♦   4. 3NT   5. 4♠ (or 3♠ now, 4♠ next).
G. 1. 1♠   2. 3♣   3. 3♦   4. 1♠   5. 3NT   **H.** 1. 2♠   2. 4♥   3. 3♥   4. 3♣ — Not forcing   5. 3♦.
Set 9 : 1. 1♠ : 2NT, 3NT : No   2. 1♠ : 2NT, 3♥ : 4♥, No   3. 1♠ : 2NT, 3♥ : 3NT, No   4. 1♠ : 3NT, No
5. 1♥ : 2NT, 3♠ : 4♥, No   6. 1♠ : 2♦, 2♠ : 4♠   **Set 10 :** 1. 1♦ : 2♣, 2♦ : 2♥, 4♥ : No   2. 1♥ : 2♣, 2♥ : 3♥, 4♥ : No
3. 1♠ : 2♣, 2♠ : 3NT, No   4. 1♠ : 2♣, 3♠ : 3♠, 4♠, No   5. 1♥ : 2NT, 4♥ : No   6. 1♥ : 2♣, 3♣ : 3NT.

34   **A.** 1. 1NT   2. 4♠   3. 2♥   4. 2♦   5. 3♥   **B.** 1. No   2. 2♦   3. 3NT   4. 3♣   5. 3♦
C. 1. 2♥   2. 3♥   3. No   4. 2♥ — with equal support, prefer partner's first bid suit   5. 2♥ — false preference
D. 1. 2♠   2. 2NT   3. 2NT   4. 3♠ — No major suit support, no diamond stopper   5. 2♠ — delayed support.

35   **E.** 1. 3♥   2. 4♥ (or 3♦ followed by 4♥ to show the club singleton)   3. 4♥   4. 2♠ — Too weak for 3♦   5. 3♦
F. 1. 3♥   2. 3NT   3. 3♠ — No club stopper for 3NT   4. 4♦ — Slam chances too good to bid only 3NT   5. 4♥.
G. 1. 1NT   2. 1♠   3. 2NT   4. 3♥   5. 4♥.   **H.** 1. No   2. No — Too weak for 2♠   3. 2♠   4. 3♣   5. 3♦.
Set 11 : 1. No : 1♠, 3♠ : 4♠, No   2. 1♣ : 1♠, 2♣ : 2♥, 2♠ : 4♠, No   3. 1♣ : 1♠, 2♣ : 2♥, 2NT : 3NT, No
4. 1♦ : 1♥, 1♠ : 2♦, No   5. 1♦ : 1♠, 1NT : 2NT, 3♠ : 4♠, No   6. 1♦ : 1♥, 2♦ : 2♠, 3♥ (delayed support) : 4♥, No.
Set 12 : 1. 1♠ : 2♥, 3♥ : 4♥, No   2. 1♠ : 2♥, 2♠ : 3♦, 3♥ (delayed support) : 4♥   3. 1♠ : 2♥, 3♣ : 3♦, 4♥ : No
4. 1♠ : 2♥, 2♠ : 3NT   5. 1♦ : 1♠, 2♣ : 2♦ (weak preference), No   6. 1♦ : 1♠, 2♣ : 2♦, 2♠ : 3♠, 4♠ : No.

39   **Set 13 :** 1. 1NT : 3♥, 4♥ : No   2. No : 1NT, 3♠ : 3NT, No   3. 1NT : 4♠, No   4. No : 1NT, 2♠ : No
5. 1NT : 4♥, No   6. 1NT : 2♥, No   **Set 14 :** 1. No : 2NT, 4♠ : No   2. 2NT : 4♥, No   3. No : 2NT, 3♠ : 4♠, No
4. 2NT : 3♥, 3NT : No   5. No : 2NT, 3♥ : 4♥, No   6. 2NT : 3NT (Do not introduce the minor suit), No.

Page

Answers and Comments

43   **Set 15 :** 1. 1NT : 2♣, 2♡ : 4♡, No   2. No : 1NT, 2♣ : 2♠, 4♠ : No   3. 1NT : 2♣, 2♡ : 2NT, 3NT (max.) : No
4. No : 1NT, 2♣ : 2♡, 3NT : No   5. 1NT : 2♣, 2♡ : 3NT (shows spades), 4♠ : No   6. No : 1NT, 2♣ : 2♡, 4♡ : No

Set 16 : 1. 2NT : 3♣, 3♡ : 4♡, No   2. 2NT : 3♣, 3♡ : 3NT, 4♠ : No   3. No : 2NT, 3♣ : 3♢, 3NT : No
4. No : 2NT, 3♣ : 3♡, 4♡ : No   5. No : 2NT, 3♣ : 3♢, 3♡ (shows 5 hearts) : 4♡, No   6. 2NT : 3♣, 3♡ : 4♡, No

47   **Set 17 :** 1. No : 1♢, 1♡ : 1NT, 2♢ : No   2. 1♢ : 1♡, 1NT : 4♡, No   3. 1♣ : 1♠, 1NT : 3♠, 4♠ : No
4. No : 1♣, 1♠ : 1NT, 2♠ : No   5. 1♣ : 1♡, 1NT : 2♠, 3♡ : 4♡ : No   6. 1♣ : 1♠, 1NT : 3♡, 3♠ : 4♠, No.

Set 18 : 1. 1♢ : 1♠, 2NT : 3♡, 3♠ : 4♠, No   2. No : 1♣, 1♡ : 2NT, 3♠ : 4♠, No   3. 1♣ : 1♠, 2NT : 4♠, No
4. No : 1♣, 1♡ : 2NT, 3♡ : 4♡, No   5. 1♣ : 1♠, 2NT : 3♡, 3NT : No   6. No : 1♣, 1♡ : 2NT, 3♢ : 3♡, 4♡ : No.

48   1. 3♢   2. 2♢   3. 2♣   4. 2NT (too strong for 2♠, too weak for 3♠)   5. 4♡ — Offering 4♠ or 4♡ choice.

49   1. 4♠ — Partner must have at least 2 spades   2. 3NT — Not enough to make slam likely   3. 3♡   4. 3♣   5. 3♠.

53   **A.** 1. 7   2. 7   3. 6   4. 8   5. 6   6. 4   7. 5   8. 7   9. 5   10. 5   11. 6   12. 4   13. 6   14. 7   15. 5.

B. 1. 2♢   2. 2♢   3. 2♡   4. 2NT   5. 3♢   **C.** 1. 2♡   2. 3♢   3. 2NT   4. 3♣   5. 2♠ — Least of evils.

D. 1. 2NT — No support, no 5-card suit   2. 3♠ — Stronger than 4♠   3. 3♡   4. 4♠ — See No. 2   5. 3♢.

Set 19 : 1. No : 2♣, 2NT : 3NT, 6NT : No   2. No : 2♣, 2♢ : 2NT, 4♠ : No   3. 2♣ : 2♢, 2NT : 3♣, 3♠ : 4♠, No
4. No : 2♣, 2♢ : 2NT, 3♣ : 3♡, 4♡ : No   5. 2♣ : 3♣, 3NT : 4NT, 5♠ : 5NT, 6♠ : 7NT — You can count 13 tricks.
6. No : 2♣, 2♢ : 2NT, 3♣ (use Stayman when you have both majors 4-4, 5-4 or 5-5) : 3♡, 4♡ : No.

Set 20 : 1. No : 2♣, 2♢ : 2♡, 4♡ (no A, K, singleton or void) : No   2. No : 2♣, 2♢ : 2♠, 3♠ : 4NT, 5♢ : 6♠, No
3. 2♣ : 2♢, 2♠ : 3♡, 4♡ : No   4. 2♠ : 3♢, 4NT : 5♡, 5NT : 6♢, 7NT — You can count 13 winners in no-trumps.
5. No : 2♣, 2♢, 3♠ : 4NT, 5♢ : 7♢, No   6. 2♣ : 2NT, 3♠ : 4♠, 4NT : 5♠, 5NT : 6♠, 7NT — 13 tricks.

56   **A.** 1. 2NT   2. 1NT   3. 2♣   4. 2♢   5. 4♠   6. 2♠   7. 1NT   8. 3♢   9. 3♣ — Too good for 2♣   10. 3♠.

B. 1. 1NT   2. 2♣   3. 4♡   4. 3♣   5. 4♠   6. 2♠   7. 3♡   8. 4NT   9. 2♡   10. 2NT (or 2♢).

C. 1. 2♣   2. 4♡   3. 2♣   4. No   5. 2♠.   **D.** 1. 3♣   2. 3♢   3. 3♣   4. 3♣   5. 4♠.

E. 1. 6NT   2. 3NT   3. 2NT   4. 3♡   5. 3♠.   **F.** 1. 7NT   2. 3♣   3. 3♣   4. 3♣   5. 3♣.

G. 1. 2♡   2. 3♡   3. 2♣   4. 3♠   5. 4♠.   **H.** 1. 3♡   2. 3♠   3. 3♡   4. 6NT   5. 4♡.

59   1. 1♠   2. No   3. 1♡   4. No   5. No   6. 1♠ — For the spade lead   7. No   8. 1♡   9. 2♣   10. No.

60   **A.** 1. No   2. 1♠   3. 1NT   4. Double   5. No   6. Double   7. Double   8. 1NT   9. Double   10. Double.

B. 1. No — Suits too weak to overcall   2. 2♢ — Suit strong   3. No   4. Double — Too strong for 1NT   5. No.

61   **C.** 1. No   2. No — despite the good support   3. 2♡   4. No   5. 3♡   6. 1♠   7. 4♡   8. 1NT   9. 2NT
10. 2♢   11. 3NT   12. 1NT — Prefer not to raise with 4-3-3-3   13. 2♠   14. 3♢   15. 2♣ — Artificial, forcing.

D. 1. No — Diamonds too weak to bother about   2. 2♠   3. 2NT — Invite 3NT if partner maximum   4. 2♢   5. No.

Set 21 : 1. (1♣) : 1♠ : 2♠, No   2. (1♡) : 1♠ : 4♠, No   3. (1♢) : 1♠ : 3♠, 4♠ : No   4. (1♣) : 1♡ : 3♡, No
5. (1♡) : 2♣ : 2NT, 3NT : No   **Set 22 :** 1. (1♢) : 1♠ : 2NT, No (2NT not forcing)   2. (1♠) : 2♣ : 2♡, 4♡ : No
3. (1♢) : 1♠ : 2♠, 4♠ : No   4. (1♠) : 1NT : 3NT, No   5. (1♡) : 1NT : 3♠ (game force with 5 spades), 4♠ : No.

65   **A.** 1. 1♠ — Too strong for a weak jump   2. 1♡   3. 2♡   4. Double — Too strong for any jump overcall   5. 2♢.

B. (1) 1. 2♠   2. 1♡   3. 1♡   4. Double   5. 1♠.   **B. (2)** 1. 1♠   2. 1♡   3. 1♡   4. 2♡   5. 1♢.

C. 1. 4♠   2. No — 3♠ will probably fail and you might defeat 3♢   3. No   4. 3♠   5. 4♡ — Worth the risk.

Set 23 : 1. (1♣) : 2♠ : No   2. (1♠) : 3♡ : 4♡, No   3. (1♡) : 3♣ : 3NT, No   4. (1♠) : 2♢ : 3♠, 4♠ : No
5. (1♣) : 2♢ : No   6. (1♡) : 3♢ : 3NT, No   **Set 24 :** 1. (1♢) : 2♠ : 3♠, No   2. (1♣) : 2♢ : 2♠, 4♠ : No
3. (1♢) : 2♠ : No — Give up early on a misfit   4. (1♡) : 3♣ : 3NT, No   5. (1♢) : 3♣ : No   6. (1♣) : 2♢ : 4♡, No

70   **A.** 1. 2♢   2. No   3. 2♢   4. 2NT   5. 2NT   6. Double   7. 2NT   8. No   9. 2NT   10. 2♣.

B. 1. No   2. Double — Looking for penalties in either minor   3. 4♡   4. 3♡   5. 4NT — Slam in hearts likely.

C. 1. 3♢   2. 3♣   3. 3♣ — With equal length   4. 4NT — Bid 6♢ opposite 1 ace and 5♢ opposite no aces.
5. 3♣   6. 5♠   7. No — Very rare decision   8. 4♣   9. 3♠ — Seeking support   10. 3NT — Good chance.

D. 1. No   2. 5♣ (or 4♣)   3. No   4. 4NT   5. No   6. 4NT   7. Double   8. 5♣   9. 3♠   10. Double.

75   **A. (a)** 1. **4♠**   2. 4♡   3. 5♢   4. 4♠   5. 1♡   6. No   7. 3♣   8. No.   **(b)** 1. 3♠   2. 3♡   3. 5♢   4. 4♠   5. 1♡   6. No   7. No   8. No.

B. (a) 1. No   2. No   3. 4♡   4. No   5. 4♡   6. 3♠   7. 4NT   8. 4NT   9. 4♡   10. 4♡.
(b) 1. No   2. No   3. 4♡   4. 4♡   5. 4♡   6. 3♠   7. 4NT   8. 4NT   9. 4♡   10. 4♡.

Set 25 : 1. 3♡ : 4NT, 5♢ : 7NT (can count 13 tricks)   2. 3♢ : 3NT, No   3. No : 4♠, No   4. 5♣ : 6♣, No.

Set 26 : 1. 3NT (Gambling) : No   2. No : 3NT, 4♣ : 4♢, No   3. 3NT : 5♣, No   4. 3NT : 6♢, No — Note this.

82   **A.** 1. Double   2. Double — 5-4 in majors   3. 1♡ — 5-3 in majors   4. No — Not double   5. 1NT — Not double.

B. 1. 1♠   2. 1♠   3. 1♠   4. 1♡   5. 2♣   6. 1♡   7. 1♠   8. 1♠   9. 2♣   10. 1NT — just OK.

C. 1. No   2. 3♠ — 4 losers   3. 3♡ — 4 losers   4. 2♠ — 5 losers   5. No — Do not rebid with a minimum.

Page	**Answers and Comments**

82 **Set 27 :** 1. (1♦): Dble : 1♥, No   2. (1♣): Dble : 1♠, No   3. (1♠): Dble : 2♥, No   4. (1♥): Dble : 1♠, 2♠ : No
5. (1♠): No : (2♠): Double, 3♥ : No.   **Set 28 :** 1. (1♦): Double : 1♥, 2♥ : No   2. (1♥): Double : 1♠, 3♠ : No
3. (1♦): Double : 1♥, 3♥ : 4♥, No   4. (1♣): Double : 1♠, 2♠ : No   5. (1♦): No : (1♠): Double, 2♣ : 3♣, No.

86 **A.** 1. 1♠   2. 1NT   3. 2♣   4. No   5. 1♠.   **B.** 1. 2♥   2. 2♥   3. 2♥   4. 1NT   5. 2♦.
C. 1. 2♠   2. No   3. 3♦   4. 3♣   5. 2♠.   **D.** 1. No   2. 3NT   3. 2NT   4. 2♥   5. 3♠ — 4 losers.
Set 29 : 1. (1♦): Double : 2♣, No   2. (1♣): Double : 1♥, 2♥ (5 losers): 4♥, No   3. (1♠): Double : 2♥, No
4. (1♥): Dble : 1♠, No 5. (1♦): Dble : 1♠, (2♦): No : 2♥, 2♠ : No. **Set 30 :** 1. (1♠): Dble : 1NT, No 2. (1♣): Dble : 1♠, No
3. (1♣): Dble : 1♠, No   4. (1♦): Dble : 1NT, 2NT : 3NT, No   5. (1♠): Dble : 2♦, (2♠): No : 3♣, 3♦ : No.

90 **A.** 1. 2♠   2. 2♥   3. 3♣   4. 2NT   5. 2♠.   **B.** 1. 4♥   2. No   3. 2♠ — Forcing   4. 3NT   5. 3♥.
Set 31 : 1. (1♦): Double : 2♠, 3♠ : 4♠, No   2. (1♥): Double : 2♥, 4♥ : No   3. (1♥): Double : 2♠, No
4. (1♣): Dble : 2♦, No 5. (1♠): Dble : (2♠): 4♥, No **Set 32 :** 1. (1♣): Double : 2NT, No 2. (1♠): Dble : 2NT, 3NT
3. (1♦): Double : 3♣, 3♠ : 4♠, No   4. (1♣): Double : 2NT, 3♥ : 4♥, No   5. (1♦): Double : (2♥), 3♠ : 4♠, No.

95 **A.** 1. No   2. Double   3. 3♠   4. No   5. 3NT   6. 3NT   7. Double   8. No   9. Double   10. 4♦.
B. 1. 3♠   2. 4♦   3. 4♠   4. 4♠   5. 3NT.   **C.** 1. 3♠   2. No   3. 3NT   4. 3♦   5. 4♣ Game force.
Set 33 : 1. (2♠): Dble : 3♥, No   2. (2♠): Dble : 4♠, No   3. (2♥): 2NT, 3NT   4. (2♥): 3♦, 3NT: No
5. (2♠): Dble : 3♣ : 4♥ (4 losers), No.   **Set 34 :** 1. (3♣): Dble : 3♥, No   2. (3♣): 3♥ (6 losers): 4♥ (3 winners), No.
3. (3♦): Double : 4♥, No   4. (3♥): No : Double: No   5. (3♦): Double : 4♦ (game force, pick a suit): 4♠ : No.

98 **A.** 1. No   2. No   3. 4♥   4. Double   5. Double.   **B.** 1. 2♥   2. 2NT   3. 2♦   4. Double   5. 1NT.
C. 1. 2NT   2. 2♥   3. 4♠   4. 3NT   5. 3♠.   **D.** 1. 2♠   2. 2NT   3. 2♣   4. 2♣   5. 2♦.
E. 1. No   2. Double   3. Double   4. 2NT   5. Double.   **F.** 1. No   2. 3♠   3. 2♠   4. 3NT   5. 2♠.
G. 1. 2♣   2. 2♠   3. 1♠   4. 2NT   5. 1♠.   **H.** 1. 2♣   2. 2♥   3. 3♥   4. 1NT   5. 3♣.
I. 1. No   2. No   3. Double   4. Double   5. 3♣.   **J.** 1. 4♦   2. 4♥   3. 3♠   4. 3NT   5. 3♠.

102 **A.** 1. 2♠   2. 2NT   3. 3♣   4. 2♠ — Too strong for 3♣ and looking for 3NT   5. 2♠ — Looking for heart support
6. 3♥   7. 2♠ — Too strong for an invitational 3♦   8. 2♥   9. 3♥ — Invitational   10. 2♠ — Too strong for 3♥.
B. 1. 3♥   2. 3NT   3. 4♥   4. 3♣   5. 4♣   6. 2NT   7. 3♦   8. 3♠   9. 3♦   10. 3♠ — Too strong for 3♦.
Set 35 : 1. 1♣:1♦, 1♠:2♥, 2NT:3NT   2. 1♣:1♦, 1♠:2♥, 3NT:No   3. 1♣:1♦, 1♠:2♥, 2NT:No
4. 1♥:1♠, 1♠:2♦, 2♥:4♥, No   5. 1♦:1♠, 1♠:2♦, 3♥:4♥, No   6. 1♦:2♠, 2♣:2♥, 3♥:3NT, No.
Set 36 : 1. 1♣:1♦, 1♠:2♥, 3♣:No   2. 1♠:2♣, 2♥:3♦, 3♠:4♠, No   3. 1♦:1♠, 2♣:3♥, 4♥:No
4. 1♦:1♥, 1♠:3♥, 4♥:No   5. 1♣:1♦, 1♠:2♥ (4th suit), 3♣:3♦ (forcing), 3♥ (stopper-ask):3♠, 4♠:No
6. 1♠:2♣, 2♥:3♦ (4th suit), 4♣ (delayed support; 5 spades, 4 hearts, 3 clubs = singleton diamond):4NT, 5♦:6♣, No.

108 **A.** 1. 1NT — Too weak for 2♥   2. 2♣   3. 2♦   4. 2NT   5. 2♥ — If you are worth 3♣, you are also worth 2♥.
B. 1. 3♦   2. 3♥   3. 3♠   4. 2NT   5. 3NT   6. 2♠   7. 3♣ — 4th suit   8. 3♠   9. 4♦   10. 4NT.
C. 1. 3♦   2. 3♥ — 4th suit   3. 4♦ — Genuine support and strong hand   4. 3♠   5. 4♥ — Freak 2-suiter.
Set 37 : 1. No:1♦, 1♠:2♥, 3♦:No   2. No:1♦, 1♠:2♥, No   3. 1♦:1♠, 2♦:2♥, 3♥:4♥, No
4. 1♣:1♥, 2♦:2♥, No   5. 1♣:1♥, 2♦:3♥, 4♦ (not 3NT): No   6. 1♦:2♣, 2♠:3♦ (4th suit), 3NT:No.
Set 38 : 1. No:1♦, 1♠:2♥, 3NT:No   2. 1♣:2♠, 2♥:2NT, No   3. No:1♣, 1♠:2♥, 2NT:3♠, 3NT:No
4. 1♦:1♠, 2♥:3♣, 3NT:No 5. No:1♣, 1♠:2♥, 3♦:3♠, 4♠:No 6. 1♦:1♠, 2♥:4♦, 4NT:5♠, 5NT:6♣, 6♦.

112 1. 1♦; 2♣; 3♣   2. 1♣; 2♦; 3♦   3. 1♠; 2♦; 4♦   4. 1♥; 2♦; 3♦   5. 1♦; 1♠ or 2♠; rebid the spades.
Set 39 : 1. 1♠:2♣, 2♥:3♦ (4th suit), 3♥:4♥, No   2. 1♣:1♠, 2♣:2♥, 3♣ (no diamond stopper):3♥, 4♥ : No
3. 1♣:1♠, 2♣:2♥, 2NT (diamond stopper):3♥, 3NT:No   4. 1♦:1♠, 2♦:2♥, 2♠ (delayed support):4♠, No
5. 1♦:1♠, 2♣:2♠, No (you have spade tolerance)   6. 1♦:1♠, 2♣:2♠, 3♣ (you have no spade tolerance): No.
Set 40 : 1. 1♦:1♥, 1♠:2♣ (4th suit), 2♦:4♠, No   2. 1♥:2♣, 2♥:2♠, 3♥:3♠ (shows 6-5 pattern), 4♠:No
3. 1♦:2♣, 2♥:3♣, 3♠ (shows 6-5 pattern):4♥, No   4. 1♣:1♥, 2♣:2♠, 2NT:3♠ (shows 6-5 pattern), 4♥:No
5. 1♣:1♦, 2♣:2♠, 3♣:3♠ (shows 6-5 pattern), 4♦:5♦, No   6. 1♣:1♥, 1♠:1NT, 2♠ (shows weak 6-5): No.

116 **A.** 1. 2♣   2. 2♦ — Clubs too weak to bother about   3. 2♦ — Too weak to reverse   4. 2♥ — Reverse   5. 4♠.
B. 1. 2♦ — Better than 1NT; too weak to reverse   2. 1NT — Weak long suits   3. 2♠   4. 2♣   5. 2♥ — Reverse.
Set 41 : 1. 1♠:2♦, 2♥:2NT, 3♠ (shows 6-4):4♠, No   2. No:1♦, 1♥:1♠, 1NT:2♦ (shows weak 6-4), No
3. 1♣:1♠, 2♣:2♥, 2NT (diamond stopper):3♠, 4♠:No   4. No:1♣, 1♥:1♠, 1NT:3♣ (strong 6-4), 3NT:No
5. 1♦:2♣, 2♦ (too weak to reverse):2♥, 3♦:4♦, No   6. 1♠:2♦, 2♠:3♦, 4♦:4♥ (shows the 6 hearts), No.
Set 42 : 1. 1♦:1♠, 2♣:2♥ (4th suit), 3♠ (delayed support):4♠, No   2. No:1♦, 1♥:2♣, 2NT:3NT, No
3. No:1♣, 1♥:1♥, 1NT:2♠, 3♣:No   4. 1♦:1♠, 2♦:3♣ (4th suit), 3♠ (3-card delayed support):4♠, No.
5. No:1♦, 1♥:1NT, No   6. 1♦:1♠, 2♣:2♥ (4th suit), 3♦ (no support for spades, no heart stopper):3NT, No.

Page   **Answers and Comments**

120 **A.** 1. 3◇ — Diamond stopper   2. 3◇   3. 3♠ — Spade stopper   4. 4♡ — Delayed support   5. 4NT — Slam values.

B. 1. 3NT — Diamonds are stopped   2. 4♣ — Diamonds not stopped   3. 3♠ — Excellent spades   4. 5♣   5. 3NT.

Set 43 (a):   1. 1♠ : 2♣, 3♣ : 3◇, 3NT : No   2. 1♠ : 1♡, 3♣ : 3♠, 3NT : No   3. 1♣ : 1♡, 2♣ : 3♣, 3◇ : 3NT, No
4. 1♠ : 2◇, 3◇ : 4♠, No   5. 1♡ : 2♣, 3♣ : 3NT, No   6. 1♣ : 1◇, 3◇ : 3♡ (heart stopper), 3NT : No.

Set 43 (b):   1. 1♠ : 2♣, 3♣ : 3◇, 3NT : No   2. 1♣ : 1♡, 3♣ : 3◇, 3NT : No   3. 1♣ : 1♡, 2♣ : 3♣, 3♠ : 3NT, No
4. 1♠ : 2◇, 3◇ : 4♠, No   5. 1♡ : 2♣, 3♣ : 3NT, No   6. 1♣ : 1◇, 3◇ : 3♠ (stopper ask), 3NT : No.

Set 44 (a):   1. 1♡ : 2♣, 3♣ : 3♠, 4♣ : 5♣, No   2. 1♠ : 2♣, 3♣ : 3◇ (stopper), 3♠ (excellent spades) : 4♠, No
3. 1♠ : 2♣, 3♣ : 3♡ (stopper in hearts), 5♣ (singleton diamond) : 6♠, No   4. 1♣ : 3♣, 3♠ (spade stopper): 5♣, No
5. 1♡ : 2♣, 3♣ : 4♡, No   6. 1♣ : 1◇, 3◇ : 3♡ (stopper in hearts), 4♠ (no spade stopper, no spade singleton) : 5◇, No.

Set 44 (b):   1. 1♡ : 2♣, 3♣ : 3♠ (stopper ask), 4♣ : 5♣, No   2. 1♠ : 2♣, 3♣ : 3♡, 3♠ (excellent spades) : 4♠, No
3. 1♠ : 2♣, 3♣ : 3◇ (stopper ask), 5♣ (singleton diamond) : 6♣, No   4. 1♣ : 3♣, 3◇ : 3♡ (heart ask), 4♣ : 5♣, No.
5. 1♡ : 2♣, 3♣ : 4♡, No   6. 1♣ : 1◇, 3◇ : 3♠ (stopper ask in spades), 4♠ (no spade stop, no spade singleton) : 5◇, No.

124 **A.** 1. 2♡   2. 2♠   3. No   4. 3♠   5. No   **B.** 1. No   2. No   3. No   4. 3♣   5. 3♣ (length difference of 6).

Set 45 :   1. 1♠ : 1NT, 2♣ : 2♡   2. No : 1♠, 1NT : 2♣, 2◇, : No (Do *not* rebid 2NT.)   3. 1♠ : 1NT, 2◇ : 2♡, No
4. No : 1♠, 1NT : 2♠, No   5. No : 1♡, 1NT : 2NT, 3♣ : No (Do *not* rebid 3NT.)   6. 1NT : 2♣, 2◇ : 2♣, No.

Set 46 :   1. No : 1♡, 1NT : 2◇, No   2. 1♡ : 1NT, 2◇ : 3♣, No (Do *not* rebid 3NT.)   3. No : 1♠, 1NT, 2♣ : 2♠, No
4. 1♠ : 1NT, 2◇ : 2♡, 4♡ : No   5. 1♠ : 1NT, 3♡ (jump shift) : 4♣, 5♣ : No   6. No : 1NT, 2♣ (Stayman) : 2♡, No.

125 1. No — 2♣ unsafe if opener replies 2♠   2. No   3. No — Too weak   4. 2♣ — rebid 3♣ over 2♠   5. 2♣.

129 **A.** 1. 3   2. 1   3. 1   4. 1   5. 1   6. 2   7. 2   8. 2   9. 1   10. 2   11. 1   12. 1   13. 1   14. 0   15. 0   16. 2   17. 2½   18. 3.

B. 1. 7; 4   2. 7½; 2   3. 4; 4   4. 7½; 4   5. 5; 5.

Set 47 :   1. 1♠ : 4♠, No   2. No : 1♡, 2♡ : 4♡, No   3. No : 1♠, 3♠ : 6♠, No   4. 1♣ : 1♠, 1NT : 4♠, No
5. (1♣) : 1♠ : 4♠, No   **Set 48 :**   1. 1♣ : 1♠, 2♠ : 4♠, No   2. 1♣ : 1♠, 2♠ : No (Note the contrast between 1 and 2.)
3. 1♠ : 4NT, 5♠ : 7♠, No   4. 1◇ : 1♡, 1♠ : 4NT, 5♠ : 7♠, No   5. (1♡) : Double : 2♠ (8 losers), No (8 losers).

133 **Set 49 :**   1. No : 1♡, 2♡ : 3♣ (trial bid), 4♡ : No   2. No : 1♡, 2♡ : 3♣, 3♠ : No   3. No : 1♡, 2♡ : 3♣, 3♠ : No
4. 1♠ : 2♠, 3♣ : 4♠ (2 club losers but maximum)   5. 1♠ : 2♠, 3♣ : 3♠, No   6. 1♠ : 2♠, 3♣ : 4♠ (1 club loser), No.

Set 50 :   1. 1♡ : 2♡, 3◇ : 3♡, No   2. No : 1♠, 2♠ : 3◇, 4♠   3. 1♣ : 1♠, 2♠ : 3◇, 4♠ (only 1 diamond loser)
4. 1◇ : 1♡, 2♡ : 3♣, 4♡ (1 club loser) : 4NT, 5♡ : 6♡, No   5. 1♠ : 2♠, 3◇ : 4♠, No   6. 1♠ : 2♠, 3◇ : 3♠, No.

136 **A.** 1. 3NT   2. 3♡   3. 3♠   4. 4♣   5. 3NT.   **B.** 1. 3◇   2. 2NT   3. 3♣   4. 3NT (maximum)   5. 4: :.

C. 1. 3♡   2. 3♠   3. 3NT   4. 3◇   5. 3♣.   **D.** 1. No   2. 3♡ — stopper   3. 3♡   4. 3♠   5. 3NT.

E. 1. 3♣   2. 3NT (maximum)   3. 2NT   4. 2♡   5. 4♣.   **F.** 1. 2◇   2. No   3. No   4. 2◇   5. 4♣.

G. 1. No   2. 3◇   3. 3◇   4. 2♠   5. 4♡.   **H.** 1. No   2. No   3. 3◇   4. No   5. No — No safe move.

I. 1. 3♠   2. No   3. 4♠   4. 3◇   5. 4♠.   **J.** 1. 4♠   2. 4♡   3. 3♠   4. 4♠ — Only 1 heart loser   5. 4♠.

139 **Set 51 :**   1. (1◇) : 2♣ : 2◇, 2NT : 3NT, No   2. (1♡) : Dble : 3♣, 3◇ : 3♡, 3NT : No   3. (3♣) : Dble : 4♣, 4♠ : No
4. 1♠ : (2◇) : 2♡, 2♠ : 3◇, 3♡ : 4♡   5. 1♠ : (2♡) : 3♣, 3◇ : 3♡, 3NT   6. 1♠ : 2♣ : (2◇), No : 3♡, 4♣ : 5♣.

Set 52 :   1. 1♣ : (2◇) : 2♠, 3♣ : 3◇, 3NT   2. 1♣ : 1◇ : (2♠), 3♠ : 3NT   3. 1◇ : 1♡ : (1♠), 2♠ : 3♡, 4♡
4. 1◇ : 2♣ : (2♠), No : 3♠, 4♡   5. (1♡) : 2◇ : 3♣, 3♠ : 3NT, 4◇ : 5◇   6. (1♠) : No : 2♠, 3◇ : 3♡, 4♣ : 4NT, 5♡ : 6♣.

143 **A.** 1. 2♡   2. 4♠   3. 3NT   4. 2◇   5. 2◇.   **B.** 1. 2♡ (or 2NT)   2. 2♠   3. 2♠   4. 2◇   5. 3◇.

Set 53 :   1. (1♡) : Dble : 4♠ (excellent suit)   2. (a) (1♠) : Dble : 2♠, 3◇ : 3♡, 4♡   (b) (1♣) : 1◇ : 1♡, 3♡ : 4♡
3. (1◇) : Dble : 2◇ (too strong for 3♣), 2♡ : 3♣, 3NT   4. (1♣) : Dble : 2♣, 2◇ (4-card suits up-the-line): 2♡, 2♠ : 4♠
5. (1◇) : Dble : 2◇ (3NT is premature), 2♡ : 2NT, 3NT   6. (1♣) : Dble : 2♣, 2♠ : 2NT, 3♡ (5 spades, 4 hearts) : 4♠.

Set 54 :   1. (1♣) : Dble : 1♡, 1NT : 2♡, No   2. (a) (1♣) : Dble : 1◇, 1NT : 3NT   (b) (1◇) : Dble : 1NT, 3NT
3. (1◇) : Dble : 1NT, 3♠ : 4♠   4. (1♣) : Dble : 1◇, 2♡ : 4♡   5. (1♡) : Dble : 1♠, 3♣ : No   6. (1♡) : Dble : 1♠, 3◇ : 3NT.

148 **A.** 1. Rdble   2. 3♡   3. Rdble   4. 4♡   5. 2NT (Truscott).   **B.** 1. 1♠   2. 2♣   3. 2♠   4. 1♠   5. 2♡.

C. 1. No   2. Dble (penalties)   3. No   4. 2◇   5. 2♡.   **D.** 1. Dble   2. 3NT   3. 2NT   4. 3♡   5. 3♣.

Set 55 :   1. 1♡ : (Dble) : 2NT (Truscott), 4♡ : No   2. No : 1♠ : (Dble), 3♠ : 4♠   3. 1♣ : (Dble) : 2NT, 3♠ : No
4. 1♡ : (Dble) : Rdble : (2♣), No : Double (penalties), No   5. 1♠ : (Dble) : Rdble : (2◇), Double (penalties) : No.

Set 56 :   1. 1♣ : (Dble) : 1♡, 1♠ : 3♡, 4♡ : No   2. 1◇ : (Dble) : 2NT, 4NT (or 4◇ forcing) : 5♡, 5NT : 6♣, 6◇ : No
3. No : 1♣ : (Dble), 1♠ : 2♣, No   4. 1♠ : (Dble) : Rdble : (2◇), No : 3♠, 3♠ : 4♠   5. 1♠ : (Dble) : Rdble : 2♣, 2♡ : 4♡.

153 **A.** 1. Dble (penalties)   2. 3♡ (Stayman)   3. 2♠ (not forcing)   4. 3NT (no stopper needed)   5. 3♠ (forcing).

B. 1. 3♣ (not forcing)   2. 2♠ (artificial, Stayman)   3. Dble (and double 2♠, too)   4. 3NT (no stopper needed)   5. 4♡.

Set 57 :   1. No : 1NT : (2♡), 2♠ — not forcing — : No   2. 1NT : (2◇) : 3♣ — not forcing, No — 3NT would be an error.
3. No : 1NT : (2♠), 3NT (too strong for 3◇; no stopper needed for 3NT)   4. 1NT : (2♡) : Double (penalties), No.

Page   **Answers and Comments**

153   **Set 58 :**   1. 1NT : (2♡) : 3♡ — Stayman, 3♠ : 4♠, No   2. No : 1NT : (2♡), 3♢ — Stayman : 3♠, 3NT : No
    3. 1NT : (2♢) : 3♢ — Stayman, 3♡ : 3NT (not 3♠), No   4. No : 1NT : (2♡), 3♢ — Stayman : 3♡, 3NT (not 3♠) : 4♠.

158   **A.**   1. Dble — Perfect pattern   2. Dble   3. No — Too much in their suit to bid again   4. 1NT — shnws 19-20   5. 2♣.
    B.   1. Dble — Better than 2♢   2. Dble — Better than 2♡   3. Nn — Too many clubs   4. Dble — Rebid 2♡ over 2♢   5. No.
    C.   1. 2♡ — Support and 0-5 points   2. 2♠ — 0-5 points because no negative double   3. 3♣   4. 2NT   5. No.
    D.   1. Dble   2. 2NT — Delayed 2NT for the minors   3. 3♢   4. Dble — And rebid 3♢ over 3♣   5. 2NT — Minors.
    Set 59 :   1. 1♡ : (2♣) : No, Double : 2♠, No   2. No : 1♢ : (2♡), No : Double, 3♣ : No   3. 1♠ : (2♢) : No, No
    4. ˙ No : (1♡) : No : (2♡), No : (No) : 2NT — Minors, 3♢ : No   5. No : (1♠) : Dble : (2♠), No : (No) : Dble, 3♣ : No.
    Set 60 :   1. No : 1♣ : (1♠), No : 1NT, 2♡ : No   2. 1♣ : (1♠) : No, 1NT : 3NT   3. No : 1♢ : (2♡), No : Dble, 3♣ : 3♢, No
    4. No : (1♠) : No : (2♠), No : (No) : Double, 3♡ : No   5. No : (1♢) : 1♡ : (2♢), No : (No) : Double, 3♣ : No.

163   **A.**   1. Dble   2. 1♠ — Only 4 spades are promised over 1♢   3. Dble — Shows both majors   4. 1♡   5. No.
    B.   1. Dble — Show the hearts before supporting a minor   2. Dble — Rebid 2♡ over 1NT, 2♢ or 2♣   3. 1NT   4. No   5. 2♡.
    C.   1. 1NT — Better than 2♢   2. 2♡ — No spade stopper for 1NT   3. 2♣ — Better than 1NT or 2♢   4. 2♡   5. 4♡.
    D.   1. Dble — For takeout. Do not sell out at 2♠   2. 3♡ — Do not sell out   3. 3♢ — Do not sell out   4. 3♣   5. Dble.
    Set 61 :   1. No : (No) : 1♣ : (1♠), Dble : (2♣) : 3♡, No   2. 1♢ : (1♠) : Dble, 2♣ : 2♡, No   3. No : 1♣ : (2♡), Dble : 2♠, No
    4. 1♠ : (2♡) : Dble — Minors, 3♣ — Much better than 2♠ : No   5. 1♣ : (1♡) : Dble : (2♡), No : (No) : Dble, 3♣ : No.
    Set 62 :   1. 1♣ : (1♠) : Dble : (2♠), No — Too weak for 3♡ : (No) : Dble — Do not sell out at 2-level : (No), 3♡ : No
    2. 1♢ : (2♣) : Dble — Both majors, 4♠ — Worth 20 points : No   3. 1♢ : (2♡) : 2♠ — Not double, 3♠ : 4♠, No
    4. 1♣ : (1♠) : Dble, 3♡ — Too strong for just 2♡ : 4♡, No   5. 1♢ : (1♠) : Dble : (2♠), No : (No) : 3♡ — = 6-9, No.

167   **A.**   1. 2♣   2. Dble — Show the hearts before supporting a minor   3. 2♡ — Not dble   4. Dble   5. 2♠ — Not dble.
    B.   1. 2♢   2. 3♡ — Too strong for 2♡ ; 3♡ shows 16-18 points   3. 3♣ — Game force   4. 3♠   5. 3♡ = 16-18.
    C.   1. 2NT   2. 3♣   3. 3♢ — Not just 2♢, which would show 6-9 points only   4. 3NT   5. 2♠ — Game force.
    D. (i) 1. 2NT   2. 2NT   3. 2NT   4. 3NT   5. 3NT.   **(ii)** 1. 2NT   2. 3♢   3. 3♢   4. 3NT   5. 2♠
    (iii) 1. 3♡   2. 3♡   3. 3♡   4. 4♡   5. 4♡. When opener replies with a major to your double, your rebid is routine.
    Set 63 :   1. 1♢ : (1♠) : Dble, 2♣ : 2NT, 3NT : No   2. No : 1♣ : (1♠), Dble : 2♣, 2NT : 3♣, No — 3♣ is better than 2NT.
    3. 1♡ : (1♠) : Dble — Better than 2♢ when holding both minors, 2♣ : 2NT — East has already shown both minors, No
    4. No : 1♣ : (1♠), Dble : 2♢, 3♡ : 4♡, No   5. 1♠ : (2♡) : Dble — Both minors, 3♠ — 16-18, 6+ spades : 4♠, No.
    Set 64 :   1. 1♢ : (1♠) : Dble, 2♡ : 4♡   2. 1♢ : (1♠) : Dble, 2♣ : 3NT   3. No : 1♣ : (1♠), Dble : 2♠, 2NT : 3NT
    4. No : 1♣ : (1♠), Dble : 2♠, 3♡ : 4♡, No   5. 1♠ : (2♢) : Dble, 3♣ : 3♢ — Game force and stopper ask, 3NT : No.

175   **A.**   1. No — Support hearts   2. No — Clubs too weak — Double   3. Suitable   4. No — Too weak   5. Suitable.
    B.   1. Dble   2. No — Hearts strong, so partner's pass must be weakness   3. Dble   4. No — Strong hearts   5. No.
    C.   1. 2♡ — 0-5 points as you did not bid 2♡ on the previous round   2. 2♠   3. 2NT   4. No — Penalty pass   5. 2♡.
    Set 65 :   1. 1♠ : (2♢) : No, Dble : No   2. 1♣ : (1♡) : No, Dble : No   3. 1♣ : (1♡) : No, Dble : 1♠ (0-5 points), No
    4. No : 1♡ : (2♣), No : Dble, 2♡ : No   5. 1♠ : (Dble) : Rdble : (2♡), No : Dble, No   6. No : 1♡ : (2♣), Dble : No.
    Set 66 :   1. 1♡ : (1NT) : Dble — Penalties, No   2. No : 1NT : (2♠), Dble — Penalties : No   3. 1♡ : (4♠) : 5♡, No
    4. No : 1♠ : (2♣), No : No   5. 1♢ : (1♡) : No : 2♡, Dble — Shows extra values : No   6. 1♡ : (2♠) : Dble, No.

178   **A.**   1. Dble   2. 2NT — Shows 10-12 points, denies 4 hearts or support for spades   3. 3♣   4. 3♢   5. No (penalties).
    B.   1. 3♡ — Shows 4 losers and 5+ hearts   2. 1NT — Shows 19-20 balanced   3. 3♣   4. 2♢ — Forcing   5. 3NT.
    C.   1. 3♡   2. Rdble — Aiming for 3NT   3. Rdble — Aiming for penalties   4. 2NT — Support and 10+ points   5. Rdble.
    D.   1. Dble — For penalties   2. 3♠ — Replacing Stayman   3. 3♡ — Not forcing   4. 3NT   5. 3♠ — Stayman.
    E.   1. Dble — Looking for penalties   2. 2♠ — Stayman   3. 2♡   4. 3NT — No stopper needed   5. 2♠ — Stayman.
    F.   1. No — Too strong in clubs   2. Dble — You were too strong for 1NT initially   3. Dble — But if partner bids 2♠,
    remove this to 3♢   4. 2♢ — Your hand is not suitable for low level penalties   5. Dble — But remove partner's 2♡ to 2♠.
    G.   1. Dble   2. 1NT — Shows 19-20 balanced and you are worth 19 with the 5th diamond   3. No   4. 2♢   5. Dble.
    H.   1. 3♠ — Too good for just 2♠   2. 3♡ — Game force, stopper ask   3. 3♡ — As for 2.   4. No — Penalty pass   5. 4♠.
    I.   1. No   2. 3♢ — Shows 13+ points and is a stopper ask   3. 3NT   4. 4♠ — Hearts cannot be better   5. 4♣.
    J.   1. Dble — For penalties   2. Dble — For penalties   3. 2♡   4. No — No reason to bid, so pass   5. 2♢ — Not forcing.

    ♢

Congratulations if you have completed all the exercises and quizzes. Please do not spoil all this fine work and learning by incorrect behaviour at the table. You want to win and you will harm your chances if you bicker with partner and continually find fault. Partner is doing the best possible and if a mistake has occurred, it cannot be changed now. You will improve your chances of winning and be a popular partner if you maintain a pleasant disposition and display cheerfulness in the face of adversity. Always make sure it is happy bridging!

PLAY HANDS FOR NORTH

(After each hand number, the dealer is given, followed by the vulnerability, e.g. S/Nil means Dealer South, neither side vulnerable)

1 N/Nil	2 E/N-S	3 S/E-W	4 W/Both	5 N/N-S	6 E/E-W	7 S/Both	8 W/Nil
♠ A6	♠ K754	♠ 63	♠ QJ973	♠ 107642	♠ 743	♠ A5	♠ Q76
♡ 843	♡ QJ1052	♡ 84	♡ J8	♡ A10	♡ 8542	♡ QJ10	♡ K8765
◇ Q42	◇ Q8	◇ QJ10	◇ J8765	◇ 1095	◇ AKQ	◇ 7654	◇ AQ
♣ AKQ52	♣ 108	♣ J108643	♣ 3	♣ A98	♣ 432	♣ A1032	♣ A64

9 N/E-W	10 E/Both	11 S/Nil	12 W/N-S	13 N/Both	14 E/Nil	15 S/N-S	16 W/E-W
♠ A10543	♠ A10642	♠ 3	♠ KJ97	♠ A96	♠ KQ52	♠ 1053	♠ KQ8643
♡ AK76	♡ Q109	♡ 9864	♡ Q106	♡ 1043	♡ Q10842	♡ 8	♡ K2
◇ Q6	◇ 943	◇ AJ43	◇ J1098	◇ KJ875	◇ 5	◇ KQ875	◇ KQ
♣ Q4	♣ A10	♣ AQ64	♣ Q9	♣ J8	♣ AJ3	♣ Q1054	♣ 764

17 N/Nil	18 E/N-S	19 S/E-W	20 W/Both	21 N/N-S	22 E/E-W	23 S/Both	24 W/Nil
♠ A2	♠ J10	♠ KQJ1098	♠ 865	♠ 93	♠ 9542	♠ 32	♠ Q1086
♡ 7654	♡ 982	♡ 964	♡ Q95	♡ K542	♡ KQ106	♡ 1094	♡ KQJ10
◇ A83	◇ A9742	◇ A	◇ KQ109	◇ AQ3	◇ J84	◇ Q962	◇ AKJ
♣ AKQ9	♣ KQ5	♣ 965	♣ 1075	♣ Q754	♣ J10	♣ KQ65	♣ AQ

25 N/E-W	26 E/Both	27 S/Nil	28 W/N-S	29 N/Both	30 E/Nil	31 S/N-S	32 W/E-W
♠ KQ	♠ 975432	♠ A93	♠ KQJ10	♠ AKJ42	♠ Q1065	♠ AKQ4	♠ - - -
♡ A83	♡ 3	♡ AK5	♡ 94	♡ J4	♡ 10984	♡ KQJ9	♡ J107
◇ Q9642	◇ A853	◇ K83	◇ A765	◇ AK	◇ 76	◇ AKQ	◇ KQ86
♣ Q107	♣ 94	♣ KQ86	♣ 853	♣ AKQ2	♣ K87	♣ A8	♣ Q96543

33 N/Nil	34 E/N-S	35 S/E-W	36 W/Both	37 N/N-S	38 E/E-W	39 N/N-S	40 E/Nil
♠ Q762	♠ 97	♠ 5	♠ 65432	♠ AK4	♠ A983	♠ 109	♠ AK42
♡ 7	♡ 8765	♡ 10865	♡ AJ1095	♡ KJ1094	♡ AJ32	♡ KJ1097	♡ A5
◇ A8432	◇ 9863	◇ 1092	◇ J	◇ J	◇ 54	◇ 105	◇ Q3
♣ Q97	♣ J109	♣ 87653	♣ A2	♣ J1098	♣ AQJ	♣ AKQJ	♣ 87642

41 N/E-W	42 E/Both	43 S/Nil	44 W/N-S	45 N/Nil	46 E/Nil	47 S/E-W	48 W/N-S
♠ J9	♠ K10964	♠ K654	♠ 8765	♠ 98	♠ 42	♠ A83	♠ AQ9
♡ KQ6432	♡ KJ	♡ KQ5	♡ - - -	♡ 653	♡ KQ10	♡ AJ10	♡ 63
◇ AK103	◇ 65	◇ 763	◇ Q984	◇ A642	◇ K1082	◇ AQJ10	◇ 1098
♣ 7	♣ 7632	♣ J73	♣ A10432	♣ AQ74	♣ Q763	♣ 853	♣ J9753

49 N/Nil	50 E/N-S	51 S/E-W	52 W/Both	53 N/N-S	54 E/Nil	55 S/Both	56 W/Nil
♠ A742	♠ J3	♠ A95	♠ AJ6	♠ 642	♠ A865	♠ 1052	♠ K3
♡ AK6	♡ KJ42	♡ AKJ93	♡ 983	♡ 862	♡ 7532	♡ 10962	♡ A8732
◇ A10732	◇ 9863	◇ K853	◇ A10	◇ K94	◇ 9	◇ Q9	◇ J64
♣ 6	♣ 1075	♣ Q	♣ KQ642	♣ KJ103	♣ 9743	♣ 10954	♣ KQ4

57 N/E-W	58 E/Both	59 S/Nil	60 W/N-S	61 N/Nil	62 E/Nil	63 S/N-S	64 W/E-W
♠ 9	♠ 743	♠ KQJ	♠ AK95	♠ AK1042	♠ AQJ3	♠ 5	♠ A942
♡ AJ10	♡ A932	♡ 10954	♡ 72	♡ 108	♡ AJ762	♡ A7	♡ 1074
◇ Q1072	◇ AQ84	◇ KQJ108	◇ KQ8	◇ Q103	◇ 10	◇ 843	◇ K10
♣ AK987	♣ J8	♣ 7	♣ Q1074	♣ J106	♣ J82	♣ KQ109873	♣ 10652

PLAY HANDS FOR NORTH

(After each hand number, the dealer is given, followed by the vulnerability, e.g. S/Nil means Dealer South, neither side vulnerable)

65 N/Nil
♠ AQ72
♥ KJ6
♦ 84
♣ K732

66 E/N-S
♠ 865
♥ J105
♦ AK982
♣ 105

67 S/E-W
♠ AQ5
♥ 932
♦ AJ1063
♣ Q8

68 W/Both
♠ 10
♥ J1096
♦ 98432
♣ K106

69 N/N-S
♠ A96
♥ 10832
♦ Q103
♣ QJ10

70 E/E-W
♠ AJ64
♥ 752
♦ J92
♣ 1083

71 S/Both
♠ K10842
♥ J9
♦ 9765
♣ 98

72 W/Nil
♠ K2
♥ AKQ3
♦ KQJ93
♣ 75

73 N/E-W
♠ 93
♥ Q1065
♦ K764
♣ Q63

74 E/Both
♠ 92
♥ K76
♦ A83
♣ AQ743

75 S/Nil
♠ AK754
♥ A86532
♦ 6
♣ 5

76 W/N-S
♠ J1087
♥ A92
♦ 10
♣ Q9874

77 N/Both
♠ J6
♥ K62
♦ KQ865
♣ Q43

78 E/Nil
♠ 73
♥ Q87
♦ KQJ108
♣ A108

79 S/N-S
♠ 92
♥ KJ1032
♦ 96
♣ A654

80 W/E-W
♠ K9843
♥ 975
♦ Q1052
♣ 7

81 N/Nil
♠ AJ1086
♥ K10
♦ 96
♣ A843

82 E/N-S
♠ 10
♥ QJ1054
♦ 10963
♣ 1085

83 S/E-W
♠ 53
♥ 843
♦ AK52
♣ AK84

84 W/Both
♠ 874
♥ 753
♦ KQ8754
♣ 4

85 N/N-S
♠ AK3
♥ Q653
♦ AQJ
♣ 872

86 E/E-W
♠ AJ108
♥ Q7
♦ 75
♣ KJ952

87 S/Both
♠ - - -
♥ 864
♦ AJ9532
♣ Q743

88 W/Nil
♠ 10982
♥ K42
♦ A964
♣ A5

89 N/E-W
♠ AKQ864
♥ K8652
♦ 7
♣ 2

90 E/Both
♠ J98
♥ QJ8
♦ 7652
♣ 1063

91 S/Nil
♠ K87653
♥ 4
♦ 63
♣ A542

92 W/N-S
♠ J107
♥ J9
♦ KQ7
♣ J10865

93 N/Both
♠ 96
♥ AQJ54
♦ A2
♣ A932

94 E/Nil
♠ A954
♥ 973
♦ KQ4
♣ Q108

95 S/N-S
♠ 9843
♥ 765
♦ J
♣ KQ976

96 W/E-W
♠ 1097654
♥ 10
♦ K9
♣ J985

97 N/Nil
♠ 107
♥ AQ10965
♦ K84
♣ A10

98 E/N-S
♠ QJ2
♥ 953
♦ A9743
♣ 54

99 S/E-W
♠ 106432
♥ 952
♦ 10753
♣ J

100 W/Both
♠ 10
♥ AKQ864
♦ 9
♣ AKQ76

101 N/N-S
♠ Q9
♥ QJ
♦ AQJ107
♣ Q985

102 E/E-W
♠ K104
♥ A54
♦ A43
♣ Q743

103 S/Both
♠ Q974
♥ A6
♦ K983
♣ A83

104 W/Nil
♠ A53
♥ AKQJ108
♦ AQ32
♣ - - -

105 N/E-W
♠ 432
♥ 42
♦ QJ1074
♣ 954

106 E/Both
♠ Q1052
♥ A76
♦ 3
♣ AK842

107 S/Nil
♠ KQ65
♥ 864
♦ Q62
♣ A93

108 W/E-W
♠ KJ643
♥ 863
♦ A104
♣ A8

109 N/Both
♠ AJ3
♥ K986
♦ A7
♣ KQ43

110 E/Nil
♠ Q108
♥ AK9653
♦ 9
♣ J102

111 S/N-S
♠ J942
♥ 10
♦ Q64
♣ AK863

112 W/E-W
♠ AQ9653
♥ 87
♦ KQ2
♣ J7

113 N/Nil
♠ 4
♥ KQ975
♦ 7432
♣ AKQ

114 E/N-S
♠ AK62
♥ AK
♦ J852
♣ AK8

115 S/E-W
♠ 1084
♥ A5
♦ 9754
♣ 9432

116 W/Both
♠ J92
♥ 109432
♦ 873
♣ 72

117 N/N-S
♠ 93
♥ AK83
♦ 72
♣ AK1052

118 E/E-W
♠ QJ1086
♥ 105
♦ K974
♣ 102

119 S/Both
♠ 8643
♥ AJ93
♦ J76
♣ 92

120 W/Nil
♠ J3
♥ AQJ983
♦ 7
♣ A1064

121 N/E-W
♠ KQ108432
♥ K65
♦ 42
♣ A

122 E/Both
♠ 983
♥ J1075
♦ 10876
♣ A9

123 S/Nil
♠ Q5
♥ KQ63
♦ 10952
♣ A62

124 W/N-S
♠ Q75
♥ A10875
♦ J83
♣ K8

125 N/Both
♠ 7632
♥ 102
♦ 984
♣ 8543

126 E/Nil
♠ 3
♥ A64
♦ AQ963
♣ J765

127 S/N-S
♠ Q10
♥ KQ953
♦ J876
♣ AK

128 W/E-W
♠ J10
♥ AK765
♦ 7
♣ AJ1085

PLAY HANDS FOR EAST

(After each hand number, the dealer is given, followed by the vulnerability, e.g. E/N-S means Dealer East, North-South vulnerable)

1 N/Nil	2 E/N-S	3 S/E-W	4 W/Both	5 N/N-S	6 E/E-W	7 S/Both	8 W/Nil
♠ KJ1095	♠ AJ	♠ Q7542	♠ 108	♠ Q	♠ 86	♠ 98432	♠ A1082
♡ 1076	♡ A864	♡ A1092	♡ A106	♡ KQ9862	♡ 7	♡ K43	♡ 10
◇ 10965	◇ A95	◇ 54	◇ 102	◇ A74	◇ 987654	◇ QJ8	◇ K1053
♣ 4	♣ AKQ3	♣ 95	♣ A109876	♣ A109876	♣ A875	♣ 64	♣ J1093

9 N/E-W	10 E/Both	11 S/Nil	12 W/N-S	13 N/Both	14 E/Nil	15 S/N-S	16 W/E-W
♠ Q98	♠ QJ3	♠ Q98	♠ 3	♠ Q73	♠ 107	♠ Q	♠ AJ9
♡ Q10954	♡ A8532	♡ 10	♡ J53	♡ A9	♡ 53	♡ KJ9753	♡ 87
◇ 9	◇ K86	◇ Q1096	◇ KQ42	◇ 64	◇ K1097	◇ A93	◇ 9652
♣ J1096	♣ Q3	♣ KJ953	♣ AJ752	♣ AK7642	♣ K10876	♣ 973	♣ QJ95

17 N/Nil	18 E/N-S	19 S/E-W	20 W/Both	21 N/N-S	22 E/E-W	23 S/Both	24 W/Nil
♠ 109	♠ 865	♠ 3	♠ AQJ4	♠ K76	♠ KQ	♠ KQ864	♠ K
♡ AQJ92	♡ J1076543	♡ QJ1032	♡ AJ10	♡ 10863	♡ AJ73	♡ A873	♡ 8743
◇ 9762	◇ - - -	◇ J87	◇ J42	◇ 9752	◇ K103	◇ J7	◇ Q964
♣ J5	♣ 932	♣ J843	♣ AKQ	♣ 108	♣ A952	♣ 42	♣ K943

25 N/E-W	26 E/Both	27 S/Nil	28 W/N-S	29 N/Both	30 E/Nil	31 S/N-S	32 W/E-W
♠ 98532	♠ AK	♠ K876	♠ A8742	♠ Q93	♠ K943	♠ J10753	♠ 86543
♡ 107	♡ K106	♡ J8	♡ 8732	♡ 76	♡ AKQ5	♡ 4	♡ 5
◇ J	◇ K94	◇ 10752	◇ Q2	◇ 9865	◇ AKQ	◇ 1098	◇ A732
♣ A9852	♣ 87632	♣ AJ10	♣ 62	♣ 10987	♣ A6	♣ Q643	♣ J72

33 N/Nil	34 E/N-S	35 S/E-W	36 W/Both	37 N/N-S	38 E/E-W	39 N/N-S	40 E/Nil
♠ A10	♠ K5432	♠ K973	♠ 7	♠ J6	♠ KQ2	♠ AK8643	♠ QJ9
♡ KJ1094	♡ J2	♡ QJ43	♡ K	♡ 73	♡ KQ7	♡ 6	♡ 74
◇ KQJ	◇ 752	◇ K3	◇ Q97542	◇ 1083	◇ J3	◇ 762	◇ AKJ94
♣ 1065	♣ AQ3	♣ KQ9	♣ 107643	♣ AKQ764	♣ K10543	♣ 1052	♣ Q95

41 N/E-W	42 E/Both	43 S/Nil	44 W/N-S	45 N/Nil	46 E/Nil	47 S/E-W	48 W/N-S
♠ 6	♠ 732	♠ Q109	♠ KQ1043	♠ 4	♠ AQJ9765	♠ K106542	♠ 87654
♡ 7	♡ A9864	♡ A987	♡ 109872	♡ AKQ	♡ 7	♡ K92	♡ A2
◇ QJ9642	◇ AK10	◇ 54	◇ 7	◇ J1095	◇ 763	◇ 8765	◇ AKJ2
♣ AQJ105	♣ Q8	♣ 10842	♣ 97	♣ 108532	♣ 104	♣ - - -	♣ AK

49 N/Nil	50 E/N-S	51 S/E-W	52 W/Both	53 N/N-S	54 E/Nil	55 S/Both	56 W/Nil
♠ Q108	♠ 8762	♠ KQJ8	♠ K	♠ KJ7	♠ 107	♠ 93	♠ AQ98
♡ QJ109	♡ Q9	♡ 7	♡ AQJ1062	♡ A9	♡ J10	♡ K54	♡ 9
◇ 65	◇ K75	◇ AQ72	◇ KQJ7	◇ QJ1086	◇ KQJ1086	◇ A1053	◇ AK753
♣ AKQ9	♣ AKJ6	♣ A986	♣ A7	♣ Q85	♣ J85	♣ 8732	♣ J87

57 N/E-W	58 E/Both	59 S/Nil	60 W/N-S	61 N/Nil	62 E/Nil	63 S/N-S	64 W/E-W
♠ AJ87	♠ K862	♠ A1093	♠ Q	♠ 73	♠ 75	♠ A1042	♠ - - -
♡ KQ54	♡ KQJ107	♡ KJ82	♡ K854	♡ 6	♡ 5	♡ KQ108	♡ 65
◇ A964	◇ 10	◇ A6	◇ 96543	◇ AK98542	◇ AK87432	◇ AQJ	◇ 876542
♣ 4	♣ A105	♣ AJ2	♣ 932	♣ 532	♣ Q94	♣ 42	♣ KQJ73

PLAY HANDS FOR EAST

(After each hand number, the dealer is given, followed by the vulnerability, e.g. E/N-S means Dealer East, North-South vulnerable)

65 N/Nil	66 E/N-S	67 S/E-W	68 W/Both	69 N/N-S	70 E/E-W	71 S/Both	72 W/Nil
♠ 10963	♠ AJ94	♠ 9873	♠ 5432	♠ K8732	♠ K10952	♠ 73	♠ 9874
♡ AQ853	♡ 984	♡ A10765	♡ A87	♡ K4	♡ J9	♡ AQ8654	♡ J10542
♢ 102	♢ 7	♢ K4	♢ KQJ107	♢ 754	♢ A643	♢ A3	♢ ---
♣ 54	♣ AK762	♣ 72	♣ 8	♣ 652	♣ 72	♣ 652	♣ QJ106

73 N/E-W	74 E/Both	75 S/Nil	76 W/N-S	77 N/Both	78 E/Nil	79 S/N-S	80 W/E-W
♠ J2	♠ A1085	♠ J	♠ A52	♠ 9	♠ 42	♠ AJ1065	♠ AQJ6
♡ 98	♡ 10	♡ Q104	♡ KJ1074	♡ J1097	♡ J106	♡ 76	♡ Q3
♢ AQ8	♢ J975	♢ QJ983	♢ 73	♢ J9	♢ A64	♢ A43	♢ 643
♣ AK9875	♣ K1096	♣ Q1092	♣ AJ6	♣ KJ8765	♣ KJ952	♣ Q97	♣ 9542

81 N/Nil	82 E/N-S	83 S/E-W	84 W/Both	85 N/N-S	86 E/E-W	87 S/Both	88 W/Nil
♠ K3	♠ A32	♠ K986	♠ AJ2	♠ Q985	♠ Q7652	♠ 953	♠ 3
♡ AJ743	♡ 92	♡ Q97	♡ A	♡ AJ942	♡ 9654	♡ KQ109	♡ AQ10865
♢ 82	♢ KQ	♢ 109874	♢ 9632	♢ 962	♢ 432	♢ Q108	♢ J5
♣ J1062	♣ AQJ643	♣ Q	♣ KQ1087	♣ J	♣ 8	♣ K109	♣ 9743

89 N/E-W	90 E/Both	91 S/Nil	92 W/N-S	93 N/Both	94 E/Nil	95 S/N-S	96 W/E-W
♠ 97	♠ A10743	♠ ---	♠ KQ985	♠ AK5	♠ KQ8	♠ K7	♠ A2
♡ Q109	♡ A642	♡ AK87	♡ AKQ862	♡ 1086	♡ J1084	♡ K932	♡ K9865
♢ KJ109	♢ A9	♢ Q1052	♢ 4	♢ J9863	♢ 985	♢ K10542	♢ 7
♣ A653	♣ 74	♣ J10876	♣ 3	♣ Q8	♣ K76	♣ J3	♣ AQ732

97 N/Nil	98 E/N-S	99 S/E-W	100 W/Both	101 N/N-S	102 E/E-W	103 S/Both	104 W/Nil
♠ KQJ3	♠ AK1097	♠ KJ87	♠ 764	♠ K865	♠ A82	♠ AK62	♠ J
♡ KJ	♡ K106	♡ J6	♡ 10972	♡ A742	♡ 97	♡ KQJ	♡ 9653
♢ AQJ765	♢ 10	♢ AKQ8	♢ K1043	♢ 95	♢ 95	♢ QJ4	♢ 9854
♣ 9	♣ 8763	♣ 875	♣ 103	♣ AJ10	♣ AKJ862	♣ K74	♣ 10854

105 N/E-W	106 E/Both	107 S/Nil	108 W/E-W	109 N/Both	110 E/Nil	111 S/N-S	112 W/E-W
♠ AQJ95	♠ AKJ	♠ 8	♠ ---	♠ Q76	♠ K9643	♠ Q1086	♠ 42
♡ K8	♡ J952	♡ J92	♡ KQJ2	♡ A42	♡ 72	♡ Q7	♡ Q54
♢ 65	♢ AKQJ	♢ K873	♢ 9752	♢ KJ10964	♢ K862	♢ 10975	♢ A63
♣ KJ106	♣ 63	♣ 108642	♣ KQJ63	♣ 8	♣ K7	♣ J105	♣ K10643

113 N/Nil	114 E/N-S	115 S/E-W	116 W/Both	117 N/N-S	118 E/E-W	119 S/Both	120 W/Nil
♠ 109	♠ QJ10	♠ AQJ732	♠ 743	♠ AQJ87	♠ AK532	♠ J9	♠ Q762
♡ AJ43	♡ J652	♡ 863	♡ 7	♡ 97	♡ J62	♡ 10874	♡ 65
♢ AQ10	♢ AKQ10	♢ 6	♢ 6542	♢ Q64	♢ 8	♢ AK1082	♢ KQJ43
♣ 10743	♣ 105	♣ AKQ	♣ Q9863	♣ Q83	♣ AQJ5	♣ 104	♣ 75

121 N/E-W	122 E/Both	123 S/Nil	124 W/N-S	125 N/Both	126 E/Nil	127 S/N-S	128 W/E-W
♠ 6	♠ 76	♠ 108	♠ K642	♠ KQ9	♠ K1054	♠ 96	♠ A
♡ AQ7	♡ 8632	♡ J10874	♡ 932	♡ A9854	♡ J1052	♡ AJ10862	♡ 1043
♢ QJ10975	♢ AK	♢ 83	♢ Q5	♢ 65	♢ 2	♢ 4	♢ KJ5
♣ K95	♣ KQJ62	♣ QJ95	♣ AQ109	♣ QJ7	♣ 10982	♣ QJ98	♣ KQ9764

PLAY HANDS FOR SOUTH

(After each hand number, the dealer is given, followed by the vulnerability, e.g. N/Both means Dealer North, both sides vulnerable)

1 N/Nil	2 E/N-S	3 S/E-W	4 W/Both	5 N/N-S	6 E/E-W	7 S/Both	8 W/Nil
♠ 83	♠ Q10863	♠ AJ10	♠ 642	♠ J95	♠ A92	♠ 7	♠ 9
♡ AKQ	♡ K9	♡ KJ53	♡ KQ94	♡ 743	♡ KQJ1063	♡ 8752	♡ QJ9432
♢ J873	♢ J10	♢ A97	♢ KQ	♢ KQJ6	♢ 3	♢ A1093	♢ J72
♣ 9763	♣ J975	♣ AKQ	♣ J542	♣ KJ3	♣ KQJ	♣ J985	♣ K75

9 N/E-W	10 E/Both	11 S/Nil	12 W/N-S	13 N/Both	14 E/Nil	15 S/N-S	16 W/E-W
♠ K72	♠ K975	♠ AJ642	♠ A8542	♠ 108	♠ A43	♠ J974	♠ 2
♡ 32	♡ ---	♡ A7532	♡ 8	♡ J875	♡ K76	♡ A1042	♡ AQJ65
♢ AK852	♢ QJ107	♢ K7	♢ 53	♢ Q109	♢ AQ6432	♢ J102	♢ AJ843
♣ 873	♣ 97542	♣ 2	♣ K10643	♣ Q1095	♣ 4	♣ 86	♣ 32

17 N/Nil	18 E/N-S	19 S/E-W	20 W/Both	21 N/N-S	22 E/E-W	23 S/Both	24 W/Nil
♠ K76543	♠ Q942	♠ 542	♠ 10973	♠ Q105	♠ A83	♠ AJ107	♠ A543
♡ 1083	♡ A	♡ K85	♡ K3	♡ AJ97	♡ 985	♡ J6	♡ 62
♢ 1054	♢ 10853	♢ KQ43	♢ A863	♢ K4	♢ A9652	♢ 854	♢ 872
♣ 4	♣ J1074	♣ AKQ	♣ J92	♣ AKJ3	♣ 76	♣ J1093	♣ 8762

25 N/E-W	26 E/Both	27 S/Nil	28 W/N-S	29 N/Both	30 E/Nil	31 S/N-S	32 W/E-W
♠ J10764	♠ 108	♠ J10542	♠ 6	♠ 106	♠ 8	♠ 86	♠ J972
♡ Q962	♡ Q975	♡ Q92	♡ KJ5	♡ KQ532	♡ 73	♡ A532	♡ 93
♢ AK3	♢ Q72	♢ A4	♢ J10984	♢ QJ43	♢ J10852	♢ J64	♢ J1095
♣ K	♣ KQJ10	♣ 752	♣ 10974	♣ J6	♣ 95432	♣ K752	♣ K108

33 N/Nil	34 E/N-S	35 S/E-W	36 W/Both	37 N/N-S	38 E/E-W	39 N/N-S	40 E/Nil
♠ K853	♠ 1086	♠ Q84	♠ 109	♠ 10972	♠ J6	♠ QJ5	♠ 753
♡ AQ8	♡ Q10943	♡ A9	♡ Q873	♡ 652	♡ 104	♡ 8542	♡ KQ10962
♢ 965	♢ AK4	♢ AQ8654	♢ AK	♢ 976542	♢ AK8762	♢ 98	♢ 862
♣ AKJ	♣ K6	♣ 102	♣ KQJ98	♣ ---	♣ 762	♣ 9743	♣ A

41 N/E-W	42 E/Both	43 S/Nil	44 W/N-S	45 N/Nil	46 E/Nil	47 S/E-W	48 W/N-S
♠ K10543	♠ 5	♠ AJ832	♠ ---	♠ AK106532	♠ 3	♠ Q7	♠ KJ103
♡ AJ109	♡ 10	♡ 6432	♡ AJ3	♡ 742	♡ 9652	♡ 86	♡ 105
♢ 87	♢ QJ9832	♢ AKJ	♢ K10532	♢ Q7	♢ QJ9	♢ 93	♢ Q73
♣ K3	♣ AJ1095	♣ A	♣ KQ865	♣ 9	♣ AK852	♣ KQJ10742	♣ Q1062

49 N/Nil	50 E/N-S	51 S/E-W	52 W/Both	53 N/N-S	54 E/Nil	55 S/Both	56 W/Nil
♠ KJ963	♠ AKQ5	♠ 643	♠ Q1097	♠ AQ3	♠ J42	♠ AJ8	♠ 65
♡ 72	♡ A753	♡ Q10	♡ 4	♡ KQJ	♡ K86	♡ J7	♡ K654
♢ KJ9	♢ A4	♢ J104	♢ 98543	♢ A32	♢ A7542	♢ KJ864	♢ Q8
♣ 873	♣ 843	♣ J10752	♣ 1098	♣ A742	♣ KQ	♣ QJ6	♣ 96532

57 N/E-W	58 E/Both	59 S/Nil	60 W/N-S	61 N/Nil	62 E/Nil	63 S/N-S	64 W/E-W
♠ Q106543	♠ AQJ10	♠ 7652	♠ 107432	♠ J986	♠ 86	♠ Q83	♠ 83
♡ 9	♡ 4	♡ 763	♡ 93	♡ AQ43	♡ 943	♡ 965432	♡ AKQJ98
♢ J85	♢ K952	♢ 75	♢ J2	♢ 76	♢ QJ96	♢ 652	♢ A3
♣ 653	♣ KQ72	♣ Q963	♣ AKJ6	♣ AKQ	♣ AK103	♣ A	♣ A84

PLAY HANDS FOR SOUTH

(After each hand number, the dealer is given, followed by the vulnerability, e.g. N/Both means Dealer North, both sides vulnerable)

65 N/Nil	66 E/N-S	67 S/E-W	68 W/Both	69 N/N-S	70 E/E-W	71 S/Both	72 W/Nil
♠ K5 ♡ 92 ◇ AK973 ♣ AJ106	♠ Q107 ♡ Q3 ◇ 10653 ♣ QJ98	♠ KJ106 ♡ 84 ◇ 72 ♣ AKJ65	♠ QJ98 ♡ 42 ◇ A5 ♣ QJ973	♠ QJ105 ♡ J75 ◇ 92 ♣ A987	♠ 3 ♡ AK43 ◇ Q108 ♣ AK654	♠ Q965 ♡ K102 ◇ J104 ♣ KJ7	♠ A653 ♡ 96 ◇ A876 ♣ AK4

73 N/E-W	74 E/Both	75 S/Nil	76 W/N-S	77 N/Both	78 E/Nil	79 S/N-S	80 W/E-W
♠ KQ108 ♡ J4 ◇ 109532 ♣ J10	♠ KQ763 ♡ A9843 ◇ K2 ♣ 2	♠ 863 ♡ 7 ◇ A75 ♣ AKJ874	♠ 6 ♡ Q653 ◇ K985 ♣ K1052	♠ KQ8743 ♡ AQ43 ◇ 74 ♣ A	♠ KQ986 ♡ AK42 ◇ 7 ♣ Q43	♠ K87 ♡ 5 ◇ 10875 ♣ J10832	♠ 1075 ♡ 102 ◇ J987 ♣ AQJ10

81 N/Nil	82 E/N-S	83 S/E-W	84 W/Both	85 N/N-S	86 E/E-W	87 S/Both	88 W/Nil
♠ 74 ♡ 962 ◇ AKJ ♣ KQ975	♠ QJ76 ♡ AK8 ◇ 875 ♣ 972	♠ AJ742 ♡ AK ◇ Q3 ♣ 9653	♠ 10965 ♡ QJ94 ◇ AJ ♣ 653	♠ J64 ♡ 8 ◇ 1053 ♣ K109543	♠ 43 ♡ J108 ◇ A986 ♣ AQ103	♠ KQ7642 ♡ A32 ◇ 64 ♣ A2	♠ KJ6 ♡ J97 ◇ 1072 ♣ QJ108

89 N/E-W	90 E/Both	91 S/Nil	92 W/N-S	93 N/Both	94 E/Nil	95 S/N-S	96 W/E-W
♠ 32 ♡ AJ743 ◇ A8 ♣ J984	♠ 5 ♡ K9753 ◇ QJ10 ♣ 9852	♠ AQ92 ♡ J10 ◇ AKJ74 ♣ K9	♠ 4 ♡ 10543 ◇ 10865 ♣ KQ97	♠ 8732 ♡ K732 ◇ 754 ♣ K5	♠ J10632 ♡ 5 ◇ AJ102 ♣ 953	♠ QJ10652 ♡ A8 ◇ A73 ♣ A2	♠ KQJ ♡ Q73 ◇ Q10654 ♣ 106

97 N/Nil	98 E/N-S	98 S/E-W	100 W/Both	101 N/N-S	102 E/E-W	103 S/Both	104 W/Nil
♠ 86542 ♡ 74 ◇ 9 ♣ J8652	♠ 643 ♡ AQ7 ◇ KQ2 ♣ AKJ10	♠ 95 ♡ AKQ1083 ◇ J6 ♣ K43	♠ J82 ♡ - - - ◇ A8652 ♣ J8542	♠ J10732 ♡ 10985 ◇ 82 ♣ 64	♠ QJ973 ♡ KQ63 ◇ KJ6 ♣ 9	♠ J105 ♡ 7542 ◇ 10652 ♣ 96	♠ 7642 ♡ 4 ◇ J6 ♣ AJ7632

105 N/E-W	106 E/Both	107 S/Nil	108 W/E-W	109 N/Both	110 E/Nil	111 S/N-S	112 W/E-W
♠ 8 ♡ 10973 ◇ AK82 ♣ AQ83	♠ 9764 ♡ 4 ◇ 9862 ♣ QJ97	♠ AJ7432 ♡ AK3 ◇ J54 ♣ 5	♠ A9752 ♡ A54 ◇ KJ3 ♣ 92	♠ K92 ♡ QJ107 ◇ 32 ♣ A652	♠ 7 ♡ J104 ◇ QJ105 ♣ 98653	♠ K53 ♡ AJ4 ◇ AKJ3 ♣ 742	♠ 87 ♡ 10962 ◇ J1094 ♣ Q85

113 N/Nil	114 E/N-S	115 S/E-W	116 W/Both	117 N/N-S	118 E/E-W	119 S/Both	120 W/Nil
♠ K752 ♡ 1082 ◇ 965 ♣ 985	♠ 9 ♡ Q109743 ◇ 643 ♣ J94	♠ K ♡ KQJ104 ◇ KJ82 ♣ J107	♠ AK ♡ QJ865 ◇ AQ9 ♣ AK5	♠ 105 ♡ Q652 ◇ A983 ♣ 974	♠ 94 ♡ AKQ97 ◇ QJ2 ♣ 864	♠ 7 ♡ KQ62 ◇ Q9 ♣ AKQ873	♠ 9854 ♡ 104 ◇ 109862 ♣ J9

121 N/E-W	122 E/Both	123 S/Nil	124 W/N-S	125 N/Both	126 E/Nil	127 S/N-S	128 W/E-W
♠ AJ ♡ 8432 ◇ A63 ♣ QJ108	♠ KQJ1042 ♡ Q ◇ J932 ♣ 103	♠ K62 ♡ A5 ◇ AQJ74 ♣ 1074	♠ J108 ♡ Q6 ◇ 10974 ♣ J762	♠ A54 ♡ KJ7 ◇ AQJ3 ♣ K92	♠ AQ976 ♡ KQ93 ◇ 7 ♣ Q43	♠ 75432 ♡ 4 ◇ K102 ♣ 10754	♠ K9862 ♡ 82 ◇ A10986 ♣ 3

PLAY HANDS FOR WEST

(After each hand number, the dealer is given, followed by the vulnerability, e.g. S/E-W means Dealer South, East-West vulnerable)

1 N/Nil	2 E/N-S	3 S/E-W	4 W/Both	5 N/N-S	6 E/E-W	7 S/Both	8 W/Nil
♠ Q742	♠ 92	♠ K98	♠ AK5	♠ AK83	♠ KQJ105	♠ KQJ106	♠ KJ543
♡ J952	♡ 73	♡ Q76	♡ 7532	♡ J5	♡ A9	♡ A96	♡ A
◇ AK	◇ K76432	◇ K8632	◇ A943	◇ 832	◇ J102	◇ K2	◇ 9864
♣ J108	♣ 642	♣ 72	♣ KQ	♣ 7542	♣ 1096	♣ KQ7	♣ Q82

9 N/E-W	10 E/Both	11 S/Nil	12 W/N-S	13 N/Both	14 E/Nil	15 S/N-S	16 W/E-W
♠ J6	♠ 8	♠ K1075	♠ Q106	♠ KJ542	♠ J986	♠ AK862	♠ 1075
♡ J8	♡ KJ764	♡ KQJ	♡ AK9742	♡ KQ62	♡ AJ9	♡ Q6	♡ 10943
◇ J10743	◇ A52	◇ 852	◇ A76	◇ A32	◇ J8	◇ 64	◇ 107
♣ AK52	♣ KJ86	♣ 1087	♣ 8	♣ 3	♣ Q952	♣ AKJ2	♣ AK108

17 N/Nil	18 E/N-S	19 S/E-W	20 W/Both	21 N/N-S	22 E/E-W	23 S/Both	24 W/Nil
♠ QJ8	♠ AK73	♠ A76	♠ K2	♠ AJ842	♠ J1076	♠ 95	♠ J972
♡ K	♡ KQ	♡ A7	♡ 87642	♡ Q	♡ 42	♡ KQ52	♡ A95
◇ KQJ	◇ KQJ6	◇ 109652	◇ 75	◇ J1086	◇ Q7	◇ AK103	◇ 1053
♣ 1087632	♣ A86	♣ 1072	♣ 8643	♣ 962	♣ KQ843	♣ A87	♣ J105

25 N/E-W	26 E/Both	27 S/Nil	28 W/N-S	29 N/Both	30 E/Nil	31 S/N-S	32 W/E-W
♠ A	♠ QJ6	♠ Q	♠ 953	♠ 875	♠ AJ72	♠ 92	♠ AKQ10
♡ KJ54	♡ AJ842	♡ 107643	♡ AQ106	♡ A1098	♡ J62	♡ 10876	♡ AKQ8642
◇ 10875	◇ J106	◇ QJ96	◇ K3	◇ 1072	◇ 943	◇ 7532	◇ 4
♣ J643	♣ A5	♣ 943	♣ AKQJ	♣ 543	♣ QJ10	♣ J109	♣ A

33 N/Nil	34 E/N-S	35 S/E-W	36 W/Both	37 N/N-S	38 E/E-W	39 N/N-S	40 E/Nil
♠ J94	♠ AQJ	♠ AJ1062	♠ AKQJ8	♠ Q853	♠ 10754	♠ 72	♠ 1086
♡ 6532	♡ AK	♡ K72	♡ 642	♡ AQ8	♡ 9865	♡ AQ3	♡ J83
◇ 107	◇ QJ10	◇ J7	◇ 10863	◇ AKQ	◇ Q109	◇ AKQJ43	◇ 1075
♣ 8432	♣ 87542	♣ AJ4	♣ 5	♣ 532	♣ 98	♣ 86	♣ KJ103

41 N/E-W	42 E/Both	43 S/Nil	44 W/N-S	45 N/Nil	46 E/Nil	47 S/E-W	48 W/N-S
♠ AQ872	♠ AQJ8	♠ 7	♠ AJ92	♠ QJ7	♠ K108	♠ J9	♠ 2
♡ 85	♡ Q7532	♡ J10	♡ KQ654	♡ J1098	♡ AJ843	♡ Q7543	♡ KQJ9874
◇ 5	◇ 74	◇ Q10982	◇ AJ6	◇ K83	◇ A54	◇ K42	◇ 654
♣ 98642	♣ K4	♣ KQ965	♣ J	♣ KJ6	♣ J9	♣ A96	♣ 84

49 N/Nil	50 E/N-S	51 S/E-W	52 W/Both	53 N/N-S	54 E/Nil	55 S/Both	56 W/Nil
♠ 5	♠ 1094	♠ 1072	♠ 85432	♠ 10985	♠ KQ93	♠ KQ764	♠ J10742
♡ 8543	♡ 1086	♡ 86542	♡ K75	♡ 107543	♡ AQ94	♡ AQ83	♡ QJ10
◇ Q84	◇ QJ102	◇ 96	◇ 62	◇ 75	◇ 3	◇ 72	◇ 1092
♣ J10542	♣ Q92	♣ K43	♣ J53	♣ 96	♣ A1062	♣ AK	♣ A10

57 N/E-W	58 E/Both	59 S/Nil	60 W/N-S	61 N/Nil	62 E/Nil	63 S/N-S	64 W/E-W
♠ K2	♠ 95	♠ 84	♠ J86	♠ Q5	♠ K10942	♠ KJ976	♠ KQJ10765
♡ 87632	♡ 865	♡ AQ	♡ AQJ106	♡ KJ9752	♡ KQ108	♡ J	♡ 32
◇ K3	◇ J763	◇ 9432	◇ A107	◇ J	◇ 5	◇ K1097	◇ QJ9
♣ QJ102	♣ 9643	♣ K10854	♣ 85	♣ 9874	♣ 765	♣ J65	♣ 9

PLAY HANDS FOR WEST

(After each hand number, the dealer is given, followed by the vulnerability, e.g. S/E-W means Dealer South, East-West vulnerable)

65 N/Nil	66 E/N-S	67 S/E-W	68 W/Both	69 N/N-S	70 E/E-W	71 S/Both	72 W/Nil
♠ J84	♠ K32	♠ 42	♠ AK76	♠ 4	♠ Q87	♠ AJ	♠ QJ10
♡ 1074	♡ AK762	♡ KQJ	♡ KQ53	♡ AQ96	♡ Q1086	♡ 73	♡ 87
◇ QJ65	◇ QJ4	◇ Q985	◇ 6	◇ AKJ86	◇ K75	◇ KQ82	◇ 10542
♣ Q98	♣ 43	♣ 10943	♣ A542	♣ K43	♣ QJ9	♣ AQ1043	♣ 9832

73 N/E-W	74 E/Both	75 S/Nil	76 W/N-S	77 N/Both	78 E/Nil	79 S/N-S	80 W/E-W
♠ A7654	♠ J4	♠ Q1092	♠ KQ943	♠ A1052	♠ AJ105	♠ Q43	♠ 2
♡ AK732	♡ QJ52	♡ KJ9	♡ 8	♡ 85	♡ 953	♡ AQ984	♡ AKJ864
◇ J	◇ Q1064	◇ K1042	◇ AQJ642	◇ A1032	◇ 9532	◇ KQJ2	◇ AK
♣ 42	♣ J85	♣ 63	♣ 3	♣ 1092	♣ 76	♣ K	♣ K863

81 N/Nil	82 E/N-S	83 S/E-W	84 W/Both	85 N/N-S	86 E/E-W	87 S/Both	88 W/Nil
♠ Q952	♠ K9854	♠ Q10	♠ KQ3	♠ 1072	♠ K9	♠ AJ108	♠ AQ754
♡ Q85	♡ 763	♡ J10652	♡ K10862	♡ K107	♡ AK32	♡ J75	♡ 3
◇ Q107543	◇ AJ42	◇ J6	◇ 10	◇ K874	◇ KQJ10	◇ K7	◇ KQ83
♣ - - -	♣ K	♣ J1072	♣ AJ92	♣ AQ6	♣ 764	♣ J865	♣ K62

89 N/E-W	90 E/Both	91 S/Nil	92 W/N-S	93 N/Both	94 E/Nil	95 S/N-S	96 W/E-W
♠ J105	♠ KQ62	♠ J104	♠ A632	♠ QJ104	♠ 7	♠ A	♠ 83
♡ - - -	♡ 10	♡ Q96532	♡ 7	♡ 9	♡ AKQ62	♡ QJ104	♡ AJ42
◇ Q65432	◇ K843	◇ 98	◇ AJ932	◇ KQ10	◇ 763	◇ Q986	◇ AJ832
♣ KQ107	♣ AKQJ	♣ Q3	♣ A42	♣ J10764	♣ AJ42	♣ 10854	♣ K4

97 N/Nil	98 E/N-S	99 S/E-W	100 W/Both	101 N/N-S	102 E/E-W	103 S/Both	104 W/Nil
♠ A9	♠ 85	♠ AQ	♠ AKQ953	♠ A4	♠ 65	♠ 83	♠ KQ1098
♡ 832	♡ J842	♡ 74	♡ J53	♡ K63	♡ J1082	♡ 10983	♡ 72
◇ 1032	◇ J865	◇ 942	◇ QJ7	◇ K643	◇ Q10872	◇ A7	◇ K107
♣ KQ743	♣ Q92	♣ AQ10962	♣ 9	♣ K732	♣ 105	♣ QJ1052	♣ KQ9

105 N/E-W	106 E/Both	107 S/Nil	108 W/E-W	109 N/Both	110 E/Nil	111 S/N-S	112 W/E-W
♠ K1076	♠ 83	♠ 109	♠ Q108	♠ 10854	♠ AJ52	♠ A7	♠ KJ10
♡ AQJ65	♡ KQ1083	♡ Q1075	♡ 1097	♡ 53	♡ Q8	♡ K986532	♡ AKJ3
◇ 93	◇ 10754	◇ A109	◇ Q86	◇ Q85	◇ A743	◇ 82	◇ 875
♣ 72	♣ 105	♣ KQJ7	♣ 10754	♣ J1097	♣ AQ4	♣ Q9	♣ A92

113 N/Nil	114 E/N-S	115 S/E-W	116 W/Both	117 N/N-S	118 E/E-W	119 S/Both	120 W/Nil
♠ AQJ863	♠ 87543	♠ 965	♠ Q10865	♠ K642	♠ 7	♠ AKQ1052	♠ AK10
♡ 6	♡ 8	♡ 972	♡ AK	♡ J104	♡ 843	♡ 5	♡ K72
◇ KJ8	◇ 97	◇ AQ103	◇ KJ10	◇ KJ105	◇ A10653	◇ 543	◇ A5
♣ J62	♣ Q7632	♣ 865	♣ J104	♣ J6	♣ K973	♣ J65	♣ KQ832

121 N/E-W	122 E/Both	123 S/Nil	124 W/N-S	125 N/Both	126 E/Nil	127 S/N-S	128 W/E-W
♠ 975	♠ A5	♠ AJ9743	♠ A93	♠ J108	♠ J82	♠ AKJ8	♠ Q7543
♡ J109	♡ AK94	♡ 92	♡ KJ4	♡ Q63	♡ 87	♡ 7	♡ QJ9
◇ K8	◇ Q54	◇ K6	◇ AK62	◇ K1072	◇ KJ10854	◇ AQ953	◇ Q432
♣ 76432	♣ 8754	♣ K83	♣ 543	♣ A106	♣ AK	♣ 632	♣ 2

INDEX